Public Administration Research Methods

The best decisions made by public sector managers are based not on instinct, but on an informed understanding of what's happening on the ground. Policy may be directed by ideology, but it must also be founded on reality. The challenge of making the right decisions as a public sector manager are often, therefore, based on the need for rigorous, actionable research. In this major new textbook, Eller, Gerber, and Robinson show students of Public Administration exactly how to use both qualitative and quantitative research techniques to give them the best chance to make the right decisions.

Uniquely, the book presents the various methodologies through a series of real-life case studies, with each chapter exploring the types of situations where a public sector manager can use research to answer specific questions, and how that research can inform future policy. Taking readers through the key concepts, from research design and sampling to interviews, survey data, and more statistical-based approaches, the book builds to provide the complete guide to using research in the public and voluntary sectors. Each chapter also includes discussion questions, class exercises, end of chapter review questions, and key vocabulary to provide students with a range of further tools to apply research principles to practical situations.

Readers of the print book will also have automatic access to an interactive electronic version, which will include not only hyperlinks to further reading, but also access to a series of data sets to enable practice using the statistical methodologies outlined in the text.

Public Administration Research Methods: Tools for Evaluation and Evidence-Based Practice is the most accessible and comprehensive research methods textbook available to students of Public Administration and will be essential reading not only to students during their studies, but also as a companion in their future careers.

Warren S. Eller is Associate Professor in the Department of Public Administration at the University of North Carolina, Pembroke, USA.

Brian J. Gerber is Associate Professor and Executive Director of the Buechner Institute for Governance at the School of Public Affairs, University of Colorado–Denver, USA.

Scott E. Robinson is Associate Professor at the Bush School of Government and Public Service at Texas A&M University, USA.

Public Administration Research Methods

Tools for Evaluation and Evidence-Based Practice

WARREN S. ELLER
University of North Carolina at Pembroke

BRIAN J. GERBER
University of Colorado at Denver

SCOTT E. ROBINSON
Texas A&M University

Routledge
Taylor & Francis Group

NEW YORK AND LONDON

First published 2013
by Routledge
711 Third Avenue, New York, NY 10017

Simultaneously published in the UK
by Routledge
2 Park Square, Milton Park, Abingdon, Oxon OX14 4RN

Routledge is an imprint of the Taylor & Francis Group, an informa business

Library of Congress Cataloging-in-Publication Data

Robinson, Scott E.
Public administration research methods : tools for evaluation and evidence-based practice /
Warren S. Eller, Brian J. Gerber & Scott E. Robinson.
    p. cm.
   1. Public administration—Research.   2. Public administration—Evaluation.
I. Eller, Warren S.   II. Gerber, Brian J.   III. Title.
JF1338.A2R55   2013
351.072—dc23   2012028047

ISBN: 978-0-415-89530-9 (pbk)

Typeset in Berthold Akzidenz Grotesk
by Apex CoVantage, LLC

Printed and bound in the United States of America by Courier, Westford, MA

Contents

Visual Tour of the Interactive eTextbook

Access your Interactive eTextbook at home, on campus or on the move*. Your eTextbook offers note sharing and highlighting functionality, as well as exclusive interactive content to enhance your learning experience. The notes you make on your Interactive eTextbook will synchronise with all other versions, creating a personalised version that you can access wherever and whenever you need it.

Throughout the text you will see icons in the margin where further multimedia resources are available via your Interactive eTextbook. These include:

 offline materials

 audio and video

 online resources curated by the authors

 testing material for each chapter

Unique to *Public Administration Research Methods: Tools for Evaluation and Evidence-based Practice* . . .

- Video screencasts demonstrating how to use STATA and SPSS for key statistical calculations

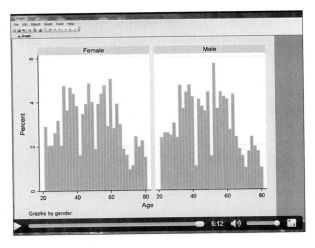

- Flashcards and multiple choice questions for each chapter

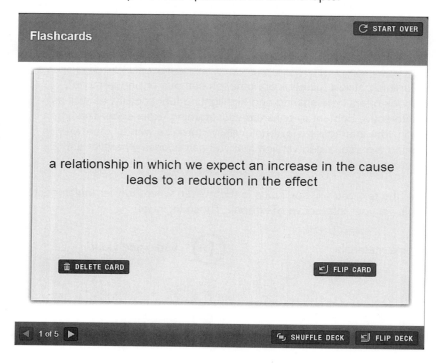

- Data sets in 3 separate formats (Excel, STATA, SPSS) to accompany the chapters on quantitative analysis
- A selection of specially tailored questions and exercises for each quantitative chapter to accompany the data sets
- Useful website links for each chapter

Many of these exciting interactive teaching and learning resources are also available for instructors to download from the following site:
http://www.routledge.com/9780415895309

*BookShelf will provide access to your eTextbook either online or as a download via your PC, Mac (OS X 10.6>), iPad, iPhone, iPod Touch (iOS 5.0>), Android app or Amazon Kindle Fire.

CHAPTER 1

Introduction: What Is Research?

Evidence-Based Argumentation

Public managers often have to make decisions about what to do or where to invest an organization's resources with very little guidance or information. Consider the following example. Public managers across the country are considering how to keep up with social media tools. Social media gurus are quick to declare that all agencies must implement social media strategies or be left in the dust. Similarly, nonprofit organizations would like to leverage Facebook™ and other social media sites to assist with fundraising. The U.S. Centers for Disease Control (CDC) and the World Health Organization (WHO) may hope to monitor Twitter™ for early evidence of influenza outbreaks. The potential for these tools is remarkable—potentially transforming the relationship between residents and their government.

At the same time, using these tools can be costly. Implementing a social media strategy would require the effort of an employee who could be working on other assignments. The alternative uses for the resources one devotes to a plan are considered the **OPPORTUNITY COSTS** of the plan. Each of these proposed uses of social media impose opportunity costs for their organization. The person overseeing fundraising efforts on Facebook could otherwise be contacting potential donors on the phone or organizing a large fundraising event. The person overseeing the Twitter feed at the CDC could be reading local reports through the traditional reporting systems. The job of the public manager in these situations is to decide whether to make these investments. Are the proposed social media investments worth the opportunity costs?

It is natural to wonder how a manager can make such a choice. A manager could decide this based on what he or she thinks will make the office look better to his or her boss. The nonprofit organization could seek to impress its board of directors, or a local planner could seek to impress the city manager. A manager can decide based on whether the choice will allow him to "look cool" among his peers at his next professional development conference. What we should hope, though, is that he will make the decision based on the costs and benefits of the potential strategies. This calls for evidence. The purpose of this book is to introduce you to the tools that one needs to collect such evidence to evaluate the sort of decisions public managers face on a daily basis.

> **Class Exercise:** What potential costs and benefits do you see to the adoption of social media technology in a local public health office?

Foundations of Research

This textbook will provide you with a set of tools to answer questions like whether to invest in social media technology. We will discuss the review of existing literatures to see if someone else has already answered your question. After all, why spend time researching the effectiveness of social media if other people have convincingly demonstrated its importance (or irrelevance)? However, literature reviews are not the focus of this textbook. The book will instead help you build the skills to answer the difficult questions that no one has already answered. This approach to public management research connects us to a long tradition of both research methodology and the scientific method.

Induction and Deduction

The heart of the scientific method lies in an ancient distinction between inductive and deductive reasoning. You are likely familiar with the term **DEDUCTION**. The most popular association of the term is with the fictional detective Sherlock Holmes. His method of reasoning was to apply a set of rules to eliminate rival explanations until only one plausible explanation remained—and that explanation must then be true.

To adapt an example, consider the famous dog that did not bark. In this case, a murder took place near a family dog who did not bark at the murderer. Deduction would be the process of using rules defining how we know the world works to eliminate implausible explanations. If we believe that a killer had to pass near a dog and that the dog would bark if someone unfamiliar passed by him, we can apply these beliefs to eliminate potential suspects. If the dog did not bark (and our assumptions are correct), then the killer must be someone familiar to the dog. This may not be enough to identify the killer, but it eliminates a number of candidates. We may have to apply other assumptions about who could have been the killer, eliminating suspects until only one remains.

The defining characteristic of this process is the combination of beliefs we have about the world (like the assumption that the dog would bark at anyone unfamiliar) with facts (the dog did not bark) to reach conclusions (the killer must have been familiar to the dog). This process productively combines rules or beliefs with facts to help us reach conclusions. However, this process does not explain where basic facts come from. Why is it that we believe that dogs will bark at unfamiliar people? This is the task of induction.

INDUCTION involves learning from the world by observation. How do we know if dogs bark at unfamiliar people? We know this if we observe dogs. We watch how dogs behave when unfamiliar people approach them. We may note how often the dog barks under these circumstances and decide whether we are comfortable with a statement like "dogs always bark at unfamiliar people."

Induction also involves the collection of new information. This is the hard part of public affairs research. Induction deals with cases where you cannot simply look up the answer to a question. You cannot read a book about social media to get the answer as to whether you should implement it within your organization. There is no single correct answer for all organizations. Instead, you will have to collect your own information, possibly specific to your own organization, to answer the question of whether to create a social media position within your organization. Most of this book will focus on how to collect information and perform disciplined inductive research.

The Scientific Method

The reliance on inductive reasoning characterizes the scientific method. By contrast, the foundations of mathematics relied on deductive reasoning. You are likely familiar with early systems of mathematics like Euclidean geometry. A set of basic definitions and principles allow you to make judgments about a broad range of subjects or problems. You know that if a triangle has two interior angles totaling 100 degrees, then the third interior angle must be 80 degrees. You can deduce this because a triangle must have a total of 180 degrees for its internal angles. Why is this the case? Simply enough, it is because Euclid defined triangles in such a way that it must be true. You can apply general rules about the definitions of a triangle and basic addition to reach such a conclusion. There is no need to actually have a triangle in front of you or to measures its angles.

This mode of reasoning was eventually challenged by the scientific revolution. Early proponents of scientific approaches to study nature did not reject the use of deductive systems like Euclidean geometry. However, they argued that there are some subjects where we can better learn by observing the world than by contemplating idealized definitions. When Mendel wanted to learn more about the ability to create strains of vegetables with desirable characteristics, he did not contemplate the ideal pea pod or debate definitions of pea pods (or, at least, he did not exclusively contemplate this ideal). He observed actual pea pods. He observed how pea pods differed when they were crossbred in specific ways (genetic engineering goes back a long way). He believed his conclusions about the best strategies for growing peas with specific characteristics because he had observed the process himself.

The essence of the scientific approach is the reliance on observation (induction) to support predictions about how the world works or to discredit predictions that don't match our observations. Hypotheses are what we will call the predictions about how the world works. We will define this term more formally in a later chapter. Holmes had a hypothesis about how dogs behave. Mendel had a hypothesis about what would happen if you crossbred pea plants with specific characteristics. The difference was that Mendel tested his hypothesis by observing the outcome of crossbreeding pea plants rather than remaining comfortable with the reliability of his own assumptions. It is the continuous prediction/observation cycle that pushes science forward from Mendelian genetics to contemporary biotechnology and from Newtonian physics to string theory.

Social Science Research

Most discussions of the scientific method focus on the study of the natural world. When people think of science, they think of biology, chemistry, physics, and a few other areas of study. However, there is nothing that prevents one from applying the inductive logic of science to subjects other than these traditional areas. Public managers can apply the scientific method to predict the behavior of people—and not just to barking dogs or pea pods. We may ask how people tend to react, given certain information. Do people use public transportation more when unemployment rates go up? This seems like a reasonable prediction/hypothesis.

Economic theory describes the conditions where one would expect people to switch to less expensive transportation options when the price of gas goes up. The specifics of the theory are not our concern here. What is important is that assumptions about the nature of consumers, the operation of markets, and the characteristics of goods can all be combined to construct reasons that people will use more public transportation when the price of gas goes up. The process for deriving predictions about purchasing behavior from basic assumptions of consumer behavior is essentially similar to the process of deriving the angles of the interior of a triangle from Euclidean assumptions and definitions.

Alternatively, we can test the hypothesis by actually observing consumer behavior when gas prices change. We could collect data about consumer behavior by talking to people from gas stations or other locations. We could talk to many people or just a few. Similarly, we could talk to users of public transportation to see if they attribute their choice of transportation mode to gas prices. Different strategies for observing behavior will have different strengths and weaknesses, but they share the strategy of learning about the world by observing the world.

> **Class Exercise:** What are examples of organizations that serve public missions? Can you think of any examples from the private sector?

Attempts to build a body of knowledge about social systems and processes using the methods of scientific observation define the social sciences. One can focus on the behavior of individuals and firms within a marketplace (as do some economists) or the behavior of voters in a democracy (as do some political scientists). Alternatively, one can focus on issues relevant to specific career paths such as work within a private sector business (as one might study in a business school) or to prepare for work in schools (as one might study in an education degree program). Whatever the specific focus, those who rely on observation to test whether predictions about the behavior of individuals can rightly share the title "social scientist."

This textbook will focus on tools of social science most relevant for people intending to work in public sector organizations. By this, we mean a broad set of organizations serving a public-oriented mission whether the organization is a government agency, a nonprofit or charitable organization, or even a unit within a for-profit firm that has a public service mission. As we have done up to this point, we will refer to the key decision maker in a public organization as the **PUBLIC MANAGER**. The next chapter will provide a series of examples to illustrate the diversity of public managers and the contexts in which they work. This textbook will teach you the skills needed to make good decisions, based on observations of the real world, in your capacity as a member of a public organization.

Purposes of Research

There are a variety of purposes that one may have in conducting research. For public managers, these purposes will all eventually lead to supporting decisions. However, the short-term purposes of specific research projects will dramatically affect your research strategies—as you will see throughout the textbook. Whether you want to answer a specific question about the effectiveness of a practice within your organization or to learn about the behavior of people that may inform the practice of public affairs, generally, will influence the choices you make in designing a research project.

Description   → background information

who are you targeting?

The simplest purpose of research is to describe the world. The first thing you will need to know in any management capacity is the shape of the world in which you are working. **DESCRIPTIVE RESEARCH** seeks to provide information about how the world is. For our current example, one would need to know what social media strategies are available. This is a simple question but an important one. Deciding which social media strategy to adopt (if any) requires much thought. Any thorough decision should consider how many residents have Internet access. If there are few residents with Internet access, there may be little reason to adopt an Internet-based social media technology. One certainly would not want to rely on an Internet-based fundraising strategy if the pool of potential donors to your nonprofit did not use these social media technologies. These are issues that require an accurate description of the world you are targeting. One way to think about descriptive research is to say that it answers questions that start with "who," "what," "when," "where," or "how many."

Many descriptive questions are trivial. Figuring out what options you have when considering different software packages (or what types of pens to stock in the office, etc.)

may involve looking at a catalog or doing a little online research. The questions become a little more complicated if you want to price shop and compare your options from different sellers. This is hardly the sort of research you need a class to teach you about, though. You do this sort of descriptive research all of the time when shopping for your own clothes, computers, etc.

Descriptive research becomes a little tougher when no one is trying to sell you something related to the information. One of the reasons shopping for software is relatively easy is that there is an entire industry of people wanting you to buy from them. It is in their interest to make your research easy. This is why you get advertisements in the mail and in e-mails. When you are seeking descriptive information that is not obviously tied to a specific purchase, you often have to collect the data yourself—this is where this textbook comes in. We will discuss how to collect your own data in those situations where people have not previously collected the data for you.

> **Class Exercise:** How would you answer the question of how many residents in your community use Facebook on a regular basis?

You may want to know (as discussed above) how many of your potential donors use Facebook. You want a simple description of your potential donors. This is not unlike wanting pricing information on software. In this case, though, no one has likely collected the data for you. You will need to do your own research to answer this question.

Descriptive research can be as specific or as vague as necessary to fit your research questions. You may want to look at specific subsets of your potential donor population. A subset is a specific group within the general group you are studying. Instead of studying all donors, you may be particularly interested in the Facebook usage of your donors sorted by age. It is a reasonable guess that younger donors may be more likely to use Facebook. You may then want to know about Facebook usage among your donors, grouped by age. A simple way to do this would be to create age categories of 10 years each. You may separate your donors into groups aged 21–30, 31–40, 41–50, 51–60, and 61+. You could try to figure out what percentage of potential donors in each of these categories use Facebook. If only the age group 21–30 uses Facebook, and they do not donate enough money to support your organization, naturally you would not want to rely on Facebook as your primary fundraising strategy.

Descriptive research can be as in depth or as simple as you want it to be. Some descriptive research will be easy to conduct because it will be easy to observe personally. You may be able to easily look up how much your office spent on computers last year. Other descriptive questions will be more difficult to answer. However, this is the starting point for most research. If you want to understand how the world works, you have to first understand what the world looks like.

Explanation

While descriptive research is the starting point, it is not the end. You will often want to know not only what the world looks like but also how the various pieces work together.

EXPLANATORY RESEARCH involves investigation of how changes in one part of the world are related to changes in other parts of the world. For example, one may want to know what it is that we do to increase the funds raised to support our nonprofit organization. This is more than description of any specific object in the world. We cannot simply ask how much money we are raising. We cannot simply ask about the demographics of the people we anticipate appealing to for funds. Explanatory research would entail linking our potential strategies (additional mailers, hiring a phone-based fund-raiser, using Facebook, etc.) to expected increases in revenue. While descriptive research is focused on the way the world *is*, explanatory research focuses on *change* and the relationship between changes. Explanatory research questions tend to start with "why" or "how."

Explanatory research is where research skills start to pay off for a manager. You want information that is useful to guide action. You want to know how you can act to accomplish your organization's goals. You can think of relationships in terms of simple machines. You want to know what will happen when you push a specific button—like starting a Facebook-based fundraising campaign. If you push the button, what comes out of the machine? If you start a Facebook-based fundraising campaign, how much money will you raise?

As you can tell, these are the sorts of research questions that really interest public managers. While descriptive research is important, it is generally a part of a process intended to generate data to support learning about explanations. We have to be able to describe our potential donors if we ever hope to understand the imaginary donation machine.

> **Class Exercise:** How would you answer the question of how much money you could raise if you started a Facebook-based fundraising effort? Did you find coming up with a research strategy to answer this question more or less difficult than the question in the previous exercise?

If we want to know what buttons to push to raise additional funds, we need a detailed description of potential donors. Explanatory research links the bits of descriptive information together to help us understand the relationship between our actions and the outcomes of those actions.

Causal Inference

The gold standard for explanatory information is causal inference. For now, it is sufficient to define CAUSAL INFERENCE as knowledge that links causes to effects. Remember that explanatory research is designed to provide information of the relationships between objects in the world. Causality is a specific type of relationship. From our machine analogy above, causal knowledge involves knowing exactly what will happen when you press a button (or start a fundraising campaign, or build bike trails in your city, etc.). Causal knowledge is the type of information we want to inform our decision about actions. Fundamentally, we want to know what the effects of our actions will be. We want to know what our actions will cause to happen. If we start a fundraising campaign, we want to know how much money we can raise. If we build bike trails, we want to know how many people will likely use these trails.

Causal relationships involve specific stipulations that are not present in general explanatory research. First, there must be some correlation between the cause and the effect. We will define correlation more formally later in the textbook. For now, **CORRELATION** simply means that there is some systematic relationship between changes in one object and changes in another. For example, posting more to Facebook may increase the amount of donations to your organization. When postings go up, donations go up. If this is true, there is a correlation. There are a variety of types of potential correlation patterns. When we expect to see an increase in the effect wherever we see an increase in the cause, we have a **DIRECT RELATIONSHIP**. We might expect a direct relationship between postings on Facebook and donations. This means that we would expect that as we see more postings that we will see more donations. An **INVERSE** or **NEGATIVE RELATIONSHIP** is one where increases in the cause lead to reductions in the effect. Increasing the number of police officers on the street may be related to a reduction in crime. This would be an inverse relationship between patrols and crime. One can imagine more complicated relationships, but this is a good starting point. If there is no relationship between supposed causes and effects, then there is no causality present. The presence of such a relationship, though, is not enough.

Second, causes must occur before effects in time. This stipulation is pretty simple. If we are to say that pressing a button results in the machine producing a toy, the toy has to emerge after we press the button. If an increase in donations occurs before we start increasing our posts to Facebook, we cannot say that Facebook caused the increase in donations. For our purposes, causal knowledge is intended to support action. If the effect were to precede the cause, there would no need for an action. The goal of our action, the effect, would already be present. This is a fairly technical requirement and does not create much of a problem for most public management research—though one does need to be careful not to make a mistake by ignoring sequences in time. If you claim that Facebook posts increased donations and someone later reveals that the posts took place after the donations, you would look silly.

Third, there must be a theory to support the relationship between the objects. This stipulation is important because it is possible to see relationships between objects and where the time-order is correct but there is clearly no causality. Every year, the number of Christmas cards sent in the mail increases dramatically between late November and mid-December. Soon after, Christmas happens. This relationship is very strong and the purported cause (cards) precedes the effect (Christmas) in time. It happens every year in recent memory. This is a strong relationship but we would not want to say that Christmas cards cause Christmas. That would be ridiculous. The presence of the relationship is not enough because we cannot construct a plausible theory that cards cause the holiday. It is clear that the anticipation of Christmas leads to cards.

Fourth, there must be no other factors that explain both the purported cause and the effect. This third "other" factor is called a source of spuriousness. This condition turns out to be the hardest requirement to meet for causal knowledge. Much of our attention to research design in later chapters will focus on eliminating spurious factors. Consider this example. Imagine that the Facebook strategy was recommended by one of your prominent donors. The donor was dedicated to your organization and wanted to see you raise more money. As one of many recommendations, she suggested you post more to Facebook to raise your profile. After making this suggestion, the big donor also went around trying to convince other people to donate to your organization—with some success. If you only looked at the relationship between postings and donations, it would look like you met the three previous conditions of causality. However, this may be an illusion. It could be that the postings had no effect at all but that the efforts of the big donor behind the scenes is why you actually saw more money coming in. In this example, the big donor caused both the postings and the increase in donations. Even though a connection between Facebook posting and donations is theoretically plausible (meeting the third condition), the connection is not a reliable basis for acting in the future. If the big donor was absent and you tried to raise funds by posting to Facebook, it might not work at all. You have to eliminate all of these potential sources of spuriousness before you can have faith that what you have learned is a sound basis for action in the future.

Spuriousness is a common problem in public affairs research. It takes a great deal of imagination and experience to identify potential sources of spuriousness. If you have recently implemented a new advertising campaign to increase the use of your public health clinics and saw an increase, you may be tempted to quickly conclude that the advertising campaign worked. However, you have to look closely for sources of spuriousness. Was the advertising campaign motivated by a major national incident, like the national attention to a prominent seasonal flu? If so, the national attention could drive people who never saw the ad campaign to the clinic. The major seasonal flu motivated both the creation of the ad campaign and the use of the clinic—even if the ad campaign was a complete failure.

It is also possible that the ad campaign coincided with some other changes that could drive use of the public health clinic. It could be that the use of the clinic was increasing every month before the ad campaign—possibly due to an economic downturn. If the trend continued, even if the ad campaign had no effect, it would look as if the ad campaign worked to increase use of the clinic. This is not an example of spuriousness because the economic downturn was unrelated to the ad campaign but is an example of a potentially confounding influence.

> **Class Exercise:** If you observed an increase in donations to your organization after the creation of a full-time position related to social media, what might explain the increase other than the new position? Which of these explanations are cases of spuriousness?

Research and Evaluation

Just as one can distinguish between descriptive, explanatory, and causal research, one can distinguish between research and evaluation. These terms can become confusing and are sometimes used interchangeably. The confusion stems from the similarity of the tool sets needed for research and evaluation. In this respect, this textbook will equip you to conduct research and to evaluate programs. The difference between the two comes in when you consider the intent behind the research activities.

EVALUATION work tends to focus on answering questions related to the success or failure of specific programs in specific organizations. The purpose of the work is not necessarily to make a contribution to general knowledge about a management strategy or policy. Instead, the intent is to decide whether a specific program did or did not work. For example, one could evaluate whether a new training program had actually increased the speed with which case workers in an organization handle their daily workload. The intent is to decide on the success or failure of the training program, not to learn something about case work or training programs generally. Evaluation work is important for the day-to-day work of managers and accountability for the use of funds. The latter has become particularly important to nonprofit and government organizations that seek external funding in the form of grants.

General research work focuses, instead, on the creation of knowledge about public affairs activities to share with other organizations. A public affairs research project might investigate whether one type of training program works better than another. The aspiration is to make a general comparison that could lead other organizations to adopt the more effective training strategy.

These two motivations for research can overlap. The evaluation of a local program can inform decisions in other organizations. The difference is in emphasis and goals. Evaluation focuses on a specific program but may contribute, secondarily, to a broader investigation. General research may start with or include the evaluation of specific projects. The activities related to evaluation and general research are so similar that we will treat them interchangeably for purposes of developing a set of skills.

Argumentation in Public Management

One way to think of any decision, such as whether to invest in a social media strategy, as an argument. Whether you have an actual argument with defenders of each option presenting a case or the debate occurs within your mind, there are basic principles of argumentation you should follow. Toulmin proposed a simple model to describe the parts of an argument to assist in this process. This model illustrates how the various components of arguments fit together and how one might use the information generated by research to make better decisions. In a way, arguments are the means by which you can put research into action.

The Toulmin Model

The Toulmin model separates arguments into three parts: claim, evidence, and warrant. We will discuss each part in turn.

Claim   The central and most obvious component of argument is the **CLAIM**. A claim is simply the statement you seek to evaluate or act upon. "Hiring a social media specialist to assist with fundraising will be cost effective" is such a statement. Forcing yourself to write out such a statement can be quite useful. You cannot start to answer questions before you can clearly state the questions. This is simply the process of asking whether a claim is true or not. Good claims will be specific, falsifiable, and relevant to the overarching purpose of your research project.

> Three characteristics of good claims:
>
> (1) Specific
> (2) Falsifiable
> (3) Relevant

First, being specific in stating the claim will pay off by making the later stages of argumentation and decision making easier. A first attempt at writing a claim relevant to our social media example might look like this:

Adopting a social media strategy will be good for my office.

This claim is actually quite vague and would be difficult to answer conclusively. It is difficult to say what "adopting a social media" actually means. It could mean buying specific software. It could mean hiring personnel. It could even mean redefining the tasks of existing employees. Each of these options would involve different costs. Some may be good while others are not. Without being specific, it will be hard to reach a conclusive answer as to whether the claim is true or not.

There is also ambiguity in the term "good." What does it mean for adopting a social media strategy to be good? It could increase revenues (for the nonprofit organization) or increase the ability of the organization to identify emerging disease outbreaks (for the WHO). WHO may be not concerned with fundraising (at least for the purposes of this research project), and the nonprofit may not be concerned with monitoring disease outbreaks. Each of these organizations has a different set of goals and a different definition of what is "good." Even within a single example, the nonprofit organization may see no increase in fundraising but an increase in name recognition related to the social media strategy. It is not clear whether this is good or not. Ambiguity in the terms of the claim can make it difficult or impossible to evaluate (i.e., to declare true or false).

The other two characteristics of good claims are easier to evaluate. You want a claim to be falsifiable, otherwise there will be no hope that you will be able to conclude your research. If a claim can never be proven false, you will never know when to stop employing the scientific method and move on to other important questions. Relevance is even more obvious. You want a clear relation between your claim and the purpose of your research. You do not want to spend your time researching claims that do not directly inform your decision. Like with unfalsifiable claims, irrelevant claims can leave you wasting time researching and arguing about topics that do not move you closer to a well-informed public management decision.

> **Class Exercise:** How could you improve the social media claim discussed earlier in this section?

Reason/Evidence   Making claims is relatively simple. I can claim, "If you buy the software I am selling, your employees will become 25% more efficient." There, that was easy to claim. It is much harder to provide a reason or evidence to convince people that the claim is true. Saying it is not enough. We require evidence to support decisions about the use of resources in public organizations—and we should.

There are generally two strategies for supporting claims. One can provide a reason or a piece of evidence. A **REASON** is a general rule while a piece of **EVIDENCE** is some observation that supports the claim—each corresponding to deductive and inductive reasoning, respectively. If I could provide an example of where an office had implemented the software I am selling and experienced a 25 percent increase in productivity, this could be persuasive evidence. If I provided an article that spoke in general terms about productivity increases related to software, this could be a source of persuasive reasons.

Reasons and evidence to support claims related to public management can be difficult to find. Instead, public managers must evaluate complex claims about predicted costs and benefits, predicted effectiveness of new policies, etc. The sorts of claims that public managers have to act upon are those about which it is difficult to collect evidence or provide convincing reasons.

We will focus on the collection of empirical observations to serve as evidence for public management decisions. As discussed above, collecting reasons involves surveying the literature for general rules. Although the book will discuss conducting literature reviews in a systematic way, the bulk of it will discuss collecting evidence. Collecting evidence is more complex than collecting reasons from the literature and will require a much more diverse and likely unfamiliar set of tools.

Warrant   Evidence does not interpret itself. The last part of an argument is the **WARRANT** wherein you explain how the reason or evidence is sufficient to provide confidence in the claim. The warrant will include the characteristics of evidence that should convince a manager to invest in a software package. Past performance could be a strong source of evidence—but only if the experience is in a similar organization. If the experience came as part of a large organization in a different field, a manager of a small organization may not find the experience to be persuasive evidence that the software would achieve similar results in his organization. If a social media strategy worked for the national office of the American Red Cross, it may not work for a small, local food bank. For any argument, you need to consider what evidence would convince you of the claim. Not just any evidence will do.

Reasons and evidence tend to require different types of warrants. A reason is a general rule, so a warrant for a reason would involve the relevance of the general rule to the specific situation. A reason to support using a social media strategy to raise funds could be that social media strategies reach new audiences and thus are likely to raise money from new donors. This seems like a plausible reason. The warrant will need to argue that this reason is relevant to your organization's specific situation. If you are a new nonprofit, there is no reason that you need to reach a "new" audience. You don't have a previous audience. This may not be a good warrant in this case. However, if you happen to notice that phone-based fundraising is bringing in the same sorts of donors (and ignoring the same populations as well), then this warrant may be persuasive in your situation. The key question is whether the general rule (the reason) is relevant to your claim.

Warrants for evidence operate differently. The warrant is the part of the argument where you explain why the evidence should be accepted as persuasive. The warrant would include why the example organization that experienced the efficiency gain is similar to your own organization. More generally, it is a reason one should accept that the presented evidence actually supports the claim. If I provided an example of a nonprofit that had hired a social media specialist and

Class Exercise: Consider the following passage related to our current example.

Nonprofit organizations must catch up to new technology by integrating social media technologies like Facebook and Twitter. We have entered a new world of media and publicity. Our tools for fundraising must change with these times. People are spending more and more time using these tools and increasingly relying on them for information about friends and organizations. We should appeal to donors wherever they are. They are now on Twitter and Facebook, so it is incumbent on us to meet them there.

Can you identify the claim, reason or evidence, and warrant in this passage?

seen an increase in donations, this might be an easy piece of evidence to warrant. One could question whether one example was enough to have confidence in the claim. One could question whether the example nonprofit was sufficiently similar to our own organization so that what worked for them will work for us. There are reasonable questions that are specific to the confidence we have in the evidence itself. The warrant seeks to address these questions.

In our example of the social media strategy, we must consider what type of evidence is available and what would convince us to invest resources. It may be enough (and clearly is for some) to find that some self-described expert has published an article saying that social media strategies are effective fundraising tools. This is the use of a reason as evidence (a general rule popularized by a management guru), and the warrant would

need to explain why that general rule would hold for our organization. Others may not be convinced, especially if that expert makes money selling services or advice related to implementing her advice. Others may want to analyze the available data to ensure that the empirical evidence supports the claim. These skeptics may want to observe actual organizations using the advice and see what happens; they prefer evidence to general reasons. We are from this skeptical crowd. The book will focus on evidence as opposed to reasons. It will teach you how to observe your

Class Exercise: Consider the following passage related to our current example.

Nonprofit organizations can benefit greatly from incorporating social media into their fundraising strategies. By reaching entirely new audiences, nonprofit organizations can raise money from a much broader pool than those reached through traditional means. In Dallas, TX, we worked with three nonprofit organizations to create a presence on Facebook and Twitter. These organizations, recently launched nonprofit organizations and then saw steady increases in their donations after implementing their social media strategies.

Can you identify the claim, reason or evidence, and warrant in this example?

organization or community systematically to generate evidence rather than rely predominately on general rules and books of general advice. These tools will help you generate your own advice.

Approach of the Textbook

The goal of this textbook is to teach you the research skills you will need as a public manager. Managers need to develop knowledge to support action. It is quite often the case that the information you need to make these decisions will not be readily available. In these situations, managers have to collect and analyze their own data. This textbook is intended to provide the tools you need to do just that.

Sometimes it is difficult to see the connection between the development of specific research skills and the practice of public management. It may be hard, for example, to see how discussions of how to conduct a survey or select a location for your research will pay off for public managers. Sometimes this is a case of losing sight of the forest (developing competency of a public affairs researcher) as we focus on the trees (specific research skills). Sometimes the tension comes from the difficulty in seeing how a specific skill would be used in practice. The textbook will address both of these problems through the use of motivating case studies and the development of a research toolbox.

Cases in Public Management Research

Each chapter (starting with chapter 3) will begin with realistic situations in which managers need to conduct their own research. There are two purposes for the cases. The first is that the cases address why it is that managers need specific skills in research methodology. It is common for students to wonder, while in the middle of a research methods class, why they would ever need these skills. Why does one need to know how to conduct an interview? Why does one need to learn statistics to analyze data? With the examples, you will see why managers need these specific skills within specific contexts.

Second, the concrete nature of the cases will provide enough details to illustrate the challenges inherent in actual research. Our goal is to let you see the complexities of the public manager's role in research. Not only will you see why research is so important to public managers, but also you will see how it is that these research projects operate and evolve in practice. You will learn how managers respond to specific research needs. This will give you a sense of how managers can conduct research as part of their work.

The case-based approach is tied to our commitment to a pragmatic view of research methods. There are a variety of philosophical approaches to the study of administrative organization and social processes. Some of the approaches question the very enterprise of building a science of social processes. Our focus is not on these philosophical arguments over issues of ontology or epistemology, but on the pragmatic needs of professional education. Our focus is on what is effective in practice, while also considering how one can define what effectiveness actually is in any given situation. Our goal is to provide managers with tools to employ in a variety of situations and some background to develop the instincts necessary for effective practice.

Toolbox Approach with Attention to Ethics

The textbook will help you develop a toolbox for research. It will rarely be the case that any research challenge you face will call for the use of all of the tools we discuss within the textbook. Instead, you will need to choose the right tool for your specific research job. Sometimes a survey will be a useful tool to answer your research questions. Other times, a survey will not get you the data you need, or it will be impossible. The key to effective research is the match between the research question, available resources, and your own set of skills. With a diverse set of skills, you will have the tools you need for a broad range of situations.

Although we concentrate on the use of your toolbox of research methods skills, we must also include a discussion of the rules of ethics that govern the use of these tools. Just as there are rules of appropriateness that govern how one should act as a student, there are rules that govern how one should act as a researcher. We will discuss these in greater detail as they become relevant to specific research subjects but consider the various kinds of rules that are at stake with research. Most prominently, there are rules governing the subjects of our research. Social science research, like much of what we do as public affairs researchers, involves human subjects; and we must respect the rights of these subjects. For example, if we collect information on specific individuals, we are obligated to protect their privacy. The rights of our research subjects must always be in our view and will involve different restrictions depending on the nature of the research strategy.

There are also ethical obligations that affect the analysis and presentation of results. These ethical obligations are closest to those with which you may be familiar as students. Analysis must be done in an honest fashion rather than manipulated to serve the interests of the researcher. Similarly, the presentation of results must be honest in the sense that the findings should not be presented in a way to mislead a reader or listener. The position of the researcher is not unlike that of a doctor or lawyer in that you are called upon to provide expert advice. The people who need your advice are vulnerable in a sense that they rely upon your expertise. Respect for the people who rely upon our research imposes ethical obligations on us to analyze and present research in specific ways. Again, the obligations as they relate to specific approaches to analysis and presentation will be addressed in later chapters.

Conclusion

This chapter has briefly previewed our approach to research methods for public affairs. It provided some of the fundamental context for research methods. You can see the logical and historical roots of research methods and how we approach these issues within the textbook. This is only the very beginning of the journey. In the next chapter, we will situate research methods in the context of public affairs and the tasks of public managers while introducing the cases. After that, we will start putting together your research toolbox.

Vocabulary

CAUSAL INFERENCE—An explanation that links causes and effects.

CLAIM—A statement you seek to evaluate or act upon.

CORRELATION—Some systematic relationship between changes in one object and changes in another.

DEDUCTION—The process of using rules that define how we know the world works, in order to eliminate implausible explanations.

DESCRIPTIVE RESEARCH—The type of research that seeks to provide information about how the world is.

DIRECT RELATIONSHIP—A relationship in which we expect an increase in the effect wherever we see an increase in the cause.

EVALUATION—A specific type of research that focuses on the success or failure of a specific program or policy.

EVIDENCE—An observation used in support of a claim.

EXPLANATORY RESEARCH—The type of research that involves investigation of how changes in one part of the world are related to changes in other parts of the world.

INDUCTION—Learning from the world by observation.

INVERSE/NEGATIVE RELATIONSHIP—A relationship in which we expect that an increase in the cause leads to a reduction in the effect.

OPPORTUNITY COSTS—The alternative uses for the resources one devotes to a plan.

PUBLIC MANAGER—A key decision maker within a public organization (including any organization serving a public-oriented mission).

REASON—A general rule used in support of a claim.

THE SCIENTIFIC METHOD—The reliance on observations of the world—rather than accepting general rules as reasons—as a basis for judgment.

WARRANT—A statement of how the reason or evidence is sufficient to provide confidence in the claim.

Flashcards & MCQs

Useful Websites

Review Questions

- What are the three parts of an argument? What purpose does each part serve?
- What are the four conditions of causal explanation?
- In the following cases, would you expect a direct or an inverse relationship?
    - Between age and Internet usage
    - Between age and volunteer hours per week
    - Between income and charitable donations

■ For any of the cases in the previous question, would you predict a more complex relationship than direct or inverse?

Discussion Questions

■ What standards would you use to evaluate an argument based on a reason—as opposed to evidence?

■ How many examples of organizations that have successfully used Facebook to raise funds would it take to convince you that it could work for your organization?

■ What sorts of ethical considerations are relevant when conducting a survey of donors about their use of social media sites?

CHAPTER 2

Evidence-Based Practice For Public Affairs

Learning Objectives

✓ Understand the origins of evidence-based practice in fields such as medicine, education, and private sector management

✓ Understand the role of research for a practicing public manager

✓ Understand the application of research within five key cases of public management research

Cases in Research

This chapter will introduce a number of examples of actual research in public management practice. Based on actual public management research projects, these examples serve to make research skills more concrete and illustrate the importance of each specific skills set. Subsequent chapters will begin with a brief discussion of two of these cases. These cases will help you see when public managers have to employ the variety of research skills taught in this textbook. You can use these case discussions to appreciate when specific skills are necessary.

The Origins of Evidence-Based Practice

Our attention to evidence parallels a variety of efforts in other areas of professional education. Students intending to practice (or to return to practice) in a field need a specific sort of training. The skills taught in a research methods textbook need to be tailored to inform practice and include practical tools. For many students, research is an activity limited to academics. This badly misleads what actual work is like in public affairs. A growing movement within public affairs emphasizes that research should be a part of every manager's portfolio. Every manager should be able to ask and answer research questions relevant to his work. We were motivated to write this textbook out of just this sort of belief. We firmly believe that public managers should ground their decisions in evidence (rather than custom, suspicion, or blind guessing). We will refer to this approach as evidence-based public management or evidence-based practice in public affairs.

> **Class Exercise:** Based on your view of what work in public affairs is like, what examples of relevant research for public managers can you think of?

The experiences with evidence-based practice in three related fields will illustrate some of the strengths and weaknesses of the approach taken in this textbook while placing evidence-based public management in context. Seeing what evidence-based practice looks like in different fields will help you understand what evidence-based public management can look like.

Evidence-Based Medicine

When we visit a doctor, we hope to receive the best possible treatment. Given how important our health is to us—and the expense of contemporary medicine—it is perfectly reasonable to have high expectations for medical care. It is little wonder, then, that the contemporary evidence-based practice movement charts its origin to the practice of medicine. When a doctor provides poor advice, prescribes the wrong medicine, or performs the wrong procedure, people can die. This is one of the professions where we have the highest expectations for the quality of care.

> **Class Exercise:** If your doctor told you that you needed a specific surgery, what sort of evidence would you hope she would base her recommendation on?

The Case for Evidence-Based Medicine   Consider the sorts of pharmaceuticals that a doctor may prescribe to you if you have a sinus infection. You want to know that this medicine works and does not have major side effects. Our pharmaceutical drug regulation system provides strict standards for how drug companies test medicines and bring them to market. The Food and Drug Administration (FDA) would not accept an expert saying, "I think this medicine will work." They would not accept an analogy between an existing drug and a proposed drug ("This new drug is similar to an old one— so just approve it."). The FDA requires an elaborate set of tests to demonstrate both the effectiveness and safety of medicines before they will allow a drug on the market. The FDA wants to observe that the drug works and is safe. In short, they demand evidence.

We may have similar expectations about the sorts of advice that any health care provider gives us. You may be surprised, though, that this is often not the case. While we have an elaborate system for approving new pharmaceuticals, individual doctors and nurses may or may not update their knowledge about the advice they give patients. Drug companies have a financial interest in getting word out about new drugs they are selling.

In the absence of someone possessing such a financial interest, we rely on doctors and other health care professionals to educate themselves continuously. Sadly, this does not always happen. Some health care professionals rely on what they were taught years, sometimes decades, before. Given the rate at which we learn about medicine and health, much of what was taught 10 years ago (much less 30 years ago) is now known to be either false or severely limited. However, many of these old practices persist among those health care professionals who have been using the same techniques for this entire time and have not kept up with current research.

The contemporary evidence-based medicine movement is a reaction to concerns about these decades-old practices. Proponents of evidence-based medicine argue that all medical practice should rely on techniques proven to be effective and safe based on strict standards of evidence (like we do for drug approvals). Such a standard for medical practice requires significant changes the in practice of medicine and the education of health care providers.

Evidence-Based Medicine in Practice   Creating a health care system that practices evidence-based medicine forces people to rethink the way we teach doctors and nurses and even what it means to be a medical practitioner. The foundation of evidence-based management is the standardization of what counts as strong evidence. This is a controversial process as we will see throughout the textbook. People have a variety of views as to what counts as sufficiently strong evidence to serve as the basis for medical practice. On the strict side of the debate, some contend that all medical practices must be tested on large groups of individuals (following strict ethical protections for the individuals, of course), using elaborate experimental methods. Others argue that studies of smaller groups using less elaborate methods can still serve as the basis for medical evidence—even if the goal is to test everything using more elaborate methods eventually. The debates over what counts as sufficient rage still.

The implications of evidence-based practice extend to the education and practice of medicine. The most significant change is the movement toward continuous education. Medical education cannot be something that a medical practitioner receives earlier in his or her career and then serves as the basis for their decisions updated only with their personal experience. While their personal experience is valuable, evidence-based medicine emphasizes that it is not enough. One needs to combine personal experience with the results of careful, rigorous studies from outside sources. This combination of personal experience and external studies forces medical practitioners to exercise judgment while continually updating what they know about medicine.

> **Class Exercise:** To what extent, if any, are the sorts of decisions that public managers have to make similar to the advice a doctor gives?

Most importantly evidence-based medicine calls for a change in how medical practitioners think about how they do their job. Every practitioner should ask themselves why he believes every treatment he recommends is safe and effective. Practitioners need to question everything they do at all times. They should not simply perform procedures because they were taught to—unless they are also aware of evidence that supports the procedures' safety and effectiveness. Furthermore, practitioners have to continually update their knowledge with new studies and learning from their own experiences.

Evidence-Based Education

Education has also been an area of professional practice that has adopted the call for evidence-based practice from its recent resurgence in medicine. Like medicine, education is seen as a policy area where a great deal is at stake. The amount of spending on education is staggering, making up a large proportion of state and local government spending. Years of struggling to develop educational reforms that would improve the success of students—particularly students of traditionally disadvantaged groups—left many wondering what could possibly be done. Seeing the promise of evidence-based medicine, some have called for a similar movement in education.

Adopting Evidence-Based Practice in Education

The logic behind evidence-based education is similar to the logic of evidence-based medicine. Before we trust schools to educate our children (and spend our money), we want to be sure that the educational strategies that they are using are proven to be effective. For example, before a school district adopts an elaborate new curriculum to teach elementary school children how to read, we should ask for evidence that this curriculum is more effective than what the school district was doing before the reform. The strategy of evidence-based education can be applied to more than curricula. One would want evidence for every aspect of educational administration, including hiring practices (What type of training best prepares teachers to help their studens thrive?), personnel practices (How can we best reward teachers as a means to improve student learning?), or even disciplinary policy (How we can design a disciplinary system to reduce disruptions?). Like with evidence-based medicine, the proponents of evidence-based education want every decision made in a school to be based on rigorous evidence.

The centerpiece of the recent evidence-based education movement has been the law entitled No Child Left Behind. While the legislation has many parts, one of the most prominent components was the requirement that states implement standardized testing at many grade levels to track the progress of students. At around the same time, leaders in the Department of Education began to promote the use of such standardized data to test the effectiveness of education reforms. They promoted using experimental studies like those popular in medical research but recognized that such research was rare (and difficult to conduct) in education. In addition to experimental studies, they recommended the use of advanced statistical approaches using data like that collected from large standardized exams. Together these efforts signaled that evidence-based education research would be influential in national education policy making.

Criticisms of Evidence-Based Education

While medical research had a long tradition of focusing on experimental trials for testing medical procedures and pharmaceuticals, education research has long included a broad range of approaches to

> **Class Exercise:** What (if any-thing) is it about education that makes it different from medicine and less likely to benefit from evidence-based practice?

research. The statements from Department of Education officials preferring experimental and large statistical studies based on standardized testing generated a great deal of opposition within the education research community.

At its heart, the criticisms of evidence-based education research argued that education is not the sort of process that one can study in the same way that one studies the effects of a new pharmaceutical. Some, for example, argue that implementing an educational program is not like giving someone a pill. Educational pro-grams are applied over time, and their success depends on a combination of the students, teachers, and curriculum (and maybe the school, parents, and even more). This is quite different than giving some a pill. Furthermore, it is not clear that we can define the goals of education. We have some consensus on what characterizes health, but there are still major debates over what constitutes a good education. Since the definition of a good education is a moving target, the tools needed to evaluate educational practices may be different than those useful in situations where the goals are clearer.

Evidence-Based Management

The arguments in favor of evidence-based practice have also begun to gain traction in business schools and research into private sector business management. Here, though, the integration of evidence-based practice has taken on a slightly different character. The private sector business management field of practice is the closest we have seen to the breadth and work in public management (though, admittedly, the fields are not identical). The experience with evidence-based private sector management provides the clearest example of what evidence-based practice in public affairs can look like.

Management Fads and Unhelpful Advice
There is a great deal of money in providing advice to private sector businesses. There are entire services that exist to do nothing more than summarize the volumes of literature published every month that provide advice on business leadership and strategy. Many within the field, though, have grown dissatisfied with the literature as a whole. While there is a great deal published, much of it is based purely on limited personal experience and a cycle of clichés. For a few years, many books will recommend that leaders need to centralize their business and that strong leadership is the key to success. This advice will eventually give way to a new wave of books recommending exactly the opposite approach—decentralized leadership, delegation, and employee empowerment. Cycles of advice repeat like this over time.

You can imagine how frustrating this can be for business professionals. These cycles are not entirely absent in medicine and education. In dietary terms, various foods come into and fall out of favor. The same holds for education where approaches to education cycle in popularity. The business literature is just an extreme example of this process.

Having seen the popularity of evidence-based practices in other fields, management scholars began to call for evidence-based management as a way to stop these cycles. If business advice had to come with supporting evidence, there would be fewer dramatic swings of trends.

The Search for Hard Truths in Management Practice and Education

The effort to ground management advice in empirical research has been a tough sell. As in the case of education research, management research had long involved a mixture of different strategies. There is a strong tradition of successful businesspeople publishing books of advice based on their years of experience. However, these texts get caught in the same cycles of reforms as the rest of the literature. The broad, sweeping recommendations tend to get caught in the wave of reform advice. As experienced practitioners think back on their experience, they do so through the filter of current trends. If it is currently quite popular to say that strong central leadership is the key to success, business leaders will look back on their life and see many examples of how central leadership worked for them. At the same time, they are likely to overlook times when delegation, the opposite of central leadership, also served them well. The books are instead filled with examples that confirm the popular trend.

The call for evidence-based management intends to correct this tendency to follow trends. Instead of merely reflecting on personal experience, proponents of evidence-based management recommend that personal experience be combined with rigorous empirical research. In the simplest terms, the evidence-based management movement recommends that you not promote a management practice until you have seen the practice work not only for your business, but also for other businesses as well. There is still room for reflecting on your own experience. However, you need to have a stronger basis before you advocate any particular approach.

The evidence-based management movement has a relatively broad view of what counts as external evidence. Part of the movement is to start a discussion of what should count as strong evidence. The starting point for the discussion is not as dogmatic as the almost singular emphasis on randomized experiments in medicine or education. A careful study of a single organization can shed light on the practice of management, as well.

Evidence-Based Public Management

The evidence-based practice movement is starting to make headway into public management as well. Just as the evidence-based practice movements have looked a little different in each of the other fields in which it emerged, it will need to take a slightly different shape within public management. In this section, we will review the specific needs of public managers and the shape that evidence-based public management must take.

The Challenges of Public Management Practice

The shape of evidence-based public management will depend on the nature of work in public management. The predisposition of evidence-based medicine for random clinical trials came from the history of medical research and the nature of medical practice. There must be a close match between the tools of evidence-based practice and the specific area of practice it is supposed to inform. You will need to understand the nature of work in public management to understand the set of tools necessary to base public management activities in practice.

This raises the question of what the practice of public management looks like. What sort of activities do public managers do? Of course, this is a difficult question to answer. Public managers do many things. In some ways, they perform tasks quite similar to managers in the private sector. Public managers may be involved in decisions such as whom to hire and whom to promote in their organization. Public managers have to make decisions about how to allocate their own time between collaborating with other organizations, working with their own employees for training and evaluation, planning for the future, etc. These are not tasks that are not peculiar to public management.

What may be peculiar to public management is the context in which some of the decisions are made. Public managers face a particular set of constraints when hiring and firing. Some of these constraints may come from the U.S. Congress or from a state capital. In all, public managers may have less discretion over their specific hiring decisions. Similarly, public organizations may have missions assigned to their organization (by a legislature or a chief executive) rather than the organization defining itself. This is easy to see if you compare a fast food restaurant to a local school. If a restaurant is not prospering by serving hamburgers, it can decide to change into a pizza place. It could even change into a convenience store. The local school cannot choose what it is. It cannot decide it wants to become a housing agency—much less a pizza place.

The lack of discretion would not be entirely unfamiliar to people within the private sector. If you are managing a regional office within a larger national corporation, you don't have the choice to redefine the mission of your organization. If you run a warehouse for Walmart, you cannot decide that your organization should instead be a movie theater. The manager of a warehouse may also face regulations on hiring from a national office. In this way, private sector management is not all that dissimilar from management in the public sector.

Another way that public management may be distinctive is the nature of the goals of public sector organizations. Public sector organizations often pursue goals that are vague and difficult to see or measure. A pizza restaurant wants to make money. It is pretty clear when it is succeeding or when it is failing. It is much harder to tell when a local housing agency is doing well. Similarly, it is hard to tell when a charity that provides meals to the elderly is doing well. The nature of the work often deals with complicated processes like homelessness, education, health, and the like. It is rarely as simple as delivering pizza and making money. Here, again, the comparisons are not as simple as they seem. While a pizza place may make a simple good and have simple goals, it is not always easy to tell whether a private sector company is doing a good job. A private sector company that writes software may have a hard time knowing whether it has done a good job until some time after it releases the software. It may be hard to tell whether the advice a private sector consulting company is providing to you is good. In these situations, the complexity and ambiguity of some private sector work may resemble the complexity found in the public sector.

It is worth emphasizing that we mean public management to include a broad range of organizations—not just government organizations. We take public management to include all organizations where public service and the public interest are core missions. This clearly includes a wide variety of government organizations including local government and city planning organizations, social service organizations, public health, and education organizations. However, it also includes a wide variety of nongovernmental organizations that also serve the public interest. This could include local or national charities including those with general community service missions and those with narrow missions like providing housing to the homeless. As you will see in the examples that follow, the tools we present will be useful for managers in a wide range of government and nonprofit organizations.

The Role of the Public Manager in Research

How are public managers actually involved in research? The proponents of evidence-based public management suggest that there are a variety of ways in which research is relevant to public managers. As the essential basis for effective decisions, evidence is the life-blood of public management decision making. Research is the process of collecting and analyzing this evidence.

Most managers are familiar with their roles as the consumers of research. It is natural for anyone making decisions, like a public manager, to want information on which to base these decisions. If you need to decide whether to add a new employee, you will want to know what that new employee can do. To continue an example from last chapter, you will want evidence to evaluate the claim that hiring an Internet fund-raiser will help bring in additional donations to your nonprofit organization (above and beyond the cost of paying his or her salary, of course).

Collecting evidence on what one can expect from hiring an Internet fund-raising specialist puts a manager in the position of consuming research. Being a knowledgeable consumer of evidence requires knowing how to collect and analyze evidence. It is easiest to understand the dangers of not being a knowledgeable consumer if you consider what happens in the absence of strong evidence-based management skills. If you cannot assess the quality of evidence, you are at the mercy of whomever you ask to analyze data for you. They become the one who decides which policies are based on sound evidence and which are not. To the extent that you are serious about basing decisions on evidence, these interpreters become influential, even powerful, in the process. You do not want to leave yourself at someone else's mercy simply for the lack of research tools.

Evidence-based management calls for more than reading research that other people have done. Many of the questions you have as a manager will not have ready answers based on sound evidence available to you. You will have to collect and analyze your own evidence in these cases. This text is designed to help you become not only a more knowledgeable consumer of research but also one capable of conducting your own research to answer the questions you run across in practice.

Cases in Evidence-Based Public Management

Throughout the textbook, we will provide examples of actual research projects related to public management. Each of these examples is based on existing or realistic projects—though the details have been fictionalized so that no individuals or communities are identifiable. We have adapted the cases so that they serve our needs of illustrating key research principles. The purposes of these cases is to show you when public managers actually face research problems as well as to illustrate practical examples of how public managers solve these problems.

A Note on Fictional Cases: It is fair to ask why we have chosen to fictionalize details of our cases if we want realistic cases at all. There are two key reasons we have chosen this strategy.

(1) When conducting the research related to the fictionalized cases, we never asked the research participants if they were willing to have their responses included in a textbook. Getting such permission is morally obligatory but impractical at this stage, years removed from the conclusion of some of the projects. We will discuss the ethics of data collection in a future chapter.

(2) The demands of writing a mixed methods textbook require a careful balancing of different research techniques and the explorations of various possible research strategies. To include the various research strategies across the cases, we needed the flexibility to add or subtract elements from the actual cases. We have, though, tried to retain as much of the factual basis (accommodating the needs for anonymity discussed above) as possible for each case.

National Helping Hands

Disasters disrupt our communities in ways that far exceed the abilities of any one government agency to fix. Preparing for and responding to disasters calls for a broad range of organizations within any community. Some of these organizations are government agencies, but not all of them. A variety of nongovernmental agencies perform functions essential to disaster preparedness, response, and relief. You are likely familiar with the American Red Cross and some other prominent organizations. The Red Cross is even written into federal legislation to lead the national efforts related to mass sheltering.

You are likely less familiar with the vast network of nonprofit organizations that provide a myriad of services to specific communities. Some nonprofits provide supporting services like feeding first responders or clearing fallen tree limbs so that people can return to stricken neighborhoods. Some of these nonprofits, many of whom are affiliated with religious organizations, are the most reliable source for critical emergency services. To a great extent, the work of these organizations is unheralded despite its important role in communities.

The National Helping Hand (NHH) organization serves as a coordinator and spokesperson for these diverse organizations. The NHH brings the various nonprofit organizations together to address shared problems. When the various organizations need a spokesperson to deal with federal organizations like the Federal Emergency Management Agency (FEMA), NHH can serve as a liaison. After decades of slowly extending its nationwide network of nonprofit service providers, the NHH has decided that it needs to publicize its work better to government agencies and the public. The NHH wants to be able to describe exactly the sort of work it does, and in what amount, to potential donors and federal agencies. The problem is that the NHH has no idea what all of its members are doing.

NHH is seeking to design a research project that will help document the work of its various members. It wants to come up with a number representing the total activity of its members. This number would then be useful as a means to justify support and monetary giving to its member organizations. Furthermore, such a number may provide support for the NHH's efforts to become more directly involved in national disaster policy making. The goal of the NHH is to evaluate its own efforts and the work of its members.

Dewey Independent School District

Dewey Independent School District (DISD) is a relatively small school district, standing on the outskirts of a major metropolitan area. For decades, Dewey served as a bedroom community for many workers who commuted downtown into the city. In the late '70s and early '80s, Dewey experienced remarkable growth as it became a trendy area in which to raise a family with a variety of family-friendly amenities including a growing and well-respected school district. This growth led to an explosion of development as the district built new schools across Dewey to accommodate this growth. As the new building went up, it required staffing as well. Dewey added a large cadre of young teachers to teach the children of these new residents.

The following decades have involved steady but slow growth for Dewey as the district became a widely respected district for its high quality teaching and well-developed extracurricular activities. In the recent years, though, the population of the district has begun to wane as young families have begun moving even farther outside of the metropolitan area. The large cohort of young teachers hired in the late '70s is now an expensive, large cadre of experienced teachers—many of whom are nearing retirement. District officials are growing concerned. The costs of having such a large cohort of highly experienced teachers combined with the potential disruption of having a massive wave of retirements in the near future have gotten their attention. The district is interested in finding out what the expected number of retirements will be over the next few years.

Grover's Corner Department of Transportation

Grover's Corner is a metropolitan city of approximately half a million residents with three times as many residents in the larger metropolitan area. Over the years, concerns have grown that the area has become more fragmented with considerable congestion emerging on some of the roads connecting Grover's Corner to its suburbs. Building additional and broader highways to the various suburbs became unsustainable both financially and environmentally. In response, Grover's Corner created a light rail network within the city to facilitate mass transit as a substitute for car-based transit. Following an increase in local sales taxes targeted to fund the development of the rail system, the Grover's Corner Department of Transportation oversaw the development and management of this system.

Attracting users to the light rail system has long been a challenge. The goal is to get people to park at the remote locations (where the parking is plentiful and inexpensive) and take the rail station into the more crowded downtown area. The result, it is hoped, will be reduced congestion on the local freeways. Part of this plan requires making the remote rail stations attractive to commuters. The Department of Transportation is charged with increasing light rail system use, in part by making the rail stations more attractive locations for commuters.

Amity Department of Homeland Security

The last decade has seen the emergence of homeland security as a major area of emphasis in policy making. While the creation of the Department of Homeland Security drew a great deal of attention, state and local offices across the country were also reorganizing to better fit within the emerging homeland security networks. Local police and fire offices were merged with emergency management offices to unify support for local homeland security preparedness and response. A large influx of money in the form of federal grants supported the reorganization of state and local offices while also providing the resources necessary to prepare for natural and man-made hazards.

A point of emphasis in the renewed funding was the training of personnel in homeland security offices (though, these offices were called many things other than "homeland security" as well). The personnel for these offices were brought together from a wide range of professions—law enforcement, fire protection, emergency management, public health, urban planning, etc. People with all of these backgrounds had to be brought onto the same page when it came to emergency response. FEMA supported the development of a variety of systems to unify these efforts and facilitate collaboration between these parties. Examples of these systems include the National Incident Management System (NIMS), the National Response Framework (NRF), and the Incident Command System (ICS). With these new systems came demands to train people across the country in their use. The Amity Department of Homeland Security is typical in this regard. Amity is a coastal community of approximately 150,000 residents (but many more in the summer tourist season). With the danger of hurricanes as well as the ever-present concern of terrorist attacks targeting the large number of people who populate the beaches in the summer, Amity's Department of Homeland Security must be prepared for a variety of hazards. Following national guidelines, the department hires a firm to provide training for the department's employees on effective practices in homeland security. Training is a key part of this process, but the director of the department wants to know: does the training really help?

Springfield Housing Department

Springfield is a large city of approximately one million residents with all of the problems common to communities of that size (tire fires, etc.). One persistent problem facing Springfield is the pattern of residential segregation present within the community and the lack of access many residents have to suitable housing. The Springfield Housing Department provides a variety of services to support residents in housing placements. Examples of these programs include managing housing vouchers and the oversight of public housing.

Conversations with case managers have revealed a suspicion that there are many more people eligible for housing assistance than are actually applying for the program. Moreover, the gaps in coverage seem to be most pronounced among ethnic minority communities within Springfield. Conversations with caseworkers and some of the recipients of the program identify an unlikely culprit: the application process. The director wants to know if it is, in fact, the application process that is driving people away from their program and how the application process can be improved to facilitate broader (and more equitable) participation in housing assistance.

Tools for Evidence-Based Research and Evaluation: An Outline for Your Textbook

This textbook is designed to provide you with a set of tools to answer questions like those faced in our cases by public managers. This section will provide a brief preview of the chapters of this textbook so that you can see how the various chapters come together to compose a complete toolbox for evidence-based practice.

Chapter 3: The Research Process

This chapter introduces you to the overall process of research, including the creation of research questions and the stages of evidence collection and analysis. It provides the rough schedule for research projects that we will fill in throughout the textbook.

Chapter 4: Conducting Preliminary Research

The best research starts by investigating what is already known on a subject. This chapter will provide techniques for conducting initial literature reviews to set the stage for effective original research—unless, of course, you find the answer you were looking for in the literature itself and the research is unnecessary.

Chapter 5: Research Design

This chapter introduces the organization of data collection in a way to account for competing explanations. The basic tools of research design apply across a broad range of research strategies.

Chapter 6: Measurement

The basic starting point of data collection is the decision of what to observe and how to interpret what you observe. This chapter will introduce standards for designing measurement strategies that are particularly useful for the sorts of research tasks public managers face.

Chapter 7: Population Sampling

After you have decided what you need to observe you have to decide where exactly you will make observations. This may mean selecting which people you will interview or where you will locate the data you need. This chapter will introduce techniques for identifying the best places to collect your data.

Chapter 8: Case Studies

Following the discussion of measurement and case selection, this chapter discusses one popular approach in detail—the case study design. In this approach, you carefully select a single example of the process or policy you want to study and subject that example to a great deal of scrutiny. This chapter will discuss the trade-offs involved in selecting specific cases and how to collect detailed data about cases.

Chapter 9: Interviews

With this chapter, the textbook moves from general issues of the design of a research project to the details of data collection. In this chapter, we introduce the use of interviews of individuals or focus groups as a means of collecting evidence. The chapter will discuss both the design of effective interview questions and the management of interview data collection.

Chapter 10: Field Research

Sometimes, you need to collect information from a specific location as evidence. This chapter provides techniques for conducting research at a specific research site. The chapter introduces the collection of documents as well as techniques related to observing behavior at field sites.

Chapter 11: Survey Data

This chapter will introduce the collection of large samples of data through systematic surveys and the use of large data sets common in organizations—such as budgetary and usage data. The emphasis is on the effective design of large data collection projects, including data management.

Chapter 12: Coding and Data Display

Having discussed the design of research projects and the collection of data, the textbook now turns to issues related to the analysis of data. In this chapter, the focus is on the analysis of small samples of nuanced data such as long interviews or field notes.

Chapter 13: Descriptive Statistics

This chapter turns from the analysis of small samples of nuanced data to the analysis of large samples of quantitative data. Here we introduce the basic representation of key public management concepts in quantitative terms and the use of statistics to describe large samples of data.

Chapter 14: Introduction to Probability and Distributions

This chapter provides the mathematics background necessary in order to understand how one can learn general lessons from specific samples of observations.

Chapter 15: Hypothesis Testing

The foundations of quantitative analysis of large samples of data continues with a discussion of a systematic process for testing whether what you observe is a reliable pattern rather than the product of randomness and error.

Chapter 16: Measures of Association

It is often interesting to see if two variables are related to each other. Is receiving training related to higher performance in a homeland security organization? This chapter provides tools for answering questions about whether there is a patterned relationship between two variables.

Chapter 17: Simple Linear Regression

This chapter introduces a popular and flexible tool for looking at relationships where the dependent variable can take on a large number of potential values.

Chapter 18: Multiple Least Squares Regression Analysis

This chapter builds on the previous one in expanding the popular least squares approach to situations where you need to control for many factors at once. For example, does training improve performance when accounting for the fact that some employees were more effective than others before their training?

Chapter 19: Mixing Research Methods

You may not be satisfied that any one research strategy will suffice to answer your research question. This chapter provides advice on why one might want to mix different research strategies together and how to do so.

Chapter 20: Managing Research and Evaluation Projects

The final section of the textbook introduces issues of research management and presentation. In this chapter, the focus is on the day-to-day planning of research projects that may take weeks or months to complete.

Chapter 21: Presenting Research

The final toolset for the textbook focuses on presenting the results of research. The best research project is useless if you cannot communicate the results. This chapter includes tools for writing effective research reports and designing research presentations.

Chapter 22: Conclusion: Bringing It All Together

The concluding chapter brings us back to the case examples introduced in this chapter. With a familiarity with the various tools of public affairs research and evaluation, this chapter revisits each case with a detailed hypothetical history to illustrate the choices that public managers may face in each of these research projects.

Conclusion

The cases provide a quick overview of the sorts of situations wherein public managers find themselves needing to consult or conduct research. The rest of the book will provide you with specific tools ranging from how to collect existing evidence relevant to your decisions, to the design, analysis, and presentation of research.

Suggested Readings

The concept of evidence-based practices has become popular in a wide variety of fields—each developing its own literature and its own critics.

Within health and education, much of the debate has taken place within the journals relevant to their discipline. In medicine, this includes such journals as the *British Medical Journal*, the *Journal of the American Medical Association*, and the *American Journal of Public Health*. A good starting point to investigate this area is a paper by Sackett and his colleagues in the *British Medical Journal* in 1996 titled "Evidence based medicine: What it is and what it isn't." You can see recent innovations in evidence-based medicine through Oxford University's Centre for Evidence Based Medicine (www.cebm.net). This is a rapidly evolving field of research, so watching webpages and journal articles is a good place to start.

Evidence-based education has been challenged more vocally than evidence-based medicine. A major turning point in the prominence of evidence-based education came from a slide presentation presented by an official of the U.S. Department of Education (available at: http://ies.ed.gov/director/pdf/2002_10.pdf). Biesta countered with a powerful critique of this practice, arguing that evidence-based practice is ill suited to the challenges of education policy. You can find his argument in *Educational Research* (2007) in a paper titled "Why what works, won't work: Evidence-based practice and the democratic deficit in educational research."

Evidence-based management (public or otherwise) is still emerging as a movement within its home discipline. An excellent starting point for applying the logic of evidence-based practice to business management is Pfeffer and Sutton's *Hard Facts, Dangerous Half-Truths, and Total Nonsense: Profiting from Evidence-Based Management*. There is less information within public management specifically, but recent issues of *The Public Manager* and *Public Performance and Management Review* are places where one can see this argument take shape.

Flashcards
& MCQs

Useful
Websites

Review Questions

- What sorts of evidence are most customary in evidence-based medicine?
- In what ways are public managers consumers of research?
- What question does the manager of National Helping Hands most want to answer?

Discussion Questions

- What might evidence-based law enforcement look like? Would it more closely resemble evidence-based medicine, evidence-based education, or evidence-based management?
- How do you think research will influence your daily work as a public manager?
- Which of the cases most interests you?
- Which of the cases do you think faces the most challenges in answering its core questions?

CHAPTER 3

The Research Process: An Introduction to Key Concepts

Learning Objectives

- ✓ Understand basic issues and processes related to initiating a research or evaluation project
- ✓ Understand core concepts associated with conducting research and evaluation
- ✓ Identify and understand different types of research approaches and strategies
- ✓ Identify ethical issues when conducting a research project that involves data collection from human subjects

Cases in Research

Case A—National Helping Hands

National Helping Hands (NHH) is a national-level organization that serves as a coordinating "umbrella" organization for a collection of separate and distinct member organizations who, in turn, provide services directly to the public after disaster incidents. That is, there are individual voluntary organizations that have their own memberships and do their own regular work serving their clients on a daily basis. When a disaster strikes, those organizations send volunteers to provide disaster relief services for the affected communities. The role of NHH is to help coordinate the efforts of a wide variety of different types of organizations who send volunteers to help in the disaster relief and recovery process. While it is clear that the work of NHH and all the various member organizations is very important, there is a basic research question: how much of an impact do those nonprofit organizations have in a disaster relief and recovery situation? In other words, how can we measure how much assistance NHH and its member organizations provide to a community after it is struck by a disaster? This is not easy to answer because the NHH is an association of distinct and autonomous member organizations who may or may not regularly track all of their service activities and are not necessarily required to do so. The director wonders where to stop in answering these key questions.

Case B—Amity Department of Homeland Security

Like all local governments in the United States, senior managers at the Amity Department of Homeland Security (HLS) are wrestling with a series of new federal policy expectations for planning and preparedness on HLS issues. In particular, the United States Department of Homeland Security has indicated that key local personnel should have an adequate level of training and expertise in specific aspects of terrorism incidents, such as chemical or radiological attacks. This training and expertise is to be developed to complement knowledge, skills, and competency in the area of more traditional hazards, such as practices related to responding to and managing emergencies and disasters (e.g., house fires, floods, severe weather). Senior management at the Amity Department of HLS want to know in as comprehensive a fashion the current level of training and expertise for all relevant public sector personnel employed by the city. They ask one of their managers to report back to them within two months on current levels of training and expertise in the city—and to what extent additional resources need to be devoted to training personnel to meet basic federal expectations in this area. Now the manager needs to design a research project to answer the question.

Research and Evaluation Processes and Strategies

As we discussed in chapter 1, the key characteristic of a scientific approach to understanding the world is to use observations to test whether a prediction, or an interrelated set of predictions about how the world works, actually holds up when subjected to empirical scrutiny. Of course, when a researcher gathers evidence, it also very likely means that she or he will find that the evidence does *not* support a prediction about things they thought were supposed to work. In other words, science is, at its core, the use of systematic methods to observe, assess, and draw inferences based on the assembled evidence—whatever that evidence demonstrates. While the techniques of conducting actual research can be complicated, and the analytic techniques used in assessing gathered data likewise can be difficult skills to master, the basic idea of how the scientific method works is straightforward.

It is also important to remember, as was noted in chapter 1, that the scientific method applies to researching the social world of humans just as it does to inanimate objects (e.g., rocks or metals or weather patterns) as well as nonhuman animate entities that we think of as lacking consciousness (e.g., plants). The basic processes of scientific inquiry are the same. But when we are talking about humans and human processes such as public policies or the operations of a large and complex organization, we can also recognize that it is often difficult to conduct experiments on human subjects or to measure complex social phenomena. (We will cover the topic of designing experiments in chapter 5 and the topic of measurement in chapter 6). Even though researching humans and human organizations can be difficult, we still use the same core elements of the research process—using theory and prior evidence to generate hypotheses, gathering data (i.e., observing and measuring) to permit testing of those hypotheses, and drawing inferences based on what those data reveal. In other words, the scientific method is the same regardless of whether the subject is relatively easy to measure (e.g., the physical properties of a plant) or relatively difficult to measure (e.g., the impacts of an education program like Head Start on long-term student achievement).

This chapter will cover five basic topics relevant to the overall process of conducting research. First, we will look at what considerations are relevant to starting a research project. Second, we will examine the basis for posing research questions and hypotheses. Third, we will provide a short preview of measurement in the research process—a preview to chapter 6. Fourth, we will briefly introduce different types of approaches or strategies in the research process. Finally, we will consider the fundamentally important issue of how to conduct research in an appropriately ethical manner—a theme that is addressed throughout this book. The chapter will close with a discussion of how the process of conducting research is relevant to evidence-based public management practices.

Basic Elements and Concepts of the Research Process

Perhaps the most effective way to understand research, including evaluation research work, is to see it as a process. To accomplish a research or evaluative goal, one will need to proceed deliberately through a series of steps. The first steps in this process and key concepts associated with them are outlined in this chapter. Getting those steps in place—that is, working through the research process deliberately—is not always easy for some researchers. You might be surprised to learn that it is not uncommon for research projects to lack clearly defined purpose statements and an effective research strategy that matches core project objectives. This may sound pessimistic, but it merely points out to the reader the importance of approaching a project in a systematic fashion. Doing a research or evaluation project using proper methods and techniques is not difficult—it is simply the case that it takes some effort to learn those techniques. Once a student learns what those methods and techniques are all about and how to employ them in practice, then doing so will strengthen the project overall and make it much more likely that the researcher or evaluator will be able to accomplish his or her goals.

All of section I of this book is devoted to explaining these basic steps and elements of conducting research in a systematic fashion. Then section II provides you with guidelines on how to collect data, and the rest of the book teaches you how to analyze those data, how to draw inferences properly, and finally, how to pull all those concepts together in producing research and evaluation projects. To start to understand the basic process of research, the rest of this chapter introduces the reader to several core concepts.

We can begin understanding these issues by first sketching out what the research process looks like in just a few sentences. All research or evaluation projects should begin with a clearly understood (and clearly stated) purpose. From that overall purpose, a central research question will need to be stated explicitly. In other words, defining an overall project purpose is not the same thing as defining a core research question. For example, understanding how nonprofit organizations play a role in community relief and recovery after a disaster might be your overall project purpose (as in our NHH case example). But we then have to be more precise in stating a specific research question. For that case example, our central research question might be the following: what is the actual monetary value of the disaster relief and recovery volunteer contributions made by NHH member organizations? Of course, that is not the only question one might ask, but it shows how the process starts to unfold. Stating a specific core research question then allows us to set out a series of specific project objectives, such as defining how we will set up the study (e.g., will we do a case study, will we study a large sample of disaster sites, or what?), defining what gets measured (e.g., will we try to measure all possible disaster service contributions, or just some specific ones?), defining who is responsible for what project tasks (e.g., putting together a project management plan), and so forth.

In the research process, we will have to make not only a series of decisions about what to measure and how to measure, but also a whole series of decisions about how to go about gathering our data. Before doing that, however, we will typically do some preliminary background examination of our topic of interest in the study—by doing things like reading prior research studies on the subject or reviewing formal documents (e.g., planning documents created by NHH). We will also lay out a key research hypothesis (or set of hypotheses) that will inform our analysis of data.

> Three stages of research:
>
> (1) Formulating Research Questions and Hypotheses
> (2) Collecting Relevant Data
> (3) Analyzing Data

Continuing down the process path, once we have gathered those data of interest for our study, we will then have to analyze those data. Data analysis requires knowledge of a whole range of analytic techniques—a whole range of which will be presented and explained in section III of the book. Further, we can also anticipate that in addition to simply describing what we have found in our data gathering, we also want to see if there is a relationship between the things we are measuring. We defined the concept of a relationship in chapter 1 (in section 1.3.3 on causal inference), but as a reminder when we speak of a relationship, we are thinking about whether one item of interest in our study appears with another and if those two items change together in some way. For example, we might want to know whether there is a relationship between the size of a disaster and the amount of effort made by voluntary nonprofits that are members of NHH. We can assess whether that relationship really does exist in reality (it seems that it would—but we cannot be sure until we measure and test the proposition!). Of course, we will learn specific techniques for how to test these kinds of hypothesized relationships later in this book. But for now, we can say that the research process wraps up by determining what our final inferences are, that is, how best to present our findings. The very final step is making decisions about how to disseminate those results.

Let's now turn to an introduction of a series of key concepts that will give us more detail and explanation to this very short sketch of the research process.

Clarifying the Purpose of Research and Evaluation Projects

The **PURPOSE STATEMENT** for a research or evaluation project is simply a statement that defines the researcher's basic intent—what he or she is attempting to accomplish with the project. Clearly defining the purpose of a research or evaluation project seems like an obvious thing to do, but in practice, this step in the process may not be easy because there can be ambiguity or lack of clarity of the research purpose. The researcher has to decide whether the project's basic intent is to *describe* some phenomena, that is, provide as comprehensive and accurate narrative description as possible, or alternatively, to *explain* some social phenomena, that is, to draw an inference about cause and effect. This distinction between description and explanation might not seem like a major difference at this point, but it is in fact an important one. As we will see over the course of this book, at times a researcher or evaluator will have a preference for one approach or the other. The purpose statement is not a restatement of an underlying problem to be studied but instead is a statement of exactly how and why the researcher intends to address some problem or question through research or evaluation.

> **Class Exercise:** Think about Case A, our National Helping Hands case, and discuss as a group how you would define the overall project purpose, and then brainstorm on different ways in which you might define the core research question for the project.

As we noted above, identifying an overall purpose for the project is not the same thing as posing the core research question for it. The core or central question of the project provides a guide to what the researcher is specifically trying to measure and assess. The central research question might seek to explain cause and effect (e.g., asking why certain outcomes are happening), or it might seek to explore a process (e.g., How is the level of knowledge of Amity government employees about natural disasters improved through training?), or it may be very descriptive in nature (e.g., How many members of National Helping Hands are in each region of the country?). In the case example of National Helping Hands, we posed this research question: What is the actual monetary value of the disaster relief and recovery volunteer contributions made by NHH member organizations? This is a descriptive question; it suggests that the answer is not easily available or well known at present. Of course, we could pose all sorts of other questions. For instance, if we wanted to pose a research question that is explanatory in nature, we could ask, why do voluntary nonprofits increase or decrease their efforts in a community after a disaster? This is an explanatory research question because it directs us toward thinking about cause and effect.

Before going any further in this chapter, it is useful to remind ourselves one more time about the distinctions one can make between research and evaluation. As was explained in chapter 1, the two terms are not equivalent (even though sometimes people will mistakenly treat them as interchangeable). The term "research" refers to project work using standard techniques associated with the scientific method, as we are discussing in this book. Moreover, we can further refine the term to focus on the idea of social science research, which is also explained in chapter 1. When we use the term "social science research," we are talking about the creation of generalizable knowledge on a subject pertaining to humans and their world of social systems and organizations. In that context, as was discussed earlier, we can think of evaluation as a specific type of research. Evaluation projects use the exact same systematic methods of social science research, but evaluation projects do not necessarily always seek to produce generalizable knowledge. For instance, an organization might be changing some internal operational process. To see if that process works better, the executives of that organization might request an evaluation to see if that is the case. What that means is that this research and evaluation might use the same types of tools, but the motives are slightly different. Social science research is motivated to produce generalizable knowledge, while evaluations are typically designed to answer a very specific question for an organization—for the precise reason of drawing a judgment about how to improve a process or a practice.

To see how the distinction between the two terms makes sense in practice, let's refer back to the research question discussion you've just read above. For an explanatory research question such as "Does the size of a disaster affect how much nonprofit groups will contribute to community relief and recovery efforts?," the emphasis and motive is to explain a broad category or even all disaster situations with respect to the voluntary nonprofit sector. That is, we are trying to see if there is a general relationship between disaster size and nonprofit effort. But think about this question from the perspective of an individual organization: Can we improve our management system to more efficiently distribute meals to disaster victims? This is an evaluation question because it is geared not to answer a question about nonprofit organizations in general but instead is intended to help make practical improvements for a specific organization.

Example 3.1—Case Discussion: National Helping Hands

Key executives at NHH have a meeting with an analyst, Melanie, who specializes in research on disasters. In the meeting, the executives tell Melanie that they are interested in whether some research work would show that disaster nonprofits have a major impact on communities that have suffered from a disaster incident. Melanie asks a few questions to try to understand the purpose of a potential research project. She asks the executives at NHH to name the key issues that they are interested in. When they mention they are interested in how much assistance NHH member organizations typically provide, Melanie asks what they mean by assistance. What is provided and how is it provided? Who provides such assistance? All member organizations? Do those organizations have to provide relief and recovery services if they are an NHH member? What exactly does NHH do after a disaster and during a longer-term recovery phase? What is the value of the research being contemplated? What use would it serve? Who would the audience be for the findings of the research project?

In other words, Melanie is trying to get a basic understanding of the nature and scope of activities by the member organizations and NHH. She is doing so in order to better understand what exact information is needed; in other words, by getting a sense of what those activities are, what the potential impacts are, and whether she will be able to help formulate a more clear and precise purpose statement for the project.

Questions about the Example: If you were an executive at NHH, how do you think you would define the project purpose? Do Melanie's questions seem to suggest that there are a wide variety of ways in which she could proceed? If so, what do you think is a reasonable way to clarify and sharpen the project focus?

Conceptualization and Operationalization

Once the purpose of a research project is clearly defined, it is necessary to identify with as much precision as possible the concepts associated with the project. For instance, if a researcher wants to study the effectiveness of employee training programs in an organization, one needs to specify the exact meaning of effectiveness. Can effectiveness be thought of as increased knowledge or skills for employees? Is it increased employee productivity? Is it an improvement in organizational performance in the aggregate? Is it some combination of all of those things? One of the researcher's first tasks is to define clearly what he or she means by a term like "effectiveness" when assessing a training program. This is critical to developing your core research question—the researcher or evaluator must be clear on what the terms mean when they state their basic question.

> **Class Exercise:** Pick a concept that is not necessarily easy to measure, such as employee productivity or disaster assistance, and brainstorm a set of indicators (i.e., specific measures) that would allow you to operationalize the concept of interest.

Closely related to the process of defining concepts is the process of operationalization. To **OPERATIONALIZE** a concept is to translate a concept into a form that can be measured. This is not necessarily an easy proposition, because some concepts are difficult to measure—even if the concept is relatively straightforward and well defined. For example, operationalizing employee training effectiveness might be captured effectively when it is measured as an effect on employee productivity—which can be captured by simple counts of an output of interest.

And by output, we means things like the number of cases processed, inspections conducted, reports filed, or similar such indicators. For example, if the employee in question is a building code inspector for a local government, one of the inspector's key tasks is to go to new building sites or building renovation sites and conduct a review of whether the construction project meets stated building code requirements. The number of inspections conducted in a month, for example, could be the key measure of interest for the study. If our research question is "Does additional training of building inspectors cause the overall number of inspections to increase?," using such a measure might be a reasonable way to try to answer the question.

However, it might not be quite that easy. Improvement in employee skill levels may be difficult to operationalize effectively because, while the concept is straightforward, finding an accurate and reliable measure (an operational definition that permits measurement) for a change in skills is not going to be as easy as simply counting increases (or decreases) in outputs. Imagine that a city conducts additional employee training for all its building inspectors, and that the training is quite effective—the inspectors are in fact better prepared to do their job. Does that mean more monthly inspections?

Project Objectives

It is essential for a researcher to define the overall project purpose, which includes crafting an explicit purpose statement, a core research question, and identifying key concepts and how they can be operationalized. It is likewise essential for the researcher or evaluator to set out a list of project objectives. A statement of objectives is a very straightforward identification of what it is the research or evaluation project hopes to achieve. Writing out a series of project objectives is useful because it forces accountability on the project; it allows the researcher to see if he or she has accomplished what it is that was intended to be accomplished. An objectives statement should be short and clearly written, using very direct and comprehensible language in order to eliminate any ambiguity as to what specific things are being attempted.

It is easy to think of what a list of objectives might consist of for most projects. These would include things such as a comprehensive review of what is known from prior research on a particular subject, creating and implementing an appropriate project research design (a subject we will learn about in chapter 8), identifying a list of essential data sources (which could be interviews with subject matter experts, policy or program documents, publicly available data sources, such as United States Census information, etc.), creating a plan for analyzing those gathered data, developing a dissemination strategy for the findings of the project, and so forth. The case discussion in Example 3.2 below provides an illustration of what the development of project objectives can look like for a specific research effort.

Example 3.2—Case Discussion: Amity Department of HLS

Heather, a policy analyst, was given a very broad task assignment: provide managers at the Amity Department of Homeland Security with an evaluation of the current levels of training and expertise in the city in order to determine whether additional funds within the city budget needed to be committed to training personnel so that Amity is in compliance with federal guidelines. Because this is a very broad task assignment, before Heather begins her work, she decides that she needs greater clarity and specificity in the core objectives of the project. She meets with key executives in the department several times to ensure her initial work plan comports with the department's evaluation needs by reviewing in detail their substantive questions and concerns. From that discussion, she determines that there are three core objectives: (1) provide a comprehensive measure of current training credentials for employees across several designated departments; (2) develop an analysis that matches employee credentials to credentials expected by the federal DHS; (3) provide an assessment of cost associated with including an additional specific percentage of employees in current training options in this area.

Questions about the Example: What do you think of these project objectives? Are they sufficiently clear? Do they need to be stated more precisely? Are there any other critical objectives that you think should be added to this list?

Theory and Prior Work

In outlining the basic process of research, we should recognize that any given project is likely to build upon previous research or evaluation work. This means asking a research question almost always based in some way on prior knowledge. For example, if we continue to consider our case of understanding the contributions of voluntary nonprofit organizations in the area of disaster relief and recovery, we can recognize that there already has been research work done by academic researchers, by government agencies (such as the Government Accountability Office), and by nonprofit organizations themselves on that subject. Such prior research has much to say about how the nonprofit sector interacts with the government sector, about how agencies—both governmental and nonprofit—coordinate with each other to provide services to the public in an atypical situation like a disaster (including why those systems may or may not work well together), or about the nature of disaster costs and the role nonprofit organizations play in a community's disaster recovery efforts.

In other words, there is very little research that is done without building on prior efforts. This is certainly true in the context of doing research and evaluation on public policies and programs—especially from the perspective of doing research to support evidence-based management practice. That is to say, most ideas that one might have about organizations and how they perform have been developed previously—at least in broad outlines. When we say that most research builds on prior research and evaluation work, what we mean is that with a new research project, the investigators are looking to see if there are new applications to examine established concepts and theories. Or they might be looking to find novel cases to examine using an established theory of how an organization or how a policy system works. Or an investigator might attempt to modify existing concepts and theory to improve explanation, and so forth.

This, of course, might prompt the reader to ask: What do we mean by theory? A **THEORY** is a set of concepts that are linked together to propose an explanation of how and why phenomena exist. In simpler language, a theory lays out an explanation of how the world works—or at least one small part of the world that is of interest. Social science generally, including research on public policies and public programs, is defined by a large body of various theories that seek to explain organizational behavior (e.g., why organizations perform as they do), individual behavior (e.g., why people engage in the political practices that they do), policy processes (e.g., how and why does policy change occur), and so forth. An illustration of a theory of relevance to public policy and public management is the idea of policy learning. The theory of policy learning suggests that major crisis events cause a significant response by policy makers, and that under specific conditions, policy improvements can be made and sustained over time by government agencies. Such a theoretic approach to understanding policy change is interesting because it provides us with very specific ideas about how and why public policy changes occur. And, in turn, we can gather evidence and see if the theory matches up with reality.

In this manner, a new research project will either build upon existing findings that have some underlying theoretic basis; or will attempt to modify that existing theoretic view in some way, including through the introduction of new evidence to change how we think about organizational performance, individual behavior, or policy processes, and so on. For example, in thinking about our Amity Department of Homeland Security case, we could use past research on policy learning to try to understand how and why a local agency would take the steps that it does in order to implement a national homeland security policy strategy. Or, perhaps we might use evidence from a local government agency like the Amity Department of HLS in order to see if key elements of policy learning actually work in practice as the theory suggests.

Understanding What to Study and What to Measure

As we have just seen in the previous section, any research or evaluation project begins by identifying an overall purpose statement and a set of specific objectives to accomplish in support of that purpose. As the researcher begins the project, there are several foundational issues he or she must address. The researcher will need to identify what exactly needs to be measured, the study's appropriate unit of analysis, the critical research questions that need to be addressed, the hypotheses he or she will want to test, how to structure the data collection process, and what type of analysis of the gathered data will permit inferences to be drawn. Structuring data collection processes—the idea of a research design—is covered in chapter 5; analysis of qualitative and quantitative data is covered throughout much of the rest of this book. Rather than tackling those subjects of design and analysis at this point in the book, we first consider the concept of identifying a unit of analysis—an important concept to understand before going any further. Then, we will introduce some preliminary ideas of measurement, and discussion ideas related to writing research questions and hypotheses in the next sections of this chapter.

Unit of Analysis

When a research project is undertaken, the investigator must make an initial decision about what is the appropriate unit of analysis for her or his study. We have established that the process of starting a research project includes identifying the overall purpose of the project, examining prior research findings and theoretic claims on the subject, and making some initial efforts at operationalizing the core concepts that are involved in the research effort. The investigator or team of investigators also has to make a critical early decision about the unit of analysis question. To what does that concept refer?

The term is a formal way of describing the fairly intuitive and simple idea of identifying what it is that is being studied or examined. We can define the term this way: a **UNIT OF ANALYSIS** refers to the entities (objects or events) being examined by a researcher. The unit of analysis can be an individual person or an organization, a city, or a type of historical event. For example, if you want to know if larger organizations have more detailed and formalized operational rules than smaller organizations, the unit of analysis is the organization. Or if you would like to know what type of person enters an MPA program as a student, the unit of analysis is an individual person. Or if you want to study the scale of economic damage caused by hurricanes in the United States over the past 50 years, the unit of analysis is a hurricane incident.

In simple terms, the purpose of the study and its core research question (or questions) dictates who or what is being studied, analyzed, compared—and hence the appropriate unit of analysis. However, in practice, selecting the unit of analysis is not always obvious. For example, if one is interested in employee training program need or effectiveness, the unit of analysis selection might seem obvious: individual persons (i.e., the employees who are subject to training). However, in a large organization, say a large city municipal government or a federal agency, there are many departments or other subunits contained within the larger organization. As a result, the researcher might want to consider training effectiveness not at an individual level, but instead might be interested in aggregating measures of training effectiveness to the departmental level. If that is the case, then the unit of analysis would be a department.

Example 3.3—Case Discussion: Amity Department of HLS

Heather's project at Amity DHS considers whether current levels of training and expertise on homeland security and other related hazards issues are sufficient to meet federal requirements. Because Amity is a large city, she could choose to examine training needs at just a departmental level for several key first response organizations—police, fire, and EMS. Instead, she decides the most effective way to address the project objectives spelled out in Example 3.2 is to measure individual employees working at the city as a whole, including not just first response agencies, but other relevant agencies or offices, such as planning and emergency management. This will allow her to gather data on individuals and consider what individual characteristics, such as experience, type of education, or type of position, have an effect on current levels of knowledge and expertise.

Questions about the Example: What do think about this decision? Do you think it would make more sense just to provide a summary measure at a department level, or would it make more sense to have individual-level measures? In other words, does the unit of analysis make sense here? What are the strengths or weaknesses of this approach?

Variables

In our discussion about identifying a unit of analysis for the purpose of gathering and assessing data while conducting a research or evaluation project, we said, for example, that a set of historical events, like hurricanes that have made landfall in the United States over the past 50 years, can serve as the unit of interest. Suppose that is the entity that we would like to study because the overall purpose of our research project is to understand how hurricane disasters affect communities in the United States. Suppose further that our core research question asks how much economic damage hurricanes typically cause in the United States on an annual basis. As the reader no doubt knows, some hurricanes are quite large in magnitude of effects, but others do not have major impacts. That is another way of saying that the magnitude of effects is not constant across all hurricane incidents. Or, we could also say that the impact of each individual hurricane varies. Recognizing this is another way of recognizing the idea of a variable. A **VARIABLE** is a characteristic of a unit of analysis that is not constant but instead varies across individual observed cases. In our example, any individual hurricane is a case, and we can measure certain characteristics of interest, such as the magnitude or category of the hurricane, how much economic damage it caused, where it made landfall, how long the incident took place, and so forth. These characteristics of our unit all vary from case to case, so we can think of each of those characteristics as a different variable.

Variables themselves are complex things—and they have their own logic and set of properties. One way to differentiate variables is to think of quantitative versus qualitative variables. A **QUANTITATIVE VARIABLE** is one where its values consist of numbers, and differences between values can be expressed in numbers. A **QUALITATIVE VARIABLE** is one where there are nonnumerical differences between categories (usually designated by words or labels). Let us think about a research question where the unit of analysis is an individual person. If our research question has to do with health issues, we might consider measuring their age, height, weight, certain physical conditions like cholesterol levels, etc. All of those measures would be quantitative variables because they are characteristics of our unit of analysis (an individual person) that can be represented clearly and easily in numeric form. What if we wanted to see if there was a link between gender and health status? We would then also measure the individual's gender. The gender or sex of the individual is a characteristic that is not inherently numerical in nature, but instead is a category in which the individual person falls—for example, female or male. This makes the gender of the unit of analysis (an individual person) a qualitative variable.

The distinction between a quantitative and qualitative variable is just the first distinction we can make. A second fundamentally important distinction is the difference between an independent and dependent variable. For a research question that we want to address by measuring variables, gathering data, and analyzing the relationships between those measures, there will be an outcome of interest. For the question of how much economic damage hurricanes cause in the United States, our outcome of interest is precisely that: a measured amount of economic damage for each hurricane that we look at in our study. We can call this outcome of interest a **DEPENDENT VARIABLE**, which is the outcome a researcher is interested in explaining and predicting. Are all hurricanes exactly the same in terms of their impact measured as economic damage or loss? Of course not. The dependent variable changes for each case (i.e., each hurricane we study)—it varies across cases.

> **Class Exercise:** As a class, identify a research project topic and a corresponding research question. Discuss what the unit of analysis would be for that question, what the dependent variable would be, and what some possible explanatory variables—that is, independent variables—might be of possible interest in explaining what causes variation in that dependent variable.

Why does the outcome of interest (our dependent variable)—in this case, the amount of economic damage from a hurricane—vary? We can think of it this way: variation in the dependent variable is considered to "depend" on the influence of other variables. In the case of a hurricane, those other characteristics would be factors such as the size of a hurricane, in terms or wind speed and area covered; the amount of flooding associated with the hurricane; whether the hurricane landed in a spot that was particularly vulnerable to damage; the number of people affected by the hurricane; and so forth. These factors can be described as variables that influence and explain variation in the dependent variable; they are called **INDEPENDENT VARIABLES** (they are also sometimes called predictor or explanatory variables because they are thought of as explaining or predicting the results of variation in the observed dependent variable).

There are also ways to make distinctions about how variables are measured. Not only can we make a distinction between measuring a quantitative variable (e.g., amount of economic damage) or qualitative variable (e.g., gender or religion), but we can also make specific distinctions between different types or amounts of information a measured variable provides. For now, we will hold off on that discussion; exactly how we measure variables in their different forms is the subject of chapter 6.

Research Questions and Hypotheses

To this point, we have considered several basic elements that help constitute key portions of the research process. We have noted the importance of identifying a project purpose and its objectives, the importance of clarifying key concepts and operationalizing those concepts, the issue of identifying an appropriate unit of analysis, and understanding the distinction between the meaning and types of variables. We turn our attention next to the issue of asking research questions and asserting hypotheses about how variables are related in order to provide an explanation of some phenomena.

Asking Research Questions

Clearly specifying a research question is a fundamental and basic part of the research process, as we have already noted. While that might seem obvious, it is important to understand distinctions between research questions and their uses. Usually, a research project will have an overarching or central question—we also referred to it as a core research question in order to convey that centrality. Of course, a researcher or evaluator will have a number of different questions associated with a project. The central research question helps guide a series of more specific subquestions. For example, let's go back to thinking about the NHH case. Earlier in the chapter we said our core question that the NHH study wanted to address was about the impact nonprofit organizations have on disaster relief and recovery. A bit more specifically, we asked how much assistance does NHH and its member organizations provide to communities in the United States after they are struck by a disaster.

That is a good starting point, but it also of course leads us to a whole series of additional questions. For instance, what is the type of assistance that the nonprofit organizations provide? Is that assistance the same across all nonprofits, or do the contributions they make differ by organization? Do the nonprofits mainly focus on relief (things like temporary housing, providing meals to disaster victims, providing counseling services), or do they mainly focus on recovery (things like cleaning up damaged buildings and removing debris or rebuilding homes)? How can we convert volunteer time and effort into a monetary value to account for a contribution value of the donated labor? How can we measure the value of an activity such as providing spiritual care to disaster victims?

We could go on, but the point should be clear: our basic purpose was to account for the impact of nonprofits after a disaster. Our central research question was to ask about how much disaster relief and recovery assistance is actually provided by those nonprofits. In turn, that leads us to ask a series of questions about what we mean by "assistance," what kinds of activities are typical, and how we can actually attempt to measure the value of those activities in order to get a sense of their impact.

Further, we can connect the nature of research questions to the basic purpose of the project. If a project has a basic descriptive objective, then the questions posed will tend to be of the "what" or "how" variety. That is, the questions will comport with the descriptive orientation of the project. On the other hand, if the project is explanatory in nature, questions will be focused on addressing the manner by which key variables are related to each other—particularly in examining how a set of independent or potentially causal factors influence variation in the outcome of interest, the dependent variable.

Writing Research Hypotheses

Another element of the research process is that after we have posed a central research question and a set of subordinate questions, the researcher also will typically pose a set of explanatory hypotheses. What is a hypothesis? A **HYPOTHESIS** is a proposition indicating how two or more factors are related to one another, and stated in a way that it can be tested with empirical evidence. What does that mean? In simple terms, we want to know if one variable is related to another, and we have to state that possible relationship in a way that we can actually measure those relationships to see if there is evidence in support, or in contradiction, of that hypothesis.

At times this can be fairly easy and straightforward. Suppose a researcher believes that nonprofit organizations let the severity of a disaster determine how much effort they will put toward relief and recovery. We could hypothesize the relationship this way: as the scale of a disaster increases, the contribution efforts of nonprofit organizations will increase. This is a useful hypothesis in that we can measure the scale of disaster (e.g., the amount of economic damage or the size of a storm or the area the hazard covered), and we can measure the amount of effort by nonprofits (e.g., the number of volunteers sent to the area or the number of organizations operating in the post-disaster area or the amount of time those organizations stayed in the disaster-affected community). It is also useful in that it does not apply to a single case, but instead lays out a general relationship that we can look at over a large number of disaster cases. In other words, we can gather data and see if this relationship really does hold up.

But perhaps this hypothesis is missing something trickier and more complicated. Perhaps there are differences based on the type of hazard. For instance, maybe nonprofits can come into a community after a flood or hurricane, but they are limited in what they could do if a community was devastated by a man-made hazard, like a major industrial accident that affects a whole community. Our stated hypothesis doesn't account for the subtle distinction, and so it might be difficult to capture the relationship of disaster size and voluntary nonprofit organizations' efforts without accounting for the nature of the hazard or disaster itself.

Regardless, we can think about the basic nature of what constitutes an effective or useful hypothesis. Any hypothesis should have all four of the following key characteristics. First, a hypothesis should be empirical. That means it should be related to the actual observation of phenomenon. Our hypothesis above meets that test because we determined that we could measure the key components of the relationship. Second, a hypothesis should be generalizable. That means it should explain a general phenomenon—not just one case. Again, our hypothesis about disaster size and nonprofit assistance effort meets the test. We were not trying to explain just one case (e.g., one really major disaster like Hurricane Katrina), but all disaster cases. Third, a hypothesis should be plausible. What we mean here is that there should be a logical reason for formulating it. Does it make sense that larger disasters would prompt greater efforts by nonprofits? That certainly at least seems reasonable. Finally, our fourth characteristic is that a hypothesis should be precise. What we mean here is that it should be able to specify the direction of the relationship for two variables. In our example, we see that a direction is stated: as disasters get larger, assistance efforts increase.

What is important to understand with this example is not that the evidence might support the hypothesis. It is very possible that things are more complicated than that, and the nature of the relationship is not so easy to determine. The key point is this: a hypothesis allows us to use our gathered evidence to test such a claim and then allow us to make a judgment about how we think the world might work. This is the beauty of learning to do research—it allows us to use evidence that can be checked and repeated and challenged in order to see how much confidence we have in saying something is to be understood as true.

Putting Knowledge into Practice: How to Write Research Hypotheses

We just gave an example of a research hypothesis when we posed this one: "As the scale of a disaster increases, the contribution efforts of nonprofit organizations will increase." The obvious question you might ask yourself is "Where did that come from?" In other words, you want to know how to write a research hypothesis.

First, we should address the question of where the idea of a hypothesis comes from. There really are several basic sources: prior research can lead you to posit a hypothesis about relationships, patterns in empirical data can lead you to positing a hypothesis stating the causal relationship, or the logic of a theory can lead to a hypothesis about the nature of expected relationships between key variables.

Let's think about our researcher, Melanie, in the NHH case illustration. If Melanie was the author of the hypothesis, why would she have posed it? For the sake of argument, let's say that Melanie had looked at nonprofit organization involvement in a series of disaster cases, some of them "routine" (e.g., Midwestern floods) and a couple of disasters that were catastrophic (e.g., hurricanes in the Gulf of Mexico). If she found that the disaster nonprofits really ramped up their efforts for the hurricane cases, the empirical pattern she observed could be the basis for the hypothesis. That is, based on past evidence, it seems that effort does increase as the size of a disaster increases.

So next, let's think about why the hypothesis is stated as it is. We want to give a direction for the relationship between two key variables of interest. In this case, our variables of interest are the size of a disaster (which we can measure by indicators such as lives lost, property losses, and geographic area affected) and the efforts of voluntary nonprofit organizations (which we can measure by the number of volunteers, the dollar value of donations, or the amount of labor contributed to relief and recovery). So when Melanie was writing the hypothesis, she stated a relationship to test (larger disasters cause greater volunteer effort)—and that relationship had a clear direction: it is a positive (aka direct) relationship because as the explanatory or independent variable goes up (disaster size), then the dependent variable, volunteer organizations effort, also goes up.

Let's think about the other elements of a hypothesis. We have established that we can measure what we need to measure, and we have defined the direction of a relationship. Next, we should ask: did the hypothesis only apply to a single case? No—it applies generally across all disasters. Finally, we can ask if the hypothesis is conceptually plausible. Clearly, this is not a crazy, off-the-wall relationship to examine. So, yes, it meets that test, too.

In sum, this is how to write a research hypothesis. You can walk your idea through these elements of a hypothesis when you are writing one. This will help you do good work in a critical aspect of the research process.

A final note: We should make the important additional point here that writing a research hypothesis is not the same as formally testing that hypothesis. Once we write a hypothesis, we need to test it and evaluate those results to make sense of what we have observed from our data collection and analysis. We will see how hypothesis testing works in chapter 15.

Approaches or Strategies

To this point, we have talked about several parts of the process of conducting research (which includes evaluation projects as well, of course). Once a researcher gets to the point of writing hypotheses, he or she is then ready to collect data and conduct an analysis of those data. We will not cover those parts of the process in this chapter. The entire second section of this book is devoted to a discussion of data collection techniques. The third section is devoted to the process of analyzing data and interpreting those results. And the last section of the book is devoted to issues of presenting results and managing projects.

What we will do at this point, instead, is provide a very brief overview of the matter of choosing a research approach. When we refer to the idea of a research approach or strategy, we are referring to the idea that there are several basic ways in which a researcher can try to answer a central research question. Briefly, a researcher can choose to answer her or his question through the use of **QUANTITATIVE RESEARCH METHODS** (intuitively, numerical measures designed to infer very specific cause and effect relationships), **QUALITATIVE RESEARCH METHODS** (intuitively, use of nonnumerical forms of data, such as narratives, ethnographies, grounded theory, or case studies to provide an interpretation of relationships within social phenomenon), or **MIXED METHODS**, which involve some combination of both quantitative and qualitative data gathering (done either simultaneously or sequentially) as part of the same project. The key consideration is whether the research approach or strategy is effectively matched to the basic purpose of the project, its central research question, and the key project objectives.

As a researcher or research team (i.e., the project investigators) lays out purpose and question statements, they will also have to map out what is the most suitable research approach. In other words, the type of research approach is a fundamental issue that must be tackled as a new project is initiated. There are three basic approaches that one might take: a qualitative, a quantitative, or a mixed methods strategy. Let us consider what each of these means.

The use of a quantitative research approach is defined by the type of data gathered and the corresponding techniques to assess those data after they are gathered. A quantitative strategy in gathering and analyzing data is characterized by the notion of using numerical measures designed to infer very specific cause and effect relationships. This is done through the use of structured measurement instruments (such as a survey questionnaire) or an experimental study (where measurements are taken under controlled circumstances).

Again, let's consider our NHH research problem to think about a quantitative approach. If we want to understand the nature of nonprofit organizations' assistance impacts, we can think about many of the related questions from a quantitative perspective. We can collect quantitative measures of volunteer hours, convert that volunteered labor into a monetary scale (i.e., the dollar value of the labor contributed), compare the relationship of the disaster damage to the value of contributions made by nonprofits, and so forth. To think in those terms of specifying key relationships in a way that can be analyzed numerically represents a quantitative strategy.

In the same way, a qualitative research approach is defined by both the type of data gathered or produced in the process of conducting a study and the types of corresponding analysis of those gathered data. Qualitative research is characterized by the use of nonnumerical forms of data—especially in service of descriptive analysis or methods of developing theory to describe and explain highly complex, not easily operationalized phenomena. This includes the use of techniques such as narratives, ethnographies, grounded theory, or case studies to provide an explanation of relationships within social phenomenon.

Again, let's think about how one might take a qualitative approach to our NHH case. What if we are interested in not just the impact of the contributions of the NHH member nonprofit organizations in terms of labor value contributed, but instead in terms of how they impact a community in ways not at all easy to measure, such as the spiritual care they provide and community cohesion. Many of the NHH member organizations are faith-based organizations, so after a disaster they are likely to provide spiritual care. Likewise, in addition to cleaning up buildings after a disaster or removing debris or reconstructing damaged homes, those nonprofits also do things like hold community social events for people to relax and enjoy themselves. There is a value to these activities, but measuring such impacts is not easy. That is, it can be difficult for a researcher to put these types of community impacts into specific quantitative terms, even though they are real and important. Precisely because it not easy to think about the impact of assistance in these areas in quantitative terms, we might want to take a qualitative research strategy, such as collecting personal narratives of disaster victims who received care and support from a nonprofit organization, in order to account for, interpret, and understand what role those important contributions play in assisting a community after disaster.

A mixed methods approach is exactly what the name implies—it is a combination of both quantitative and qualitative data gathering. That is, both forms of data collection and analysis are part of the same overall research project. A mixed methods strategy has the advantage of using the strengths of both approaches. For instance, as we have just seen, some aspects of nonprofit assistance are relatively easily captured by a quantitative strategy, but other aspects are more appropriately addressed using qualitative methods. As we will learn throughout the course of this book, there are strengths and weakness to each approach.

It is useful to recognize that a mixed methods approach to gathering data and information can be done either simultaneously or sequentially. In our NHH example, we might have part of our investigative team collecting and analyzing the quantitative aspects of assistance from the disaster services nonprofit organizations (such as accounting for the value and impact of volunteer labor). At the same time, other project team members might be conducting qualitative data gathering and analysis (such as interviews with disaster victims about the value they perceived gaining from coping with a disaster through spiritual care and community events provided by the nonprofit organizations). In this way, the two approaches to research can be conducted as parallel processes and the information combined in final reporting on the results of the study.

Ethics and the Research Process

Throughout this book we consider a range of ethical issues in the research process, specifically as they relate to the subject matter being discussed in a particular chapter. Any discussion of general issues in initiating research and evaluative projects, of course, includes a wide variety of potential ethical issues. Because we cover those issues in other chapters, here we would like to pay particular attention to the matter of gathering data from human subjects.

It is critical for any researcher to understand the importance of protecting the rights of other persons in any project that involves gathering any type of data from other persons. There is a very disturbing and unpleasant reason why we point this out: in the past, medical and social science research on human subjects has seen abuses of the most serious nature. Among the most well-known incidences of abusive research is the infamous Tuskegee Syphilis Study, which ran for 40 years, from 1932 to 1972, when it was finally forced to be discontinued. Essentially, the study involved intentionally withholding treatment for diseases from poor African American sharecroppers for the ostensible purpose of examining the progression of the disease over time. This meant that not only was appropriate treatment intentionally withheld from the subjects, but those men then transmit-ted the disease to their wives, which lead to a number of children being born with congenital syphilis. As ethically wrong as this research was, it is important to note that a public health researcher specializing in the study of venereal disease, Peter Buxton, attempted through official channels to get the study stopped. However, remarkably, he was unsuccessful and only when he acted as a whistleblower by reporting the situation to journalists (which attracted news media attention and, in turn, congressional hearings) was the Tuskegee study stopped. From a historical perspective, this suggests how weak institutional safeguards for the rights and protections of human subjects were at the time.

The Tuskegee study ultimately helped prompt the Belmont Report, which was written in 1979 and helped develop specific federal guidelines for biomedical research. However, the Belmont Report had broader impacts than just that type of research and helped usher in a system of human subjects protections more generally. The main mechanism for university research to follow good practice of human subject protection is an Institutional Review Board (IRB), which serves as an internal review process to ensure research is done ethically and without harm or a lack of informed consent from study participants. With such reform, research on human subjects is considerably safer than it had been several decades ago precisely because of more careful and effective regulation of research projects.

Whenever a researcher is seeking to solicit informed consent from a potential study subject, there are some basic elements that any such request should contain. A subject should be told what the purpose of the study is, about both any potential risks and benefits from participation, that participation is voluntary, and that the subject has a right to end that participation at any time. The subject should also be made aware how long his time in the study will take and that the study has undergone IRB review. If this information is presented to a potential subject, then he or she can be considered to make an informed decision to participate. In some cases, an IRB will ask for a formal notice to participate (such as a signature). In other cases, such as a telephone survey interview, the subject's verbal agreement to continue with the interview is deemed sufficient to indicate consent.

Conclusion: How the Research Process Relates to Evidence-Based Public Management Practices

This chapter provided the reader with an initial overview of what the process of research is about. We introduced some of the core concepts of that process, such as asking research questions and writing research hypotheses, while other key concepts and elements of the process will be covered in other parts of this book, such as the mechanics of gathering data and testing hypotheses.

The last topic we will address is how basic concepts of the research process are related to the practice of evidence-based management practices. As discussed in chapters 1 and 2, the concept of evidence-based management is fairly straightforward. Public managers operate in a difficult environment: they have many competing demands made on them by the public, by elected officials, by the courts, and so on. For public managers in government, or the executives or managers of a nonprofit organization, there are also significant expectations about performance and accountability. As a result, evidence-based public management is premised on the idea of using the best available data and empirical analysis to inform decisions about agency operations and resource allocations.

Within such a context, making decisions based on evidence—as opposed to intuition or even ideology—is not only a sound practice, it is increasingly a basic expectation. This is why it is necessary to understand the basics of the research process. If a public manager does not know how the research process works, he or she will not be able to make decisions effectively in terms of utilizing empirical evidence in critical decision-making situations.

Much of this chapter is introductory in the sense that most of the specific steps needed to complete a research or evaluation project are covered in detail in subsequent chapters of this book. But we can see the relevance of the concepts that are covered here to effective evidence-based decision making in the public and nonprofit sectors.

For example, it is critical that clearly defined purpose statements are made for a project not only in order to ensure effective project development, but also because doing so allows for transparency and accountability when the public examines the work efforts of public agencies. Similarly, having clearly defined project objectives flowing from a well-stated research question makes it easier for outside observers to assess the work activities of a public agency or a nonprofit organization. In this way, not only does the project proceed more effectively as it properly follows the core elements of the research process, it also makes it easier for the broader public to understand how a government agency or nonprofit organization came to develop the evidence that it did when making decisions. This gives greater legitimacy to decisions made by public agencies precisely because those decisions were made on the basis of evidence gathered through a proper process.

Suggested Readings

There are a great many research methods and statistics textbooks that can offer excellent treatments of the basics of the research process. In fact, there are far too many to try to cite here! But instead of looking at other methods textbooks, the interested student might begin getting a feel for how research and evaluation looks in practice by going to several sources of original research. Two excellent journals that publish very rigorous and useful articles on policy and public administration are the *Policy Studies Journal* and the *Journal of Public Administration Research and Theory*. For a greater emphasis on public management issues, take a look at the *Public Administration Review*. To get a feel for how evaluation research proceeds, go to the website of the American Evaluation Association, http://www.eval.org/, as well as taking a look at the *American Journal of Evaluation*. Simply perusing these resources will help you to understand what research and evaluation studies look like in published form.

Vocabulary

DEPENDENT VARIABLE—The outcome a researcher is interested in explaining and predicting.

HYPOTHESIS—A proposition indicating how two or more factors are related to one another, and stated in a way that it can be tested with empirical evidence.

INDEPENDENT VARIABLE—A variable that influences and explains variation in the dependent variable.

MIXED METHODS—The use of a combination of both quantitative and qualitative data gathering techniques, performed either simultaneously or sequentially within the same research or evaluation project.

OPERATIONALIZE—The process of translating a concept into a form that can be measured directly.

PURPOSE STATEMENT—A statement that defines the researcher's basic intent for a project—what he or she is attempting to accomplish with the project.

QUALITATIVE RESEARCH METHODS—The use of nonnumerical forms of data, such as narratives, ethnographies, grounded theory, or case studies to provide an explanation of relationships within social phenomenon.

QUALITATIVE VARIABLE—A variable whose measurement is designated by placements in a category, which is to say, there are nonnumerical differences between those designations.

QUANTITATIVE RESEARCH METHODS—The uses of numerical measures and associated analyses designed to infer very specific cause-and-effect relationships.

QUANTITATIVE VARIABLE—A variable whose measurement is designated in numerical terms, which is to say its measurement values consist of numbers and differences between those values can be expressed in numbers.

THEORY—A set of concepts that are linked together to propose an explanation of how and why phenomena exist.

UNIT OF ANALYSIS—The collection of elements (data) representing observations for one phenomenon of interest.

VARIABLE—A characteristic of a unit of analysis that varies across individual observed cases.

Flashcards
& MCQs

Useful
Websites

Review Questions

- What is a unit of analysis—and why do your research objectives determine the selection?
- What is the difference between independent and dependent variables?
- What are the four key characteristics of a research hypothesis?
- What does it mean to operationalize a concept?
- What are the differences between quantitative and qualitative research approaches?
- What is the idea of human subject protections?

Discussion Questions

- In conducting research, how might there be differences between research on human subjects in medical studies versus social science studies, in terms of risks to the study participants?
- Are variables inherently dependent (i.e., always an outcome of interest) or independent (i.e., always)?
- Why is it important to have clearly defined purpose and objective statements to guide a research project?

CHAPTER 4

Conducting Preliminary Research

Learning Objectives

✓ Understand initial tasks of research and evaluation, such as writing a literature review or creating an annotated bibliography

✓ Understand techniques in obtaining general background information, such as conducting preliminary interviews with key informants or subject matter experts

✓ Identify and understand some basic concepts of types of data gathering techniques

Cases in Research

Case A—National Helping Hands

The executive staff at National Helping Hands (NHH) is interested in conducting an evaluation of internal processes at the national office level, including how the national office interacts with member organizations. The national office staff is a critical link between the member organizations and state and federal government agencies during a disaster incident and during the early recovery period following a disaster. The executive staff believes they can improve coordination both among member organizations and between members, government agencies, and the national office. The purpose of the evaluation is to examine internal processes and better understand coordination practices between governmental and non-governmental organizations. Before they begin to embark on a large research project, the director of NHH wants to know what the literature suggests are the best approaches to develop coordination between offices in an organization like this.

Case B—Springfield Housing Department

Among the services provided by the Springfield Housing Department is the management of housing assistance vouchers and general oversight of public housing. What the Department has come to learn is that even though Springfield has a number of people eligible for public housing assistance, the percentage of eligible program participants is quite a bit lower than would be anticipated given the socioeconomic profile of Springfield. This leads senior executives in the department to question why this is the case, and thus, initiate some basic evaluation work on the service delivery methods used by the department.

Starting Points in a Research Project

To this point, we have covered a series of foundational concepts associated with empirical research work. In chapter 1, we learned about the idea of the scientific method and conducting social science research. As that chapter explained, conducting research allows one to describe, explain, and produce causal inferences of social phenomena of interest. What that means in practical terms is that, if we want to know if a policy or program is working, or if we want to know if one operational method is better than another for an organization in trying to meet some service goals, then we must use basic research methods practices to answer such questions. It is important to recognize that those research methods, that is, the collection of data following specific practices associated with what we identified earlier as the scientific method, allow us to describe, explain, and make causal inferences when we tackle our research questions.

This book continuously builds on concepts in order to help you see how to get to that point. So in chapter 2, we saw how the practice of gathering evidence can be used for more effective management practices in organizations, including government agencies and nonprofit organizations. In chapter 3, we started learning about the processes involved in conducting a research or evaluation project by tackling such ideas as how to establish project objectives, write research questions, and specify hypotheses.

Here we continue the discussion by elaborating on some basic practices that you as a researcher will undertake in the early phase of a project. This chapter will cover several basic topics. First, we will provide an overview of a task that is applicable to most research projects: conducting a review of previously published research findings, which frequently takes the form of a literature review. Second, we will consider some additional issues of gathering background information in ways beyond reading through existing reports or published articles. One important technique is to interview persons who have specialized knowledge and expertise in the substantive area of interest. Third, we will consider a variety of data gathering techniques to familiarize the reader with these concepts as a means of preparation for the rest of the material covered in this book. We will close by considering some ethical considerations related to these processes, and we will likewise consider how these preliminary research efforts are related to evidence-based management practice.

Getting Started with a Literature Review

As we saw in chapter 3, the process of conducting research (which includes evaluation projects as a particular type of research) starts with clearly stating the project's purpose, asking a core research question, and defining a set of objectives to accomplish with the project. We learned in that chapter that very little research starts as a kind of tabula rasa—as a blank slate. Instead, nearly all research work—at least any research or evaluation work done in the public sector—is built on prior efforts at understanding some public policy or program questions, or how individuals interact with such public systems.

To understand what kind of prior research work has been done, either directly or indirectly related to the topic in question, one common way to become familiar with the existing knowledge in a research area is to produce a literature review. What is a literature review? A **LITERATURE REVIEW** is a reasonably comprehensive survey of previous research studies related to a specific research topic area. The scope and breadth of a literature review depends almost entirely on the needs of a project. If the research work is intended for an academic audience, the literature review is likely to be more extensive and to take note of certain types of studies—mainly other prior academic studies. If the work is intended for a practitioner audience, there is likely to be less of a need for anything approaching an exhaustive summary of prior work in the area, but in most cases there would be sufficient treatment of prior research to give the report's readers a solid grounding in the key substantive issues being addressed. If the audience is even a narrower one, for example, the executives at a public or nonprofit agency who will be reading an evaluation report, the scope of a literature review depends on the needs of the report and the expectations of those key readers.

Regardless of the nature of the audience, there are some basic functional elements common to a literature review. Those elements are considered below, along with some discussion of how to capture source material and what source materials are typically relevant in understanding the basic substantive information needed to undertake a research project.

Purpose of a Literature Review

Starting a research study report with some sort of discussion of prior theoretic and empirical work and findings (whether it be an applied research project report, an evaluation, or general purpose academic research) is a fairly basic norm or expectation. There are several different functional purposes that a literature review plays. First, it provides a substantive introduction to core issues associated with the research being presented in a report. For instance, if an evaluation report for NHH seeks to understand how inter-agency or inter-sector (i.e., organizational interactions between government and nonprofits) coordination occurs, there is a large body of prior research on such questions. An evaluator providing a report to NHH would no doubt seek to highlight several critical operational and management issues and/or challenges on inter-organizational coordination and provide a review of prior findings about what works and what doesn't in that area.

A second functional purpose of the literature review is to explain to the reader why the research topic is important. This may seem obvious to the person or persons writing the report, but it is by no means obvious to many or most readers. It is important to recognize that research projects typically have a very narrow focus. Given that, relatively few readers will have specialized knowledge of the particular issues covered by the report or research paper. Thus, the literature review provides a short educational purpose for the reader as to why the contents of the study matter, why they are important, and why the reader should pay attention to the results presented.

A third function of the literature review is to provide a broader explanation of the context within which the research took place. Again, most readers will not have a comprehensive knowledge of the historical background for a given subject. The literature review can provide historical context so the reader can better understand the implications of key findings presented. Doing so also helps situate the research in a broader tradition of inquiry for a given subject area.

> **Class Exercise:** Take an example of a policy research article published in an academic journal, such as the *Policy Studies Journal*, and compare it to a policy research report published by an agency like the Government Accountability Office. Compare and contrast how the background literature reviews are presented.

Example 4.1—Case Discussion: Springfield Housing Department

Christina is a senior program manager at the Springfield Housing Department. She knows a great deal about all aspects of housing programs and policy issues at the local, state, and federal levels of government. However, she would like a thorough review of several recent federal-level evaluations of relevant grant and pilot programs managed by the U.S. Department of Housing and Urban Development, several recent academic studies on equity issues in housing markets and the efficacy of public assistance programs in the area of housing, as well as several white papers produced by a low-income housing advocacy organization. Christina directs one of her junior staff members, Morty, to collect and provide her with a review of these recent research findings in this policy domain.

Questions about the Example: Given that Christina has directed Morty to summarize some specific reports to keep her abreast of recent research findings, would you consider this a literature review? If you were Morty, how would you go about summarizing the requested material? Would you do so by theme? By research authorship? Some other approach?

Annotated Bibliographies

It is important to make clear that a literature review is not equivalent to an annotated bibliography. An **ANNOTATED BIBLIOGRAPHY** is a comprehensive listing of major research articles, reports, books, and other similar sources of information about a specific topic. An annotated bibliography is not the same as a bibliography, which is the listing of sources (books, journal articles, etc.) that one has cited in a research document. A bibliography serves the purpose of presenting prior works references; an annotated listing in the annotated bibliography contains a brief summary description of the content of the research presented, typically including comments on focus, methods used, and major findings. Annotated bibliographies can be thought of as a resource or reference guide rather than as an analytic or critical review and synthesis that highlights key themes and questions (i.e., what a literature review does). In this regard, the functional purpose of an annotated bibliography is to collect and summarize prior research as comprehensively as possible, in part to assist in making sure the literature review that is presented is thorough and has not missed any important prior work in the area.

So we can see that a literature review is used to identify themes, highlight questions, and represent a summary of what is known in the field relative to the question posed by a research project. In this way, a literature review is presented as part of a report or a journal article or some other type of formal research presentation. In contrast, an annotated bibliography is not presented as part of a research paper or report. Instead, it serves as a resource to be used by the project investigators (i.e., the research team) as they do their work; it is an internal document for use by the research team to be aware of prior studies on the subject. (It is not particularly common for annotated bibliographies to be published, but they occasionally are.)

In this sense, creating an annotated bibliography serves three important functions. First, it directs the researchers to perform a careful review of, and documentation of, prior research findings on the research topic. Second, to the extent the writer(s) of the annotated bibliography entries also include an evaluation of findings, and not just mere summaries, it helps the research team see key themes in the research and assists in developing research questions and research hypotheses. And third, as mentioned, once created it serves as a reference document for the team of investigators as they complete their work on the project.

Putting Knowledge into Practice: How to Create an Annotated Bibliography

Creating an annotated bibliography is quite straightforward. After identifying as comprehensively as possible a set of prior works relevant to your research subject (books, research articles, policy reports, evaluation studies, newspaper articles, etc.), you create a summary listing of each of those items. The entry for each item may be limited to just a short summary of what the prior study covered and what its major findings were. But sometimes the entry might also include an assessment of strengths or weaknesses of the research approach, or include key questions left unanswered.

If we use the NHH case study as an example, here is an illustration of two published articles that might be relevant to that project. (Note: the sample entries are simply illustrations; an actual entry can and should provide additional details on the nature of the data gathered and associated analysis and, as noted, might also provide key questions or issues not addressed in the published paper.)

Sample Entry

Brudney, J.L. & Gazley, B. 2009. Planning to be Prepared: An Empirical Examination of the Role of Voluntary Organizations in County Government Emergency Planning. *Public Performance and Management Review*, 32(3): 372–399.

Paper examines the role of voluntary nonprofit organizations (and individual volunteers generally) in local disaster management planning processes. Authors rely on a national survey in the United States, measured at the county government level, to assess the extent of voluntary organization active participation in planning for emergency and disaster response. Key findings include a positive relationship between level of voluntary organization participation and overall reported preparedness levels for a jurisdiction, as reported by local officials.

Sample Entry

Robinson, S.E. & Gerber, B.J. 2007. "A Seat at the Table for Nondisaster Organizations." *The Public Manager* 36 (3): 4–7.

Authors focus their assessment on the relationship between nontraditional response organizations, such as nonprofit organizations who provide relief and recovery services, and traditional response organizations (first responders, such as police and fire, and emergency management offices) at the local level. Authors examine those relationships in two states, Texas and West Virginia, and find several critical barriers to effective cross-sector integration, including organizational structure and organizational culture. Authors provide several illustrations of successful efforts at improving preparedness relationships between these different types of organizations.

Of course, not all relevant research materials are published as academic journal articles. Various organizations (think tanks, advocacy groups, etc.) will publish policy reports. Below is an example of an evaluation study done for a disaster services nonprofit organization. The evaluation was done by two university researchers and is available on the nonprofit organization's website.

Sample Entry

Eller, W.S. & Gerber. B.J. 2010. "Voluntary Nonprofit Organizations and Disaster Recovery: Assessing the Value of the Nonprofit Contribution to the 2009 Alaskan Rivers Flood Recovery Effort." www.nvoad.org

This study evaluates the direct contributions to the successful community recovery by nonprofit, nongovernmental organizations for a flood disaster in a remote area of Alaska. Several members of National Voluntary Organizations Active in Disaster, along with other nonprofits in Alaska, provided disaster relief and helped rebuild and repair homes damaged by the flood waters in the brief two-month window available before winter endangered residents in the villages. Exceptional collaboration with FEMA, which altered its protocols to expedite provision of building materials and to support the volunteer labor, was a key factor in the success, the report found. The value of services provided by the nonprofits was calculated by the researchers to be $3,818,865—92 percent greater than a traditional approach to accounting for volunteer contributions, which originally estimated the value at $1,992,000.

Source Materials

The process of gathering source materials to either generate an annotated bibliography for the purpose of creating a comprehensive reference list, or for use in creating a literature review (if one chooses to skip the creation of an annotated reference list) can require some amount of time and effort. If the researcher is to be thorough and careful, it does require him or her to comb through a variety of different types of source documents. Of course, this is not necessarily as arduous as it was in the past, given the availability of resources via library search systems, such as electronic indices, or other search engine tools available to anyone with access to digital resource materials and the World Wide Web. While conducting searches from a technology standpoint is not particularly challenging with today's information technology resources, understanding the sources of prior research work is extremely important. Not all material has the same standards of carefully following proper research methods practices and rigor in making sure that evidence is appropriately related to the claims made. Therefore, let's discuss how to understand different types of research documents.

Typically the most rigorous standards for published research are a double-blind peer-review process. This means that neither the author nor the reviewer of a research study is aware of the other party. This process of review is common for most academic journals that publish empirical research; and as such, the reader can have confidence that a research finding has been subject to such a scrutinization process.

Using academic research journals is one form of understanding critical explanatory relationships for questions of interest. Let's consider the NHH research question posed at the start of this chapter, which is the matter of understanding what types of mechanisms are most effective in producing interorganizational coordination. One source of information that the evaluators can look to is prior examinations of those issues in policy, public administration, or management research journals. That is a standard approach to finding prior research findings. Of course, there are other sources. Peer-reviewed research articles share similarities with academic books (i.e., a book published from a university press), which are often subject to similar review processes. Similarly,

> **Class Exercise:** Find an academic journal article on a subject and then find a second paper on more or less the same subject—but this time from an advocacy organization, such as a think tank with a clear ideological agenda. Compare and contrast the nature of the claims made in the two documents. Discuss how it is important to understand research motives when research findings are presented.

published research conference proceedings and doctoral dissertations go through peer-review processes to ensure scientific rigor and quality. Again, it is important to remember that while the level of rigor of review varies across these sources of information, none reaches the same level of double-blind peer review.

Advocacy organizations and think tanks also produce research, but these types of studies vary from very sound and rigorous to clearly and ideologically biased. It is difficult to generalize—which is one of the values of learning the basics of research methods: doing so allows you to understand the quality of an empirical assessment. Research produced by a think tank, for instance, if the group has a clear ideological bent, may have some value but the reader needs to be aware that standards of objectivity are potentially not applicable in such work.

Finally, another major source of research findings is government reports. This type of research work tends not to attempt to posit broad theoretic claims or test theoretic hypotheses. It tends to be grounded in a more direct, applied evaluative approach that is geared toward examining processes outputs, and outcomes rather than theoretic arguments that are typical of academic research. This is by no means a shortcoming—just the opposite—if one is interested in the fine-grained details of public policy and public programs. Evaluative reports like the ones produced by the U.S. Government Accountability Office or by inspector general offices at a government agency are often invaluable sources of information about how and why public programs function as they do.

Gathering Background Information

Reviewing prior research findings is by no means the only way to develop the background knowledge and information needed for a project. Another important means of acquiring basic information on a policy question or how a program operates in practice is to conduct preliminary or background interviews with knowledgeable individuals. These can be done as a simple general conversation to gain familiarity with a subject. Or an investigator might conduct a more formal, structured interview. Just like reviewing prior research work, having formal or informal conversations with knowledgeable persons in order to gain new or additional substantive understanding of a policy or program is a fundamental part of the research process. As a result, a researcher or program evaluator often will seek out persons with specialized knowledge of a policy or program or persons with direct programmatic or administrative responsibilities.

Conducting Background Interviews with Subject Matter Experts

The strength and value of a formal interview with a knowledgeable person is that it allows for detailed discussion, clarification of critical points, and discovery of unanticipated issues. When we talk about a knowledgeable person, we often use the term **SUBJECT MATTER EXPERT**. A subject matter expert is a person with knowledge, expertise, and experience within a particular policy domain or program area, or one who has general knowledge of systems, processes, products or technologies, or both. As a result, a subject matter expert can be an invaluable resource in identifying core research challenges and critical questions to pursue in support of a research goal or objective.

There are a few basic steps one should take in preparation for conducting a formal interview that is being recorded (either through note taking or an audio recording device). First, as was discussed in chapter 3, such interviews are subject to human subjects protections. As a result, a researcher should gain an approved review of the study protocol and the interview questions by an Institutional Review Board (IRB). Part of that process is to make clear that the interview subjects are willing participants and have granted permission to be a part of a research study. That means in addition to having IRB approval for the study, before an actual interview is conducted, participation consent must be made clear.

Second, as the actual interview proceeds, it is important to define the purpose of the interview in order to define its scope. If the purpose is to gather some general information about a policy or program, that will lead the interviewer to produce a list of general topic questions to discuss. If the purpose of the interview is to get some very precise information, what is required of the interviewer is the formulation of a much more precise set of questions. Third, whether the purpose is broad or narrow, the interviewer should come prepared with at least some general working knowledge of the policy or program, along with a set of prepared questions. Some general knowledge will facilitate a better discussion and permit more thoughtful follow-up questions when pursuing a particular line of inquiry.

During the interview, there are also some basic practices that prove useful to producing richer information. For example, it is important to understand which questions are most critical, and which are merely helpful, in the event the interview has time constraints. It is important to balance the time allotted for questions, as very few interviews will have the benefit of large amounts of time. Another good technique to use during an interview is to paraphrase and repeat responses stated so as to both reinforce your own understanding of the material and to convey your attentiveness to the subject. Chapter 9 will provide much greater details on the processes and issues related to interviews.

Data Gathering—Preview

As the rest of this book makes clear, there are quite a few different ways and techniques for gathering data that are then used in order to describe and explain some phenomenon. The next section of this book, section II, provides detailed explanations of processes involved in several specific data gathering techniques, such as data collection through survey research. For the benefit of the reader, we preview some of those data gathering techniques here. We do so in order to provide you with some context as we turn to issues of research design, measurement, and sampling in the next several chapters.

Field Research

The idea of **FIELD RESEARCH** refers to data gathering that takes place in a natural setting. While the term originates in the natural sciences (the term implies a literal origin of making observations and collecting specimens in the field), it can be applied to a social science context as well. Subjects of research interest, such as the example of evaluating coordination issues within the NHH, can be treated as field research if the researcher or evaluator goes into the "field"—that is, if the researcher spends time directly observing individuals in the member organizations to see how their operational practices relate to issues of coordination. The researcher typically will have some organized plan for what to look for, how to capture information (often informally through note taking about what was observed), and a plan for what to do with the information that is gathered. It is important to recognize that human subjects approval might well be needed for this type of data gathering.

Surveys

A very widely used and well-known technique for gathering data is to conduct a survey. Surveys have a great number of advantages, some disadvantages, and a wide array of techniques for drawing a sample from which to collect information, for measuring underlying concepts, and even for performing complex research designs. How surveys work is covered in a full chapter later in this book. For now, it is sufficient to note that data collection using a survey is typically done for two reasons: first, because the number of potential information sources is much too large to accomplish through individual interviews; and second, when there is an express desire to collect information from a large group of subjects that are of interest. On this latter point, the basic notion is that a research project has a complete set of subjects that is the object of study, referred to as a population. Measuring all those subjects is referred to as a census; taking a small subset of that population is referred to as a sample. Survey research is typically premised on the idea that the population of interest is quite large, and conducting a census is not practicable or feasible. As a result, to represent the nature of critical relationships in the population is effective to conduct a survey with a sample of the population, which allows for inferences to be made about the population. Example 4.2 below provides some insight as to that logic.

Example—4.2 Case Discussion: Springfield Housing Department

Christina follows up her request for Morty to produce a review of recent research findings with a second request. She would like Morty to draft an initial survey instrument to distribute to the target population of the housing assistance program. In addition to writing a useful survey instrument, the challenge for Christina to resolve is to decide how many surveys to distribute and how to contact the appropriate persons for inclusion in the study. This is difficult because while current program participants can be identified easily from program records, those nonparticipants are not going to be so easy to identify. Christina will have to devise a plan for how to sort out those members of the Springfield community that are eligible for the program but who are not currently participating in order to conduct survey interviews with them. Her plan to resolve this challenge is to use U.S. Census data to identify low-income areas of Springfield and to attempt to draw samples from residents in those areas. [The techniques for taking such an approach will be explained in chapter 7.] The survey data collection process will have to involve some initial questions from survey respondents in order to screen whether the subject is appropriate to continue with the interview.

Questions about the Example: How important do you think it is that the survey of the eligible program participants includes both current participants and current nonparticipants? If Christina only drew a sample of persons who are already in the housing assistance program, what kind of challenges would that present in terms of addressing her central evaluation question? Finally, is doing a survey, which entails interviews with a large number of individuals in order to gather information of how and why the make use of program services—or not—a reasonable or necessary approach given the question at hand? Would some other approach, such as doing in-depth one-on-one interviews with a small number of persons from the target population, be a viable or even superior approach?

Existing Data Sets

An extremely common approach to data gathering is to utilize information that is already publicly available. For example, it is very common for government agencies to develop and maintain data sets that are of use to the public; a researcher can, of course, use that information as they need for specific informational purposes in their own project work. A **DATA SET** is simply a collection of data, organized into a table (usually in a spreadsheet or similar tabular form that is amenable for use in a statistical software package), with information presented in columns as individual variables and rows typically representing the observations made on an individual unit of analysis (i.e., an individual case) in the study. Sometimes these are readily available general sources of information such as those produced by the U.S. Bureau of the Census. Sometimes these are existing collections of relevant data or information maintained by a specific government agency, such as an annual assessment conducted by a state audit bureau. And sometimes it is common for a federally funded research project that the participating agency requires that once a researcher or research team completes its work, to make the resulting data set available to the public for use.

Using an existing data set is convenient because of the no-cost (or at least low-cost) access to those data. While convenient and useful, the potential downside of using an existing data set is that it very likely was created with some research purpose that is not an exact match with your own needs, given your research question. If, for instance, a researcher has a need for a very specific variable measure or two, and even if the data set contains all other relevant information, if it does not contain the specific item, the researcher will not be able to answer his or her key questions. On the other hand, a nice feature of working with existing data is not only the cost and convenience advantages, but also that it permits a researcher to check or replicate prior work in the research area.

Creating an Original Data Set

Finally, a researcher may wish to create her or his own data set. This is an extremely common effort, because existing data sets often do not permit a very precise and specialized research question to be addressed. Moreover, much or even most research is motivated by the need to collect unique and specific information on a very specific problem.

There are two basic processes in creating an original data set. One is a process of aggregating existing information. What that means is that there are records available in the public domain that exist but are not organized into a data set in a coherent way that permits analysis and review. For example, an environmental regulatory agency, such as the U.S. Environmental Protection Agency, will maintain its records on regulatory enforcement actions. These records might be obtained from the agency by a simple request for records, or if the agency does not maintain a public database or have the personnel to provide those records immediately upon request, obtaining the information is accomplished through a Freedom of Information Act request (i.e., a written letter to the agency that asks for it to provide you, as a member of the public, specific information about its activities: in this case, a report on enforcement actions). Once those records are obtained, the researcher is likely to want to combine them with other information. Say, for example, he or she organizes those enforcement actions by state. They could then collect pollution data on a state level for the time period corresponding to the enforcement records. Say they had requested records on air quality enforcement actions. They could then look at records of state air pollution emissions during the corresponding period to see if greater amounts of pollution indeed do prompt greater levels of regulatory actions. Doing such a process of records and information aggregation is a common part of the research process.

The other process is to create original measures and compile them into a data set. Our brief introduction to survey data collection illustrates this process. When a researcher writes a new and unique survey instrument, he or she is creating unique and original data that did not exist anywhere before. So in Example 4.2, where Christina from the Springfield Housing Department is performing a survey to measure participation in a public housing assistance program, and she determines what measurement items to include in the survey instrument, she is creating unique and original data that did not exist before.

Ethical Considerations

In chapter 3, we noted the important ethical considerations in association with doing research that involves human subjects. As was discussed, a fundamentally important principle of conducting research is to ensure the protections of the study subjects. In the context of social science research, that means following established practices about protecting the safety of subjects, including exposing them to no unknown risks. That principle of protecting research subjects of course also applies to the case of background or preliminary research. As we've noted, one common initial research effort is to interview subject matter experts. Given these are most likely to be interviews to gather information on public policy matters or organizational performance issues, there is little chance that conducting such interviews would pose any physical or emotional risks to the subject. However, there could be adverse professional consequences if a subject reveals damaging information about his or her organization. As a result, it is critical that the researcher follow standard practices of gaining consent and protecting subject confidentiality in all instances. If the researcher feels it might be useful to use direct quotes or a paraphrase of a subject's remarks, then she or he must obtain explicit consent from the interview subject to do so.

As we think about the early stages of the research process, we can also think about another fundamental principle that should guide all research project efforts: transparency. The principle of transparency as it pertains to ethical conduct in research is the idea that for any reporting about a research study and its findings, the researcher needs to be completely explicit and transparent about her or his methods used in the study. This means that the consumer of a report should have no ambiguity in her or his mind about how data were collected for the study, how key ideas were measured, or how the gathered data were analyzed. So for instance, if a study made use of subject matter expert interviews, any presentation of study results should make clear the types of organizations or professions represented in that interview data. This can be a delicate balancing act: if subjects were promised strict confidentiality, you will not want to indicate that an interview was done with a key executive of a named public agency, for instance. This could lead someone to reasonably surmise that a specific individual was the source being referred to in the study report. However, if the report explains that subject matter expert interviews were conducted with public sector officials with knowledge of a policy or a program, the reader can understand that the source of information is a professional expert source—without knowing exactly who the individual was who granted the interview.

This illustration reinforces the larger point: the critical ethical consideration is to make sure the reader or consumer of a research study understands the methods used and the nature of those data gathered. Because human subject confidentiality always must be protected, there are appropriate ways to indicate the nature of the data gathering without revealing specific individuals.

As we will see in later chapters, key decisions over research method choices must also be made explicit to conform to the principle of transparency. This is not only an ethical consideration, but it is also critical to the scientific method. If we are to gain knowledge about a subject, other researchers must be able to understand completely how a study was conducted in order to evaluate the merits of the claims being made. Without transparency, we cannot be confident of the results that are presented—and thus we cannot afford them credibility.

Conclusion: How Conducting Preliminary Research Tasks Relates to Evidence-Based Public Management Practices

In this chapter, we covered several elements of the initial stages the research process: reviewing prior research on a subject, producing annotated bibliographies, writing literature reviews, and conducting formal or informal interviews with subject matter experts. We also previewed some of the ways in which data are gathered. How does this material relate to evidence-based public management practices? There are several key points to recognize.

First, if research is to be used to inform decision making, it clearly has to be situated in prior research work on a given subject. As we noted above, very few subjects in the world of public policies and programs have not been examined in some way previously. As a result, if evidence-based decision making is to be followed in practice, it is of course necessary to have as comprehensive an understanding as is possible about what is known in a given subject area. Second, engaging in preliminary work on a project by interviewing subject matter experts is important to evidence-based practice because while those persons are experts in the substance of what they do, that expertise is not necessarily always widely known or disseminated throughout an organization or a policy domain. In fact, the precise reason to engage in research and evaluation in a public management context is to ensure that that sort of knowledge and expertise is made a critical part of the decision-making mix.

Third, it is also important to understand that it is both a common and sound practice for government agencies at the state or local level to perform peer comparisons to guide decision making. For example, local government agencies tasked with making recommendations on developing new land use zoning requirements or planning new building code regulations or even something as simple as fees for household pet licenses will look to similarly sized communities, either within their state or outside their state, to see what those policy practices look like, or what experiences those other communities have had with their programs or regulations. This kind of peer comparison is very common and is a critical piece of background information that is gathered as an agency goes through its analysis to inform its decision-making process. In other words, the kind of preliminary research work discussed in this chapter is directly relevant to evidence-based management practice.

To this point, we have covered a wide range of important concepts in order to get a basic feel for, and understanding of, what the research process is all about. Our next chapter, on research design, begins to move to more specific techniques you will need to learn in order to execute an actual research project.

Vocabulary

Flashcards
& MCQs

Useful
Websites

ANNOTATED BIBLIOGRAPHY—A comprehensive listing of major research articles, reports, books and other similar sources of information about a specific topic.

DATA SET—A collection of data, organized into a table with information presented as a combination of variables and the specific observations made for individual cases in the study.

FIELD RESEARCH—Data gathering process that takes place in a natural setting, that is, in the place where the activity that is to be observed and measured actually occurs.

LITERATURE REVIEW—A reasonably comprehensive survey of previous research studies related to a specific research topic area presented as part of a research report.

SUBJECT MATTER EXPERT—A person with knowledge, expertise, and experience within a particular policy domain, program area, or who has general knowledge of systems, processes, products or technologies, or both.

Review Questions

- What are the core purposes of producing a literature review?
- How do annotated bibliographies differ from literature reviews?
- What is a subject matter expert?
- What does it mean to conduct field research?

Discussion Questions

- Look at an academic journal article on some subject of interest. How did the author(s) present his or her literature review? Was it detailed and comprehensive, or did it cover just a narrow set of specific themes? Was it adequate in explaining the broader context in which the research took place?

- Think about the utility of conducting a subject matter expert interview. How would information gathered from such a process differ from simply doing a thorough background reading of policy or program materials? How do you balance the expert's information with his or her subjective views on the relative importance of information relevant to your research?

CHAPTER 5

Research Design

Learning Objectives

✓ Understand the core concepts related to the design of an evaluative project
✓ Understand the different types of experimental and quasi-experimental research designs
✓ Identify key issues of validity associated with a range of research design types
✓ Identify ethical issues with the research design choices

Cases in Research

Case A—National Helping Hands

Melanie is continuing her research project looking at the nature of National Helping Hands (NHH) member organizations' contributions to disaster relief and recovery. She decides she will do a survey of those members after the next large natural disaster incident in the United States. Of course, the challenges she will face include, among other things, deciding who to survey, when to implement a survey, how to identify an effective sampling and respondent contact strategy, and so forth.

Case B—Amity Department of Homeland Security

Colton was asked to lead an evaluation team in developing a research design that would permit assessment of the effectiveness of National Incident Management System (NIMS) training among relevant Amity government personnel. While Amity has done a good job of making sure that a broad range of municipal offices have been included in training activities, including police, fire, emergency management, public health, and city planners, the question of how well personnel have retained knowledge and familiarity with NIMS is of concern to executives at the city. Colton and other team members need to identify a design that will allow them to see whether the training approach used by the city can be described as effective or whether there should be changes to the training approach. Therefore, Colton is going to have to define a means by which he can measure effectiveness and a design that will be able to permit inferences as to whether the existing training system produces benefits to employee knowledge of NIMS.

Case C—Grover's Corner Department of Transportation

The Grover's Corner Department of Transportation has tasked one of its analysts with an evaluation of commuter usage behavior for the various light rail stations in the metropolitan area. Three years ago, Grover's Corner invested in a series of upgrades to several select stations, including increasing available parking at those sites along with leasing some available space for commercial activity (e.g., coffee and food vendors at the station site). The analyst has a basic challenge: to see if there is evidence to support the proposition that targeted improvements at the light rail stations have improved commuter usage at those locations.

Research Design

Following our discussion to this point, the general purpose of conducting research is to produce clear and meaningful understanding and explanation of social phenomena. In simpler language, we use the research process following the scientific method to figure how and why things work as they do. For our purposes in this chapter, we have a bit more of a specific intent: we wish to understand how to produce research that supports the notion of evidence-based public management. Our preceding chapters outlined the basic logic of the research process—what it is and how it is used—and some essential starting points for initiating a research project or process. Chapter 4 provided you with a preview of several different ways in which data might be collected. What we need next is a basic understanding of exactly how to approach the data collection process when we are attempting to evaluate or assess some program or policy. Doing so is the basic notion of **RESEARCH DESIGN**, which simply refers to the process by which data gathering efforts are structured and defined. That is, the research design defines what is to be studied and how, which includes what variables are to be included in the study, how they are measured in relation to one another, and how those data are gathered.

Perhaps the best way to recognize the importance of how the data are collected for some project—its underlying research design—is to refer back to our prior discussions

→ an explanation that links
     causes & effects

of causal inference in chapters 1 and 3. In the context of evidence-based management, we are commonly interested in asking whether a program or policy had some discernible or measurable effect (or perhaps whether we can predict a certain effect). What is important to understand is that how one answers the question is based on the nature of those data you have collected. In other words, it is important to recognize and understand— and this is key—the way in which those data were gathered, as this directly affects what kind of answer one can actually give about program effects. What we will see in this chapter is that the way in which you collect information or data to assess a program determines the nature and quality of any possible causal inference you might attempt to make. We will explore those issues in detail below, but that is the reason for learning about and understanding research design issues.

Further, having a sound grasp of research design issues is necessary for anyone interested in conducting, or even simply reading, policy research or program evaluation studies used for evidence-based management practices. As we will see below, designing a research or evaluation project is a challenging endeavor, one made more so when dealing with public policies and programs. Data are often difficult to obtain, and more important, there are meaningful limitations on what and how public programs can be studied. Thus, careful attention to the process and nature of data gathering can improve the quality of decisions over program management functions by making reasonable decisions about the value and use of those data.

This chapter provides you with an introduction to basic concepts and issues associated with designing an assessment or evaluation of a public policy or program. It fits into our discussion of the research process in chapter 3 because it is the way in which we define how data are going to be collected. By the conclusion of this chapter, the reader should have developed an understanding of what research design is, how design affects the meaning of data and its subsequent analysis, and how those issues are relevant to evidence used in a public management context.

Basic Concepts for Research Design

Before examining a selection of different types of research designs, along with the discussion of other key issues related to validity and design type, we must first cover some basic concepts that underlie those design types. We can do so by first considering the notion of an experiment.

In simple terms, an **EXPERIMENT** can be described as an activity where a researcher controls or manipulates the conditions under which some sort of subject is examined in order to observe and measure a specific cause-and-effect relationship. We can think of an experiment as a collection of subjects who are randomly assigned to either an experimental group, who receive a treatment, or a control group. The term **TREATMENT** refers to some variable or condition that the researcher introduces into the experiment in order to see whether it has an effect on the subjects. For example, let's say a state government agency develops a new home energy efficiency program. It is interested in testing the effects of the new program to see if it really helps reduce energy consumption at the level of an individual household. The treatment group would be those participating subjects who receive specific adjustments to their house to improve energy consumption. The **CONTROL GROUP** is those subjects in the experiment that do not receive the treatment. That is, the control group would be those subjects that did not receive any planned adjustments to their home structure.

In the classic case of an experiment, the researcher will start by randomly assigning the study's subjects into one of two groups: either the treatment group or the control group. Next, he or she will measure all subjects—the treatment group and the control group—before the treatment is introduced. During the experiment, the researcher will hold constant all conditions experienced by the subjects. And then, the researcher will again measure all subjects after the treatment has been introduced—in order to see if there is a difference in outcomes between the treatment and control group subjects.

Each of these elements of the experiment has an important function. A control group allows the researcher to examine possible unique effects from a treatment that are exclusive to the treatment group. The random assignment of subjects is important because it minimized the possibility that the process of selecting subjects affects the observed outcomes of the experiment. The pre- and post-measurement allows the researcher to see if there was a discernible effect from the treatment. Holding all the conditions constant for all subjects during the experiment—other than the introduction of a treatment—allows the researcher to see if the only difference in the final measured outcome between control or experimental group subjects was the effect of the treatment itself. What this all means then is that if there was a meaningful difference between the treatment group and the control group subjects at the end of the experiment, then we can draw a very clear inference that there is a cause-and-effect relationship for that treatment. This is the power of experiments: they are great tools for helping to see if there are cause-and-effect relationships at work.

That said, we do need to keep an equally important notion in mind. Even if we do observe a difference between treatment and control group subjects at the end of an experiment, there is a possibility that it is not the result of the treatment. Instead, the researcher might have seen an outcome of the experiment that was simply due to random chance.

Does that mean researchers everywhere should despair? That they should worry that they can never quite be sure what results of their research mean? Thankfully, the answer is no. This is the power (and beauty!) of statistical analysis and why we are studying these issues in this book. As we will learn in section III of this book, we have very useful tools of statistical analysis that will allow us to see how likely it is that the results of our research work are due to random chance. For example, if you are 99.9 percent sure that the effect of the treatment is meaningful, you could be wrong—but you would only be wrong 1 time out of 1,000. This means that a researcher can be quite confident that the treatment really does have an effect.

We can summarize this section by recognizing that the idea of an experiment is central to grasping the basic concept of research design. That is because in thinking about the elements of an experiment as just described, we can see how the data collection process, structured in a particular way, matters to how we can interpret the results of a study. Even though experiments can take on much more sophisticated forms and can be applied to both human and nonhuman subjects, the basic elements of pre- and post-measurement, controlled conditions, specificity of treatment introduction, and random assignment of treatment and control groups are the essential elements. Thus, we can think about which elements are present in a study—as well as which elements are lacking—when we examine how the data used in a study were collected. In doing so, as we'll see in a moment, we can better understand what our data are able to tell us, and more importantly, what we must be cautious about in drawing inferences of potential cause and effect.

Variables, Measurement, and Measurement Error

In outlining the concept of an experiment, we were introduced to the idea of a treatment, which was described as a variable that a researcher believes might cause some discernible change in a subject in the experimental group. When we use the term **VARIABLE**, as discussed in chapter 3, we are referring to a characteristic of the unit of analysis that changes or varies; that is, it does not have a constant value. Variables can be quantitative (i.e., measured in numeric form) or qualitative (i.e., measured as categories identifying some nonnumeric characteristic). Our next chapter, chapter 6, goes into greater depth on issues and concepts related to variables and variable measurement, but for now, we will consider the distinction between independent and dependent variables. A **DEPENDENT VARIABLE** is the outcome of interest for a researcher. For instance, if a researcher wants to know whether employee knowledge of administrative requirements improves with training (see Example 5.1 below), the outcome of interest is employee knowledge of those requirements; that is, it is the dependent variable or outcome of interest. Because that knowledge level is not constant across employees, in that it varies, we have to ask ourselves what causes or explains that variation in our outcome of interest. Those variables that we believe to be responsible for causing or explaining observed variation or changes in the outcome of interest, the dependent variable, are referred to as **INDEPENDENT VARIABLES** (they are also sometimes referred to as explanatory or predictor variables). Independent variables are thought to be responsible for explaining changes in the dependent variable across each case we are looking at in a study's data set.

It might be a surprise to someone new to the research process, but in many cases measuring a variable is not necessarily straightforward. Many of the concepts we care about in terms of public administration and public management are not quite as easy to measure. Concepts like equity and efficiency might seem straightforward, but translating those ideas into concrete measures can be quite difficult. For example, let's take perhaps an even easier concept to measure: employee performance. While it might seem like that would be easy to measure at first glance, when you think about it, employee performance can mean many different things, which is to say, the concept has multiple dimensions. What is necessary is to settle on a definition through which the concept can be put into measurable form. This is the notion of **OPERATIONALIZATION**. Employee performance might be operationalized as some specific measure of productivity in the form of a count of outputs, for example.

Of course, whenever you measure something, even if the operationalization is as sound as it can be, there is going to be some degree of imprecision when gathering the

operationalization – making the concept a measurable form

actual data. **MEASUREMENT ERROR** refers to the idea that no matter what is being measured, there is likely to be some amount of error involved in the process. Sources of error include the fact that a measurement instrument might lack precision; there might be mistakes in the use of the instrument, or in the recording of the information gathered; or other random factors. There are two types of measurement error: systematic and random. Systematic error can also be referred to as **BIAS**, which means that the measurement error occurs in a specific pattern. On the other hand, random measurement error is nonsystematic, which is to say it does not have any particular pattern. As we will see later in the book, **RANDOM ERROR** does cause statistical estimates to be less precise than they otherwise would be, but it is not otherwise problematic necessarily. Systematic error or bias, on the other hand, prevents us from making valid, reliable estimates, and hence is quite problematic.

While we introduce these ideas here—so the reader has an understanding that when collecting data there are going to be questions over the effectiveness of any measurement process—we do so only briefly. In chapter 6, we will discuss concepts and issues of measurement in greater detail.

Example 5.1—Case Discussion: Amity DHS

Colton has been given the analytic task of assessing the relative effectiveness of training for the National Incident Management System (NIMS) among relevant Amity government personnel. This presents a basic measurement question: how can one operationalize the concept of training effectiveness? Colton believes that effectiveness can be measured effectively by comparing the pretraining scores of individuals on a questionnaire of NIMS knowledge to the scores on the same instrument following employee completion of the NIMS self-study course. This is a quantitative measure of performance: one that Colton argues is a reasonable indication of effectiveness. Further, by looking at the change in scores by employee occupation (e.g., first response personnel versus public health personnel), Colton will be able to investigate whether general knowledge of emergency management issues is relevant to training effectiveness.

Questions about the Example: What do you think of Colton's decision regarding the operationalization of training effectiveness? Is it likely to measure what he thinks it is measuring? Are there weaknesses to this approach? What other alternative measurement strategies might you suggest?

Reliability and Validity

After we have identified our variables relevant to our program evaluation or policy analysis task and have operationalized them, we need to ask ourselves about the nature of reliability and validity as we gather our data. **RELIABILITY** is a straightforward concept having to do with measurement consistency. Imagine you know the true value of something we want to measure. A measure is reliable to the extent that it produces the same value if it is measuring the same object. For example, if you are weighing an object on a scale, and the object hasn't changed and the scale is reliable, the reported weight should be the same each time you measure it. In other words, we want to know if our measurement instrument yields consistent results whenever it is applied. This might seem straightforward, but it is not. There are numerous complications when we try to measure things in the social world. If we are using a telephone survey to collect data, the telephone interviewers might vary greatly in how they interact with interview subjects, for instance. Or if we are gathering agency data and have some output measure of interest, those data might not be reliably measured from case to case. For example, if we are looking at car crash incident data, or if we are tracking the impact of a change in speed limits on state or federal highways, the fact that different areas might record accident information differently, or that there may be definitional changes over time in how the accident information is recorded, make it clear that there are questions about the reliability of the data we are working with.

VALIDITY, on the other hand, refers to the idea that some operationalized measure of a concept is in fact measuring what it purports to measure. The key question to ask is, how good is the fit between the concept we are trying to measure and the actual operationalized measures we are using? That is, we can think about the gap between a concept and measure as a question of validity. We can also extend that simple concept to an experiment or research design overall: When we design a study, are we really getting at what we think, or say, we are getting at? For instance, if we say we intend to measure employee performance by a count of some kind of output, then we can ask whether that is the best way of capturing the core features of the performance concept. Employee performance also has to do with creative contributions to the organization, the ability to work well with fellow employees, consistency of effort, and so forth. A process count for an employee might work well in some circumstances, but it might not be a useful indicator of performance in another.

What is the relationship between reliability and validity? We can say that an unreliable measure cannot be valid. That is, if the measurement approach is inconsistent and unreliable, we can never be sure if we are actually measuring the underlying concept we want to measure (i.e., we can never have confidence in the validity of our data precisely because they are unreliable). But, a measure can be highly reliable (i.e., highly consistent) but still not at all valid. For instance, what if we wanted to use height as a measure of a person's political ideology? We could have a highly reliable measure of a person's height, but that in no way is a valid representation of the core concept of ideology.

We will return to the subject of reliability and validity in chapter 6 to provide additional information about those concepts. That chapter focuses on concepts related to measurement and within that discussion, we will see how a researcher can assess the reliability and validity of a given measurement approach.

Example 5.2—Case Discussion: Grover's Corner DOT

The Grover's Corner DOT analysts are interested in measuring commuter light rail usage over time—as it relates to specific station locations. The DOT office does have specific records of ridership activity. At present, they are able to measure both numbers of unique rider cards (cash card purchases from on-site vending machines) and monthly rider numbers (riders who purchase monthly optical scan cards) at all stations on the light rail system. However, given the DOT wants to track usage over time, the analysts are presented with a dilemma: several years ago, the rail system used a method to estimate ridership numbers rather than report exact user totals. This is because persons previously were required to purchase a ticket before riding but did not have to pass through turn-stiles. Instead, the rail system used a method where there were only spot checks of passenger ticket purchases by agents during the ride. Clearly, there is reliability issue with a comparison of rider numbers over time. The current period has measured ridership in a more precise way than an earlier period where the spot check method was used and only drew estimates of ridership numbers.

Questions about the Example: What does this measurement issue in this case example tell you about reliability concerns? Are there any alternative measures the Grover's Corner DOT office might use to ensure reliability in the ridership measurement? Likewise, are there any validity concerns with the way the analysts are trying to assess light rail usage?

Randomization, Control, Confounding Effects, and Generalizability

As noted above, an essential element of an experiment is the **RANDOM ASSIGNMENT**, or randomization, of subjects to either the experimental group or the control group. What that means is that each subject has an equal probability of falling into either category; there is no systematic selection process at work. In our example of the professor's experiment of feedback, we noted that she made the selection of the treatment and control groups completely random; she selected from a randomized list of numbers that were attached to each individual student.

On the other hand, the concept of **EXPERIMENTAL CONTROL** serves quite a different purpose. Experimental control refers to the situation where the researcher is able to deliberately hold constant the conditions experienced by the study's subjects during the conduct of the experiment. In our example of the instructor feedback experiment, we saw that the professor attempted to maintain experimental control through a conscious effort to treat all students exactly the same during the course of the semester. In that sense, she was attempting to exert experimental control by keeping classroom conditions constant for all students. At the same time, she also systematically introduced the treatment—the written feedback—in a controlled way (i.e., only applying the treatment to the selected group). This other element of experimental control is seen when the researcher introduces a variable designed to produce an effect—or at least a variable that can be observed to see if an effect is actually produced.

While randomization and control are key elements of the experiment, it is possible that there are other variables that can affect the study results even though the researcher attempts to limit this possibility. Let's consider an example from one of our cases highlighted in this chapter: the effort to evaluate the effectiveness of emergency management training programs in Amity. Suppose the researcher wants to know if the length of an employee's tenure in a position is related to post-training scores. The premise would be that more senior personnel will have a greater ability to do well on the training comprehension instrument. There might be a relationship there, but it would be difficult to isolate that effect given the way the researcher is studying this question. That is because there is also a possibility that other factors are driving performance scores, such as occupation (e.g., employees from the emergency management office might perform differentially better than employees from the public health office, regardless of job tenure). This is the idea of a **CONFOUNDING EFFECT**, which can be described as a variable related to the key research variable of interest that affects or "confounds" the observed results. What this means is that if the research does not take occupation into account in the analysis, then we cannot be sure whether it is job experience or occupation type that is affecting training comprehension scores. Put another way: we cannot be sure there is not some other variable having an effect on the observed outcome if we have not accounted for its possible effects. This is a major problem if the researcher has not been able to isolate the treatment effect—the key independent or explanatory variable. Failure to account for possible confounding effects means the researcher has failed to account for competing explanations, and we cannot be sure of the accuracy of any causal inferences that are offered.

> **Class Exercise:** Discuss the challenges of determining external validity for one of the case examples presented in this chapter. What about the research problem might make the results externally valid, or what factors might limit the external validity of the findings?

Our last key concept to discuss is the issue of generalizability. Generalizability is a term that is nearly self-explanatory: it simply refers to the degree to which results from a study can be generalized to other places, time periods, subject populations, and the like. This is also referred to as **EXTERNAL VALIDITY**. A key question that any research analysis is likely to address is whether the results are externally valid. For example, if we consider the example of the instructor feedback experiment, it is entirely reasonable to ask if the findings are externally valid—that is, whether they are generalizable to other settings. There are likely a whole host of questions to address before we can be confident the results are externally valid. For example, can we generalize from a single class of 30 students in a university setting to the impact of written feedback on student performance in any classroom setting? A statistics course might be more difficult than some other courses, which means the degree of feedback from an instructor might not matter as much in courses that are not very challenging or uncomfortable for students. What if the course is a graduate level one? Are graduate students similar to undergraduate students in how they interact with faculty? These are the kinds of questions to assess when one considers the external validity of a study's findings.

Issues of Validity and Inference

Earlier we defined validity in terms of the quality of a variable's operationalization; we noted it was the degree to which we are measuring what we think we are measuring. Importantly, we can extend that basic concept by applying it to research design overall, as opposed to an individual variable measure. The extent to which a research design is able to account for, or rule out, competing explanations (i.e., something other than our treatment or key causal factor) is the notion of **INTERNAL VALIDITY**. In simple terms, when examining a program or policy, we want to know if that program (which we can think of as the treatment) is having the effect the results our study suggests it is. In other words, if our research work is designed to attempt to identify and explain a causal relationship, the study is internally valid to the extent that we are confident that the relationship we have observed is accurate and that we have ruled out other possible explanations for that observed relationship. Of course, we have to be aware of what sorts of things might make it difficult for us to draw a causal inference.

In a seminal book on the subject, Campbell and Stanley (1963) identify a list of factors that represent threats to internal and external validity. By threats we mean that there is something not accounted for (i.e., controlled for) in the design that can be confused with the effects of the treatment. If a research design does not account for these threats, then the researcher cannot be sure any inferences of treatment effect are valid.

There are different ways to list all possible threats to internal validity. The next section provides you with a list of threats that are common to internal and external validity. To reiterate, the point of understanding these threats is to understand how the research design that determines a data collection strategy might affect our ability to make appropriate causal inferences from the analysis of those data.

Threats to Internal and External Validity

A first threat to internal validity is history, which can be defined as some external event that occurs during the course of the experimental period—between the pre- and post-measurement—that presents a potential rival explanation for any observed change in the experimental group. If we are looking at a public program over multiple years, it is very possible that some event occurring that is beyond the researcher's ability to control its introduction can affect the post-treatment measurement. For instance, if one is examining a community economic development program, a stock market crash at the national level would introduce an effect on the results that is distinct from the program itself.

A second threat to internal validity is maturation, which can be defined as any changes to the subject in the study that occurs simply as a result of time passing. This is not the same thing as history, which refers to an external event(s) that changes overall measured outcomes, potentially. Maturation is a change in the subjects themselves directly as a consequence of being studied over time. For instance, a longer-term study would result in natural changes in subject's attitudes, beliefs, or physical conditions that might cause effects on the outcome of interest—again that are separate from the treatment effects. This is true not only for people but also for entities of interests such as public agencies, whose personnel and leadership and the political dynamics affecting it no doubt do not stay constant over time.

A third internal validity threat is testing, which refers to the effect that occurs when a subject taking a test at one point in time (e.g., a pretest) might have an effect when the same subject takes a test at a second point in time (e.g., a posttest). That is, the individual subjects might remember question items from the first test, or they might have discussed the subject matter with others between point A and point B in the testing period. Further, the very existence of a pretest can provide a cue to subjects that they should pay more attention to the subject matter. Or, the initial measurement might provide a cue to the subject as to what is being examined and thus affect their performance as measured in the later test. The famous illustration of this validity threat is referred to as the "Hawthorne Effect" because of the factory site of an experimental study where the subjects modified their behavior in response to being continuously observed by researchers during the production process, even when treatment changes were modified.

Instrumentation refers to some kind of change occurring to the measurement instrument during the course of an experiment or a change in who collects the data or how the data are measured. For instance, if the study involves some degree of subjective interpretation in the collection of data, changes that observers witness during the study can affect the study results. Likewise, it is not uncommon for there to be slight changes in the operational definition of some measure of outputs used by a government agency; this presents a validity threat because those data over time may not be exactly comparable.

Regression to the mean is another internal validity threat. It refers to the notion that if subjects are chosen for inclusion in a study because of an extreme score, there is a possibility that over time, those subject scores will regress to their average or mean score (i.e., they regress to their mean). For instance, if students are put into an advanced or gifted study program based on placement tests it is possible that their scores might decline. This does not necessarily indicate the gifted program is functioning poorly, but instead, the placement scores may have captured an unusual set of scores, and the scores will have a tendency to "fall back" to their more typical level. This is a danger of one shot measurements: the researcher may not be sure if there is a regression to the mean effect occurring.

A common and significant challenge to researchers is the idea of selection bias, which refers to the idea that selection in a study is not random or of an equal probability among the study subjects. This is a problem of a lack of random assignment of study subjects. When the researcher or evaluator cannot control randomization of subjects, then there is the distinct possibility that inclusion in a study is driven by some process separate from the study.

To put it another way: it is not uncommon that there is a problem of self-selection of the study subjects. When study subjects volunteer for a program (e.g., think of a city deciding to participate in some voluntary grant program offered by the federal government, there is a process by which some cities are more inclined to do that while others not), the factors that drive participation may be critical to the outcome of interest, but those factors are often not captured by the study itself. In that way, the researcher cannot know for certain whether the treatment caused an effect or whether the self-selection process is what was driving the end result.

Similar to self-selection is the problem of mortality. This is where a subject drops out of study of his own volition, as opposed to self-selecting in. Subjects who drop out of an actual program or study might have unique characteristics that are affecting the outcome results. Hence, the researcher cannot be sure of whether the outcome would have been the same had those participants not dropped out.

The above list of items all refer to threats to internal validity. Any design also has implications for external validity, again, which refers to whether results can be generalized to other settings beyond the specific sample gathered for the purposes of conducting a given study. External validity can be adversely affected when the study itself is different from a larger generalization that a researcher may want to make; that is, if there is something about the study design or data gathered that precludes generalizing to other settings or situations. These involve interaction of the nature of the study (and its treatment) with specific aspects of conducting an experiment (i.e., an interaction between treatment and testing). What does that mean? It simply means that the effect of the treatment might be different when you have pretreatment measurement—precisely because when you have pretreatment measurement, the subjects become aware of the fact they are being measured, and this affects their behavior.

Now that we have a basic understanding of the key concepts associated with research design, we will turn to the question of how to put research design choices into practice. That is, we will address exactly what research design types look like and how they function.

Research Design Types

To this point, we have talked in broad terms about the idea of a treatment as an intervention introduced by a researcher conducting an experiment in order to see if that intervention has a discernible effect. What is critically important to understand is that a research design approach and the notion of a treatment is not just applicable to a controlled experiment. For our purposes in the world of public agencies and nonprofit organizations, the experiment and its design do not occur in a controlled laboratory setting. Further, the treatment usually takes the form of some specific program (e.g., we can look at an economic investment effort in a community), a management activity (e.g., a new training package for employees), or a specific policy action (e.g., adoption of a new regulation). Rather than some activity in a laboratory, given our interest in evidence-based public management, the research designs described below can be understood as applicable to public programs and policies. In fact, as you might have guessed by now, analyzing public policies or programs or organizations very seldom allows for a laboratory experiment.

Instead, we must recognize that research designs can be taken as an experimental approach—but it is much more likely in a public sector research or evaluation setting that the investigator is going to take a quasi-experimental or nonexperimental design approach.

Why is that so? Keeping in mind the elements of a controlled experiment, it is important to recognize that conducting a true experiment is generally difficult in the context of studying public programs or policies. It is often not possible to withhold a service or program benefit to the public, which precludes the notion of randomly assigning subjects to an experimental or control group. Likewise, the nature of random selection of subjects themselves is often difficult. As a result, researchers can specify designs that deal with nonrandomization or the inability to create a control group by instead matching subjects as closely as possible and defining that as a comparison group instead. In this way, the design is described as a quasi-experiment. Further, as we will see below, it is often extremely common for researchers and evaluators to use a nonexperimental approach. That term will be defined below, but the short version of the story is this: sometimes a researcher will simply take a set of measures at a single point in time and then use statistical techniques to account for a range of possible explanations. This is a very powerful approach to take because it can offer the possibility of resolving some of the challenges researchers face when they cannot set up a controlled experiment.

True Experiments

We have discussed earlier in the chapter the basic features of a controlled experiment. What exactly does that look like in practice?

An example of a true experimental design is the classic pretest pos-test control group design. It is a classic design because it is simple, straightforward, and contains all the essential elements of an experiment. As Figure 5.1 shows, subjects are placed into either an experimental group, which receives a deliberately introduced treatment, or placed in a control group, which does not receive the treatment. The placement in either of the two groups is done via random selection. Likewise, there is a pretreatment (i.e., pretest) measurement of all subjects and a pos-treatment measurement of all subjects. The beauty of this design is that if experimental conditions are properly controlled, then we are able to isolate effectively the nature of the treatment effects. If there is an observed effect for the treatment, then we can infer with a high degree of confidence that there is a meaningful causal relationship between the treatment and the outcome of interest, the dependent variable. Of course, it is also possible that the observed effect occurred by chance. However, as we will see later in this book, we can also utilize statistical techniques to check that very possibility as well. We can also note that the statistics course instructor's feedback experiment is represented by the diagram shown in Figure 5.1. That is, we can now see that the instructor conducted an experiment using the classic pretest–posttest control group design.

	Pretest	Treatment	Posttest
Experimental Group	O_1	X	O_2
Control Group	O_1		O_2

Figure 5.1   Pretest–Posttest Control Group Design

Quasi-Experiments

As noted above, one nontrivial problem with experiments for evidence-based management in the public and nonprofit sectors is that it is relatively uncommon for a researcher or evaluator to be able to create a true experiment. It is worth reiterating that this is so because in the real world of public programs and policies, a researcher or evaluator cannot always simply assign control and treatment groups, nor can they otherwise control an experimental setting.

Why would that be so? Consider the idea of a public program (e.g., a social welfare program such as food assistance to families living below a designated poverty line) as a treatment. How would a researcher be able to assign some households or families, randomly, to receive the program? The short answer is that the researcher cannot typically make such controls of who receives such a treatment. Likewise, consider the idea that if our outcome of interest for a study of the effects of an antipoverty program (through basic food assistance) was whether an improved health status occurred, then how would a researcher be able to control for possible conditions within which the study's subjects lived during the period the research took place? Again, the short answer is that the researcher cannot generally control conditions in the same way that researchers do in many true experimental designs. As a result, we relax some of those conditions of a true experiment and proceed from a quasi-experimental design perspective.

There are numerous variations of the true experimental design shown in Figure 5.1. Likewise, there are numerous variations of quasi-experiments as well. The first of two illustrations presented below looks a great deal like the true experimental design depicted in Figure 5.1. However, there is an important difference. In the design shown below in Figure 5.2, the reader will note that we do not have a control group but instead we have a comparison group. This indicates that there is not a random assignment of subjects. Instead, because random assignment is not possible, the researcher will identify a comparable set of subjects who have not received the treatment but are otherwise very similar to the experimental group in all other respects. In this way, the comparison group, though not selected at random, functions as close to a control group as possible. One way to illustrate this design is to think of a state where some cities have adopted a specific pollution control program endorsed by the state government while others have not. A researcher looking to study the effects of that program over time could match cities who are quite similar to the participating programs in all other respects (size, demographics, etc.) but for the fact that they do not employ that particular pollution control program. Assuming that the state has reliable measures of pollution outputs at the municipal level,

	Pretest	Treatment	Posttest
Experimental Group	O_1	X	O_2
Comparison Group	O_1		O_2

Figure 5.2   Pretest–Posttest Comparison Group Design

	Before		Treatment	After	
	$O_{E,t-2}$	$O_{E,t-1}$	X	$O_{E,t+1}$	$O_{E,t+2}$
	$O_{C,t-2}$	$O_{C,t-1}$		$O_{C,t+1}$	$O_{C,t+2}$

Figure 5.3   Interrupted Times-Series Comparison Group Design

the researcher could reasonably isolate the effects of the pollution control program to see if the pollution control performance is, in fact, superior in those participating cities.

Another type of quasi-experimental design is shown in Figure 5.3, an interrupted time-series comparison group design. This design is one that tracks some kind of program or policy effects over an extended period of time (i.e., a time series or a longitudinal study). Figure 5.3 indicates that there are data collected at multiple points in time before a treatment (e.g., the adoption of a policy change) and multiple points in time after the treatment. The figure shows, $O_{E,t-2}$, which is indicating the experimental group being measured at two time periods prior to the introduction of the treatment. Again, this design does not have a randomly assigned control group but instead has a comparison group that is as similar to the experimental group as possible.

A time-series design is interesting and useful because it reduces or removes any potential bias seen from only collecting observations at a single point in time. That is, by collecting observations over an extended period of time, we are able to observe trends and thus better identify whether a treatment at a given point in time has had a specific impact.

Example 5.4—Case Discussion: Grover's Corner DOT

The analysis team at the Grover's Corner DOT has set up a times-series design of commuter usage at the selected stations (treatment) in comparison to the other stations that did not receive the additional parking and customer services upgrades. The station improvements are considered the treatment. As mentioned above, not all stations received these improvements, and as a result, the research team can create a comparison group of otherwise similar or matching stations to those that received the upgrades. The team takes monthly data for 18 months prior to the station upgrade and 18 months after. They take the same amount of observations for the matching stations that did not receive the upgrade. This large number of time period observations allows the team to account for any other trends in commuter rail usage (e.g., seasonal effects) as well as to see if the station upgrades had any apparent changes in attracting greater use—and whether those higher use patterns have stayed consistently higher.

Questions about the Example: While such a posttraining evaluation approach is extremely common, what do you think the major weaknesses of such an approach are?

Nonexperiments

An experiment has several essential features, which include random assignment to experimental and control groups, pre- and posttreatment measurement, and control of experimental conditions. Generally speaking, if the key element of randomization is missing (i.e., we cannot randomly assign subjects to a control or treatment group, or we cannot even create a control group), then we think of the design as quasi-experimental. But if most of those characteristics are missing, then we can describe the design as "nonexperimental." A classic and common example of such a design approach is a one shot case study design. In this design, there is no random assignment of subjects to experimental or control groups; indeed, there is no control group at all. Likewise, there is no pretreatment measurement of subjects, and there is no controlled introduction of the treatment itself. In effect, what this design captures is the notion that some event occurs, which constitutes a treatment. It could be a policy change or it could be a specific event associated with a given program, for instance. After that treatment has occurred, the researcher measures some sample of subjects. Example 5.5 provides an illustration of how this design might occur in practice.

	Treatment	Posttest
Group	X	O

Figure 5.4   One Shot Case Study Design

Example 5.5—Case Discussion: Amity Department of HLS

A nonexperimental approach might be simply to ask employees about training satisfaction after they completed it. That would be the design structure illustrated in Figure 5.4 above. There would be some utility in knowing how employees felt about their training—that is, an important piece of information a manager might want to consider. However, in terms of telling us much about effectiveness, there are real limits. We cannot know if some employees are just favorably disposed to all training or some unfavorably disposed to all training, for instance. We cannot know if this particular set of training materials was more effective or less effective. In other words, there are limits to what we can infer

Questions about the Example: While such a posttraining evaluation approach is extremely common, what do you think the major weaknesses of such an approach are? In terms of analyzing those data that are collected, what utility would such data provide to you if you wanted to assess its effectiveness?

There are two other research design terms that you almost certainly will encounter if you end up either doing original research or are in a management position that requires your organization to conduct research and evaluation studies to meet key organizational tasks and goals: cross-sectional designs and longitudinal designs. These two terms can be used in several different ways, but you might be most likely to encounter them in discussions around research designs used for survey research. A great deal of the data that are collected for the purpose of studying public programs and organizations are gathered through the use of surveys. Hence, it is important to understand how data collection for a survey is designed.

Overwhelmingly, the most common research design for survey data collection is a **CROSS-SECTIONAL DESIGN**. It is called a cross-sectional design because the sample of the subjects is taken at a single point in time (a cross-section), which is why sometimes you will hear it said that a survey is simply a snapshot in time. The phrase "single point in time" in our definition does not mean all survey data are gathered simultaneously. Instead, a survey may be completed by a survey lab in a matter of hours (which is unusual), or a matter of several days (which is common), or even over several weeks. Especially in the case of mail surveys (as opposed to a telephone survey), the time to execute the data collection can take more time. But because the survey is completed in as short a time period as is practical, we think of it as a "single point in time"—though that is not quite literally true. Cross-sectional research designs are nonexperiments because they do not have the other elements

A variation of this design strategy is to take the same basic approach, but instead of collecting data at only a single point in time, researchers will attempt to collect data (including survey data) over time. Doing so is a called a **LONGITUDINAL DESIGN**, which indicates the same measurement items are collected at two or more points in time. What that means is that if you are collecting data from an agency, you are measuring those same items over a period of time (for instance, it could be a selection of weeks, months, or years).

If you are talking about individual persons in survey data collection, there are two ways to conduct a longitudinal study. One way is to take repeated cross-sections of the same population. (We will get into much greater detail on the nature of sampling in chapter 7, but the very short meaning of the term "population" here is the universe of cases we are interested in studying, such as all adults in the United States. A cross-sectional survey might take a sample of 1,000 adults in January, and then a sample of another 1,000 in April, then again in July, etc, if this were a quarterly survey of U.S. adults.) This is sometimes referred to as a trend study because the point is to observe trends over time in the data collected. Another way to conduct a longitudinal study is take the same set of study subjects (e.g., a set of individuals) and measure them at repeated points over time. This would be referred to as a panel study (i.e. a panel of subjects are measured to see how they do or do not change over some set period of time).

Again, we will tackle these issues in greater detail in the chapter on sampling and the chapter on survey data collection.

Putting Knowledge into Practice: How to Choose a Research Design Type

In this section of chapter 5, we have provided the reader with a very brief introduction to the basic categories of research design type: experimental, quasi-experimental, and nonexperimental. You should be aware that this is only the most brief of introductions, for these questions have produced a large number of textbooks and monographs on the subject.

While we cannot cover all aspects of research design in a single chapter, we should also address a basic question: How does one choose a research design approach for a given research or evaluation project? There is good news and bad news in answering the question. The bad news is that there is not a simple or easy answer to cover all situations. The good news is that there are some general principles that one can follow that will inform the selection of a research design type.

To see what kinds of considerations come into play when you are making a choice over a research design strategy, the reader can look for additional practice problems and exercises in the Interactive eTextbook version. There you will find several sample exercises that illustrate the kinds of common questions that most investigators face when making research design choices.

Fill in
the
Blanks

Example 5.6—Case Discussion: National Helping Hands

Melanie decides that as part of her research project, she will do a survey of NHH member organizations to find out what kind of post-disaster assistance they provided. After a major hurricane in the Gulf region, she goes into the field with a survey of member organization executives. She initiates the survey of about 50 individuals about a month after the disaster. She asks a series of questions about their respective organization's efforts in the first week after disaster response operations were concluded. She contracts with a university survey lab to conduct the survey via telephone.

Questions about the Example: Do you see any difficulties with the research design strategy for this data collection effort? Is a cross-sectional survey the most effective way to try to understand member organization contribution impacts? What about the time frame involved? Do you think it might limit the usefulness of those data that are gathered? If so, how?

We have just seen three types or categories of research design, described as true experimental, quasi-experimental, and nonexperimental. If the researcher has the ability to randomly assign study subjects to treatment and control groups and to have control over where and when the treatment is introduced, then we are looking at a true experimental design. This is fairly uncommon in public or nonprofit sector research and evaluation because the treatment of interest is usually a public policy or specific program; and, as such, they do not lend themselves to direct controlled experiment conditions.

If the researcher cannot control the experimental environment and cannot randomly assign subjects to either a control or treatment group, then we are dealing with a quasi-experiment. As discussed above, quasi-experiments are common in public sector research work. But also common are nonexperiments. For instance, if a major event happens, and a researcher gathers data to assess what happened, that can be described as a nonexperimental one shot case study design. Chapter 8 is devoted entirely to the topic of case studies, which are nonexperimental in nature but widely used in practice for research and evaluation work.

Validity Threats Applied to Designs

With those three categories of research design approaches in mind, we turn next to this question: When a design type is used, what are its implications for validity and inference?

The essential feature of understanding the utility of any research design is recognizing what about it might limit our ability to draw a causal inference. Each of the threats to internal and external validity could potentially apply to any of the research designs as well as to the many other possible variations of designs in each of those three categories outlined in previous sections. It is critical that the researcher in charge of a project be well aware that these validity threats exist, but more importantly, that he or she be aware of exactly which threat is relevant given the nature of the design employed and how the study data were gathered under that design. To illustrate this fundamental point, we will consider the three illustrated designs and how internal or external validity threats might be applicable.

For the One Shot Case Study Nonexperimental Design (displayed in Figure 5.4), we can say that there are lots of potential challenges to validity, and as a result, as a nonexperimental design, any causal inferences are unlikely to be sound. First, we can note that several validity threats do not apply because of the nature of the design. For instance, maturation and testing effects are probably not applicable because there is only a single point in time for the measurement of subjects. Instrumentation changes may or may not be applicable, depending on how the data were collected. However, depending on when the post-treatment measurement is taken, there may be history effects that the researcher cannot account for; there may be selection effects that the researcher cannot account for; and because of only a single point in time measurement, we do not know if we have inadvertently captured a set of extreme scores (i.e., we cannot necessarily account for any possible regression to the mean issues).

The classic pretest–posttest control group design shows the power of a true experiment. The various threats to validity listed above are generally accounted for. For example, random assignment makes selection bias a limited concern. The inclusion of a control group allows us to consider whether there are any testing or instrumentation effects (depending on the particular way the experiment is conducted, of course). History is accounted for because if some external event occurs, then both the treatment and control groups will be affected in the same way. The pretreatment measurement for both groups gives us at least some leverage over the risk of regression to the mean effects. In short, while some validity threats may exist the nature of a true experiment is that their likelihood is dramatically reduced.

The interrupted time-series comparison design has a number of strengths, as noted above. However, in terms of possible validity threats, we can mention a few. The use of a comparison group always raises the possibility of a concern over any selection bias because it might be difficult to obtain an appropriately matching comparison group, which at least raises the idea that there might be pre-experiment selection processes at work. The design does not offer any specific protection against mortality, which is most relevant when a study is longitudinal in nature. The researcher must take care to investigate whether that threat is an issue. Finally, regression to the mean is something that is a potential concern, especially when there is a very short time series (a limited number of time period observation points). That is, if by random chance a short series started with a higher than typical mean score, the researcher might have a difficult time discerning a regression to the mean effect from any actual treatment effects. Fortunately, if the design is implemented appropriately, the researcher should have sufficient information to check whether that is the case.

Putting Knowledge into Practice: How to Identify Threats to Internal Validity

Let's go back to Melanie and the National Helping Hands case. She has conducted a survey of voluntary nonprofit organizations. As we saw in Example 5.5's Case Discussion, it was a classic cross-section design approach: she took a survey of NHH member organization executives at a single point in time. The case discussion did not make clear the exact strategy for selecting and contacting those individuals (that is a question of sampling, which we will cover in chapter 7), but we do know that the survey included about 50 people, was done via telephone from a survey lab, and that the respondents were asked about their organizations' activities during a specific time period (the first week after the disaster).

Presumably, Melanie is going to use those data she collects to try to draw generalizable inferences about the nature of voluntary nonprofit organizations and their efforts to provide post-disaster assistance. The question we need to ask ourselves is, what can we say about the internal or external validity of the findings that Melanie reports?

In answering that question, we can think about a general practice that we should always follow in assessing validity issues for any research effort—that is, going through an assessment of validity is not just for this particular case.

The way to proceed is to systematically go through our list of validity threats and assess whether there are problems or concerns that we need to explore further. Let's assume that the survey was completed over a matter of a couple of days. Further, for sake of argument, let's assume that it was a relatively short period of time to complete the entire survey interview (say about 12 to 15 minutes). Those conditions of the survey implementation mean it is unlikely that threats such as history, maturation, or mortality would be a concern for this study. Because we have not yet discussed methods of selecting a sample of individuals for the purpose of doing a survey—and because the case example did not give specific details on the matter—we cannot know if there was a problem of selection bias. Here is how selection bias could be a problem in this case: if Melanie only selected executives from larger nonprofit organizations, or if she selected only those organizations that were most active in providing services after this particular disaster, then selection bias would be a very significant concern here. It would call into question both the internal and external validity of the findings.

When conducting any survey, testing effects are an important internal validity threat. A testing effect would be something to guard against here because the survey respondents are obviously aware that they are representing their organization and thus have a motive to cast their organization's activities in a positive light (either consciously or subconsciously). Similarly, instrumentation is a possible concern depending on how the interviews were conducted. If the respondents were asked a very structured set of questions, then instrumentation is likely not a validity threat to be concerned about. But if there was a lack of consistency in the questions asked or the manner by which those interviews were conducted, then instrumentation would appear to be a significant concern to investigate further.

There are other potential issues to consider, but given the short example, we would need much greater detail on the specifics of the study and the exact particulars of the data that were collected. Of course, you will learn a great deal more over the rest of this book that will help you to understand and identify how to interpret and assess the quality of a research study's findings. What this short "how to" box shows is the process that you will learn to use in being effective in assessing and interpreting how data are gathered and used.

Ethics and Research Design

It is important to recognize that while selection of a research design is a technical question, research and evaluation in the public sector occurs within a political context. Most any evaluation of a public program will carry with it nontrivial political consequences. As such, attention to potential bias and conflicts of interest in the conduct of a research or evaluation study is a paramount concern. Biases can take a variety of forms, and human beings, of course, have their personal, experiential, and ideological lenses through which they view results. That subjective element cannot be removed; it is an inherent condition. However, it is important to recognize that merely using standard social science techniques in no way immunizes a researcher from personal bias in the collection, analysis, and interpretation of results. Thus, the researcher is under an ethical obligation to be explicit and transparent about all steps in the research and evaluation process so others can see and understand what choices were made—and whether those choices were reasonable and had any inappropriate effect on the results presented. Likewise, that basic principle of transparency applies to the notion of conflict of interest. A researcher should always disclose any actual or potential conflicts of interest.

The issue of human subjects protections were discussed in chapter 3 but are worth reiterating here. A researcher has an ethical obligation to follow standard human subjects protections protocols in all instances. Of course, much of the kind of work done in the context of research relevant to public management does not involve significant potential harms to individuals participating. However, the possibility of adverse employment consequences or the like are real concerns, so particular attention to full explanation of study design, intent, and purpose is important. Securing explicit consent for participation is important in all cases of research but is important to emphasize here because subjects in the kind of research we are contemplating in this book are likely to be most at risk of risk of public scrutiny, more so than other kinds of potential harms.

Finally, the American Evaluation Association provides guiding principles for the conduct of evaluation research of the type that we are examining in this book. The five guiding principles can be summarized in the following way: evaluation research should follow basic principles of systematic inquiry; evaluators should engage in professional competent behavior in their work; the evaluation process should be one of honesty and integrity; the evaluation work should respect all people involved in a project; and evaluation researchers should take into account considerations about the general public welfare. While these are very broad principles, they can be used to inform any effort at setting up a research project or evaluation. They reflect the notion that a researcher is bound by an ethical obligation to be honest and transparent in his work, to follow accepted professional standards in conducting research, and to consider the public welfare associated with any given project.

Conclusion: How Research Design Decisions Relate to Evidence-Based Management Practices

Understanding the manner by which data are collected is absolutely critical to assessing the quality of a potential causal inference. As we have seen in this chapter, the way in which the design of data collection is structured is critical to how we can ultimately interpret the meaning of a study's results. There are three important implications of the information in this chapter for evidence-based public management practices.

First, evidence-based management necessarily is based on the quality of the data gathered, so of course it is essential for both a researcher and the managers involved in decision making to have a basic understanding of research design. That knowledge permits one to understand the strengths and weaknesses associated with those data gathered under a particular design approach. Second, public sector management represents a unique challenge for research work: there are very significant limits on the ability to do experimental research. As a result, public sector research is most commonly a question of designing quasi-experimental analyses. We mentioned earlier in the chapter that there are limits on design options because of flexibility across the federal system as to how governments make decisions about policies and programs. That can create challenges in finding comparable units; similarly, randomization of subjects is commonly not possible in public sector studies. This all simply means that understanding the logic and particulars of research design issues is critical to good research practice as related to public management.

Last, careful attention to research design is important to evidence-based management practices due to the reality that understanding key causal relationships in the world of public policies and programs is quite complex. For our purposes, what we typically consider a treatment—a public program—is not as simple to examine as a treatment in a controlled experiment. That is, it is difficult to find underlying causal relationships when the treatment is some kind of public program. Think about the possible relationship between student performance in a public school setting and a program intervention, such as an additional after-school reading program. Does that program have a beneficial effect? Well, what constitutes good learning is an incredibly complex mix of school environment, community environment, parental involvement, individual aptitude, peer effects, teacher quality, and testing accuracy. If a researcher wants to evaluate the effects of the presence of an after-school program on overall student achievement, he or she is operating in a very difficult research environment. It will not be easy to identify the unique effects and any specific impacts of such a treatment. The program may well be worthwhile, but establishing whether there is empirical evidence to show that becomes very tricky. That means getting the research design right is a very important task!

Suggested Readings

Students in this course might wish to get even more detailed information about the nature of experiments and research design issues. One of the best ways to proceed is to review a series of three books that represent classic statements on the subject. Campbell and Stanley's (1963) *Experimental and Quasi-Experimental Designs for Research* is absolutely considered a classic book on the subject, and it was followed by Cook and Campbell's (1979) *Quasi-Experimentation: Design and Analysis Issues for Field Settings*. Just over two decades later, those two books were followed by *Experimental and Quasi-Experimental Designs for Generalized Causal Inference*, published in 2001, by W. R. Shadish, T. D. Cook, and D. T. Campbell. These three books represent classic statements on the nature of research design and threats to internal and external validity. If the student wants to see how research design is used in a public management context, a very good book on the subject is Bingham and Felbinger's (2002) *Evaluation in Practice: A Methodological Approach*. That book is useful because it presents more examples of different research design types than we can present here in a single chapter. Further, it illustrates how research design issues are explicitly linked to the nature of performing program evaluations.

Vocabulary

BIAS—Measurement error that occurs in a systematic or specific pattern.

CONFOUNDING EFFECT—A variable related to the key research variable of interest that affects or "confounds" the observed results.

CONTROL GROUP—Subjects in an experiment that do not receive the experimental treatment and are placed in that category through random selection.

DEPENDENT VARIABLE—The outcome of interest in a research question; its variation is thought to depend on the influence of a set of independent or explanatory factors.

EXPERIMENT—An activity where a researcher controls or manipulates the conditions under which a subject is examined in order to observe and measure a specific cause-and-effect relationship.

EXPERIMENTAL CONTROL—The conditions experienced by the study's subjects during the conduct of the experiment are held as constant as possible by the researcher.

EXTERNAL VALIDITY—The degree to which results from a study can be generalized to other places, time periods, subject populations, and the like.

INDEPENDENT VARIABLE—A variable that is believed to be responsible for causing or explaining the nature of the changes in the outcome of interest, the dependent variable.

INTERNAL VALIDITY—The extent to which a research design is able to account for, or rule out, other explanations that compete with the experimental treatment as the explanation of an observed outcome.

MEASUREMENT ERROR—Regardless of what social phenomenon is being measured, discrepancies occur either in a random fashion or in a systematic fashion between the true underlying value and the recorded value

OPERATIONALIZATION—The process by which a concept is translated into a measurable form for the purpose of data collection.

RANDOM ASSIGNMENT—Each subject in an experiment enjoys an equal probability of falling into categories of treatment or control. and there is no systematic selection process.

RANDOM ERROR—Measurement error that is nonsystematic—that is, error that does not have any particular pattern.

RELIABILITY—The extent to which an instrument produces the same value if it is measuring the same object.

RESEARCH DESIGN—The process by which data gathering efforts are structured and defined.

TREATMENT—A variable introduced into an experiment in order to see whether it has an effect on an outcome of interest.

VARIABLE—A characteristic of a unit of analysis that takes on different values across different cases.

Flashcards
& MCQs

Useful
Websites

Review Questions

■ What is the difference between validity in measurement and internal validity in assessing an experiment's results?

■ What is a treatment, and how is the concept of a treatment in a research design used in the context of evidence-based public management?

■ Explain the similarities and differences between a control group and a comparison group.

■ What does "history" mean as a threat to internal validity?

■ How are selection bias and mortality validity threats similar or dissimilar?

■ What does IRB stand for, and what is its relevance to the research process?

Discussion Questions

■ What argument would you give for the strength of a true experimental design versus a quasi-experimental design?

■ Why are quasi-experimental designs particularly useful to the study of government programs and policies?

■ If a research study is done on college students, are those results likely to be externally valid, or would you have concerns about their generalizability?

■ What are the core ethical challenges in conducting research on a public sector program?

CHAPTER 6

Measurement

Learning Objectives

✓ Understand basic issues of measurement in social science research
✓ Understand the core concept of levels of measurement
✓ Learn to determine the appropriate level of measurement for a variable
✓ Understand and identify the nature and sources of measurement error

Cases in Research

Case A—National Helping Hands

Because National Helping Hands (NHH) is interested in evaluating the scope and scale of the contributions of its member organizations, it must devise some system of measuring those members' activities. This is not as easy as it might seem, for the member organizations of NHH are autonomous organizations who each provide different types of services during and after a disaster. Further, many of these members are faith-based organizations who see providing disaster relief and recovery services as part of their spiritual and charitable mission—and thus do not typically do a careful accounting of services provided because they do not seek governmental reimbursement for services provided. Thus, when the senior executives wish to provide a quantitative estimate of the value of the contributions their members make each year for disasters in the United States, they realize they have a series of measurement challenges to grapple with.

Case B—Springfield Housing Department

As mentioned earlier, the Springfield Housing Department manages housing assistance vouchers and provides general oversight of public housing. One major question of interest for the department is how individuals and families utilize housing services available to them. That is, while there is a target population for public housing assistance, not all eligible persons take advantage of the program. This leads to the question, why not? What is it about the process of reaching out to potential program clients that has led to significant numbers of Springfield residents not taking advantage of the program? Answering those questions presents not only a substantive challenge but also a challenge in developing sound measures that allow for accurate answers.

Measurement in Research

You should recall from chapter 3 the idea of a **UNIT OF ANALYSIS**. We defined a unit of analysis as the entity being examined by a researcher (which could be an object, an event, or a person). Whatever the unit of analysis might be, it will have some set of characteristics that are of interest to the researcher. Say, for instance, that a researcher is interested in whether the unemployment rate in a city is associated with the level of crime rate in a city. The unit of analysis is a city because that is our object of interest. Unemployment rate and crime rate are simply two characteristics of a city—two characteristics that matter to the question of interest (whether a city's employment rate affects the city's crime rate). Certainly, it is easy to recognize there are many other characteristics of an individual city that vary that might be relevant to answering this research question. For instance, city characteristics such as population size, geographic location, types of key economic activities within the city, poverty rates, education levels of residents, and so forth, all seem like they would be relevant to our research question. Further, we can also recognize that if the hypothetical researcher examined 50 cities for her study, those data gathered would reflect the fact that each observed value for unemployment rate and each observed value for crime rate would be unique values. That is, those observations will vary across each unit (i.e., each city measured in the study).

Thinking about measuring social phenomena in this way helps make the concept straightforward and easy to understand. **MEASUREMENT** can be defined simply as the process by which a researcher assigns either a name or number to the differences that are observed for a given variable, represented in qualities or amounts. For our researcher interested in the relationship between unemployment rates and crime rates in a city, we would assign a numeric value (a quantity) for those two variables. But as we have seen earlier in this book, a variable need not be measured only as a numeric quantity. As we just saw, another characteristic of a city that might affect the level of criminal activity is geographic location. We would not assign a quantity to that characteristic; instead, we would say that location (by region perhaps, such as Northeastern or Southeastern) is not something that can be usefully described as a quantity but instead can be more usefully thought of as a quality or category.

Let's continue with another illustration of this difference between quantitative measures and qualitative measures. Say we are interested in the political beliefs of individuals as related to their religious affiliation. Our unit of analysis would be an individual person, and one variable of interest would be an individual's stated religion. This is a quality that is not numeric in nature; religious affiliation simply is a set of categories that one would be placed into (Catholic, Protestant, Jewish, Buddhist, Atheist, etc.). Thinking about those two types of characteristics, quantitative (such as unemployment rates), or qualitative (such as what religion a person is) demonstrates the key point that we can systematically measure items of interest in the process of gathering data to answer research or evaluation questions, regardless of whether the measure of interest is qualitative or quantitative in nature.

What is important to understand is that deciding how to measure some phenomenon of interest is critical to the research process because it helps determine whether the data you then collect will be useful in trying to answer your research question. If measurement is done poorly, such as when there is a gap between the concept and the way in which that concept is actually measured in practice, then a researcher's ability to draw reasonable inferences from the data they've collected will be compromised. What you are able to observe, the nature and quality of the variable measurement, and the process by which those measures are collected all have important effects on the nature of what you can infer, as we discussed in our previous chapter. In very simple terms, if you measure something poorly, you will not be able to tell with very much accuracy what is really going on in the world, and you won't be able to explain what you want to explain!

In this chapter, we address several key issues of measurement in greater detail than in our prior chapters. We will describe basic ideas of measurement such as operationalization and discuss different types of variables and levels of measurement. We will also present a short introduction to the idea of assessing measurement quality.

Understanding the Basics of Measurement

Before talking about how the level of a variable's measurement is a reflection of the type and nature of information it conveys, it is useful to revisit the basic characteristics of variables—and how we create or define a variable in the first place.

Operationalization

As was discussed earlier in both chapters 3 and 5, the process of **OPERATIONALIZATION** is where a researcher translates some concept of interest into a form that can be measured. This is important because it is necessary to define with a great deal of precision exactly how measurements are to be made. A failure to do so leads to a variety of problems of validity and reliability, as we just learned in our previous chapter.

To see why that is so, think about one of the issues facing our analysts at the Springfield Housing Department. Those persons intended to be eligible for the housing assistance program—the target population for the program—will fall into the classification of "poor." Of course, that points us to the challenge of operationalizing poverty, either on an individual basis or on a community-wide basis (depending on what kind of question one wants to address). On an individual level, poverty might seem easy to operationalize: simply measure the person's annual income. But doing that introduces the challenge of defining at what level that income can be described as poor. Of course, the federal government provides a defined income level for individuals and families, but that may or may not be reasonable for the purposes of a research project. (In the case of the Springfield housing question, it would seem to be reasonable—it is typically used as the best or most effective measure of poverty.)

On the other hand, if we want to operationalize poverty on a community scale, we could look at the percentage of households living below the federally defined poverty level. While this is a standard approach, a researcher might consider other ways to understand what share of a community is struggling economically and what share can be considered poor. Alternative operational definitions might include the percentage of the community on food stamps or other types of food assistance. It might include the percentage of the community that can be classified as long-term unemployed. The key point to understand is that there are different ways for a researcher to operationalize a concept, and the choice depends on the particular needs of the research question being addressed.

If a researcher measures their concept incorrectly—that is, if he or she has an ineffective operational definition used to measure the concept and gather data—then they might have a problem of internal validity (not measuring what they think they are measuring) or reliability (not measuring their concept in a consistent fashion). For instance, what if an analyst at the Springfield Housing Department has a survey data set of residents from the Springfield area (drawn from a random sample of household phone numbers)? Say she wants to compare poor and nonpoor households on a question related to home energy use. However, a problem exists: the survey instrument did not ask telephone respondents to report their annual income, but instead simply asked respondents to classify themselves as poor, middle class, or upper class. What would be the problem with that? Well, there are a large number of problems, but let's consider just two obvious ones. First, it is not a very precise operationalization of the concept of poverty—that is, we don't really know to what degree someone's income or wealth is actually associated with one of those three categories. Second, there is the problem of a very realistic chance that many respondents would not want to identify themselves as "poor" because it has negative connotations. At the same time, a household with a very substantial annual income (say $190,000) might be much higher than the average or median household income in the United States (that is nearly four times as much as the median income in the United States around the time of the last national census). But the respondent from that household might not consider himself wealthy (though that annual income would put the household within the top 10 percent of annual income in the United States) and so would call themselves middle class. That is, there is a bias in both directions for people in the United States to label themselves as "middle class," and this makes the operationalization an ineffective one. As a result, the analyst does not really have a very accurate picture of whether any individual case in the data set can be considered low income or poor for the purposes of doing an analysis on potential differences in home energy use.

Example 6.1 below provides an additional illustration of some of the challenges of operationalizing concepts that are key to a research or evaluation project.

Example 6.1—Case Discussion: National Helping Hands

Ella manages several key program areas at National Helping Hands (NHH). Her supervisor assigns her the task of trying to measure the value of member organizations' contributions to disaster relief and recovery efforts in the United States. Ella decides that the best way to proceed is to collect the number of volunteer hours each organization has donated to disaster incidents over the past year. Then, she decides to assign a labor market value to volunteer hours as a means of placing a dollar value on those voluntary contributions. She believes that while there are a number of contributions items missed, this is the best and most practicable way to proceed in collecting the needed data.

Questions about the Example: The first question we can ask: Is assigning a wage rate per each volunteer hour a sound operationalization of "contribution value"? Second, it seems that just assigning a wage rate to volunteer hours might miss a great deal of what the member organizations do. For instance, what about in-kind contributions of goods, supplies, and organizational supports that do not get counted as direct volunteer hours in the field? Third, is it safe to assume that all volunteer hours can be treated as having a consistent rate across different types of skills and activities?

Types of Variables

By being able to measure a concept, we are able to observe how that measured concept changes over our selected unit of analysis—over however many cases that are included in our study. It is worth repeating our definition of a **VARIABLE**: it is simply a characteristic of the unit of analysis that changes or varies across observations.

Let us further make two distinctions about variables. The first distinction is what form a variable can take on. Variables can be either quantitative or qualitative in form. When we say a variable is **QUANTITATIVE**, we are simply saying that the operational definition of the concept of interest is measured in a numeric form. That is, we are able to represent the concept through a numeric value when we make our observation of that concept (i.e., when we are gathering our data). On the other hand, a variable might be **QUALITATIVE** in nature. This merely means that the operational definition of our concept is measured as a category, which is used to identify some nonnumeric characteristic of the unit of analysis.

One can again think of an individual person as a unit of analysis. If the amount of income an individual earns in a year is of interest to the question we are addressing in our study, we would measure each individual person's annual income, and we can say that this is a quantitative variable. Likewise, if we are doing some research where the sex of the individual was of relevance, and we measured that variable across the cases in our study, we would say that the gender of the individual is a qualitative variable—it falls into one of two categories: female or male. If a person's political party affiliation was of relevance to the study, then we might have a longer list of categories on the variable's scale—which simply means the possible values the variable can take on. For a party affiliation variable, the categories might be Democrat, Republican, Independent, Green Party, Libertarian, and so forth.

A second distinction that we can make when considering variables is not the measurement form they take but instead their functional meaning in addressing a research question. That is, the way in which a variable is used to describe or explain some phenomenon of interest is a functional use distinction. As we have mentioned in previous chapters, a variable can be used as an independent variable or as a dependent variable. A **DEPENDENT VARIABLE** is the outcome of interest for a researcher; observed variation in that variable is thought to depend on, or that it can be explained by, the influence of other variables. For instance, if we consider our illustration of a quantitative measure just mentioned above—an individual person's annual income—that income measure becomes our dependent variable or outcome of interest. As you will of course know, income levels vary greatly across individuals, and because of this, a researcher might want to try to explain why one person has a high income and another has a lower income. In other words, we can ask, what factors explain why income levels vary from person to person? What does income depend on?

As a result, we can then say that an **INDEPENDENT VARIABLE** is a variable that is believed to be responsible for causing or explaining the nature of the changes in the outcome of interest, the dependent variable. That is, when we observe our dependent variable, it changes across our set of observations—it has variation. What explains that variation? The most general answer is that it is an independent variable or a collection of independent variables. So for our income example we might consider what independent variables explain the variation in income level across any set of individuals (i.e., what

> **Class Exercise:** Consider this research question: What explains student performance on a mandatory standardized test administered annually in public schools at the K–12 level? First, can you identify the unit of analysis for this analytic question? What would be the dependent variable? What might a list of possible independent variables that potentially explain the observed variation in the dependent variable look like? For each of those variables, discuss how it would be operationalized.

variables can be understood as explanatory factors)? Variation in income most certainly can be explained by a set of independent variables (aka explanatory variables) such as education level, occupation type, geographic location, seniority in a position, gender, ethnicity, and so on.

It is important to understand that a variable is not inherently independent or dependent in nature. Let's go back to one of our illustrations of a qualitative variable: political party affiliation. Suppose we want to understand why some individual person is a Democrat or a Republican. There are a lot of different factors that might cause or explain an individual person's choice of party affiliation: their educational background, their political ideology, their income, their occupation, the party affiliation of their parents, and so on. For this question—why does a person choose a particular political party to affiliate with?—party affiliation is the outcome of interest, that is, it is the dependent variable we are interested in analyzing and explaining.

But now think about a different question: Why would someone vote for an incumbent president in an election or for one of the incumbent's challengers? In other words, here is our research question: Why does a voter choose one presidential candidate over another? Again, there are a lot of reasons that seem obviously relevant to any answer: the state of the economy, a person's ideology, perceived competency of the candidates, and so forth. Of course, another major factor in the choice is whether the preferred candidate is of the same party affiliation as the voter making the choice. In this illustration, the dependent variable is the vote choice (e.g., did a voter choose Obama or McCain in the 2008 presidential election?), and party affiliation is now an independent variable—perhaps an extremely important independent variable to explain our dependent variable. However, for our earlier research question, party affiliation was our dependent variable.

Again, the point of this illustration is that when we talk about a functional use distinction in terms of dependent or independent variables, any given variable could be one or the other. It simply depends on the particular research question at hand.

Example 6.2—Case Discussion: Springfield Housing Department

Christina is a senior program manager at the Springfield Housing Department. She wants to know why some eligible families are participating in the housing assistance program and why some are not. She decides that the participation decision is the variable she wants to explain. That is, this question of who participates represents her dependent variable. By making this choice, her analysis is going to focus mainly on individual-level characteristics of the members of the program's target population. This means she will need to gather information to discern which factors promote participation (or not) in part by gathering data on both current participants in the assistance program and those who are eligible but do not participate at present.

Questions about the Example: There are several questions to think about here. Is Christina's approach sound—that is, does it make sense to try to focus on individual-level characteristics of members of the target population for the program? Is there another way that one might consider proceeding? What about assessing the Housing Department's internal service delivery approach? How will she go about gathering the kinds of individual-level measures she will need to understand why an individual (or his family) participates in the assistance program?

Levels of Measurement

Just as there are different ways to classify or categorize a variable (quantitative vs. qualitative, independent vs. dependent), we can also draw another important distinction between the specific measurement properties of a variable. We can distinguish variables by their **LEVEL OF MEASUREMENT**, which is a term that we use to identify a given variable's key measurement property, including the type of information it contains and what types of mathematical operations can be appropriately used for that variable. There are four levels of measurement: nominal, ordinal, interval, and ratio. Each of these is discussed below.

Nominal Variables

A **NOMINAL VARIABLE** is one that simply indicates placement in a category, in a class, or as having a particular quality. Nominal variables are also sometimes called categorical variables, and that is a useful way to think of this level of measurement: some inherently nonnumeric characteristic of a unit of analysis can be placed in a category. Our discussion above of political party affiliation is an illustration of a nominal level of measurement: a person falls into one category on the variable's measurement scale (e.g., as a Democrat, Republican, or Independent, or some other smaller party). Other examples might be favorite a color (e.g., red, blue, green), or occupation type (e.g., machinist, nurse, lawyer, full-time graduate student), type of geographic location (e.g. urban, rural, suburban), and so forth.

It is important to recognize that at a nominal level of measurement, there is no inherent numeric meaning to these category values on the variable's scale. This can sometimes be confusing when one sees a data set and there is a numerical value used for a nominal variable. For example, think of a dichotomous variable (meaning a variable that takes on only two values) like gender. In a data file, the research might use this code for the measure: 1 = Female and 2 = Male. Of course, there is no reason that we could not reverse that coding, if we wished, to the following: 1 = Male and 2 = Female. Or for that matter, we could use this coding approach: 3 = Female and 5 = Male. The point to understand is that even if there is a number assigned to the categories on the nominal variable's scale (female and male being the two available categories for the gender variable's scale), the actual number chosen is arbitrary—it has no numeric meaning. It is just a convenient way to represent the variable scores—rather than using a typed-out word (which will be labeled as a string variable in a spreadsheet or in a statistical software package) in the data file.

In terms of mathematical operations, a researcher can really only do a simple count of observations that fall into each category on the response scale. For example, if we have 10 voters, we can count how many fall into the possible categories on our political party affiliation variable: 3 Democrats, 3 Republicans, 4 Independents. However, making a frequency count of the number of observations falling into those categories does allow one to make comparisons of which category has the most observed values.

Example 6.3—Case Discussion: Springfield Housing Department

As discussed in Example 6.2, Christina, the senior manager at the Springfield Housing Department, decides to provide overall research and evaluation direction to her staff. As a first step in the data gathering process, she instructs a member of her staff to identify both the roster of current program participants, and using U.S. Census data, an estimate of how many individuals and families in Springfield are eligible to participate. This information will allow Christina to receive a reasonable estimate of the percentage of eligible participants who are not using local housing assistance services. Her staff member, in conducting this initial step, is gathering data on a dichotomous nominal variable: participation and non-participation in the program.

Questions about the Example: Is the measure we are considering here a quantitative or qualitative variable? Is it a reasonable operationalization of Christina's key concept of interest: program participation? That is, do you see any potential gaps between looking at a count of current program participants and the use of Census data to estimate the number of nonparticipants in Springfield?

Ordinal Variables

An ordinal variable contains a bit more information than a nominal variable. **ORDINAL VARIABLES** also use name categories, but those categories have a ranked order of placement. For instance, a variable that shows a ranking from highest to lowest (e.g., first place, second place, third place) is considered ordinal. You might see in a survey questionnaire a ranking of the survey respondent's attitude toward a particular question as captured in the response scale: strongly agree, agree, disagree, strongly disagree. The variable is ordinal because it shows a ranking ranging from strong agreement to strong disagreement. (As an aside, these types of measurement items in a survey are called Likert scale questions, named after the researcher who devised the measurement technique, Renis Likert.)

In this way, an ordinal variable has a greater amount of information contained in it when placed in comparison to a nominal measure. Think of the situation this way: if we have a nominal measure that indicates a respondent is a student, we have no information beyond that categorical status. However, if we have a variable that measures amount of years of education, we could use this ordinal ranking: graduate student, undergraduate student, high school student. From that measure we know that a graduate student has more years of formal education than an undergraduate and the undergraduate more years of formal education than the high school student. In other words, the ordinal level of measurement conveys more information than the nominal level.

In terms of mathematical operations, a researcher can do a count of categories (and make a comparison of relative frequencies for observations in those categories) for an ordinal variable, just as with a nominal variable. However, the researcher can also make a computation of differences and average values for the ranks.

Interval Variables

At the next level of measurement is an **INTERVAL VARIABLE**. An interval variable is one with a constant unit length between adjacent points on the measurement scale. For instance, taking the measurement of a person's height is an interval variable. The units on the measurement scale are constant—each inch on the measurement tape is equivalent. In this way, we know that a person who is 5 feet 10 inches is exactly 3 inches taller than a person who is 5 feet 7 inches. In this way, an interval measure contains as much information as an ordinal variable, as well as providing even more information. A rank placement such as first place and second place tells you an order, but it does not give an exact unit measurement of the placement between those two points on the scale. An interval measure, of course, does provide that additional information. If you are measuring the performance of people in a race, we can get an exact time to finish at the interval level of measurement but only a rank order of finish if we are at the ordinal level.

Interval variables, thus, provide us with more information and as such, make more mathematical operations possible. Not only can we perform the operations made possible with an ordinal variable, we now can perform addition, subtraction, multiplication, division, square root, and so on. This gives us many analytic options in using our gathered data to describe and explain phenomenon of interest, as we will learn later.

Ratio Variables

A **RATIO VARIABLE** has the same properties as an interval variable but also includes one more piece of information: a true zero point. This is sometimes confusing, but it need not be. A researcher simply needs to recognize whether a variable has a true or absolute zero point on the measurement scale. A perfect example to illustrate this point is showing two different temperature scales. The Fahrenheit scale has a score of zero, but that zero point is arbitrary—it is not a true or absolute zero, meaning it does not indicate no temperature at all. It might be cold, but it is not an absolute zero point. However, the Kelvin temperature scale does have a true zero value. A value of zero on the Kelvin scale means that all thermal motion ceases (i.e., there is zero kinetic energy at that point). We, of course, see lots of common ratio variables in social science research: a GPA can have a true zero point, as can duration of time, the population size of a community, an agency budget, and so forth. In terms of mathematical operations, a variable at the ratio level of measurement permits all the same operations at the interval level, but it also allows for the computation of meaningful or true

Class Exercise: Consider the case of athletes competing in a foot race at a track and field meet, such as the 100 meter dash. Discuss how you would represent a variable at each of the four levels of measurement presented above for the outcome of the sprint contest.

ratios (which is, strictly speaking in a mathematical sense, not appropriate for an interval measure that does not have an absolute zero).

Putting Knowledge into Practice: How to Code Variables at Different Levels of Measurement

Previous sections have provided you with a discussion of how we can distinguish between variables based on level of measurement. It is also helpful to keep in mind the link between operationalization and level of measurement. That linkage can be stated this way: a challenge for a researcher is to translate a concept into a measurement form (i.e., operationalizing a concept) and when she or he does so, he will often have to make a decision about how to code information at a certain level of measurement.

To see what it means in practical terms to code information at each level of variable measurement, the reader may go to the Interactive eTextbook version. There you will find several sample exercises that illustrate how researchers code information in a way that matches up with each level of measurement.

Determining the Level of Measurement

It is not uncommon for students learning research methods and statistics for the first time to have difficulty in recognizing which level of measurement is which for a given variable. One simple way to resolve any uncertainty is to ask yourself a series of questions about the measure. First, if the measurement scale for the variable is in categories, then the variable is at the nominal level of measurement. For instance, if the categories are "female" or "male" for a dichotomous variable measuring gender, it is nominal. Next, you can ask yourself if the values on the scale can be ranked. For instance, can gender be placed in a ranked order? It cannot, so it is nominal and not ordinal. However, a variable like the year in an undergraduate degree program, "senior," "junior," "sophomore," and "freshman" can indeed be in a meaningful rank order, so the measure is ordinal.

If the variable is displayed in numeric form, such as 1, 2, 3, you can ask yourself whether the values on that scale have a constant unit of measurement. For example, if 1, 2, 3 indicate first, second, third place, then the variable is ordinal—because we don't know the exact distances between values in that ranking. But if the 1, 2, 3 values on the scale measure something with a constant unit, such as inches on a ruler or a tape measure, then we know the variable is an interval level measure. That is, if you were measuring the length of a board, and the measurement scale was denoted in feet, you would know that a board exactly three feet long is exactly three times the length of a board one foot long.

And finally, we can ask whether a given variable has a true or absolute zero point on the fixed, continuous units measurement scale as we described for the case of interval measures. Obviously, if there is an actual zero value on that scale, then we can recognize that at the ratio level of measurement. As we noted above, when we use language such as actual zero value, we are really indicating that the scale must have an absolute zero point or, to put it another way, a substantively meaningful value of zero. For example, as we noted in the temperature scale illustration above, you can ask yourself in that particular case: What does zero mean on the Fahrenheit scale? As we noted, it is not an absolute zero value, which is to say, it really does not have a substantive meaning equivalent to zero on the Kelvin scale. Thus, the Kelvin temperature scale is at a ratio level of measurement, while the Fahrenheit temperature scale is at an interval level, but not ratio. Thinking about that substantive meaning of zero, consider another familiar example: a student's grade point average (GPA). If a student receives all letter grades of "F" for all courses, he or she will not receive any course credit at all. Thus, the value of zero is substantively meaningful on the scale (i.e., not located at an arbitrary point).

Putting Knowledge into Practice: How to Identify Level of Measurement and How to Select the Most Effective Level of Measurement to Use

Up to this point in the book, we have not yet covered methods of the statistical analysis of gathered data. The importance and significance of choosing a level of measurement will become much clearer in just a few more chapters. However, there are a few things we can say at this point to help the reader understand measurement level identification and use. The best way to clarify in your own mind what level of measurement is being used is to run through the four levels of measurement by asking what information is conveyed by the variable in question. If you ask whether a measure only provides an indication of a category, then it is a nominal measure. If you ask whether a measure provides a rank ordering, it is ordinal; but if there are fixed units on the scale that allow comparison of distances or quantities on the scale, then it is an interval measure. And if you ask whether the interval measure has a true (i.e., absolute) zero point on the scale, then it is a ratio measure.

A second matter to consider is what level of measurement should a researcher or evaluator use when gathering data or conducting statistical analyses? This seems like a question with an easy answer: the operational definition used to measure the concept is what is reflected as the level of measurement. However, it is more complicated than that in practice. At times, the researcher will have the option of deciding at what level to measure a concept—for example, he or she can make a decision as to whether to construct an ordinal measure or an interval measure or some similar decision. At times, the researcher is working with an existing data set, and he or she has no control over the way the variables were measured in the first place. In other words, you as the researcher might prefer to have some concept measured at the interval level, but the existing data set might only have measured as an ordinal variable, and you will just have to work with that. But, it is very common for a researcher to modify existing variables for a particular analytic reason. For example, you might have an interval measure like city population, but for a specific reason, the researcher might want to reduce that to an ordinal measure of three size units: small, medium, and large cities (based on some population thresholds).

To see how these issues play out in practice, the reader may refer to the Interactive eTextbook, and there, can go through several exercise problems that will give you a chance to test your ability to identify a variable's level of measurement and several exercise questions to demonstrate what a researcher must consider in deciding what level of variable measurement to use for particular research and analysis problems.

Issues of Measurement Error

We have established that variable measures are operational definitions of concept; that is, we put some idea or concept that we are interested in into a measurable form to permit data to be gathered and research questions to be addressed. When we measure some phenomenon and gather data, we need to concern ourselves with the quality of those data. In our previous chapter, we introduced the concepts of validity and reliability. It is useful to return to both of those ideas in this section and the next. As we learned before, when we collect data, we can say that the measure is valid to the extent that it actually captures what we are intending to capture and is reliable to the extent that it produces consistent results over repeated measurement applications.

Before discussing validity and reliability in more detail, it is also useful to return to the concept of measurement error, which we introduced briefly in our previous chapter. Measurement error indicates an acknowledgment that any measurement process is not perfectly precise; we may not always see the exact measurement scale value applied perfectly to the specific unit in our study. For example, if we are trying to measure a person's height, and we are using a mark on a wall and a tape measure, we might get the true value of the person's height—but we also could be off in making the mark (we might hold the tape measure in a crooked fashion, etc.). Or we might ask that same person to tell us his annual income, and the person might give us a completely accurate report (perhaps he just completed his annual tax returns), or it is also possible that he does not want to report the exact amount, so he might offer a value higher or lower than the true or actual value of his income. This measurement imperfection can be thought of measurement validity. When there is relatively little difference in the assignment of values in the data collection process, we can say measurement validity is high and error is low. For our height measurement example, the error might be relatively low, but because people tend to be uncomfortable talking about their income, for that variable the measurement error might be relatively high. **MEASUREMENT ERROR** thus can be defined as the difference between what the true value is for an individual observation and what is collected or recorded in our data set.

We can recall from our previous chapter that there are two basic types of measurement error: systematic and nonsystematic. **SYSTEMATIC MEASUREMENT ERROR** occurs when factors create error in the measuring process itself or errors influencing the concept being measured. One way to think of this type of measurement error is to recall *Research Design Types* in the previous chapter. In our discussion of threats to validity, we noted the idea of a testing effect as occurring when subjects know they are being studied and thus react to that process and change their behavior—which leads to a mismeasure of what the researcher is trying to study. This can sometimes be referred to as a reactive measurement effect—which simply means that human subjects change their behavior when they know they are being observed for the purpose of a study, and thus the researcher cannot measure their "true" behavior—the kind of behavior they would normally engage in. Similarly, experts on survey research methodology have established quite clearly that survey respondents have inherent tendencies to do things like agree with a survey question posed to them—regardless of the actual content. That is, people taking surveys tend to consistently exhibit a bias toward agreeing with whatever is asked of them. Likewise, people being asked questions that are of a sensitive nature, or that might put them in a position of expressing a socially unpopular or undesirable view, will consistently exhibit a bias toward expressing a response that is considered "socially desirable." An easy example: roughly about 50 percent of the eligible voters actually cast a vote during any presidential election year. But when surveys are done after an election, a much higher percentage of respondents in a sample say that they voted. Why this gap? Because people perceive that they are supposed to vote—that it is their civic obligation—so some percentage of the population will be biased toward giving a socially desirable response. Because this occurs so consistently, we identify it as a systematic measurement error issue.

While those are examples of measurement error that occur systematically, we can also talk about nonsystematic or random measurement error. **RANDOM MEASUREMENT ERROR** can be defined as an error that is not directly related to the process of measuring a concept. What that means it that there are simply chance errors that occur in the data collection process that do not repeat themselves in any systematic fashion. Think of someone entering data for a study into a spreadsheet. The person might accidently enter a number incorrectly. There is nothing systematic about that—chance errors like that simply occur from time to time, but that does not create any systematic error pattern that would create a problem for analyzing that data the researcher has collected. You can also think about how chance factors in a human subject's environment could affect measurement of a concept. For example, because a respondent in a survey might be in a particularly bad mood at the time he is contacted (he or she might be angry about something else), that respondent might give a more negative assessment to a question than that person otherwise would. The opposite of course is also true—a respondent might have a not-so-favorable assessment of a policy (e.g., health care reform) or an elected official (e.g., the incumbent president), but because of entirely unrelated circumstances, she or he might have a particularly positive mood at the time contacted, and so he or she would give a higher rating than is his or her typical or true feeling about the matter.

These are ways to think about how measurement error can occur in a way that is random. The very nice feature of random error is that it does not bias our measurement in any particular way or direction. For our data entry error, if the true value to be entered was a value "5," the person entering the data is every bit as likely to make an error by entering "4" or "6" instead. This random error has no meaningful impact on our assessment of the data we gather. However, systematic error does create a bias that has very negative consequences for how we try to understand our subject. Say, for instance, we wanted to measure the American public's attitudes toward tax policy reform. Let's further say we gathered our data by conducting a landline-only telephone survey. Given younger people and lower-income households use cell phones exclusively at much higher rates than the overall population, we would systematically fail to capture or represent those types of persons in our data collection process. Further, older persons are more likely to rely on landline telephones and not cell phones. Thus, we would systematically overrepresent those kinds of persons in the data we gather. Thus, we have a bias toward older (and likely wealthier) persons in our sample—and that means we will have a much more difficult time in trying to create an accurate estimate of how the American people as a whole feel about policy questions toward possible tax reform options.

Assessing Measurement Reliability and Validity

Given the preceding discussion of measurement error, it is obvious to ask next about the quality of our measures by asking about their reliability and validity, concepts we discussed in chapter 5. It is useful to think about reliability and validity within our current discussion of measurement because we know that measurement error can and does occur, either systematically or randomly. As a result, we will want to know how and whether an error (random or systematic) affects the reliability and validity of a measured concept. There is both a nice answer and a not-so-nice answer to this question. Let's start with the not-so-nice news first.

When we measure a concept, there are no easy and direct means of assessing the validity of our operationalization. In effect, to assess the validity of a measure is to draw a subjective judgment about whether the operationalization makes sense. There are several ways in which we can attempt to do so.

One common way to approach variable quality assessment is to try to judge its face validity. **FACE VALIDITY** simply asks: On its face, is this variable a valid operationalization of the concept it intends to measure? It is not a rigorous assessment, but sometimes it is sufficient to judge the quality of a measure. In the simplest terms, you can ask whether the operationalization of a concept is plausible. For example, say we are interested in trying to measure the degree of democratization in a country. If a researcher suggests he or she will operationalize countries' levels of democratization by examining voting participation rates in the countries selected for study, we can immediately suggest that this measure has a validity problem; that is, we can recognize that a simple face validity assessment is sufficient to identify this measurement approach as problematic. Why? Democratic countries often have low voter participation rates because voting participation is voluntary. In contrast, authoritarian countries—nondemocratic—often have compulsory voting rules that frequently mean that authoritarian countries can have much higher voting rates. We do not have to perform any more rigorous analysis than a simple face validity check to know that the proposed operational measure of degree of democracy is serious flawed and will not lead to a valid inference about whatever the researcher is interested in examining (in this case, assessment of democratization).

Another way to check a variable's validity is to consider the question of content validity. What **CONTENT VALIDITY** means is to assess whether a variable measure is actually capturing all the various aspects of the specific information needed to draw an inference about an underlying relationship. For instance, if a scholastic achievement test (a set of individual measures) is attempting to test knowledge and skills that one should expect of a senior in high school, then one can examine those measures to ensure that those knowledge and skills are actually appropriate for a high school senior. The assessment might find that the skills and knowledge measures actually are too weak (i.e., they capture skills at a much lower grade level), too demanding (i.e., they capture knowledge and skills at a higher grade level, such as an undergraduate level) or that those measures are at exactly the right grade level. We will say more about these issues in the next section.

In contrast to subjectivity-based assessments of validity, there are several different methods of quantifying an assessment of measurement reliability. Recall from our previous discussion that reliability really is just the idea that the operationalization of a concept produces consistent measurement results. In other words, **RELIABILITY** is a straightforward concept: if you measure the same object of interest repeatedly with the same or very similar measurement item, do you get the same or extremely similar results over those repeated measurements? If results are repeated in this way over those repeated measurements—assuming there is not some other external event that could cause a substantive change—then the measure being used can be understood to have a high degree of reliability.

One very common and straightforward approach to checking on a measure's reliability is to perform a test-retest reliability assessment. A test-retest assessment is exactly what the name implies: it means that a researcher will collect measurements on the unit of analysis at a point in time, then collect measurements from the same unit of analysis (a person or some entity being studied) at a second point in time. The researcher then can measure the degree of consistency between the two sets of measures. The reader will learn about the statistical concept of correlation in a later chapter, but the basic idea is that the observed correlation value accounts for how closely related the two measurement results are, on a scale of 0.0 to 1.00. The closer to 1.00 for the correlation value, the greater the reliability of the measure. In other words, at a value of 1.00, there is no difference at between the two measurement results, and so the measure being used is perfectly consistent.

This is a check of consistency over time (with at least two points in time where the measurement results are compared). A researcher can also check a measure's reliability by looking at the degree of equivalence among measures of a concept. One way to do such an equivalence assessment is to create two separate forms of a measure, but intentionally as similar as possible. The two forms of the measure are each applied to the study subjects and again compared to see how high the correlation is for the results.

Another way to check for measurement equivalency is the idea of intercoder reliability. The idea of intercoder reliability is also simple and straightforward: when you have more than one researcher measuring some unit of interest, those measurement results can be compared to see if they are consistent across the researchers doing the measuring. A common use and illustration of this reliability assessment approach is when researchers will take a public document of some sort (e.g., a planning document, a policy statement, a speech by an elected official) and extract certain items of interest. In other words, the researcher will assess and analyze the content of the document. To do that, the researcher must develop a coding scheme so the content assessment is done consistently across the documents; this coding scheme is developed before the actual content analysis occurs. In this way, more than one researcher can go through the documents to extract the measurements of interest. The group of researchers then can examine their individual coding efforts of the material and thus can check to see if the coding scheme resulted in consistent results. If the results are consistent across the researchers, then the coding scheme can be deemed reliable.

Example 6.4—Case Discussion: National Helping Hands

Ella has decided to contact her organization's 30 or so national members to ask them for estimates of volunteer hours donated. She collects those total volunteer hours estimates for the past year from each organization. She then takes an average hourly wage rate for a moderate skill-level laborer and computes a dollar value to estimate the contribution value for each organization. Creating an interval level measure allows her to calculate an estimated average contribution value for the member organizations.

Questions about the Example: Is the measurement approach taken by Ella a reasonable operationalization of the concept of contribution value? What might be some limitations of this approach? Are there any problems of measurement error that you can see?

Conclusion: How Measurement Issues Relate to Evidence-Based Management Practices

The significance of sound practices in measurement is intuitive: if we want to understand what is happening in the world through social scientific research methods, we need to have valid and reliable measures of the concepts in which we are interested. In this chapter, we presented several basic issues that are important to understanding measurement. Of course, this material is simply an initial overview of the subject of measurement. For instance, professional researchers spend a great deal of time and effort developing and exploring very fine-grained details of the reliability of specific measurement instruments. In other words, measurement is a field of study in and of itself, and we have made only a small scratch on the surface of the subject.

However, even with this broad overview, it is also easy to understand the implications of measurement for evidence-based public management practice. If you are interested in public management issues, you likely are well aware of the importance of performance measurement in the public sector. Performance measurement is tricky within the public sector because much of what government and nonprofit organizations do does not have an easy evaluative metric like a private sector organization—that is, a private, for-profit firm performs well ultimately if they are profitable. It is of course more complicated than that, but it is useful to draw this contrast: public agencies often are operating on a set of activities that are designed to minimize a social problem that does not have a nice easy resolution like a set of discrete private market transactions.

For instance, take the world of emergency management. Emergency management agencies at all levels of government have responsibilities associated with preparing for emergencies and disasters. How does one measure whether preparedness efforts are effective? That is not at all straightforward. Operationalizing the concept is difficult, and it is perhaps even more difficult to link the measurement of preparedness to specific outcomes when a disaster strikes. There are many reasons for this: the disaster response is shared across a large number of actors (making the performance of one local agency difficult to separate out); the specific nature of the disaster might have characteristics that were not easily planned for; the evaluation of performance is a measure of response effectiveness in terms of damages or harms minimized, not necessarily prevented, and that become very difficult to measure accurately. We could go on, but the key point is this: measuring concepts correctly to improve evidence-based management practices is fundamental. For future public managers and nonprofit leaders, learning the ideas and techniques covered in this book is important to meeting the challenges of improving public organizations by using evidence to support decision making and improved practices.

Vocabulary

CONTENT VALIDITY—An assessment of whether a variable measure is actually capturing the specific information needed to draw an inference about an underlying relationship.

DEPENDENT VARIABLE—The outcome of interest in a research question; its variation is thought to depend on the influence of a set of independent or explanatory factors.

FACE VALIDITY—The process of assessing a variable's degree of valid operationalization of the concept it intends to measure by a simple inspection of plausibility.

INDEPENDENT VARIABLE—A variable that is believed to be responsible for causing or explaining the nature of the changes in the outcome of interest, the dependent variable.

MEASUREMENT—The process by which a researcher assigns either a name or number to the differences that are observed in a given variable, represented in qualities or amounts.

MEASUREMENT ERROR—The difference between what the true value is for an individual observation and what is collected or recorded in our data set.

NOMINAL VARIABLE—A variable that simply indicates placement in a category, in a class, or as having a particular quality.

OPERATIONALIZATION—The process of translating a concept into a form that can be measured directly.

ORDINAL VARIABLE Variables that use name categories, but those categories have a rank order.

QUALITATIVE VARIABLE—The operational definition of a concept of interest is measured as a quality and is represented in a nonnumeric form.

QUANTITATIVE VARIABLE—The operational definition of a concept of interest is measured in a numeric form.

RANDOM MEASUREMENT ERROR—Error that is not directly related to the process of measuring a concept.

RATIO VARIABLE—A variable with the same properties of an interval variable, but one that also includes a true zero point.

RELIABILITY—Assessing whether repeated measures of the same object of interest with the same or very similar measurement item produces identical, or at least extremely similar, results over those repeated measurements.

SYSTEMATIC MEASUREMENT ERROR—Measurement error that occurs when factors create errors in the measuring process itself or errors influencing the concept being measured.

UNIT OF ANALYSIS—The collection of elements (data) representing observations for one phenomenon of interest.

VARIABLE—A characteristic of a unit of analysis that varies across individual observed cases.

Flashcards
& MCQs

Useful
Websites

Review Questions

■   What is the difference between qualitative and quantitative variables?

■   What is the difference between an independent and dependent variable?

■   What are the four levels of variable measurement?

■   What does it mean to operationalize a concept?

■   What is measurement error and measurement validity?

Discussion Questions

■   What are the several ways in which a researcher can distinguish key characteristics among variables?

■   What does the concept of "levels" of measurement imply? That is, why do we see more information among one type of variable measurement versus another?

■   How do the concepts of validity and reliability apply to variable measurement?

CHAPTER 7

Population Sampling

Learning Objectives

✓ Understand the logic of sampling and of case selection
✓ Learn several types of sampling strategies and how they differ
✓ Learn different case selection strategies
✓ Understand and identify the implications of different sampling strategy choices

Cases in Research

Case A—National Helping Hands

National Helping Hands' interest in evaluating member organization contributions is not only a measurement challenge in terms of operationalizing the nature of voluntary contributions, it is also a data collection challenge because of the wide range of organizations involved and their involvement in emergency and disaster incidents on a small scale (e.g., local emergencies) to a very large scale (e.g., national disasters). As a result, National Helping Hands' executive director decides to work with a university partner to lead a research effort. Melanie, at Great State University, decides she needs a sampling strategy to measure effectively the nature of member organization activities. That is, she recognizes that she cannot measure everything each organization does, so she needs to devise a way to take a sample and provide a valid and reliable measure of member organizations in that way.

Case B—Grover's Corner Department of Transportation

As described in chapter 5, several years ago the Grover's Corner Department of Transportation upgraded a portion of stations in its light rail system. These upgrades included expanded retail sites, such as additional coffee and food vendors; and expanded parking space to improve the accessibility of the rail system to commuters. The department would like to review customer satisfaction with these changes. Further, it also has the even more ambitious interest in understanding basic usage behavior among the residents of the Grover's Corner metro area.

Sampling from a Population

In chapter 5, we learned how to specify a research design for a research over evaluation project. This simply means making a choice over the specific strategy and process for gathering those data we will need to answer our question of interest. That is, the research design spells out a series of explicit choices over what is to be studied and how. Then, in chapter 6, we learned about the basic process of measurement, where the research or evaluator assigns either a name or number to the differences that are observed for a given variable, represented in qualities or amounts. Taken together, those chapters provided you with two critical elements in understanding how to engage in data collection: structuring your data collection and the assessment approach and how to measure appropriately those phenomena in which the researchers are interested. In this chapter, you will be introduced to basic concepts and principles associated with sampling, a third critical element of data collection.

As we will learn below, sampling is important to understand because many research and evaluation projects do not allow us to measure all possible elements or units that we wish to study. Intuitively, this is easy to grasp: we can see, for instance, that if we want to study attitudes or behaviors of college students in the United States, it would be very costly and difficult to try to contact and measure each of those individuals. Instead, as we will discuss below, taking a sample of those U.S. college students will allow us to address research or evaluation questions of interest—and permit us to make estimates about what the overall population of college students looks like. Learning about sampling is important because this is a powerful tool at a researcher's disposal; if a researcher had to measure an entire population, very little research or evaluation work could ever be accomplished.

And when we talk about sampling, we are generally talking about drawing a subset (which could be in small numbers or large) and measuring quantitative or qualitative features of our unit of analysis. We will start this chapter with a presentation of some basic concepts that are fundamentally important to understanding sampling. We will then proceed to review the basic logic of sampling as well as different types of sampling designs. We will wrap up this chapter with a brief discussion of ethical considerations in sampling.

Some Basic Concepts Associated with Sampling

While the material below provides more details on the substance and process of sampling, let us begin with a few terms to help familiarize you with the subject of this chapter. When we talk about sampling, we have to first understand the idea of a **POPULATION**, which we just alluded to above. A population is the aggregation of all individual units of interest relevant to a study. To see what this means, let's think about a particular research topic. Say you are interested in how views on health care policy reform might affect a presidential election in the United States. Would your population be all residents of the United States? It would not. The research question pertains to how policy views might affect voting; thus, our population of interest would exclude nonvoters—or more precisely—those who are not eligible to vote (e.g., children, noncitizens, felons). Our population of interest then is all eligible voters in the United States.

Clearly, however, it is not practicable to measure policy attitudes of all eligible voters. To measure all members of a population of interest is to conduct a **CENSUS**. There are two really strong reasons for not conducting a census when we do research: first, it is in most cases where we have a large population, so it is not feasible. It is the time and cost and practical logistics of conducting a census of a large population that precludes us from conducting a census. (Think about how expensive and logistically challenging it would be to try to contact every single eligible voter in the United States—over 200 million people—just to answer a simple research question!) Second, and more important, as we will learn in section III of this book, principles of sampling and probability will show that we do not really need to measure a population in its entirety. In most cases, a census will not be perfect—there will be significant measurement error just because of the practical difficulties associated with measuring a large population (e.g., there are well over 300 million residents of the United States). As a result, it is more practical and as we will learn in a few more chapters, every bit as useful and meaningful, to take a sample of a population in order to estimate the characteristics of the units within that population.

This begs a question: What is a sample? A **SAMPLE** is simply a subset of a population. For instance, we wouldn't try to measure directly all 200 million voters in our example under consideration. Instead, we would draw a sample of a given size that would allow us to estimate the effects of policy views on presidential voting preferences based on the information contained in the sample. Chapter 15 will provide you with the specifics on how the accuracy of such estimates are made; here, we will just discuss the overall logic and process of sampling.

Of course, when we draw a sample, it is important to recognize that doing so can be done in one of two ways: it can be drawn as a probability or a nonprobability sample. A **PROBABILITY SAMPLING** approach is where each of the units in your population of interest has an equal probability of being selected. So for our example, we might use a list of available telephone numbers and take a random draw from that list. The beauty of probability sampling is that a random selection of members of the population of interest, in general, will produce a representative sample of the population. **REPRESENTATIVENESS** simply means that the characteristics of the sample closely resemble the characteristics of the population from which the sample was drawn. In other words, a probability sample of all eligible voters, based on a random selection of a small subset of those voters, will allow us to make an accurate estimate of what the overall population really does look like—without having to take a full-blown census of the population.

However, not all sampling is based on a process of random selection based on an equal chance of selection for all members of a population. Instead, sometimes a research might use a **NONPROBABILITY SAMPLING** process, where the members of a population do not have an equal chance of being selected, so we cannot infer that the sample we do in fact collect is representative of the overall population. Why would one want take such an approach? We will discuss this issue in more detail in section, but the short answer is that sometimes it is not possible to take a true probability sample from a population, and in other cases, it is either not necessary for the purposes of the research effort or it is not even desirable.

> **Class Exercise:** Think of several research questions of interest to you. Identify specifically what the population is for each, and then discuss whether you think a probability sample might be feasible. If taking a probability sample does not seem possible, explain why not.

Finally, there are two more terms that we should introduce here, as they will be used throughout the rest of this book. If we want to describe a characteristic or attribute of a sample in numeric terms, we can refer to this as a **STATISTIC**. If we want to measure or estimate a numeric value in the overall population of interest, we refer to this as a **PARAMETER**. Therefore, when you see the term "statistic," you can know that it is referring to information that summarizes a sample, and if you see the term "parameter," you can know that it provides information that summarizes a population.

With these initial concepts described, let us turn next to the basic logic of sampling.

The Logic of Sampling

The underlying logic of sampling is quite straightforward and intuitive—as implied by the discussion above. Consider a population of interest, and that you as a researcher want to collect information about that population. The population of interest could be all adults in the United States if your research question pertains to the policy preferences of the American public. It could be all persons who are eligible for benefits under a program like food stamps if you wanted to know something about the nature of benefits utilization for that program. It also could be, of course, a population of inanimate objects, such as all bridges above a certain size, or of a certain type, if you were interested in issues related to transportation infrastructure in the United States. If all the units (the individual members, a person, or an inanimate object, whatever the case may be) were exactly the same or identical—meaning no variation in any of their characteristics—then we would not have a need to sample. Instead, if all our population members were identical, one single case would be sufficient to describe all other units.

Of course, for just about all questions in which we would be interested, the members of the population are not identical. As we noted above, we are seldom in a position to perform a census on a population, nor do we typically need to do so. Instead we can draw a sample from a population. If it is a probability sample (equal chance of selection for all members), then it is likely to be representative of that population. By that we mean that the sample contains approximately the same patterns of variation that exists in the population itself. We say "approximately" because any probability sample is not going to be a perfect or exact representation of the population. However, random selection of population members allows us to avoid any kind of bias that would adversely affect the sample's representativeness. We have discussed the idea of bias above, but in simple terms, it refers to anything that has a negative impact of whether the selection process allows for representativeness. For example, if we only took a sample of females for our study of eligible voters, we would be missing all males in the population. If a researcher at a university only drew a sample of other students who were over 18 and eligible to vote because they were convenient to contact, we would not have a representative sample because most voters are not currently enrolled university students.

Beyond the utility of avoiding bias through random selection of units that have an equal likelihood of being selected, there is a second advantage of probability sampling. As we will learn in chapter 15, we can use techniques that allow us to estimate with a known precision how likely it is that our sample is an accurate representation of the population. In short, this means that we can draw a sample and make an estimate of how likely it that sample is to be equivalent to patterns in the population itself. This is a powerful feature of probability sampling that rescues us from having to conduct a census when we have a research question that we wish to pursue.

Example 7.1—Case Discussion: Grover's Corner Department of Transportation

Larry is a research and program evaluation specialist at the Grover's Corner DOT. His manager tasks him with preparing an assessment of customer satisfaction with the Grover's Corner light rail system in general, and with particular attention to satisfaction with individual station improvements. About 50,000 commuters use a monthly pass, and Larry has access to that list and has acquired permission to contact those rail users for the purposes of measuring satisfaction.

Questions about the Example: How do you think Larry should try to sample from this list? What would your approach be? Even more important, what do you think the implications are of using just the list of monthly pass rail users? Would Larry be missing someone important from the population of interest? And further, is that population of interest clearly defined?

Probability vs. Nonprobability Sampling

While probability sampling allows us to make sense of what is going on in a population without having to measure the entire population itself, we also have encountered the term "nonprobability sampling." If a probability sampling approach allows us to draw representative samples of the population, then why would researchers ever take a nonprobability approach? There are a variety of reasons for that. One reason is that collecting data is a costly and difficult undertaking. Therefore, a researcher might rely on readily available subjects, an approach that can be called a convenience sample. Think about a university professor who wants to test some theory of behavior. He or she might take a sample of students from a large class. The researcher knows this is not a representative sample, but the purpose might simply be to test out an idea that the researcher has. In this way, the researcher is not really interested in making a claim about how things actually are in the population; instead he might simply want to get some preliminary sense of how his idea works in practice as a means of developing further and more precise research efforts.

A second reason is that there are populations of interest that do not lend themselves to a simple random selection of members. A classic example of that is research on the homeless. There are no existing lists of homeless persons. Unlike taking a list of telephone numbers and making a random draw of some quantity from that list, you cannot make a list of homeless persons and then randomly select from that list—because such a list does not exist. Indeed, even the concept of homelessness is not entirely straightforward; there are different types or conditions of transient housing, which means there is some subjectivity in defining the population itself.

The problem with nonprobability sampling is that we do not have representativeness (i.e., we cannot be confident that the data we have gathered are an accurate representation of the population we are interested in assessing). Nonprobability sampling, in other words, has inherent biases and does not allow accurate inferences about a population. As we just stated, that might be allowable, depending on several circumstances. The researcher might not need for his or her specific research needs, to make a general statement about the population. Further, as we noted above, it might not be possible to create an effective list of population members to draw from to permit a random selection process.

> **Class Exercise:** Think of several research questions of interest to you. Identify specifically what the population is for each, and then discuss whether you think a probability sample might be feasible. If taking a probability sample does not seem possible, explain why not.

This last point introduces another new concept: the idea of a sampling frame. When we draw a probability sample, as opposed to a nonprobability sample, you might have a question as to how it is accomplished in practice. The process of selection in probability sampling is to first create a **SAMPLE FRAME**, which can be defined simply as the list of population units of members (the word "elements" can also be used) from which a sample—of some defined number—is drawn. What that means is that the researcher either takes an existing list (e.g., using a list of published phone numbers if he or she wants to sample possible voters) or creates a list (e.g., compiling a list of bridges of a certain size if he or she wants to do a study of current infrastructure quality) and then samples a certain number of elements or units from the list.

Types of Sampling Designs

While the basic concepts of sampling are relatively straightforward, it is not necessarily an easy or simple proposition to conduct actual sampling from a population, be it a probability or nonprobability sample. Just as was the case with our discussion of research design choices in chapter 5, there are a variety of considerations that come into play when drawing a sample from a population. Ideally, if you want to draw an inference about a population you would take some type of probability sample. There are a variety of different probability sample types, which we will explain below. But there are differences in the nature of populations themselves that might cause a researcher to favor one sampling strategy over another. Further, there are also instances where it is less important to draw a population inference, such as if the researcher is merely testing out some initial research ideas or pretesting a measurement instrument. Likewise, there might be complicated circumstances in the data collection process that prevent the researcher from constructing a meaningful sample frame itself, which would limit the options the researcher has at his or her disposal. We will discuss these considerations below.

Simple Random Samples

A **SIMPLE RANDOM SAMPLE** is no different than the idea we used to define the concept of probability sampling. It is when we select a subset of the population based entirely on random chance, and each member in that population has exactly an equal probability of being selected for the sample. What that means is that for any possible sample we could draw of a given size, one such sample has the same chance of being selected as any other sample. Random samples are seen as very powerful because it does not take a terribly large sample to tell us a great deal—meaning an accurate representation—about the overall population.

An easy way to see why this is so is to think about public opinion surveys. You probably have heard or read a phrase such as "the survey had a margin of error of plus or minus four percentage points." What that means is that is the margin of error is a statement on how much confidence we have that the sample is an accurate estimate of the overall population from which it was drawn. The smaller the margin of error, the more confidence we have that the sample is an accurate reflection of the population. At the same time, we should also understand that a sample (like the ones taken for a public opinion survey) also has a confidence level. The most common confidence level used is 95 percent. What that means is that if you had a 4 percentage point margin of error, and you took a question from a public opinion survey, the results for that question would be within 4 percentage points of the answer you would see if you were measuring the population directly—and that would be the case 95 times out of 100. You should also be aware that this means that 5 times out of 100, your results could be very, very different from what the real value is in the population. Generally speaking, researchers rely on the "bet" that their results make sense—because they are confident that the results are accurate at a 95 percent level (which is a chance most people would take if they were gambling!).

We'll learn more technical details on this subject in later chapters on probability and inferential statistics. But for now, we can take note of the basic principle that larger samples produce more accurate representations of the population. There are general rules for sample size and margin of error. Again, without getting into a technical explanation at this point, we can say that for any population that is large (e.g., eligible voters in the United States), a sample of about 300 people would have a margin of error of 6 percentage points. (As an aside, we use the notation "n = 300" to refer to sample size.) A sample size of n = 700 would produce greater accuracy of our population estimates, with a margin of error of 4 percentage points. If you increase the sample size to n = 1,000, then the margin of error will be 3 percentage points. To reduce the margin of error down to 2 percentage points, you would have to have a sample of about n = 2,400.

Another way to think of this issue of error is that as a rough rule of thumb, as sample size quadruples, the error associated with the size of a sample is about cut in half. For instance, if n = 100, the error will be about 10 percent. If you increase the sample so that n = 400, then the error drops down to about 5 percentage points. While there are different ways sampling error can be computed, one simple formula looks like this:

$$S = \sqrt{P \times Q / N}$$

Where N = number of cases and P and Q = population parameters.

With this short background in mind, you can see that it does not take large samples to give a pretty accurate account of what is going on in a large population. Let's stay with the example of eligible voters. Say the survey we took had a question about rating the current state of the economy. Further, let's say that 50% of the sample rated the economy as good. If our sample size was 1,000 people, we could say with 95% confidence that the true rating in the population was 50%, plus or minus 3 percentage points (i.e., that we are confident that 95 times out of 100 we would see such a result). This means that we are 95% sure that the true rating of the economy as "good" by all eligible voters in the United States falls somewhere in the range of 47% to 53%. In other words, taking a sample of just 1,000 eligible voters allows us a fairly precise estimate of how all voters rate the economy (just at that given point in time, of course). In this way, we can see the power of sampling. It allows us to obtain an estimate of what is going on in a population—without having to measure the population in its entirety.

Finally, we can also take note of the idea of **MULTISTAGE RANDOM SAMPLING**, which is closely related to the idea of simple random sampling—or more accurately—it is another version of that approach. A multistage random sampling approach refers to the idea that a researcher can take a series of simple random samples in stages. Usually, the way such an approach works is that the research starts with a large (in geographic terms) study area, such as entire country. The researcher divides that area into smaller units (e.g., regions) and then takes a random sample of those regions as the first stage. In the second stage, a random sample of smaller units within the regions (e.g., counties) is taken. In the third stage, another sample of smaller units (e.g., cities) is taken from the second stage units. If that third stage unit, cities, is the focus of the study, the researcher then can stop and he or she has taken the random sample that is desired.

Example 7.2—Case Discussion: Grover's Corner Department of Transportation

Continuing with Larry's sampling challenge, we established that Larry has access to a readily available sample frame of monthly light rail users. This provides very straightforward cases of simple probability sampling. He decides that he has a research budget large enough that he is able to take a sample, n = 800, of those monthly riders. He is going to ask them questions about their history of use of the light rail system, how they perceive its utility at present, and what they think of recent changes/upgrades to various stations in the system.

Questions about the Example: Similar to our previous example questions, the key issue seems to pertain to the population of interest and whether Larry is sampling it properly. One could reasonably ask, if Larry samples from a list of monthly pass users, isn't he missing a whole host of other users? For instance, people who ride regularly but don't necessarily use a monthly pass? Or those who only ride occasionally? How do you think missing these persons would affect the results of the study?

Putting Knowledge into Practice: How to Create a Sample Frame and Make Random Selections

There are several different considerations in creating an actual sample frame before making a random selection of units. One is whether you are generating a frame from a completely original list. For example, say a researcher wants to sample local government transportation planners from across the United States—that is, the counterparts to the personnel working in the Grover's Corner transportation planning office. While there are directories of local government officials, there might not be a specific listing of transportation planning personnel. Thus, the researcher will have to create an original list if he or she wants to draw a true probability sample of such individuals. Another consideration is what to do if you have an existing list of units to sample. Let's say instead of selecting individual planners, you simply want to sample 50 cities from across the United States in order to then take a look at transportation planning

Once you have created a sample frame, you need to take a random draw of the units listed. One easy way to do this is to make use of a spreadsheet (e.g., MS Excel). Let's take the selection of 50 U.S. cities. Perhaps you want to select 50 cities from the possible list of cities with a population size of more than 100,000 persons. You could simply go the U.S. Census website and pull a list of all cities with a population greater than 100,000. Once you do that, you can list those cities in an Excel spreadsheet and you have a sample frame. To randomly select 50 of those cities, you can then use the random number generator function in Excel to assign a random number to each unit. After you have randomly assigned a number to each individual unit, you can then sort your list by the random number attached to each unit (i.e., each city name) in either ascending or descending order. (It does not matter which sort you choose precisely because the numbers have been randomly assigned.) Then you would select the first 50 cities of the sorted list and, voila!, you have a simple random sample of U.S. cities with a population of greater than 100,000 persons.

To try this random selection exercise yourself, the reader may go to the eTextbook in order to try several additional exercise problems that will give you a chance to practice generating sample frames and to take random probability samples from those frames.

Systematic Sampling

Another probability sampling approach is the idea of **SYSTEMATIC SAMPLING**. The basic idea of systematic sampling is quite similar to simple random sampling—very nearly the same, in fact. In systematic sampling, however, the researcher does not simply select a certain aggregate number from a sample frame. Instead, the researcher takes every *kth* unit or element from the sample frame list. Image that you work for a small company with 500 employees and that you are tasked with evaluating performance across the whole of the company; you might work from that employee list and take every 10 employee to draw a sample of 50 employees to measure. To avoid any bias in the selection, you would make the first selection at random, then select every 10th case.

If the list of employees was randomized, then this would be equivalent to a simple random sample. However, researchers can find themselves in situations where it is not entirely easy to create a randomized list of elements in a sample frame. Imagine a case of a temporary housing encampment following a natural disaster, such as an earthquake. Say a researcher wants to conduct an evaluation of public health conditions in the camp by taking a random sample of the temporary occupants. If there is a basic row structure to the tents, the researcher might take every *kth* tent and measure a series of health indicators for an occupant, or perhaps all the occupants, of the selected tent. This approach might be superior to trying to taking a random draw overall from the temporary encampment, precisely because it might not be practical to create a list of encampment occupants and then draw a sample from a randomized listing of those occupants.

Stratified Sampling

For some research or evaluation problems, there are groups that are distinct from one another and are likely to vary quite a bit on the subject of interest between those groups. In this sense the population can be considered heterogeneous (i.e., there will be major differences in variation across the groups within the population when we take our measures of interest)—as opposed to a homogeneous population (i.e., no major discernible differences across any subgroupings in the population). For example, let's think about the case of the Amity Homeland Security Office that we have discussed from time to time. If we had as a research project an assessment of how communities responded to their hazard risk profile, we might expect that cities that are smaller than 10,000 people in population are quite different in their actions than cities that are larger than 500,000 in their resident population. From a sampling standpoint, we might want to separate out categories based on community size before we take a sample. In other words, when you have a heterogeneous population, it makes sense to engage in a **STRATIFIED SAMPLING** strategy. The subgroupings idea we've referenced can be called strata, and what the researcher does is take a sample from each stratum (subgroup), usually with the size of the sample taken from each strata being proportional to the size of the strata in the overall population. For instance, to take our homeland security assessment project, if 5% of all cities in a country are over 500,000 in population, and 70% of all cities are less than 10,000 in population, we would want a final sample that had about 5% of our cases to be large cities (>500,000 residents) and about 70% to be small cities (<10,000 residents).

There are several reasons for taking a stratified sampling approach. As we have already discussed, if we have an expectation of a heterogeneous population regarding our research question of interest, it makes sense to sample accordingly—precisely because we would likely want to make comparisons across the subgroupings (each stratum) when making inferences about the overall population. A second important reason: it makes our sampling strategy more efficient. What that means is this: if we took a simple random sample of about 200 cities for our homeland security study, where our sample frame list was all cities in the United States, we would likely draw a large number of very small cities (because they far outnumber large cities). In this way, we guard against any possible "unrepresentative" sample outcomes, and at the same time, we ensure that we have a sufficient number of elements from each strata that we can compare across subgroups in our analysis of the data after they have been collected. There is really only one major disadvantage to a stratified sampling approach: it potentially requires more time and effort to establish the proper sample frame arrangement.

Example 7.3—Case Discussion: National Helping Hands

As we noted above, Melanie is a professor at Great State University and is working with National Helping Hands to examine the nature of member organizations' contributions to disaster relief and recovery efforts across the United States. One of the challenges is that member organizations at National Helping Hands are spread out over the United States, vary greatly in size, vary in terms of the services they provide, and vary in terms of the types of emergency or disaster incidents that they respond to. Melanie decides that the critical issue for understanding member contributions to disaster relief and recovery is organization size: larger organizations respond all over the country while medium and small organizations tend to be selective in terms of where and when they respond. Medium and small organizations also tend to offer a narrower range of services. Because getting detailed measures of organization activity is going to be difficult, Melanie thus decides to take a small stratified sample of organizations and then create very detailed accounts of activities for the sampled cases. She stratifies on organization size, operationalizing size based on organization full-time disaster relief and recovery budgets (small, medium, and large).

Questions about the Example: There are several questions to think about here. Is Melanie's stratified sampling approach sound? Would you approach sampling differently than Melanie? What do you think are the main advantages of this stratification method? Are there any obvious disadvantages?

Cluster Sampling

Related to the notion of stratified sampling is the idea of **CLUSTER SAMPLING**. A cluster sampling approach can be defined as one where the population of interest is divided into groups or clusters, and then a random sample of the clusters is selected. Each of the individual clusters are mutually exclusive and once a cluster is selected, then all the individual units or elements within that cluster are part of the final sample. This is not equivalent to stratified sampling because in that approach there is a random selection of units within each strata. In the cluster sampling approach, you select complete, mutually exclusive clusters and use all the elements contained within. And to be clear: no units or elements from the clusters *not* selected are part of the final sample.

> **Class Exercise:** Think about Melanie's sampling approach discussed in Example 7.3. Discuss how her sampling approach would look if she decided to take a cluster sampling approach instead. How could that approach make sense given her project?

To see how the cluster sampling approach works in practice, let's consider an example again related to our homeland security research problem—except instead of selecting cities, for this illustration, let's say the researcher wants to collect data from individual first responders (e.g., police, firefighters, emergency medical services). Suppose you want to survey first responders in a given area to find out about their perceptions of homeland security policy effectiveness in their communities. If you had a given area, say a larger metropolitan area, or even an entire state, if you took a simple random sample of all police, firefighters, and emergency medical personnel, you might have to contact all (or at least a very large number) of different fire departments or police departments, or the like. That might make the survey effort more difficult and costly to effectively administer. However, if the researcher first selected a certain number of fire and police departments within the defined geographic area to be included in the sample, and then conducted survey interviews with personnel at those departments, then the survey might be easier—and thus more efficient—to administer. In this way, cluster sampling offers the advantage of efficiency, especially if the cluster units can be seen as something like a "natural" cluster unit (e.g., a fire department) and the area of interest (say a large metro area or a state) is geographically dispersed, and conducting the interviews might be administratively difficult to accomplish in practice.

Purposive Sampling and Snowball Sampling

The previous four sampling strategies discussed are all examples of probability sampling. But as was discussed earlier, not all sampling is probability sampling. There are occasions when a researcher either does not want to, or cannot, attempt to draw some type of random sample from a population. If a researcher is trying to test out a new measurement instrument, she or he might simply draw a sample of convenience—that is, selecting readily or easily available subjects—and that might be sufficient for their objective of testing the instrument. Or, if the population is hard to define or even impossible to create a sample frame—such as a study of homeless persons in a given community—then a probability sample is not possible.

The key issue is to understand that, regardless of whether a nonprobability sample is drawn for convenience reasons or because true probability samples are not possible, such samples do not allow for representativeness of the population. In other words, when a researcher is using a nonprobability sample, he or she cannot generalize about, or make accurate estimates about, the population from which it is drawn. This is important to understand if you are attempting a research or evaluation project: if you do not have a probability sample, you will not be able to draw an accurate inference about the population. Further, the process of determining how precise sample estimates are of the population (further developed in more detail in chapter 16) is not possible. However, there are in fact a number of occasions where we would use a nonprobability sampling approach—and not just for convenience or because creating an actual and accurate sample frame is impossible or impractical.

One common nonprobability sampling approach is **PURPOSIVE SAMPLING**. A purposive sampling approach can be defined as a nonprobability sample that is drawn specifically based on existing knowledge of population characteristics in order to serve a specific need of a study question. What that means is that a researcher might want to ensure a sample with wide variation across key characteristics on units in the population. This is an extremely useful approach that researchers and evaluators employ regularly. Consider this example: say an analyst at the Amity Department of Homeland Security wants to look at several policy performance indicators to see how Amity stacks up with other cities across the state. She does not have the time or resources to construct a true probability sample to select other cities for comparison. Further, the performance indicators in which she are interested are going to be difficult to gather for they will rely not on public documents, but on direct interviews with top administrators in the homeland security units for each city. Thus, our analyst wants to limit the size of her sample—but she does want to see if community size and corresponding budgetary resources have an impact on performance issues. Therefore, she takes a purposive sample of four cities smaller than Amity, four of about the same size, and another four larger cities (and she assumes that the budgets for emergency management issues correspond roughly to community size). When she looks at her performance measures of interest across those dozen other cities, she now has the ability to check to see if community size and budgetary resources are related to performance. She cannot generalize to the overall population of cities and homeland security performance because she did not randomly sample from a list of all cities in the state—she merely purposively selected a handful of cities based on population size. However, while that limits her from making estimates and inferences about the overall population, she does have some basic information about population and budget effects on performance. So long as she is cautious and clear in explaining that we cannot generalize to the population with certainty, she can discuss her findings as providing us with some preliminary understand of the potential effects of size, budget, and how Amity is performing in relation to other cities.

Another commonly used nonprobability sampling approach is to engage in **SNOW-BALL SAMPLING**. A snowball sampling approach can be defined as a nonprobability sample that is used when it is difficult to identify members of a population, and the researcher relies on initial contact with several population members and asks them to identify other members. An example will illustrate this technique. Let's stay with our policy analyst in the Amity Department of Homeland Security. Say she wants to not only take a look at the effects of budget and community size on policy performance, she also wants to know how the emergency management and homeland security offices interact with groups in their respective communities to enhance general community preparedness for emergencies and disasters. If she wants to know about the nature of preparedness activities and types of involvement by community groups, she is going to have to talk to some sample of representatives of those groups. But of course, there is no existing comprehensive list that she can turn to in order to develop a sample frame—thus, she is not able to do a probability sample. Further, involvement in networks relevant to emergency preparedness is often a fairly loose network of individuals and organizations. Thus, the way our analyst decides to proceed is to talk first about community group involvement with emergency management and homeland security personnel in each city and ask them about the main groups that they routinely work with. She then contacts a key person (or persons) at those identified organizations to ask them about their emergency preparedness activities. But she also asks them about other groups in the community with whom they work or interact on these issues. By repeating that process of asking one person or organization to identify other relevant actors for this research question, our analyst accumulates a sample list over the course of doing her interviews (hence, the term for this approach—the sample accumulates just like a rolled ball of snow). Again, while there are limits on being able to generalize to an overall population because of the nonprobability nature of the sample, in many research settings this is the best available approach to try to gather data useful to your research question.

Ethical Considerations in Sampling

At first glance, the preceding discussion of sampling logic and sampling design might not seem like it raises questions of ethics, but in fact, sampling can, and does, present ethical questions. In at least some situations, there is an important ethical balancing act that researchers should be aware of and should address when sampling from a population where human subjects are the unit of analysis. We have noted in this chapter that there is a research need for maximizing external validity for a study—that is, for making the results as generalizable and representative of a population as possible. However, at least in some circumstances, that generalizability imperative can conflict with the need to take seriously the costs and risks that the data collection process presents to a study's subjects.

Take, for example, the activities of social work professionals—certainly an important government function. In the provision of various types of assistance to the public, a social worker's ethical obligation is to maintain professional integrity, to provide services to clients, and to protect the rights of those clients. If a social work organization decides to conduct a program evaluation, then the need to ensure the rights and benefits of those same clients does meet the challenge of trying to maximize participation in the evaluative study. That is, if we want a representative sample to be able to draw generalizable inferences about the program's target population, then we want as many subjects to participate as possible. However, if we are talking about particularly vulnerable populations (such as those who are economically disadvantaged, those with emotional or cognitive disabilities, children, prisoners, and so on), then the benefits to the individual participant might not exceed the costs of their participation. As a result, a researcher or program evaluator should consider whether maximizing external validity of results presents any undue burden on subject participants, especially those from vulnerable categories.

Closely linked to those questions is the matter of ensuring diversity of participation in a study. In simple terms, there is the question of what kind of sampling approach, including sample size, should a researcher take to ensure a diverse level of subject participation. For instance, if sample sizes are set too small, then the nature of the sampling effort might exclude the participation of some population subgroups. If the sample size is too large, then the researcher might run the risk of placing too many demands on subjects.

There is not a simple rule that will resolve all such questions. The best way to approach these matters is to follow sound practices of human subjects protections, to make sure all risks and costs to a study's participants are minimized, and to not intentionally exclude diversity of participation in a research effort. Those three principles provide general guidance on how to approach the particulars of any individual challenges a researcher might face in a given study.

Conclusion: The Relationship of Sampling to Evidence-Based Public Management Practices

As we noted above, along with research design and measurement, sampling is fundamental to the data collection process. As such, sampling is fundamentally important to evidence-based management practices. If a sampling strategy or sampling design is not sound, then the data gathered will be problematic for any executive wishing to use those data to support decision making or other organizational management processes. Consider, for instance, the case of the Grover's Corner Department of Transportation provided in this chapter. If the research analyst is tasked with understanding customer behavior and attitudes as a means of helping develop an investment strategy in the light rail system designed to increase future usage, then that analyst has an obligation to produce the most representative and accurate picture of the population as is possible.

Given that research need, consider the idea that the analyst merely conducts a convenience sample as opposed to some form of a probability sample (which might be a simple random sample, or it might be a slightly more complex design such as a stratified sample based on geographic areas of the rail system). Clearly, a convenience sample is a poor approach for several reasons. First, it will not be a representative sample of the population, so it will not provide useful insights into what the behaviors and attitudes are of current and potential users of the light rail system. Second, an obvious downside of convenience sample is that respondents are biased—nonrepresentative—but we might not easily know the exact nature of that bias. Again, this makes it virtually impossible to have a sound empirical basis for decisions based on the data gathered. And third, there is not a good justification for taking a convenience sample approach given the terms of the case presented. That is, there are not such incredible constraints that would prevent some probability sampling approach.

This is not a straw man argument that we are making. It is not uncommon to see a poor data collection strategy—such as the use of convenience sampling—in part because of resource constraints (i.e., an agency might not be able to budget for a rigorous and systematic study) or in part because executives in decision-making authority either do not understand the principles of evidence-based management or do not value that kind of approach, or both. This is a mistake, for public and nonprofit sector organizations can only benefit from sound and appropriate data collection and analysis to support their goals and responsibilities.

Vocabulary

CENSUS—The direct measurement all members of a population of interest.

CLUSTER SAMPLING—A sampling approach where the population of interest is divided into groups or clusters, and then a random sample of the clusters is selected, and all members of the selected clusters comprise the final sample.

MULTISTAGE RANDOM SAMPLING—A sampling approach where a researcher can take a series of simple random samples in stages.

NONPROBABILITY SAMPLE—A sample where each of the units in the population of interest does not have an equal probability of being selected due to a lack of random selection.

PARAMETER—A measure that describes a characteristic or attribute of a population.

POPULATION—The aggregation of all individual units of interest relevant to a study.

PROBABILITY SAMPLE—A sample where each of the units in the population of interest has an equal probability of being selected.

PURPOSIVE SAMPLING—A nonprobability sample that is drawn specifically based on existing knowledge of population characteristics in order to serve a specific need of study question.

REPRESENTATIVENESS—The characteristics of a sample closely resemble the characteristics of the population from which the sample was drawn.

SAMPLE—A subset of a population of interest.

SAMPLE FRAME—The list of population units of members or elements from which a sample—of some defined number—is drawn.

SIMPLE RANDOM SAMPLE—A sampling approach where a subset of the population is selected entirely on random chance and each member in that population has exactly an equal probability of being selected directly from an original sample frame.

SNOWBALL SAMPLING—A nonprobability sampling approach used when population members are difficult to define; a researcher relies on initial contact with several population members and uses their knowledge to identify other population members.

STATISTIC—A measure that describes a characteristic or attribute of a sample.

STRATIFIED SAMPLING—A sampling approach where a researcher divides a heterogeneous population into several strata and then takes a sample from each stratum, usually with the size of the sample for each strata being proportional to the size of the strata in the overall population.

SYSTEMATIC SAMPLING—A type of probability sampling where a researcher takes every *kth* unit or element from the sample frame list.

Flashcards
& MCQs

Useful
Websites

Review Questions

- What is the difference between a probability and a nonprobability sample?
- What does the concept of representativeness mean?
- What is the difference between a sample statistic value and a population parameter value?
- What is a stratified sample?
- What is a snowball sample?

Discussion Questions

- What are the key advantages of a probability sampling approach over a nonprobability sampling approach?
- Why would a researcher want to take a nonprobability sampling approach?
- How do stratified samples differ from cluster samples?
- How does purposive sampling differ from a probability sampling?

CHAPTER **8**

Case Studies

Learning Objectives

- ✓ Understand the basic principles of case study research
- ✓ Learn several types of case study design approaches
- ✓ Learn different case selection strategies
- ✓ Understand and use several approaches in analyzing data collected from a case study research effort

Cases in Research

Case A—National Helping Hands

The Executive Director of National Helping Hands has contracted with an evaluator to assess all member organizations' disaster relief activities. Melanie, the evaluator from Great State University, has undertaken a survey of all member organizations. However, she also recognizes that there are limits to the amount of information she can gather from those organizations in a survey. She feels it is important for her assessment to also examine in greater detail how a typical member organization interacts with a community during the relief and early recovery stages of a disaster. Thus, she decides to take a typical member organization and do a much more detailed examination of how that organization functions in providing disaster relief services.

Case B—Springfield Housing Department

The Springfield Housing Department has an interest in the manner by which individuals and families utilize housing services, given its responsibilities in managing housing assistance and general oversight of public housing. Managers at the department have general data available to them regarding the demographic characteristics of residents in public housing, historical patterns of availability and use of public housing, and similar objective measures pertinent to the administration of the program. However, recent changes in Springfield's housing voucher program have those managers interested in how individual families eligible to receive a housing voucher are likely to adapt to those changes. Rather than relying solely on survey data, the managers would like to have an evaluator produce a set of case studies to provide detailed explanations of how individual households understand, and are adapting to, program changes.

Case Studies in Research and Evaluation

In chapter 7, we learned about the basic logic of sampling and several different approaches a researcher might take in trying to assess a question in order to draw an inference about what is happening in some defined population. As we saw in that chapter, our discussion of sampling was organized around a basic premise: if we have a large population of interest and we cannot measure all units in that population, then we must take a subset or a sample from that population.

However, this is not the only way one might approach understanding and addressing questions about subjects within a given population of interest. Drawing probability samples in the manner described in chapter 7 permits a researcher to draw generalizable inferences about a population—and generalizability is a key strength and benefit of such an approach. At the same time, quantitative studies that are produced from a large "n" sample do not allow for detailed exploration of very subtle contextual factors that affect some phenomenon of interest—and this is a limitation of that approach. As a result of difficulties in accounting for the not-so-easily quantifiable aspects of a research question, qualitative measurement approaches offer their own explanatory strengths (as we have discussed earlier in this text). A detailed, context-rich account can be accomplished by conducting a research or evaluation effort based on a single case or some relatively small selection of cases. This case study research approach is explained in this chapter.

Before covering the various elements associated with case study methods, it is useful to note what case studies are trying to accomplish within the area of public management research and evaluation. For the purpose of generating evidence to support public sector decision making, case studies are often used in order to understand systems of actions. They might also be used to study specific behaviors or actions of individuals or groups of individuals, but broader systems evaluations are perhaps more common in the area of government program evaluation and assessment. When a system of action like a specific public program (e.g., a public housing voucher program) or how an organization participates in a community-wide activity (e.g., a voluntary organization providing disaster relief services) is the general question of interest, then the program or organization becomes the unit of analysis.

Further, as we will define the use and methods of case studies below, it is useful to clarify a point of confusion that sometimes arises when the term "case study" is used. Case study research is not equivalent to teaching from case studies. Courses of instruction will sometimes use cases as a teaching tool. Cases are presented not necessarily to generalize to a range of phenomena, but instead to illustrate a very particular point or lesson. It is a subtle but important distinction to make: research with cases is not equivalent to teaching with cases. One might note that case study research is sometimes criticized for a lack of rigor or form limits in generalizability (i.e., limits on the external validity of a single case). However, if case study research is done properly, it can have explanatory value and can be useful in generalizing to broader inferences about how the public sector world functions. The rest of this chapter provides an overview of how case study research can be performed.

Basic Concepts Associated with Case Studies

As chapter 7 outlined, selecting a large sample from a population generally lends itself to quantitative analyses. As we learned, by "large n," we mean the sample is of some nontrivial size such that we can compute a margin of error in our population estimates that is only several percentage points. However, we do not always want or need to draw a large "n" sample. There are times where a researcher has different data collection or explanatory needs. At times, a research or evaluation project might seek to utilize a case study to answer critical questions. A **CASE STUDY** is just as the name implies: it is an account that describes, explains, or explores details about an organization, a program or policy process, or an institutional arrangement.

Robert Yin, in a classic book on the subject (*Case Study Research: Design and Methods*) notes that a case study approach to research can essentially take one of three forms. A first form is an **EXPLORATORY CASE STUDY,** where data collection on some organization and its processes or programs—or some similar object of interest like a specific public policy decision—is undertaken before well-defined research questions or hypotheses have been developed by research in that area. In other words, it is an initial effort to try to understand some very basic properties of the object of study. One can think of an exploratory case study as representing a pilot study, which is to say it is an initial effort to shape a basic understanding of an organization and its processes, or a program and its processes, when there is little prior examination to allow for specific understanding. For example, if the senior managers at the Springfield Housing Department cannot locate any prior research information about the voucher program they are attempting to adopt, then an exploratory case study of possible household responses to the program change might be one effective way to proceed.

Celebrations ARE BETTER AT BUCA

Buca di BEPPO Italian Restaurant

FEBRUARY 2019

A second type is an **EXPLANATORY CASE STUDY**, where the account of an organization, system, or process is designed specifically to provide a causal explanation that addresses the basic research question posed. Explanatory case studies are quite different than exploratory studies. We have discussed causal inference previously (see chapter 5, for instance). Thus, one can use a case to explicitly examine specific possible causal relationships between variables. If the data are gathered under specific standards of rigor, it is possible to draw inferences about the nature of underlying variable relationships. Sticking with our Springfield Housing program example, the evaluation work might be focused on the degree to which certain critical features of a household (e.g., how much education the adults in the home have, or, how well developed a social network the adults in the household have) are related to choice and utilization of program benefits. In other words, the explanatory case study is geared toward trying to illuminate specific possible causal relationships between key variables.

A third type or form is a **DESCRIPTIVE CASE STUDY**, which is one that is designed not to make a specific causal argument about some observed outcome, but instead, to provide a detailed descriptive account or overview. In this type of case study, the intent is not to explore some system or process that is not well known (from a research perspective), nor is it trying to examine a hypothesized relationship of the intent. Instead, in order to produce a sound documentary account of the organization, system, or process, the descriptive case study attempts to provide as much reliable detail as is possible. The value and utility of such a case study is that it allows researchers or evaluators to understand the internal logic and operations of a given system or program. This, in turn, facilitates other research or evaluative efforts because the process or program is clearly understood and accounted for. Again, referring back to the Springfield Housing Department, a descriptive case study might simply be a documentary report on how the program change was developed and implemented.

The Logic of Case Selection

It is important to recognize that the unit of analysis for a case study can be a system of action (for instance, a program that is implemented by an organization, or a policy process, or some other specific aspect of an organizational or organized activity), rather than a set of individual persons (e.g., eligible voters) or individual objects (e.g., objects like a sample of bridges, as was mentioned in reference to an infrastructure study). This is important because when a researcher is thinking about selecting a case, it is not done in the same way as a random probability selection from a large population. Considerations other than constructing a sample frame in preparation for a random draw of units comes into play.

Selecting cases for research can be thought of as similar to the logic of nonprobability sampling discussed in chapter 7. For example, a purposive sample is an approach where cases are selected specifically to offer contrasts (e.g., small cities in comparison to large cities, coastal communities versus interior communities, experienced employees as distinct from new employees) that permit the information gathered to best answer the research question posed. The approach a researcher takes to selecting a specific case for analysis is much the same: she or he will want to select a case that maximizes the information gathered in terms of providing a casual explanation of some outcome based on actions that have occurred, a useful description of a system or process, or a useful opportunity to explore what question or relationships are most relevant to further systematic inquiry.

Perhaps the most common criticism of case study research is that a single case is inherently limited in the sense that one should not, as a basic rule, try to generalize to a whole population from a single case. In an informal sense, it is common to see case study research treated as if it were equivalent to an anecdote. However, this is frequently an unfair criticism, and depending on how careful and thorough the research is conducted, and how the case (or cases) is selected, the information presented can provide critically important information that illustrates a great deal about a system or organizational processes (and thus is very different from the limits of a simple anecdote).

There are three principles relevant to a case selection strategy. First, a researcher can select a case (or several cases) specifically based on the critical implications of the chosen case—including whether the case results do have something to say about other similar cases (i.e., a principle of generalizability). While it is true that a single case is not necessarily the best strategy for generalizing to a larger population of cases (which might be very dissimilar if their details are examined as well!), the selection process should consider whether the case to be examined constitutes something of a typical case for the phenomenon of interest or whether it is relatively atypical. For example, if a researcher is looking at an environmental agency and its regulatory enforcement of a statute, and the researcher knows that the majority of enforcement actions are of a specific type, then a detailed case study of a typical case provides a basis for understanding very detailed information about the process of a typical regulatory enforcement action. Likewise, if the researcher knows that another type of regulatory action is seldom observed, selection of that atypical case can provide detailed explication of precisely why such cases are very different than the more common enforcement actions to which it is being compared.

A second principle of case selection is the potential research productivity of the case. Given case study research is a time-consuming process of gathering fine-grained details and information and collecting data in a wide variety of ways (e.g., interviews, document reviews, reviews of records), the case selected should be one that is going to productively illustrate what is intended to be accomplished. For example, if the case study is exploratory in nature, the researcher should perform a preliminary review to make sure that there is sufficient material of interest that will facilitate future research question and hypothesis development. If the intent of the case study is to provide an explanation of a system or process outcome, the researcher should conduct a preliminary investigation to ensure that the case being considered will yield adequate information to answer a causal question. That is, if it is necessary to have some combination of interviews and records relevant to making a causal judgment of key relationships, the researcher should investigate whether such records are available for collection and review and if such interviews are feasible. If critical information is unlikely to be obtained for a particular case, then this should dissuade the researcher from selecting it.

A third key principle of case selection pertains to the principle of replication. Replication simply refers to the idea that evidence from one study can be used to compare results to a prior study to see if they are similar or essentially match. A case may be selected with the specific intention of replicating prior work. Further, at times a research-er might want to select multiple cases in order to see if system or administrative process operate similarly across different settings or situations. We can think of this multi-case selection design approach as permitting pattern matching across organizations or set-tings. That is, if the researcher observes consistent evidence across those cases, then he or she can be more confident that the results are robust and that stronger inferences about key relationships can be made.

Example 8.1—Case Discussion: National Helping Hands

Melanie has completed her survey of member organization relief and recovery ef-forts. She has some interesting results and decides she wants to take a much more detailed look at three organizations (a large one, a small one, and a medium-sized one). She wants to compare how each of the three organizations handles two key issues: management of disaster volunteers and management of the internal deci-sion-making process for determining which incidents to respond to and at what effort level. She plans a multiple case study approach to compare these processes across the three organizations.

Questions about the Example: How would you describe the case study ap-proach? Is it exploratory, descriptive, or explanatory? Are there any issues or concerns you might have about the nature of this research design approach? How do you think Melanie should proceed in terms of conducting data collection for this question?

Case Study Design Strategy

Why are case studies used, as opposed to an experimental or quasi-experimental design, or some other type of large n sample? There are several reasons. First, one was men-tioned in the preceding section: at times, little might be known about a system or process, and an exploratory case study is the first step in a larger research or evaluative effort. The exploratory case study can be quite helpful to establishing more precise research ques-tions, to developing testable research hypotheses, and to general theoretic development on questions where only very little explanatory theory might be available to a researcher. A second reason is that the experimental or quasi-experimental research designs can be quite difficult to manage in practice. That is, there are potential situations where it is not practicable to conduct either type of design. In that case, performing a case study design might represent an effective and practicable alternative assessment approach. Finally, as the previous section indicated, the research or evaluation at hand might simply require that a case study be performed. For example, if the evaluative need is to produce a thor-ough account of actual program practices—where none might exist previously—then conducting a descriptive case study is an appropriate way to respond.

We have considered the basic logic of how one might proceed in terms of selecting a case. We turn next to the decision over whether to design a study from the perspective of a single case or as a set of multiple cases.

Single Case Design

Given a researcher intends to conduct a case study on an obvious question, he or she must address whether a single case is sufficient or whether multiple cases are needed. Choosing to select and analyze a single case is similar to conducting a single experiment. According to Yin in his *Case Study Research*, choosing a single case can be justified on several grounds. First, a researcher or evaluator may select a single critical case. This refers to the notion that a single case may represent all the necessary (i.e., critical) information or characteristics that permit the researcher to examine and draw inferences about key theoretic propositions.

A second rationale for a single case is that the investigator (i.e., the researcher or evaluator) is able to identify an extreme or particularly unique case. The value of an extreme or unique case is that precisely because it is so unusual, it is worth documenting. This is not uncommon in medical or clinical psychological research. Documenting extreme cases is also useful in a public policy or public management context precisely because doing so helps illustrate how exceptions to a rule demonstrate how more typical or average cases are handled. Similar to a unique case rationale is a revelatory case rationale. This is a situation where a researcher is presented with an opportunity to study and observe a situation where previously such access had been unavailable. For instance, imagine a federal intelligence agency that doesn't typically allow nonclassified access to its program operations. If for some reason a researcher had an opportunity to examine and assess some activity associated with that agency, this would be described as a revelatory case.

Finally, one can also keep in mind that if the case selected is a typical case—that is, if we have reason to believe it represents something of a modal case, then we can draw inferences about what typical cases are like across a program or across a policy domain. In other words, if we want to describe, explore, or explain if the investigator is on sound footing in demonstrating that most cases are like the one selected to be profiled, then we can draw inferences about how a program or system typically functions.

Multiple Case Design

In contrast to a single case, selecting multiple cases is sometimes viewed as being more robust in terms of generalizability. A multiple case approach is sometimes referred to as a comparative case method, because as the term indicates, selecting multiple cases allows the researcher or evaluator to draw direct and explicit comparisons across those cases and the evidence being analyzed. There are both advantages and disadvantages to the multiple case design approach.

A strength of a multiple case approach is that by collecting evidence in more than one situation, it makes it easier for the investigator to posit more general causal claims. That is, if the investigator sees a relationship not just in a single case, but across a series of cases, it is easier to argue that the observed relationship is likely to be observed in many instances. Indeed, precisely because a relationship has been observed across multiple settings, it is more plausible to assert a general relationship. This can also be described as strength through replication. That is, if an investigator sees a critical relationship in a first case, or if there is a specific claim about a policy or program that the first case indicates evidence in support of, then the additional cases can provide greater support that there is indeed evidence for that proposition.

To understand what potential weaknesses there are in a multiple case approach, one must recall what the very purpose of single case design is. Single cases are often justified precisely because they are unique or critical or revelatory. By definition, unique or revelatory cases are mainly applicable to only a single case. Thus, a potential disadvantage of multiple cases is that they would not permit a clear explication of uniqueness. Further, it is also important to understand that conducting multiple case studies around a single question is more difficult in practical terms—it takes more time for the researcher, more expense, and so forth.

However, one can rightly note that there can be more than one extreme or unique case, for example—especially when we are talking about a distribution of activities or outcomes for a program or policy. That is, there is a typical or modal case, and then there are some cases that deviate quite a bit from what is common or typical. But what a multiple case design approach does offer is something analogous to conducting multiple experiments rather than taking a random sample. In this way, the multiple cases might provide common evidence (i.e., the evidence in the cases might all support a similar interpretation or inference), but this should not be confused with a random probability sample from the population of all cases.

> **Class Exercise:** Discuss why a researcher or evaluator would want to choose a single case design or a multiple case design. Discuss the strengths and weaknesses of both approaches by creating a hypothetical example and walking through how an analysis would differ if multiple cases were compared as opposed to a single case.

Collecting Data and Case Study Analytic Methods

To this point we have discussed the several different types of case studies, how one might go about selecting a case (or cases) for examination, and considerations in selecting a single or multiple cases. In the next two sections of this chapter, we take a look at basic issues in collecting data for case studies—especially in order to ensure that the process of data collecting is conducted systematically and with rigor—as well as some basic considerations in reporting the results of the case study research or evaluation work. Before concluding the chapter, we take a quick look at the use of logic models in case study research.

Data Collection Practices

In addition to sound practices in case study selection and design choices, it is also imperative that a researcher or evaluator use sound practices in actual data collection. There are four key principles in terms of gathering evidence for a case study. First, prior to collecting data, a well-defined protocol for collecting data should be established. A **DATA COLLECTION PROTOCOL** refers to the notion that a researcher or evaluator must have a well-defined set of procedures for how to gather evidence and rules for what evidence is appropriate to be included (or excluded) for the purposes of completing the case study.

A second principle for the researcher or evaluator to follow is that she or he should use a variety of sources and methods in gathering the case study data. By sources, we are referring to documents, records, and other data resources. Using the term "documents" covers a lot of ground. The researcher or evaluator could be looking at administrative documents, formal policy or strategy documents, memoranda, newspaper articles, press releases, and the like. Similarly "records" refers to a wide range of evidence, such as archival records from a program, budget statements, personnel rosters, organizational charts, or other organizational records. Other data resources refer to things like survey data or other public sources such as measures provided by the U.S. Census Bureau or other federal or state agencies that provide measurements relevant to the case.

The methods used in case studies typically include interviews, direct observation, and participant observation. Interviewing subject matter experts or key informants is a critical part of most research or evaluation work—case studies included. These can be **FOCUSED INTERVIEWS**, which refers to a typically short interview designed for the subject to answer a very specific set of questions—usually to confirm data gathered elsewhere. A **STRUCTURED INTERVIEW** is similar to a focused interview in that it relies on a defined set of questions. However, rather than being largely confirmatory in nature (as is the case for a focused interview), a structured interview is more expansive and investigative; that is, it covers a broad range of topics and is designed to collect original information, rather than mainly confirm prior information. **DIRECT OBSERVATION** refers to making an actual site visit where the researcher or evaluator observes practices and processing in person. The reliability of direct observation is improved when more than one investigator is present to produce observation notes on the site visit. And **PARTICIPANT OBSERVATION** refers to the process by which the researcher or evaluator is directly involved in the processes or activities that she or he is studying and from which she or he is recording observations. An example of participant observation is a researcher studying or evaluating a political campaign as well as participating in campaign activities. This method of collecting data is potentially very problematic in many instances, for it can compromise the neutrality and objectivity of the study, and it might also create an inherent bias in the nature of data gathered for the assessment.

All of these topics are covered in much greater detail in the four chapters in section II of this book, which explains key practices and techniques of data collection.

According to the third principle of collecting data for a case study, the researcher or evaluator should also develop and follow explicit rules for documenting the exact nature of the data gathering processes. Doing so is extremely important for the reliability of measurement and for clarity of interpretation and inference of the data collected. We discussed several means of measurement reliability testing in chapter 6. Likewise, we emphasized that any external assessment of validity is based on primarily subject judgments about how effectively the operationalization captures the underlying concept. Thus, a careful documentation of data collection processes is important for these types of judgments to be made.

The fourth principle is that the researcher or evaluator should develop and follow a principle of data maintenance. That is, he or she should create and maintain clear records for use in future work and for replicability—that is, to allow for another researcher or evaluator to attempt to replicate or "re-do" the research or evaluation work in order to check to see if she or he gets a similar result. Replication is not extremely common in social science research work, but it is done at times. Case study research, like other research techniques, should allow for such replication in order to check the validity of results and interpretation.

> **Class Exercise:** Discuss the differences between a focused interview and a structured interview. What kinds of information would the researcher be able to garner from those two different interview approaches? Why would a researcher choose one versus the other?

Pattern Matching

As we have discussed above, there are different types of case studies. Exploratory case studies allow us to obtain a preliminary understanding of some phenomenon (e.g., a new program, a particular set of organizational activities, the implementation of a policy). Descriptive case studies allow us to answer the question of how some program or policy works, how services are delivered, or how target populations behave or interact with a program. To address the question of why a policy or program works as it does, or why individuals behave as they do, explanatory case studies are employed.

Regardless of type, it is important to recognize that case studies generally attempt to capture and account for multiple perspectives in their subject analysis. That is, for most research or evaluation topics, the case study will incorporate a variety of sources of evidence types (as just described in the preceding section) and will account for the perspective of a wide range of actors, including accounting for who constitutes the most relevant actors (as pertains to the analysis) and the interactions between those actors—as well as their interactions with formal administrative systems or processes.

Further, one should also recognize there are various ways that a researcher or evaluator might proceed in addressing that very complex list of considerations just described. One particular way is to use a pattern matching technique. **PATTERN MATCHING** is a technique used to link the data gathered to a theoretic proposition. What that means in practice is a researcher or evaluator will have a core theoretic proposition (or set of propositions) about how a system or process (or whatever the key question for the case) functions in practice. He or she then uses several key pieces of information to see how closely related they are to the key proposition. The evaluator or researcher then draws an inference about whether the evidence provides support—or not—for the proposition.

Example 8.2—Case Discussion: Springfield Housing Department

Christina, a senior manager in the Springfield Housing Department, is interested in a comprehensive evaluation of the impact of recent changes in Springfield's housing voucher program. She is particularly interested in how individual families are interacting with changes in those administrative processes. As a first step, she tasks one of her staff with contracting with an evaluation firm to perform case studies on several families. Part of the work the staffer must do for the assigned task is to specify a detailed set of expectations about the data collection protocols and about the analytic approach the contractor might use.

Questions about the Example: If you were the staffer, what would you define as critical to the data collection protocol? Would you specify the need for interviews, housing records, or what else? Is there a particular type of information that you might think most important to focus on? And what kind of key propositions might the contractor be told to examine specifically?

Reporting Results

Case study research is sometimes criticized for a lack of rigor. That can be a fair criticism if the work is done poorly. For example, if there is not a sound rationale for the case selection, or if the data gathering process does not follow the principles outlined earlier in this chapter, then the work might be of poor quality. But it is unfair if the researcher or evaluator takes care to think about the potential implications of their work, such as whether the results might help with building a generalizable theory on a subject.

Still, it is not uncommon for case studies to be approached in a non-rigorous way. In other words, a researcher or evaluator might be asked to examine a question, and he or she will produce a case study, often because this is perceived as a convenient way to proceed. If that case study does not have a good case selection rationale, a well-specified data collection protocol, and if it does not consider carefully the strengths and weaknesses of different analytic approaches, then this is not a rigorous approach and deserves criticism. However, case studies need not be approached in such a sloppy fashion—there is nothing inherent to case study methods that mean they should be done poorly. Indeed, examples of sloppy, poorly designed quantitative analyses are incredibly abundant.

Part of being rigorous and careful in using case study methods is to produce an effective report of the study effort's results. Yin's class case study text suggests there are five criteria for an effective case study report: (1) the research or evaluation work should be significant, (2) it should be thorough and complete, (3) it should have considered multiple perspectives and alternative explanations, (4) it should present sufficient and compelling evidence for key claims, and (5) it should be presented in an engaging manner. How can one present the case study results? We tackle that question in the next section.

Structuring a Case Study Report

The manner by which case study results are reported depends on several considerations. The foremost considerations are the following: the nature of the report should be determined by the type of case study work being offered (exploratory, descriptive, explanatory), the audience for the report, and the ultimate substantive purpose of the report.

There are several different means of arranging a case study report. If a case study is exploratory or descriptive, it is likely appropriate to present the results of the data gathering effort in a simple linear and/or chronological structure. By linear structure, we mean to indicate that if a program or policy process is being described, for example, then the presentation could be arranged so that it takes the reader from the very first elements of the process through its conclusion in that process. By a chronological structure, we mean to indicate that if a series of events over time are key to the case description, then the report can be arranged by essentially starting at the initial point in time (on a calendar) and end with a logical stopping point on a calendar. (For example, if a program began at the start of a decade and is being evaluated 10 years later at the end of the same decade, and that time period is significant to the case analysis, we would describe that as a chronological structure to the report.)

If the case study is explanatory in nature, then the structure is likely to require a different approach. One way the finding could be presented could be along specific themes in the results, and these themes could be used as part of building toward a broad theoretic claim about causal relationships. Likewise, there might be some basic comparisons that the evaluator wishes to present. Thus, rather than a chronology of events, the results are presented as a means of comparing issues within a case, between several cases, or in comparison to previous findings.

In the end, the basic purpose of the report and its intended audience are the critical determinants of how the investigator should shape its presentation.

Logic Models and Case Studies

A logic model is not a necessary part of an individual case study or case study methods in general. In fact, it is often true that a given case study report will be presented without any reference to a logic model. So what are logic models, and why do we bring them up in a chapter on case studies? A **LOGIC MODEL** is a graphical summary (much like a flow chart) that depicts how the core activities of a program or an organization are connected to the intended outcomes of the program, or the central goals of the organization. A logic model is sometimes described as a theory of change, which is to say, it explains in summary form exactly how a program's activities are intended to produce specific results.

If a researcher is conducting a case study project, he or she does not need to include a logic model as part of the overall assessment effort. However, if the intent of a project is to evaluate an organization or specific program, as in an explanatory case study, then a logic model can be an extremely helpful tool. Providing a graphical summary representation that clarifies the underlying processes of an organization or program is likely to improve the quality of a case study report.

Further, if you recall from earlier in the book, we distinguished evaluation projects as a special category of research. Program evaluation projects are often intended to produce assessment information specific to a program or organization. Such assessments may or may not be intended to be generalizable to other settings (i.e., the purpose of the project might be to provide some information specific only to the organization that has commissioned the evaluation). Further, an evaluation often has the specific intent of producing information that can help an organization or program improve practices. Generally speaking, social science research does not usually carry with it the specific intention of producing information to improve operational practices for some organization.

Keeping that distinction in mind, it is easy to see why a logic model would be a helpful element in the production of a case study. For instance, if the program evaluation required an explanatory assessment (i.e., if it was trying to identify and explain causal relationships), then providing a logic model would assist in explicating how the organization's program efforts are intended to produce a specific result. Think about our Springfield Housing Department case. If the senior manager, Christina, asks an analyst on staff about how changes to the voucher program are intended to work, the analyst might well lay out a logic model to describe and characterize the theory of change in a summary form. For instance, the analyst might well lay out a summary of how prospective clients are supposed to utilize the voucher program and how the voucher system should result in a more efficient allocation of housing. Then, the analyst's case study evidence is used to explore how well the theory of change matches up to the real world application— actual utilization behavior by clients and what that implies for possible efficiencies in the program.

The nice feature of this kind of tool is that developing a logic model is fairly straightforward. The evaluator determines the scope of organizational or program processes to assess. For example, consider a narrower scope: if the researcher is looking only at how stakeholder meetings contribute to information used in a decision-making process for a significant program change, then we would see this as a logic model applied to only one aspect of a broader set of program development and implementation processes (how stakeholder meeting impact program processes). But if we considered the entire program— holding stakeholder meetings to gather their ideas, and feedback is just a single activity— then we would be producing a logic model that is comprehensive in scope, which means we look at all inputs and activities with respect to program outcomes.

To see what this scope distinction really means, consider that a logic model should have these four components at a minimum: inputs, activities, short-term outcomes, and long-term outcomes. By inputs, we mean the resources (human, financial, administrative, etc.) used to create and implement a program. By activities, we mean the formal and actual operational actions undertaken by personnel responsible for a program. This means an identification and assessment of the daily work of staff within an organization

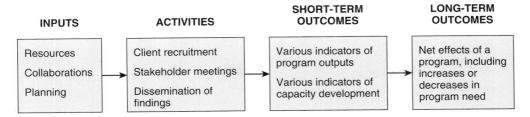

Figure 8.1 Core Elements of a Logic Model

that is directly related to providing a program's key service or services (e.g., meeting with clients, delivering actual services, planning activities, human resource activities such as employee evaluations if those evaluations relate specifically to individual employee goals, and objectives that pertain to the program). By short-term outcomes, we mean the direct tangible and measurable results of activities (e.g., number of cases processed, number of clients served, increases or decreases in dollars spent on given services or staff activities). By long-term outcomes, we mean the net effects of a program (i.e., whether the program produces a particular substantive and intended result).

Figure 8.1 is the most simplified version of what a logic model might look like. We could produce a more complex logic model if needed and if the analysis warranted that such additional distinctions be made. For instance, sometimes a logic model will include three categories of outcomes: short, intermediate, and long term. Likewise, the overall policy and program environment can be part of a more nuanced characterization of the input element. Likewise, we could also have a separate category or element for outputs—especially if we want to distinguish between outputs (e.g., things like the number of cases processed or number of clients seen), and different types of outcomes (e.g., whether there has been a net change in the number of people in a community needing program assistance).

There are several benefits to including a logic model as part of a case study. First, if the case study is intended to serve a program evaluation effort, then the logic model can be a useful device in shaping the way the evaluation is conducted. It helps both the evaluator and the organization being evaluated come to a shared understanding of what are the essential features of a program or organizational effort. In that way, the logic model can both help clarify key features for assessment focus, but it also can lead to greater common understanding of program activities and purpose. Another benefit is that not only by guiding or shaping an evaluation effort, it can also assist collective learning about the organization. In other words, it can help assist in putting measures and data into context so there is a greater ability to provide a useful critique of where a program or organization is successful and where it can be improved. And finally, one should not underestimate the power of a simple graphical display of key relationships. Such visual displays are useful precisely because they convey critical information in a way that is concise and understandable. In other words, a logic model is powerful because it makes the scope, purpose, and implications of a program comprehensible to a wide range of potential audiences.

> ## Putting Knowledge into Practice: How to Create a Logic Model
>
> As the discussion above indicated, there are several basic elements to cover in creating a logic model. After determining exactly what to depict with the graphical display—the overall activities of the organization being evaluated versus a very specific component of a policy or program—the basic steps to develop a logic model are fairly straightforward. (Again, please refer to Figure 8.1 to consider the basic components.)

Conclusion: How Case Studies Relate to Evidence-Based Management Practices

Case study methods are an important part of general research and of program evaluations. As we have seen above, there are a number of reasons to take a case study approach: it might be helpful for the purpose of theory development, it might be necessary to create a careful descriptive record of a policy change, or it might be useful in examining some aspect of a program or organization that does not translate well to easy quantifiable measurement.

For these reasons, case studies are widely used in the assessment of public programs and organizations. They have a great deal of utility and value because they are widely used. Quite frankly, because many people do not have formal training in quantitative research methods, information from case studies is often powerful because it is accessible to a wide audience of information consumers.

For these reasons, it is important that researchers and program evaluators follow sound practices of case study methodology. If a researcher clearly defines purpose, selection, and design strategy, and carefully documents the data gathering effort, a case study can be a very useful tool to contribute to an overall approach of evidence-based management. Further, if the case study is of an explanatory type, this can provide powerful data to help inform an organization's decision making on a given subject.

Suggested Readings

While there are various monographs devoted to the subject of case study research, perhaps the best place to start is to look at two books by Robert Yin. Yin's *Case Study*

Research: Design and Methods is a classic on the subject. Further, Yin's more recent effort, *Applications of Case Study Research*, will illustrate the concepts briefly overviewed in this chapter. Additionally, for a subject like creating a logic model to characterize the work of an organization and its processes as the subject of the case study, there are a large number of web-based resources to help one go about doing that work. Two places where a new researcher might want to go is the Harvard Family Research Project, located at www.hfrp.org; or the program evaluation resource center at the University of Wisconsin's Cooperative Extension, located at http://www.uwex.edu/ces/pdande/index.html, in order to see how logic models are used in actual research and evaluation projects.

Vocabulary

CASE STUDY—An account that describes, explains, or explores details about an organization, a program or policy process, or an institutional arrangement.

DATA COLLECTION PROTOCOL—The notion that a researcher or evaluator must have a well-defined set of procedures for how to gather evidence and rules for what evidence is appropriate to be included (or excluded) for the purposes of completing a research or evaluation project, such as a case study.

DESCRIPTIVE CASE STUDY—A case study that is designed to provide a detailed descriptive account or overview of an organization, a program or process, or the actions and behaviors of individuals.

DIRECT OBSERVATION—A data gathering technique where an investigator makes actual site visits to observe and document, in person, practices and processes of relevance to the project research.

EXPLANATORY CASE STUDY—A case study where the account of an organization, system, or process is designed specifically to provide a causal explanation that addresses the basic research question posed.

EXPLORATORY CASE STUDY—A case study that is undertaken before there are well-defined research questions or hypotheses precisely in order to help shape or define future questions and additional research efforts.

FOCUSED INTERVIEW—Typically a short interview designed for the subject to answer a very specific set of questions—usually to confirm data gathered elsewhere.

LOGIC MODEL—A graphical summary depicting how the core activities of a program or an organization are connected to key intended outcomes or goals.

PARTICIPANT OBSERVATION—The process by which the researcher or evaluator is directly involved in the processes or activities that he or she is studying and recording observations.

PATTERN MATCHING—A technique used to link data gathered in case study research or evaluation work to a set of theoretic propositions.

STRUCTURED INTERVIEW—An interview using a defined set of questions designed to collect original information rather than to confirm mainly prior information.

Flashcards
& MCQs

Useful
Websites

Review Questions

- What does a case study refer to?
- What are several considerations in selecting a case for research or evaluation?
- What are the three basic forms of case studies?
- What is the difference between a single case and a multiple case design, and why would a researcher choose one approach over the other?
- What does "pattern matching" in case study research refer to?
- What is construct validity, and why is it a challenge for case study research?

Discussion Questions

- Why can case studies be described as taking a nonprobability sampling approach?
- What are the relative strengths and relative weaknesses of case studies in general, and as opposed to probability sampling specifically?
- How can sound techniques in case study selection methods improve the generalizability of case study findings?
- What are several key considerations in selecting a case to address a research question?

CHAPTER **9**

Interviews

Learning Objectives

- ✓ Understand the role of interviews as a data collection tool
- ✓ Differentiate between types of interviews including structured, semi-structured, and unstructured interview strategies
- ✓ Learn how to design and implement an interview protocol
- ✓ Understand the ethical implications of interview research—and the obligations these place on researchers

Cases in Research

Case A—National Helping Hands

It is time for the director of National Helping Hands (NHH) to start collecting some data. She wants to know who was involved in disaster response in selected situations. This seems like a simple question to ask people about. Based on her previous thoughts on selecting respondents to ensure an appropriate sample, she needs to design questions about the respondents' experiences with disaster response. This can include questions about with whom they interacted or whom they saw in their response efforts, but it can involve a great deal more. She is also interested in questions related to the difficulties (and successes) each respondent identified following their experiences in disaster response.

Case B—Grover's Corner Department of Transportation

Without users, a new train station will fail. The director of the Department of Transportation wants to know what sort of amenities will draw people to use a new train station. Do people want food on their way into or out of work in the morning? How important is it to have a convenience store? With what sort of supplies would such a store need to be stocked to be useful to riders? How important are amenities compared to other potential barriers to use of the train station, including location, parking availability, etc.? These sorts of questions seem like ones where a simple interview with users could prove fruitful. Now the director needs to tackle the significant challenge of developing just such a research protocol.

The Fundamentals of Interviews

One of the most intuitive ways to collect data is to talk to people. Public affairs research often involves the opinions or attitudes of various people. This could include the employees within a local agency or residents of a specific community. This chapter introduces how to gather information to answer key research questions for public managers. It will introduce the basic logic of interview data collection along with its strengths and weaknesses. The next sections provide specific advice on the design of interview research protocols, including the writing of effective interview questions. The final section will discuss the ethical implications of interview research.

The Logic of Interviews as Data

Interview research projects must start with the basics of research design discussed in previous chapters—including research design and measurement. We start with a research question. That question motivates us to seek the answer by observing the world. Interviews are simply one strategy to get a look at the world. Interviews tend to be most useful in situations where the information is not otherwise easy to see. If we need to get a sense of local gas prices, we can simply drive around and write down what you read off of gas station marquees. This would be an easy case of data collection. That part of the world is easy to observe. In fact, there is a strong incentive for gas stations to make sure you know what their prices are. If you want to know what people are thinking or how they will react to potential policy changes, you have no simple analogue to posted gas prices. People don't wear signs that reveal their attitudes (though bumper stickers can be a telling sign). If we can't just look around us, we have to use data collection techniques to observe otherwise unobservable parts of the world. When the part of the world we want to observe is inside the heads of potential research subjects, we may want to use interviews to get a look inside.

Of course, interviews are only appropriate in cases where people are aware of the answer to the question you are asking. If the answer you are looking for is not something that your respondents can offer, then the interview will not likely work. It is distressingly common (and an all-too-common approach in news programs) to see polls that ask questions to which the respondents can't possibly know the answer. A news organization may ask people, "Did the recent national policy reduce unemployment?" The true answer to this question, if knowable at all, is likely to require extensive, careful research by teams of highly qualified economists. A randomly sampled respondent to a phone poll is not going to have the information necessary to answer that question. They may provide an answer. You may be able to summarize the responses. However, that does not reveal what the answer really is. At most, you reveal a reflection of the respondent's attitude toward the policy (which may be interesting but is not exactly what you asked). More troubling, it is common to see poll questions about the guilt or innocence of a person accused of a crime— where the people taking the poll don't have access to all of the information that will be present in a trial. To avoid this confusion, it is important to only ask people questions to which they are likely to know the answer.

> **Class Exercise:** What examples have you seen lately of poll questions—often political polls— where the respondents do not likely know the answer?

Strengths of Interview Data

There are several reasons you may want to use interviews to observe the world.

(1) **Ease**—The largest selling point of interviews is that they can be easy to administer. Of course, well-designed interview protocols require a great deal of work (as we detail later in the chapter). However, people can easily imagine what interviews look like. After all, we see them on television all of the time. Instead of a journalist interviewing a politician, we may be interviewing a worker in a nonprofit about his ideas to improve the organization. Regardless of this difference, we have the model of what an interview looks like in our mind.

(2) **Natural language**—Interviews tend to be conducted in natural language. Interviews allow people to express themselves in their own language. We don't have to impose categories for respondents to use. The result is a research protocol that is easy on the respondents in that they won't grow frustrated by imposed response categories. In the transportation department interviews, respondents can use whatever language they want to describe the amenities they would like at the train station. If they want to say "coffee shop," they can use that language. If they want to name a specific coffee shop chain, they can do that instead. It is up to the researcher to leave this in its original form or to translate the language into either quantitative form for later statistical analysis or to group similar responses together. Analysis strategies for this sort of data are discussed in the next section of the book.

Weaknesses of Interview Data

Of course, interviews have some important weaknesses as well. You must keep these weaknesses in mind when considering whether interview research is appropriate to address your research question.

(1) **Responder bias**—The simple fact of hearing or seeing an interviewer may influence the sort of responses that a person provides. A respondent may be less likely to admit illegal or unpopular activities when he or she has to report the activity to a specific interviewer. This makes interviews about sensitive subjects like personal finances, crime, sexually transmitted diseases, and childhood trauma difficult to conduct. In an extreme example, a victim of rape may not want to talk about it—especially to a stranger like an interviewer.

Even when a respondent does not mind talking about a subject, he may change his answers based on the knowledge that someone is listening to him (and possibly looking at him across a table). Studies have documented that people exaggerate their income when interviewed, likely as an attempt to impress the interviewer (or avoid embarrassment). Similarly, there is a well-documented pattern of people reporting that they voted in recent elections when they did not (as demonstrated by the voter rolls). These simple examples illustrate a larger point. When respondents may want to impress or meet the expectations of an interviewer, their responses may be subject to **SOCIAL DESIRABILITY BIAS**.

(2) **Language uncertainty**—Interviews involve communication in natural language. This is actually one of the strengths, but it is also a weakness. The uncertainties and ambiguities of natural language also introduce uncertainties and ambiguities into interview research. When a word may be misinterpreted, it may prevent clear analysis of interview data. Unclear language may also interfere with the comparison of responses across multiple respondents. If two respondents in interviews about potential amenities at a train stop both say that they want coffee "if it is not too expensive," it is not clear that both respondents would define "too expensive" in the same way. One person may think that $3.00 is too expensive for coffee while another thinks that $3.00 is fine but $5.00 is too much. Follow-up questions can clarify this ambiguity, but often some amount of it still remains.

(3) **Implementation costs**—Interviews are often time intensive and thus expensive. As we go through the process of designing an interview protocol, you will see how much effort it takes. In the simplest terms, the interview itself may only take 5 minutes for each respondent but may take 15 minutes between each person as the interviewer transitions from one respondent to another. Of course, a 5 minute interview can only include a small number of questions. For longer lists of questions, interviews often run from 30 minutes to an hour or longer. This takes personnel to staff (with interviewers) and may require compensation for the time you are asking of the respondent. When you have completed that interview, you have one more

[handwritten margin note:] May not be as upfront about the success of a program. Mentally-ill in the criminal justice "sector" is a very sensitive subject

data point (though an intensely detailed one). As a result, it is incredibly expensive to conduct interviews with a large number of people. If you need a large sample of data, interviews will be an expensive way to collect those data.

Types of Interviews

Interviews are a popular research technique and take on many forms. The first step in designing an effective interview protocol is to define the type of interviews you will conduct. At one extreme, interviews can be completely open to any sort of conversation and go in whatever direction the respondent wants to take. At another extreme, the interview can involve a specific set of questions in a scripted order that is repeated for every respondent. Of course, the choice of interview type depends on your goals for the interview protocol.

The discussion of interview types naturally raises questions of the design of specific interview questions. This chapter will introduce the issues related to question wording. A later chapter on survey design will address more specific issues of the design of questions for survey administration.

Structured Interviews

The most strictly designed forms of interviews are called **STRUCTURED INTERVIEWS**. In structured interviews, one scripts all questions in advance, asks all questions in the same order to every respondent, and uses the same questions and order for all respondents. This approach does not allow for follow-up questions, clarification (though this restriction is often relaxed), or any changes to the protocol. A structured interview for the train station research would include a series of questions like "What amenities would you like to see at this train station?" One could not stop to ask follow-up questions. Strictly speaking, one would not be able to provide clarifications such as defining what one means by amenities. Instead, the interviewer is supposed to read the exact text of each question in order, record responses, and do nothing more, other than sometimes recording the actual words used and sometimes translating those words into a code from a prepared list of anticipated responses.

The chief advantage of this is that each respondent's experience is as similar as possible. If some people are getting the term "amenities" clarified and others are not, it may make the responses of some respondents incomparable with the responses of others. If you ask questions in different orders, you may similarly change the interview experience and influence the responses that you get. If comparability of the respondents' experience is an important part of the research design, a highly structured interview protocol may be in order.

Another advantage of structured interview protocols is the ease for interviewers. If your research requires a large number of interviewers, you may not have the time or money to train each interviewer extensively. You may have to rely on having an interview instrument that is easy to implement. A structured interview transcript is about as easy as it gets. You can tell respondents to simply read the question text (often set off in bold or in boxes) and then to record responses. They may also read the specific response options so that respondents can choose from the available options. They don't have to improvise at all by providing follow-up question, adapting the interview to the respondent, or clarifying anything in the questions. All they do is read the text exactly as it is printed in front of them (whether on paper or on a computer screen).

Unstructured Interviews

The polar opposites of structured interviews are, unsurprisingly, unstructured interviews. Of course, all interview protocols have some amount of structure. You can't go into an interview without some idea of the topic of the interview. In this way, even unstructured interviews are at least partially structured. The goal is not the absence of structure but the minimization of structure and the maximization of flexibility.

[handwritten margin note: Same questions will be asked but with expected follow-up]

Instead of comparability, the goal of unstructured interviews is to probe as deeply as possible to ensure complete understanding of a respondent's answers. Instead of ensuring that the interview experience is the same from person to person, you want to adapt the experience to the needs of every respondent. You can tailor the experience by providing extensive clarification, adjusting question wording, jumping ahead to questions as they come up naturally in the interview, and providing follow-up questions. In this way, an unstructured interview more closely resembles a conversation than the formality of the structured interview.

Unstructured (or loosely structured more accurately) protocols are generally useful for exploratory phases of research. When you know very little about the subject of the interview and you want to explore the topic, there is no strong basis for choosing specific question wording or question order. You need to listen to your respondents to learn more about the topic before you can even start creating a uniform experience for interview respondents.

When facing a research project with such pervasive uncertainty, one can prepare a topic guide instead of a highly structured interview protocol. The topic guide provides information to the interviewer about what basic understanding the research team has of the research topic, anticipated areas of discussion, and general guidelines of what should be covered in the interview. The guidance provided by a topic guide can be particularly helpful for interviewers who may be unfamiliar with the context of the larger research project—as would be the case if you hired interviewers or had assigned new researchers to this task.

Semi-Structured Interviews

Between these extremes lie a series of compromises. No interview protocol is completely structured in that no experience is entirely comparable to any other. Similarly, no experience is completely unstructured. Having a topic imposes at least a minimum of structure. All protocols actually choose a point between these extremes. In the middle of this range lies the semi-structured interview.

Semi-structured interviews start with a pool of predefined questions. It is often the case that you start with a set of introductory questions. These are often highly structured questions that just serve to establish the identity of the respondent. From the basic introductory questions, the interviewer can branch in a number of directions. Possibly following a rather open question, the interviewer chooses from a pool of follow-up questions depending on where the open-ended questions lead.

In the NHH example, the director only has a general topic of interest: the participants in disaster recovery and barriers to participation. In such a situation, the director could start with structured questions about the identity of the respondent and the respondent's organization. These would be simple questions. A general question could follow about what other organizations the respondent worked with during disaster response followed by specific follow-up questions about those collaboration experiences. This branching logic means that every interview is a little different depending on the number of partners the respondent discusses. The next phase of the interview can start with an open question about barriers to participation in disaster recovery. Follow-up questions can clarify what the respondent means with each identified barrier—possibly asking for examples.

This interview would be semi-structured in that it combines a standardized strategy with some flexibility in the implementation of the interview. The clearly defined topic, defined pool of questions, and strategy for branching are structured aspects. The ability to branch, follow-up questions, and clarifying probes are unstructured aspects of the interviews.

Putting Knowledge into Practice: Designing an Interview Protocol for the Department of Transportation

The director of Grover's Corner Department of Transportation wants to know what amenities users of the community's rail service would like at a local rail station. There are a relatively small set of potential amenities based on models around the country. Many rail stations have coffee shops and convenience stores, for example. Few rail stations have pet stores—and for good reasons. Given the relatively small number of previously defined options available to the department, the interview protocol asking respondents of their opinions can be highly structured. The interview can include a small number of questions with limited flexibility and still answer important questions about the relative priority of food service or a convenience store, for example.

If the director wanted to leave the options completely open to see if respondents would generate entirely new ideas, a semi-structured protocol would be appropriate. There would need to be some structure to focus respondents on amenities rather than, say, train times and the condition of waiting areas. However, the discussion of amenities can allow flexibility to follow respondents' interests. Such an approach would equip interviewers with a topic guide rather than a strict set of questions and response options.

Focus Groups

People often assume that interviews are between a single interviewer and a single respondent. Grammatically, we have assumed this in the previous discussions. This is not necessarily the case, though. One can conduct interviews with multiple respondents (or using multiple interviewers). If interviewing a smaller number of respondents (2–5) at a time, there are not many changes with how one conducts the interview. The nature of the exercise changes once respondents start reacting to each other's statements—but the practical administration of the interviews may be quite similar to single respondent approaches. Once one gets to a slightly larger number of respondents, one is conducting a **FOCUS GROUP**. In a focus group, the goal is to collect data from multiple respondents (typically 5–10 but sometimes as many as 20) at one time.

The first advantage of focus groups (as opposed to interviewing each person individually) is the shorter period of time needed to carry out the interviews. It may require 10 hours to conduct individual interviews where a single focus group session of 1–1.5 hours will suffice. This reduces the time one has to pay an interviewer or reduces the complexity of scheduling because all the focus group takes place at a single time and location. Of course, there is the added complexity of scheduling many people to appear at one time or at one location.

The second advantage is more subtle. Focus groups involve the simultaneous interaction of each of the respondents. The result can be the equivalent to brainstorming and piggybacking. A comment one respondent makes can remind another respondent of something. If one conducted a focus group of users of the train station, one respondent may mention that he would like a way to buy the morning newspaper at the station. This might inspire another to make a related recommendation like that he would like a full magazine stand. The result is that focus groups may better represent the set of attitudes of the group than individual interviews would otherwise.

At the same time, there are some potential biases built into the same social processes in focus groups. Just as respondents may piggyback on other group members' comments, those comments may influence other people. It may be that people are too shy to comment when they feel that their opinions are in the minority. Alternatively, they may endorse an opinion to join in that majority. These other possibilities lead people to provide different answers than they would if interviewed individually.

There are also dangers in spreading the attention of the interviewer over too large a number of focus group members. Some argue that focus groups should not include more than 10 people to ensure that all people have a chance to contribute. You have likely experienced this with group discussions in classes. With classes including more than 15 or so people, group discussions often devolve with only a few people dominating the discussion. The same can happen in focus groups. Even with a diligent interviewer coordinating the focus group, a large group (more than 10 or so people) can often result in only a few people actually talking. Other people, even if prompted, may give short and unhelpful answers that do not reflect their true opinions.

Developing Interview Questions

The heart of the interview protocol is the set of questions the interviewer asks. Even in unstructured interviews, great care should be taken to be prepared with a wide variety of questions and a deep familiarity with the language one will use to ask questions. For this reason, you should take great care—and devote considerable time—to the preparation of questions for your interview research.

Goals of Question Development

Before you start writing interview questions, you need to consider what it is that makes some questions better than others. There are two general standards you will want to meet for any questions you write: relevance and clarity.

Obviously, you want to limit yourself to questions that are relevant to your research question. This is harder to achieve than it may seem at first. You will need a clear idea of your research topic and a thorough understanding of the existing body of knowledge on the subject. We have implored you to invest time in honing research questions and conducting preliminary research. Now that work will start to pay off. The expense of interview research makes asking useless or irrelevant questions quite costly.

The most difficult of the standards of good questions to meet in practice is clarity. Your goal is to make sure that every respondent will understand each question in the same way. You may think that asking someone, "With what organizations did you collaborate during disaster recovery?" is clear. However, there is a great deal of ambiguity in that question. Different respondents may think of different actors as "organizations." Just about everyone may see the Red Cross as a relevant organization. However, if a couple of people from a local religious community show up to help, would you count the religious community as an organization? Similarly, respondents may vary in what they define as "collaboration" or "disaster recovery." Academics who study collaboration between public organizations still argue over what counts as "collaboration" and what is "coordination" or "partnerships." Any similar ambiguity in your question can leave respondents using different definitions to answer your question. Respondents who had identical experiences could provide different answers. The end results may be mere noise or systematic bias in the responses you hear.

> **Class Exercise:** What alternative words might you use to investigate partnerships between organizations in the National Helping Hands case?

Given the goals of relevance and clarity, you want to take great care in writing questions and to follow a process to reduce the chance that you make an error.

Types of Questions

When writing your specific questions, you must start by deciding on a type of question you want to ask. There are two basic types of questions to choose from. You can ask

OPEN-ENDED QUESTIONS that allow respondents to answer in any way they choose. Alternatively, you can ask CLOSE-ENDED QUESTIONS where you force respondents to choose among a set of acceptable response options (this approach is popular in situations where the data will eventually be subject to statistical analysis). The choice resembles that between structured and unstructured interviews. You will have to decide how much freedom you want to offer respondents.

Close-ended questions are the simplest to administer but may be frustrating for some respondents. The goal is to support the clarity of the question and ensure the comparability of results across respondents by defining a small set of response options for them. Imagine that you ask someone, "How old are you?" We can imagine a variety of potential answers (here exaggerated to serve as a vivid example) including: "24 years old," "young," "old," or even "I would prefer not to answer that question." It is difficult to compare "24 years old" to "young." I may consider 24 to be young but a 10-year-old child would not.

To avoid these problems, close-ended questions provide response options among which the respondent must choose (if he chooses to respond at all). Instead of simply asking a person's age, you might ask him to mark a box next to the range that includes his age. If you only needed a general category of age, your response options may include broad ranges such as "18 to 35 years old" or "65 years or older." If your research question involved precisely measured ages, you may instead ask for a person's birth month and year. You could go so far as asking for a specific birth date—but you are likely to encounter considerable resistance for security reasons.

In public affairs research, the potential response categories may be difficult to define. In the train station interview, you could ask which amenities a respondent would like to see at the train station and then list the following options: coffee shop, news stand, full-service restaurant, DVD rental kiosk, Internet café, etc. You could then instruct respondents to check all of those that they would like or some specific limited number ("choose up to three"). The advantage to this approach is that the response options serve to further clarify the question. Perhaps the respondent did not know exactly what you meant by amenity (maybe he thought that "more frequent arrival times" is an amenity). Once he heard the options, he would have a pretty good idea of what you mean. You could then use the answers to address questions about which amenities are the most likely mentioned.

The danger of close-ended questions is that you may end up with either too long a list (which leads to people not paying attention to the question anymore and possibly quitting the interview entirely) or an incomplete one. It can be quite frustrating to encounter a close-ended question where the answer you want to give is not present. A late night talk show host had a popular joke where he would ask people whether they thought the president was "a great president" or "the greatest president." He strictly enforced the close-ended nature of his questions and would not let people provide any other answers, even if they did not support the president. On a smaller scale, respondents in the train station interviews could experience the same frustration if they really want to see a bank ATM but that is not an item on the list.

One solution to this frustration is not to provide response options at all and leave it up to the respondent. In this case, you would rely on open-ended questions. People could answer the questions in any way they see fit. In the transportation example, you would simply ask, "What amenities would you like at the train station?" and record the responses. This approach is particularly attractive when you are not sure about the range of possible answers that you will get. If you are not confident that you can list all of the amenities that people will want at the train station, the open-ended question makes a great deal of sense. If you are pretty sure that all of the options will be within a narrow range, the close-ended questions have a compelling simplicity. It is possible to follow up with the recorded answers (in the language chosen by the respondent) to group the responses based on the research needs of the project. This approach is discussed in more detail in a later chapter as data coding—which we leave to the section of the book focusing on the analysis of data.

With open-ended questions, you have to be even more careful that your question is clear and easy to answer. If a respondent was not sure what you mean by "amenities" in the train station interviews, he could provide answers that don't fit your intent with the questions ("more trains," "better weather," "lower prices"). If you were employing a semi-structured interview protocol, you may be able to clarify or follow up to redirect the respondent to the sorts of amenities that interest you. In a structured interview or if your interviewers do not have the training to properly follow up, these answers would simply stand until you later analyzed the responses. Then you would likely have to throw out the responses and may grow frustrated that you missed an opportunity at more interesting responses.

Open-ended questions may also result in ambiguous answers that will be frustrating for you in the later analysis period. Recall that "young" and "24 years old" would be difficult to compare. With the train station survey, people may refer to coffee shops in a variety of ways. This will raise a question later as to whether you can combine them all under one heading. It so happens that I do not drink coffee. I would never answer such a question with "coffee shop." I might say something like "somewhere I can get a drink" if asked an open-ended question. You will have to decide later whether to combine my answer with "coffee shop" and "Starbucks" (or other specific company names). Combining may be dangerous. It could be that someone used the term "Starbucks" to stand for any place where one can buy coffee. Another person could really mean Starbucks and only Starbucks. The advantage of open-ended questions is the beautiful diversity of the responses you can get. The challenge for later analysis is this same diversity.

There are also methods to balance the advantages of open-ended and close-ended questions. A **HYBRID QUESTION** involves a series of specific response options that includes an open-ended option. You can list various potential amenities for the train station survey but also include an "other" option. If the respondent says "other," the interview simply asks for him to provide an option to record. This provides the clarity supporting functions of the close-ended question with some of the flexibility of open-ended questions. This approach does introduce some problems, though. People tend to rely on provided options and rarely use the open-ended option if they can avoid it. You can think of this as respondent laziness. If they can simply choose one, two, or three options and move along—they will often choose an option read by the interviewer rather than choosing "other" and providing additional information (even when their true answer would call for such specificity). Other, more expressive respondents (or those who want to make very fine distinctions) may use the "other" category to indicate a choice that others would have included under one of the listed options. For example, one person may say "other—Starbucks" when there was an option for "coffee shop." The use of hybrid questions does not eliminate the need to analyze the resulting data with great care.

An alternative approach is to include both close- and open-ended questions. Many national policy surveys ask two versions of questions about what respondents think are the most important problems the country faces. One of the versions is open ended. The other lists a standardized set of potential problems from which the respondents choose. Interviews can use the same approach. This approach ensures that you do not misidentify patterns in responses that are a product of your choice of questions type. However, the approach is rarely used in interview research because it takes a great deal of time. This approach doubles the time you are spending to get answers to one core question. If your research project requires an extreme amount of care for a specific question, this may be warranted. If your research project calls for a broad range of questions, you may not have the time needed to ask questions twice.

Putting Knowledge into Practice: Designing Parallel Questions for the Transportation Survey

The interviews related to rail station amenities could call for two question strategies. The director would like to hear unprompted suggestions from the interview respondents. However, it may be the case that the respondents will not provide any suggestions at all until prompted. To balance these two concerns, the interview protocol starts with an open-ended question that asks, "What sort of amenities, shops, or services would you like to see added to this rail station?" The interviewer is directed to write down any response. This question is followed by a closed-ended question including specific options that the director's research has suggested are popular elsewhere. This question is worded as, "Other rail stations include amenities different than what are available here. Please rate your level of interests in each of the following amenities on a scale of 1 to 10, where 1 means that you are not at all interested and 10 means you are very interested: (1) coffee shop, (2) fast food restaurant, (3) convenience store, . . ."

Situational Characteristics of Question Development

Developing questions of any type also requires specific consideration of the context of the interviews you are conducting. We will discuss two categories of considerations: interview characteristics and respondent characteristics.

Interview Characteristics

The nature of your interview will affect the question writing process a great deal. The chief characteristics of the interview relevant to question wording is the length of the survey. If you are only planning to interview respondents for a short period of time, you have a small number of questions you can ask. Furthermore, open-ended questions are likely to eat up more time than close-ended questions. You will have to choose question types in a way that balances the information you hope to get from the answers with what is feasible given your time constraints.

One should also consider the environment in which the interview takes place. You need to ensure that the respondents will be comfortable or they will not participate. You will need to maintain this comfort throughout the interview. If you are conducting your interviews in an office with respondents seated comfortably around a table, you may be able to ask a series of questions about disaster recovery lasting half an hour without the respondent noticing any discomfort. If you interview people standing outside in a train station, you will have to keep the interviews short. Not only are your respondents likely waiting for a train, they may not be comfortable standing around answering questions for very long. You may even encounter adverse weather like rain or snow. As you can imagine, people are not keen to answer many questions when doing so involves them standing in the rain waiting for their train. The weather itself can provide an obstacle for your interview.

Respondent Characteristics

You must also consider the nature of the respondents to your interviews. There are two rough categories to consider: **ELITE RESPONDENTS** and **MASS RESPONDENTS**. Elite respondents include any interview subjects who possess specialized knowledge of the field in which the interview is taking place. If we interview a director of a Red Cross office about disaster response and recovery, that respondent is an elite. If we interview the same person about nuclear power, the respondent will not be an elite respondent for the purposes of that subject. Mass respondents are the remainder—respondents with no particular expertise in the field of the interview.

The nature of your respondents affects the design of your questions. With elite respondents, you can rely on the respondent to be familiar with specialized vocabulary for the field—**JARGON**. If one were interviewing a disaster response professional for the NHH project, one would not be able to rely on the respondent to be familiar with terms like "emergency management coordinator" or "NIMS" (a specialized system for managing various governmental efforts in emergency management). Chances are, you do not know what NIMS is. This is not a course on emergency management, and you do not need to know these sorts of details. You are a mass respondent when it comes to emergency management. This just illustrates how one cannot make the same assumptions about vocabulary for elite and mass respondents.

The Process of Question Development

Given these considerations, you might wonder how you can tackle the difficult problem of writing interview questions. The answer is to develop questions slowly and deliberately. You must treat question writing as a process.

You can start the process by generating an initial list of candidate questions. With these candidate questions, you want to make sure that you have enough questions to collect the data you want. You do not need to worry a great deal about the potential pitfalls of question wording or choices like whether to use close-ended or open-ended responses. At this initial stage, you just want to brainstorm a large variety of options.

After you have developed a pool of potential questions, you can start to sculpt the questions. You can draw each question for the pool and give it an initial look for question wording problems. Read each question to make sure that all of the words in it are appropriate for your audience (either elite or mass). Consider whether the questions are clear. Then you can decide whether to have close-ended responses or not. If you do, generate a list of potential responses and test them for comprehensibility in the same way. You can even try multiple versions of individual questions and retain the questions you like.

After you have given each question this initial pass, you should circulate the full list of questions to the full research team. The research team should read each question with the intent of finding problems with them. At this stage, the research team is like quality assurance for a video game company. Your goal is to read the questions in all of the possible strange ways they can be read to eliminate sources of ambiguity. Just like video game quality assurance processes involve making sure that your character cannot jump to some areas not intended for a level or that some combination of button pushes will not crash the game, the research team tests questions to make sure that they will not bring interviews to a halt as respondents scratch their heads trying to figure out what the question means. You can gather the research team following their individual readings of the questions to have a group discussion of any problems. The group can then address the problems and propose alternative, clearer question wordings.

You should not move from this internal review process to the interviews themselves. Your research team is still coming from a specific perspective that may lead it to miss problems with question wording. If nothing else, your team likely consists of a series of experts in the field of the interviews. There is a very real danger that your team may assume that people are familiar with terms with which respondents—particularly mass respondents—are not familiar. To address this problem, you want a second stage of question review. This can either be an outside set of readers of people familiar with question wording issues (but, preferably not familiar with the jargon of the interview subject) or to some group as similar as possible to the eventual sample for the interviews. Each of these rounds of review should be followed by a team review of any problematic questions identified by the question testers.

Only after going through these various rounds of review will you draft the actual list of questions. With interviews, the respondents do not actually see the list of questions (in either a structured, semi-structured, or unstructured protocol). You need to make sure that the question list is easily understood by interviewers, but the aesthetics of the question list is not paramount.

Putting Knowledge into Practice: Circulating a Draft Interview Protocol

The director of the National Helping Hands program is well aware that some of his member organizations are less familiar with the jargon and vocabulary of disasters and emergency management. For this reason, he asks Mel to write the interview protocol with this limitation in mind and to circulate the interview questions broadly to identify potential problems. Mel starts with a series of drafts within her office at the NHH. She specifically asks everyone who reads the draft to look for words that could be misunderstood by people unversed in the field's jargon.

An internal round of reviews is not enough though. Mel also circulates the list of questions to a colleague she knew in school who works in a local transportation department. She knows that her school colleague knows about the fundamentals of writing questions but not the specifics of disaster policy. Her colleague will provide a valuable perspective.

Implementing Interviews

After developing the interview question list, you have only just begun the process of interviews. The work continues as you actually carry out the various interviews. This section will cover some of the administrative details important to a successful interview protocol. We will defer discussion of how to analyze the resulting information until a later section of the book that includes a variety of analytic options including data display approaches.

Recruiting Interview Respondents

The first stage in the implementation of an interview protocol is the recruitment of potential respondents. As the previous chapter on sampling techniques made clear, the selection of your research subjects is of vital importance to any research project. This is just as true for interviews as it is for surveys, field sites, or any other type of research.

Since interviews involve human subjects, the selection of a sample involves recruiting specific people to take part in the interview process. Given that interviews are time consuming and expensive, great care must be taken to make sure that you get the right set of respondents. What the right mix requires will depend on the nature of your research question.

> **Class Exercises:** If you wanted to get diverse respondents in your community, who would you want to include? How might you recruit them?

If your research question involves finding the range of opinions or attitudes on a specific matter, you will want a sample that is as diverse as possible. This could be the case if you wanted interviews to identify the range of potential amenities that the train station could include. Since the focus is on getting as diverse a list as possible—not necessarily to represent the proportion of supporters for different amenity options within the community—a maximally diverse set of respondents would be appropriate.

If, instead, you wanted to find out which amenities are most popular within the community of potential users of the train station, you will need a sample that resembles the potential population of users as closely as possible. A sample of respondents that is maximally diverse may not resemble the community very much at all. Of course, getting a sample that resembles the population is quite difficult with a small sample. If the Grover's Corner Department of Transportation serves 100 thousand residents, it will be difficult for a mere couple of dozen of interview subjects to represent everyone. It is for this reason that research questions that focus on proportions in the population, popularity of policy options within the community, etc., tend to rely on research methods that allow for more respondents with a smaller investment of time than interviews require.

Getting people to participate in interviews at all can be tricky. Interviews typically take a significant amount of time coordinated with an interviewer. If you are going to ask people to attend a specifically scheduled interview session, many may expect some form of compensation. Even if they do not expect it, providing compensation may make some people more likely to actually show up for interviews. Compensation rates vary by the area and the amount of time that you expect respondents to participate. You may be able to get people to participate in a short interview on demand (say, 5–10 minutes) without anything more than thanks in return. If you want to have people sit down for an interview or a focus group for an hour, you may need to provide $20–30 worth of compensation—possibly in the form of a popular gift card. Of course, the rates and expectations for compensating respondents will vary in different countries and communities.

Of course, providing compensation may create some biases in itself. If you promise compensation, people for whom the compensation represents a significant amount of money may be more likely to participate. People with sufficient disposable income that the offered compensation is not significant may be less likely to participate. As a result, you may stack the deck toward interview subjects with specific characteristics. Of course, compensation also increases the cost of each of the interviews. With compensation, you no longer only have to worry about paying for a skilled interviewer. Of course, now you do have to budget for compensation payment for each respondent.

Conducting Interviews

Once you have selected the interview subjects, your attention can turn to the actual interview period itself. The decision to implement either a structured, unstructured, or semi-structured interview will potentially influence the entire interview experience. Regardless of your choice of interview type, there are a few guidelines for conducting interviews that remain important.

First and foremost, it is essential that interview respondents be comfortable in the environment of the interview. If you are conducting interviews standing outside of a train station in the heat of the afternoon as people are in a hurry to get back to their homes, they are likely to provide as short an answer as possible (even if they have agreed to participate in the interview in the first place—which may be unlikely). Even in environments where people can be out of the elements, an environment that is unclean or disorganized may make respondents uncomfortable. Be prepared for the environment of the interview to change; as with the beginning of a rainstorm. You should plan for comfort, as discussed earlier, but you have to be prepared to make changes in the conduct of the interviews if the conditions unexpectedly change.

The need to keep interview respondents comfortable extends to the conduct of the interviewer him- or herself. Skilled interviewers are able to keep people at ease through the entire interview process. This is some of what makes famous interviewers on television the subject of such attention. The best interviewers turn interviews into conversations in which the respondents are comfortable talking. The result is the sort of frank dialogue that provides the best data. Of course, it is still important to keep to the script and provide a consistent environment across different interviews. The interview experience should be as consistent from respondent to respondent as possible.

Documenting Interviews

An important part of the interview process is actually recording the responses. There are a variety of options you can take. Two approaches are more popular in public affairs— audio recording and note taking. Each of these approaches has its own strengths and weaknesses. A key part of documenting interviews, though, starts before the respondent answers even the first question.

Interview Codes

It is vitally important that you keep track of all of your interviews. You will need to be able to organize your data in various ways, including the date of the interview, the identity or organizational affiliation of the respondent, the identity of the interviewer, and other information about the interview itself. These basic bits of information about the interview are called **INTERVIEW CODES** and represent the equivalent of meta-data for the interviews— just as MP3 and other digital music files save ancillary information to the music itself. As you may have noticed, MP3 files can keep track of the name of the artist, the name of the song, the name of the album, etc. This information is stored in the meta-data in the sense that it is not part of the actual music. Similarly, interview codes provide some summary data for the interview but are not the core data of the interview—which consists of the respondent's statements. It is important to differentiate interview codes—which identify the context of the interview—from substantive codes that involve the substance of the responses the interviewer records. Substantive codes are the subject of a later chapter on the process of "coding."

The specific interview codes you need will depend on your specific research project. It may be important to know the time of day, location, or gender of the respondent in an interview. In many cases, though, none of these are of central importance. If you are conducting interviews at the train station for the amenity research project, you will likely want to know the time of day of the interview. Riders in the morning may be different than riders in the afternoon—especially if you are more likely to catch people waiting for trains than those who have arrived at their final destination. At some point (possibly using the techniques we discuss later in the book), you can compare the morning interviews to the afternoon interviews if you are suspicious that there are differences. This is only possible if you have kept the time of the interview (even approximate) in the interview codes.

In public affairs research, we recommend the following codes as a starting point. First, you will always want to record the date of the interview in any protocol with interviews on multiple dates. If there are changes in the world relevant to your research question, you will want to know which interviews happen before or after this event. In the NHH research, if there is a disaster event in the community you are studying in the middle of your protocol, you will need to know which interviews happened before or after that event. The event itself may influence the responses of your interview respondents. To understand the responses later, you will need this context. This sort of disruptive event does not happen often in research protocols, but you will want to be prepared in case that it does.

The second set of interview codes you will want to record are interviewer characteristics. The easiest way to do this is just to track the name of the interviewer. You will be able to reconstruct the interviewer's age, level of training, and race later (or whatever interviewer characteristics are relevant for your research). There is some research suggesting that respondents are less likely to provide certain answers to interviewers of specific genders or races. For example, you are less likely to hear people describe women in negative ways if the interviewer is female. If this is an important part of your research project, you will want to know the gender of the interviewer. This is not a primary concern in most public management research but there is another characteristic that you will definitely want to track: level of training. If you have multiple interviewers with different levels of training, they may be implementing the survey questions in different ways. With highly structured interviews, this may be less of a problem (unless one interviewer is implementing the structured protocol in a loosely structured way). It could be that one interviewer is providing prompts and explanations while another is not. If you have tracked the identity of the interviewer, you will be able to check whether one interviewer reports responses that are much more detailed and thorough than others. Only if you recorded the interview codes can you later investigate why.

Note Taking

The simplest form of note taking involves writing down notes as the respondent answers questions. Such notes can take many forms depending on the degree of structure in the interview protocol. In a highly structured interview, this may be as simple as marking down which of the response options to close-ended questions a respondent chooses. It may even be as simple as circling the chosen response. In highly structured interviews with close-ended questions, the interview resembles a survey in which the person recording the answers happens to be an interviewer rather than the respondent him- or herself.

In relatively unstructured interviews, the process is much more complicated. Even with close-ended questions, an unstructured protocol with branching questions can lead to complications in recording responses. Where the question order changes from interview to interview, the difficulty of recording the answers increases. The interviewer will need to be careful jumping from question to question to record answers to all of the core questions.

In unstructured (or semi-structured) interviews with open-ended questions, the interviewer has to be quite careful in recording responses. It is often difficult or impossible to record every word that a respondent offers following a question. The result is a need to take careful notes. It would be appropriate to provide some training on note taking for interviewers in this case. You cannot likely train people in a full shorthand system for a research project, but you may provide some key shortcuts for commonly repeated words or concepts. Even a dozen or so shorthand replacements for common names or concepts can remarkably speed up note taking.

Note taking is easy to implement but has its dangers. The greatest danger is that note taking may misrepresent, or miss completely, a key response by the interview respondent. If the interviewer is only able to capture a fraction of the responses, it may be that the important part of the response falls between the cracks. If the interviewer uses shorthand or some other strategy for summarizing responses, it may be difficult to reconstruct the original responses months, or even days, after the interview itself.

In a situation where you rely on taking notes, two strategies may help support your analysis of the data later in the process. First, you should return to your notes as soon as possible after the interview. It is best if you can return to the notes on the same day as the interview. You can transcribe the interview notes to eliminate anything that will be hard to understand later (shorthand, sloppy handwriting, etc.). You can also produce a short memo summarizing what you see as the key notes. It is easiest to produce this initial summary memo if the interview itself is fresh in your mind. This memo may serve to jog your memory when you return to the data weeks or months later in the analysis phase.

A second strategy is to take your notes (transcribed to use entire words and sentences rather than shorthand) back to the interview subject. You can ask the interview respondent if the interview notes represent his or her intent in the various answers. Of course, this is only possible if you have access to your interview respondents at a later point in time. This is more often the case with elite interviews than with mass interviews. The respondent can confirm his or her intent or point out where note taking may have generated errors.

Recording

The most popular alternative to note taking is to record the interview. One can record the interview with either video or audio recording devices. For public affairs research, an inexpensive audio recorder is generally sufficient. One can find a digital audio recorder with remarkable quality for less than $100. You only need to use more expensive recording devices (like video recording) if the technology is essential to your research question. Child psychologists may need to videotape play sessions, for example. If you are deeply concerned that nonverbal responses are important to your interview (like smirks, smiles, eye rolling, etc.), you can use video recording techniques. You should not feel obligated to use the most expensive available technology if there is no specific reason to do so, though.

Recording seems like an easy choice given that it provides a highly accurate account of the interview. However, there are some reasons that recording may not be an option or would cause additional problems for your research project. First, some interview respondents are reluctant to be recorded. Some individuals may become less open and more reserved in answering questions if they know that their answers are being recorded in detail. This is particularly a problem with public officials who may feel that recorded statements are more likely to be used against them later. Second, recording requires a certain amount of technology. You will need to develop plans for what happens if the recorder fails in the middle of the interview. If you are lucky, the recorder will fail in a way that will be obvious (an audible click indicating that it has stopped, the recording light going out, etc.). However, you want to consider how you will handle finding out only later that the interview you conducted was not actually recorded because the recorder failed in a nonobvious way (including having quiet respondents whose voice is just the right tone for the microphone to not pick up their voice).

Recording also raises the possibility of transcribing the interviews. It is generally easier to analyze interviews that are in some textual form. You can transcribe a recorded interview by creating a document that recounts every word in the response. With some research questions, you may even want to record pauses, audible sighs, or other non-word utterances. The result will be a text you can analyze (a topic I reserve for later chapters). This process can take a great deal of effort. Software packages that automatically translate audio files into text are notoriously unreliable despite dramatic improvements over the past decade. If you were to transcribe interviews from the NHH interviews about disaster recovery, the respondents are likely to use a variety of acronyms and similar short names of agencies. The automatic transcription software will not realize that the phonetic "fee maa" is actually FEMA. It will instead replace the term with the closest guess it can make. In any case, you will have to read back through any software transcribed interview to ensure accuracy.

Transcription services are available to provide human-assistant transcription. These services often mix an initial pass through software transcription with a follow-up human transcription process to fix errors. Even here, the human transcriber will not know jargon associated with a specific field. They are likely to know FEMA but may not know what an EMC is (as an example of a field-specific jargon term). This will require a read through by a team member even if there has been a human transcription phase. These services can also be quite expensive and time consuming. The prices vary with the number of speakers (how many interviewers? How many respondents?) in each recording and the length of the recording. Of course, the more interviews, the more expensive the service will be. Even a modest interview protocol including 20 interviews of about 30–60 minutes each will cost thousands of dollars to transcribe and may take a week or two of time.

If your project has the resources to transcribe or hire such a service, it can be a great help. However, this is not always an option for short projects or ones without large budgets.

Ethics and Interviews

The previous sections have reviewed how to carry out an interview protocol. The discussion focused on how one can conduct interviews. This final section will grapple with serious questions of how one ought to conduct interviews. Specifically, this section will consider the obligations that we, as researchers, have to the respondents in our interview protocols. This section will discuss standards of ethical conduct when it comes to interview protocol.

Informed Consent and Interviews

One might wonder why a discussion of the ethics of interviews is so important. Interviews do not involve violence, and people rarely see them as risky activities (though we will see soon how there can be risks). For some readers, then, ethics are not an obvious concern. However, we have an obligation as researchers to respect the rights of the subjects of our research. This means being careful with how we collect and analyze data. We must treat people in our research—including respondents, interviewers, team members, funding agencies, etc.—with proper respect. For the purposes of interview research, the primary obligation is to ensure that the respondents provide **INFORMED CONSENT** to participate in the research project.

The term "informed consent" is tricky but of paramount importance in research. Consent is a cornerstone of many ethical theories. For research purposes, it is essential that every participant in a research protocol consent to his or her participation in whatever specific form it takes in the research project. This implies that you have to be extremely careful to explain what participation means to a respondent. This is where the notion of being informed comes in. The respondents have to be fully informed as to the nature of their participation.

The importance of informed consent implies that there are some cases that require a great deal of care. Situations where informed consent will be difficult to obtain or is suspect in nature require special safeguards. For example, one must take special precautions when conducting research on prisoners. This is a population that is detained and where there has been a history of abuse. For these reasons, additional safeguards are required to ensure that informed consent is present for any prisoners participating in a research project. Research on children is even more problematic. Children cannot give their own consent—in large part because they cannot be informed of what that consent entails. Parents can provide consent on behalf of their children, but this secondary nature of the consent creates additional concerns and warrants additional protections. Interestingly, there are often special exemptions from additional scrutiny for research conducted on children in classrooms where the research pertains to education, curriculum, and related materials. If you conduct research on populations like these where informed consent is difficult to ensure, you will need to investigate the rules for your specific community and organization about how to establish additional processes to ensure the safety of your participants.

Just telling someone that he will be part of an interview is not sufficient. Instead, you need to explain in great detail what his participation will include. You need to explain the purpose of the research project and the subject matter of the interviews. It is important that respondents know what they will (and will not) be discussing in the interview. You should also provide a sense of how long the interview will take. Of course, this is a guess, but you should provide a credible estimate of the length of time. Finally, you should provide contact information if the respondents have any follow-up questions about the research project or their rights as participants. Some research organizations require more information, but this establishes a bare minimum.

You should be prepared to document the informed consent of each participant. This generally consists of a consent form that lists all of the important information about the project and the signature of the respondent. You should then keep these signed forms safe if there are any questions about informed consent later in the project. Admittedly, this can be an inconvenience for the interviewer and the respondent. However, it is important to go through these processes out of respect for your respondents—whether they feel the forms are tedious at the time of the interview or not.

This means that part of planning the interview process itself is planning the process of obtaining informed consent. At a minimum, you must prepare forms for people to read and sign. This can be tricky for short interviews with a large number of respondents in a short period of time. You may also consider providing detailed information sheets to complement the consent forms and providing all of the material in advance for the respondent. Presumably, with additional time, the respondent will have a better chance to carefully consider his participation, and the informed consent will be more meaningful.

It is also important to note that informed consent is not a blank check for the research project. If someone has agreed to participate in the interview, she can change her mind at any time—in whole or in part. Consent is not something that the participant turns over when she signs the consent form. You must maintain the informed consent of the participants through the entire protocol. They have to know that they can quit at any time, and you must make accommodations for them to do so. This means that they can opt not to answer specific questions that make them uncomfortable or to simply end the interview at any time.

Interviews and Difficult Subjects

All of this attention to the rights of respondents may be curious to you. Why do we spend so much time and effort ensuring the rights of respondents to interviews? It is an ethical practice per se, but it is also important given the nature of interview research. It can be traumatic to talk about some subjects. This can be a form of harm to the participants if they feel coerced into discussing a subject with which they are not comfortable. With this in mind, it is particularly important to be careful when interviewing respondents about subjects that may be uncomfortable or can place the respondents at risk.

There are some areas of discussion that will rather obviously risk placing interview respondents in an uncomfortable position. Interviews about personal sexual experiences, traumatic events in one's life, or illegal activities may make interview respondents uncomfortable. Protocols on these subjects require additional scrutiny to ensure that the rights of the respondents are protected.

It can be difficult to tell what will be an uncomfortable subject for a respondent or what sort of subjects will put respondents at risk. Beyond the obvious cases listed above, seemingly innocuous subjects can become uncomfortable for some respondents—and unpredictably so. In the train station interviews, one may include a question about where people are parked. This would seem innocuous. However, this question may create discomfort if there are respondents who are illegally parked. You may not have intended for the protocol to identify people who are illegally parked, but the question can result in that identification. This is where informed consent can provide some protection. If people are uncomfortable, they should be able to refuse to answer specific questions or to end the interview entirely. If the respondent had not anticipated that a question about her use of the train station would include a question about her parking, she can decide when the question is asked that she would like to skip that question.

In public affairs research, the boundaries of interview research can be tricky. If you are interviewing public officials about the operations of their offices, the answers may be of interest to political opponents or simply journalists looking to drive circulation with an embarrassing story about a local official. Questions about mundane subjects like trash pickup and human resource policies in the planning office can become politically contentious. You must remain sensitive to how just about any subject can become uncomfortable to public officials—even when they seem like innocuous subjects to you.

Anonymity, Confidentiality, and Data Protection

Preventing the release of the data resulting from an interview is an additional layer of protection for our research subjects. The goal is for any specific statement not to be traceable to a specific respondent by the readers or anyone outside of the research team. You can see how important this can become in situations where the answers a person provides can create risk for the respondent. If one of your respondents in the train station survey indicated that he had parked illegally, it does not present a risk to that person if it is not possible to identify who it was specifically who had said this. **DATA PROTECTION** involves the steps taken to protect the data that respondents have provided after the data collection effort is complete.

The strongest form of protection is **ANONYMITY**. Anonymity involves data where any link between the identity of a respondent and the data she provided is absent. If the train station interviews never recorded who was interviewed at any given time, the interviews are anonymous. The interviewer does not know the identity of the respondent, and no one can later figure out who it was that provide a specific set of responses. It is important to emphasize that the absence of a link between the identity of the respondent and the data must be absolute. If even the interviewer knows who the respondent is, the protocol is not anonymous.

True anonymity is quite rare in public affairs research—especially with elite respondents. If you are interviewing people because of their expertise in a specific field, you likely know the identity of the respondent. Anonymity is even lost if the respondent provides answers that make it possible to identify himself. If in the course of the NHH interviews on disaster recovery, a respondent refers to his superiors in the national Red Cross office, the data are now identified. The protocol itself may not have required a respondent to identify himself, but he may do so accidentally or knowingly.

CONFIDENTIALITY is a lower standard for data protection. Confidentiality only requires that any link between a respondent and his or her responses be protected from release and known only to the research team. You could assign each respondent a specific identification number. The research team can keep track of which respondent is number 100 and which is number 150. If you never release the list linking respondents to their identification number, the responses are considered confidential. All that anyone will ever know is that respondent #150 provided a series of answers to the questions. As with anonymity, confidentiality can be lost if a respondent provides answers that identify him- or herself. If you never release the data from interviews, then confidentiality is possible as long as whatever is released is not linkable to a specific respondent (even if members of the research team know who said what).

The standards of anonymity and confidentiality are important as part of how you process your data after collection but, sometimes, before analysis. These standards focus your attention on protecting respondents from preventable risks. This typically means eliminating all identifying references that one can. If your data are anonymous to begin with, this is easy. No identifying linkages exist for you to have to worry about. If your protocol was based on confidentiality, though, you have to plan for how to process the data to eliminate any unnecessary identifying references.

The first step in eliminating identifying information is creating nonidentifiable codes for each of the respondents. You may have already created these as a simple system to index your interview data. The key is taking these codes and replacing all references to a specific respondent with their respective codes. If the only identifying information is a single question in the interview or in the interview codes, this can be a simple process. If individuals refer to each other in the middle of the interview, this can be much more challenging. In the NHH interview example, you may want to replace references to the Red Cross with a code such as "organization #12." This is a simple way to sever identifying linkages. However, you may have to go through every interview and replace every reference to the Red Cross with the same code. Otherwise, people reading the data may be able to piece together who "organization #12" was using clues in the references other people make.

Of course, breaking the identifying linkages changes the nature of the data. Reading interviews with all of the people and organization replaced with codes may eliminate important contextual information necessary to understand the responses offered. It may make a difference in reading a statement whether you know which organization is the Red Cross and which is not. It may not be possible to move beyond confidentiality for

NHH and retain data with any interesting information—especially if the identity of the actors is central to what your research question. Mass interviews related to the train station project are probably easier to scrub of identifying information. You probably don't need to know anyone's name in that project. Even if you kept a person's name so that you did not interview the same person twice, you can destroy the data with names as soon as you complete interviews. This may require deleting a file with the list of names or it may mean taking a black marker to physically obscure the written names.

Conclusion

Interviews are a popular component of public affairs evaluation and research. The simplicity of the techniques and the breadth of questions interviews can address make the technique an important part of any researchers' toolkit. However, the familiarity of interviews does not mean that the research technique is easy. One must take great care to design an effective and ethical interview protocol. This chapter has provided you with the basic skills you need to add this popular tool to your repertoire.

Suggested Reading

There are many resources to help you build on this foundation for conducting careful interview studies. I recommend you first turn to Weiss's masterful *Learning from Strangers*. This book focuses on developing basic skills as an interviewer through many specific examples of interview transcripts. The book is quite accessible and can serve as an excellent starting point for anyone who wants to learn more about interviews.

The subject of question wording has occupied the attention of social scientists for many years—but mostly those who write survey instruments rather than interviews. An interesting starting point for question design is Wills's *Cognitive Interviewing*. This technique uses interviews as a means to prepare effective questions for surveys. The advice, then, can support the development of interview protocols as well as surveys. A more technical treatment is available in Tourangeau et al.'s *The Psychology of the Survey Response*. This is also a book that focuses mostly on survey questions (privileging, for example, close-ended questions in a highly structured protocol) but provides a state-of-the-art review of the potential pitfalls in question design. The examples largely focus on health questionnaires—but the exploration of the processes through which people answer questions is valuable.

The administration of focus groups has been the subject of specific attention. I recommend Krueger and Casey's book *Focus Groups* as a general introduction. While most of the advice on interviews is applicable to focus groups, this book provides a detailed discussion of the concerns specific to focus groups. Based on decades of experience with focus groups, this is a superb place to start before you consider implementing your own focus group protocol.

Vocabulary

ANONYMITY—A data protection plan that involves having nothing to tie the identity of a respondent to his or her responses.

CLOSE-ENDED QUESTIONS—A question for which the respondent is asked to choose among a small number of responses.

CONFIDENTIALITY—A data protection plan that involves restricting access to all information that can link respondents to his or her responses.

DATA PROTECTION—A plan for controlling the release of data from your research project—typically to ensure the protection of the participants in your project.

ELITE RESPONDENTS—Respondents in a research protocol who possess specific expertise in the subject matter of the survey.

FOCUS GROUP—An interview protocol that includes multiple interview respondents simultaneously (often 5–10 participants).

HYBRID QUESTION—A question in which respondents are offered a short list of potential responses and at least one that allows him or her to add his or her own answer.

INFORMED CONSENT—The obligation researchers have to ensure that participants understand the risks present in their participation and that participants will only continue to participate if they choose to.

INTERVIEW CODES—A set of codes describing each interview and the participant (or participants) in that interview.

JARGON—Specialized language used by members of a specific community—often including acronyms, shorthand terms, etc.

MASS RESPONDENTS—Respondents who possess no particular expertise in the area of the survey.

OPEN-ENDED QUESTIONS—Questions where respondents are free to provide responses using any approach they wish.

SOCIAL DESIRABILITY BIAS—A bias built into question where respondents may change their answers to meet the perceived expectations of the interviewer.

STRUCTURED INTERVIEWS—Interviews in which the question wording and order is highly prescribed.

Flashcards
& MCQs

Useful
Websites

Review Questions

- What distinguishes structured, semi-structured, and unstructured interview protocols?
- Name three interview codes that you should always include.
- What distinguishes anonymity from confidentiality in an interview protocol?

Discussion Questions

■   If doing elite interviews for the housing case study, what sort of jargon terms might you be able to use in questions that you could not use with a mass interview protocol?

■   What are the sources of ambiguity in the following question: "How often have you seen a doctor in the past year?"

■   Under what conditions would you want to use a highly structured interview protocol for the train station research project? When would you want to use an unstructured approach?

■   Unstructured protocols are more common with elite interviews. Why might this be the case?

CHAPTER 10

Field Research

Learning Objectives

✓ Understand the basic logic of data collection in a field setting
✓ Develop a plan for document collection from a field setting
✓ Conduct participant observation in a field setting including detailed note taking

Cases in Research

Case A—National Helping Hands

Disaster locations are complex and confusing. The director of National Helping Hands (NHH) is not convinced that reading reports of activities or interviewing people long after the event is going to tell the whole story of disaster recovery. Instead, she would like someone to collect data on location of the disaster event itself. Her hope is that data collected on site will be richer and more reliable than after-the-fact recollections or rationalizations documented later as after-action reports. Of course, collecting data at the site of the disaster presents its own challenges.

Case B—Grover's Corner Department of Transportation

If you want to know what challenges that users of public transportation face, there is no substitute for using the services themselves. While interviews and surveys can provide valuable information regarding services that the users of your public transportation system would like to see at their train stops, visiting the train stop itself could provide invaluable data. A visit to the train station can provide insight into how people behave while they are waiting for the train, which existing facilities they use, and how long people tend to wait. Simply observing the direction from which people are entering the train station may raise questions about the availability of legal parking, as well as ethical concerns about how to address suspected illegal parking.

The Logic of Field Research

Many research techniques create a great deal of distance between the researcher and the subject of research. If you conduct interviews, you often take people out of their natural settings to conduct the interviews. The interview may involve questions about activities that took place weeks or months (even years) earlier. This separation creates specific challenges. Similarly, a survey may take weeks or months to get into the field and may be filled out in a number of environments quite removed from the activity of interest. This separation of research from the subject of study has led to the development of techniques for data collection with a close connection to the research subject. The goal is to conduct research in a setting that is as close as possible to the natural setting of the research problem.

Field research involves the collection of data from a specific location related to the subject of study. If one wants to study how people use public transportation, it is irresponsible not to visit transit locations. It is essential that you understand the basics of the services you are researching. You want a strong operational sense of what goes on. In some settings, such an operational sense can be hard to get. In the NHH case, the research focuses on disaster recovery. Some phases of recovery may involve dangerous or unstable locations (like locations that have recently flooded). Visiting these locations may not only be dangerous for you as a researcher, but you may get in the way of the people whose job it is to assist disaster victims. Just these two examples illustrate the promise and the complexity of field research.

Field research involves a unique set of skills. In many ways, a good field researcher has a skill set analogous to a tracker. A tracker tries to figure out where an animal has gone without actually observing the animal moving. Instead of simply watching the animal (probably because the animal passed through the area before the tracker arrived), the tracker has to look for evidence of where the animal traveled. A broken branch may provide evidence that an animal passed through the area and give a sense of direction (though it may have been broken by a different animal, a strong wind, natural decay, etc.—you can't always be sure). Tracks in soft dirt may provide more conclusive evidence.

Example Public Affairs Research Sites

A public school
A community health clinic
A public park or playground
A community receiving development grants

A good tracker has to collect all of this indirect evidence to infer where the animal went. In field research, you will have to rely on similarly indirect evidence of the social processes you are studying.

You can think of people at the location of your research as constantly creating data without intending to do so. Just as an animal may pass through an area and leave tracks without thinking for a moment that these tracks will later indicate their presence, people may leave behind evidence of their attitudes and behaviors unintentionally. When someone writes a memo at work, he may choose words that convey his attitudes in ways he doesn't intend. People congregating in specific areas of a train station may not intend to announce a preference about where they want to stand waiting for a train, but a trained field researcher may note their behavior. The unintentional quality of the data may make the results less prone to manipulation by the research subject—but it also makes the interpretation of any piece of evidence potentially unclear.

The focus of this chapter is on techniques for collecting data from specific field locations like the disaster site in the NHH case or the train station. The chapter will discuss how to get access to these locations and the variety of sources of data useful at different sites. This chapter does not discuss the analysis of the data you collect from a research site—a topic discussed in later chapters.

Types of Data in Field Collection

Just as an animal can leave many different types of evidence of its passing, field research must look for different types of data in the field. One could conduct interviews, as we discussed in the previous chapter, but interviews can also take place later or off site. This chapter will instead focus on collecting the data in forms that were never intended to be data.

The most obvious data to collect are documents. When someone writes a memo, he is not intending for a field researcher to come along later and pore over the wording looking for implicit attitudes toward authority, etc. The field researcher who later reads the memo is not the intended audience. However, the memo may reveal a variety of assumptions of attitudes of the author. In the disaster recovery case, one may collect memos written during the event to assess which actors were considered part of the formalized response activities. Simply reading documents to see who was included in the "to" field of such memos may provide insight into this question.

One need not limit oneself to physical documents, though. Some field researchers specialize in directly observing activities at a site. The train station is not a site where there are many documents (though one could consider any handouts or posters at the site to be documents). However, a skilled observer might instead watch the behavior of users of the trains. Careful observation of where users stand waiting for the train, which seats they use (and which they do not), or the sorts of

Class Exercise: Imagine that you were a field researcher visiting your own classroom to study how college classes operate. What sort of remnants of class activities would you find?

material they carry with them onto the train could all be useful to a transportation manager. If you notice that there are long lines at the restrooms, you may learn something about the demand for that particular amenity. Noticing that many people are carrying coffee cups may also provide some useful evidence. What is relevant depends entirely on the research question at hand.

Challenges for Field Collection

Field research involves great potential and great challenges. The flexibility of field research to include a wide array of data also creates a great deal of uncertainty about on what a field researcher should focus. Should a field researcher at a disaster site focus on patterns of communication (who is talking to whom), the nature of the activities that each person is conducting (support services like feeding other actors vs. actively participating in search and rescue activities), or nonverbal aspects of communication (who is deferring to whom)? It is not always clear going onto a site what it is on which you should focus. The artistry of field research is observing just the right patterns among all of the innumerable options present.

The flexibility of field research creates problems with replication of research. It is not at all clear—in fact, it is unlikely—that any two field researchers will focus on the same patterns at a site. If there is a formal collection of documents, this might not be much of a problem. If, however, the research relies on the personal observations of a field researcher, the observations may depend on which field researcher you send to the site. A person trained in an anthropological tradition of field research may focus on social interactions at the site. A person trained in organizational field research may focus on the decorations and informational posters placed around the site. Training may drive what you look at—which means, in this case, the results of the research depend on the identity of the researcher.

Finally, field research calls for a fine balance between involvement of the researcher in the site or community of interest and separation that may be useful for external critical judgment. A popular variant of field research techniques is **PARTICIPANT OBSERVATION**. The paradox of participant observation is embedded in its name. Field researchers are both asked to participate in social processes at a site and observe those processes. At a disaster site, one may be asked to assist with the organization of disaster response activities while one is also researching the response activities themselves. It would be fair to ask whether one can independently and critically assess the quality and nature of disaster response activities if you are part of those activities. Critics of field research allege that by being present on a site, the researcher may change the behavior of the people on the site itself. Again, this is less of a problem for formal document collection (where the documents were written without any researcher in mind) but can be quite a dilemma for the on-site observation of individual behavior. Simply put, the train riders may act differently at the train station if they notice that there is someone standing around watching people and writing notes on a clipboard. Furthermore, participating in the social processes at a site (say, by participating in disaster recovery services) may influence the judgment of the research.

Gaining Access to Research Sites

The first step in field research is gaining access to the field. Field researchers often choose this approach because of the closeness they feel between themselves and the site when they are in the field. Of course, this requires having access to the physical site. In some cases, access to the site may be trivial. If the site is a public location, there is nothing preventing you from accessing the site. Similarly, if the manager of the physical site has hired you, or you are studying a site where you work, you will not likely have problems getting access. However, if you are an outsider to the field location, you will need to seek access.

Gatekeepers and Access

Gaining access to a field site typically requires the permission of some person—a person we will call a **GATEKEEPER**. A gatekeeper may be a person with formal or legal authority to give you access to a site. Gaining access to a disaster response location may require legal permission from a person like an incident commander. If you wanted to study the Department of Transportation at its main office (rather than the presumably public train station), you might require formal permission of the office manager to even visit the location.

The process of gaining access begins with identifying the important gatekeeper. There is not always a single person who is an obvious gatekeeper. Instead, you may have to devote some time to figuring out who it is that can authorize your visit to the study location. You will need to start by contacting any person identified as a building manager or public information officer/press relations officer. It is seldom the case that you want to start your search for a gatekeeper by contacting the person who looks like he or she has the highest position on the location (like a chief executive officer, university president, etc.). Instead, look for a person whose job responsibilities include dealing with information requests from outside groups like journalists. These are the people who will not only be more likely to listen to your request; they will likely know the process for getting permission for your visit.

Once you have made contact, you must make your research plans clear to the potential gatekeeper. From an ethical standpoint (as discussed in the previous chapter), you will need the informed consent of the gatekeeper. This requires that the gatekeeper fully understand the nature of your request for access to the site, what you will be doing when you visit the site, and the implications that might be present for the organization. Transparency in your request will also reduce potential conflict when you arrive at the field site. If the gatekeeper knows who you are and what you are going to do (in as much detail as possible), he can deflect many questions or challenges to your presence. Gatekeepers are only capable of deflecting such conflict if they are aware of why you are doing the research and what you will be doing when you visit the location.

The difficulty of gaining access to a site varies widely depending on the nature of the site itself. If you are working for an organization, getting access to that organization's sites may not be a problem. Similarly, public locations are easy to access. However, you may find yourself wanting to research locations that present other challenges. In extreme cases, you may encounter resistance in your attempt to get permission to visit a site because such research would by risky. If the location is an active disaster site, the site itself may be dangerous. If the location is the site of an active flood, anyone present may be in danger—particularly people without proper training. Consider an extreme case: an active criminal investigation. A field researcher wandering around behind the infamous yellow tape would risk contaminating or destroying evidence, leaking information about the investigation, and overall just getting in the way of the law enforcement officials. Similar problems could be the case at the site of a disaster.

An active criminal investigation site is surely an extreme and exotic example. However, the example serves to illustrate why some people are reluctant to give field researchers access to their site. Without a gatekeeper on your side, you might look like just another distraction and bother by the people trying to work at the site. It is incumbent on you to recruit a gatekeeper by explaining what, exactly, you will do at the site and how what you do will not interfere with normal operations. Better yet, you may be able to argue that the resulting research will help improve the work being done at the site in the long run.

> **Class Exercise:** Again, consider the possibility of studying a college class as a research site. Who would you need to contact to get permission to conduct field research at your school?

Putting Knowledge into Practice: Cultivating Gatekeepers

At National Helping Hands (NHH), Mel knew that she wanted to conduct field research at a specific disaster site. This created some interesting challenges. She did not know where the next disaster would be. She did, though, know that there were some regions that were more likely to experience disasters in the next six months because the country was entering hurricane season. Without knowing where a hurricane would make landfall—if one even did—she sought contacts in a wide variety of actors. She contacted many regional directors for the areas of the country most likely to experience a disaster in the coming months. From this set, she identified a few actors who seemed most interested in working with NHH to conduct field research. At this point, she just had to wait for a disaster to occur in a region where she had a well-placed gatekeeper.

It turned out that it did not take long for her work developing a stable of gatekeepers to pay off. A hurricane emerged in the ocean and headed toward land. Mel contacted her gatekeepers in the likely affected areas and began the process of getting permission to conduct field research at the site of disaster response and recovery. This required the permission of local emergency management and law enforcement officials. However, Mel relied on her gatekeeper to help get her permission to conduct research on site and to recruit people for on-site interviews. It would have been tough for Mel to get this permission herself. However, with the help of her friend in the regional office, she was able to get access to the disaster site to conduct her research.

Rapport

Once you are on site, you need to develop a sense of **RAPPORT** with the people at the location. Rapport is your sense of connection with the people at the site you are studying. Your purpose in studying a site is to record behavior and other characteristics of a site. If the behavior of the people at the site changes because they notice that there is a strange outsider watching them, you will never see what would have happened at the site in the absence of your research. To avoid changing the nature of the behavior of the people at the site, you need to blend in and become a normal part of the location.

Anthropologists who employ field research techniques, often called **ETHNOGRAPHY** in those situations, face the greatest challenges in establishing rapport. You can imagine how hard it would be for a Caucasian graduate student from an Ivy League school to blend in among the native population of a Polynesian fishing community. If the ethnographer hopes to see how people behave in the village, he may instead find that the members of the village either avoid him or simply stop what they are doing and stare. By standing out so much, the researcher has undermined his own purpose for being on the site.

Field research in public affairs is not likely to encounter as dramatic a set of challenges as these sorts of anthropological ethnography. Still, it is important for field researchers to consider how they will blend in to the location enough that their presence will not disrupt the site. The most obvious consideration is clothing. If you visit a disaster site in a suit and tie, you are likely to stand out. The site is filled with people who are working in trying environments and generally wear clothes that make manual labor comfortable. On the other hand, if you visit an office where "business formal" is the dress code while wearing a short sleeve shirt and blue jeans, you will stand out. In both cases, standing out so dramatically from the local dress codes (or norms) will continually draw attention to your position as an outsider and reduce the chance that people will act normally around you. Even standing around and taking notes may draw attention to you and mark you as an outsider. For this reason, some field researchers avoid taking any notes or doing anything atypical that would draw attention to

Class Exercise: Once more, consider the possibility of studying a college class as a research site. Would you recommend a blending-in strategy or an insider introduction strategy? If you use an insider introduction, who could realistically put people in the class at ease? If you use a blending-in strategy, what could you do to blend in effectively as you take notes in a college classroom?

their presence. Others still take notes, but use small notepads or other devices to reduce how much they stand out. Your strategy for collecting data will need to be consistent with your rapport with people at the site.

The need to establish rapport can lead to two widely divergent strategies. You can seek to blend in as unobtrusively as possible (matching local attire, limiting behaviors that may seem odd like note taking, etc.). Alternatively, you can address the problem head-on and seek your gatekeeper's help. Instead of hiding what you are doing, you can directly address your role as researcher to the group with the help of some representative of the site you are studying. The representative (possibly the same person who serves as your gatekeeper) can introduce you to people on the site, explain your presence, and ask people to act normally. Of course, this makes your presence clear and runs the risk of putting people on edge. However, people may act in a manner closer to normal if they know that the researcher has the endorsement of one of their colleagues. Which strategy is better (try to blend in subtly or make your presence known with an insider endorsement) depends on the specific nature of the site.

Rapport and Objectivity

Efforts to establish rapport reveal a fundamental trade-off in field research. Rapport involves becoming a (likely, partial) member of the community that you are studying. Being a member of the community brings with it a number of advantages. You can rely on people within the community to be more frank with you and to let you travel freely throughout the site. This advantage comes at a price, though.

If you really become a member of the location community, you will find it difficult to step outside of the community to offer an objective description. You are a member now and may find it difficult to discuss any unflattering aspects of the location. In the NHH case, imagine that you had a gatekeeper who provided you access to the disaster site and vouched for you (reassuring people that you were conducting research and not trying to write some sort of "gotcha" journalistic story). In the process of observing activities on the site, you overhear the gatekeeper make a series of racist statements about some of the disaster victims. These statements could explain a pattern of behavior you have observed and may be important to your understanding of what is going on at the site. However, revealing that you overheard these statements would both embarrass the gatekeeper (possibly exposing him to legal or administrative action) and may cost you access to the site in the future. Naturally, if you embarrass your gatekeeper, you may lose access to the site. It would be a hard choice to either censor yourself and not reveal what you have heard or jeopardize the research project by losing access.

While this is a dramatic example (though by no means the most excruciating dilemma I have heard of in field research), it reveals a tension inherent in field research. The more that you are a

> **Class Exercise:** Imagine that you wanted to conduct field research in the teachers' break room at a local high school. What would be the danger of not establishing rapport? How might you go about establishing rapport with the teachers?

member of a group, the more you tie yourself to the group. These ties may start to limit what you are willing to report, or they may influence how you interpret the behaviors you observe. It may be hard to argue that you are observing a site objectively or even critically if you are a member of that group.

One could argue, though, that objectivity is not what we should seek anyway. Objectivity assumes a strict separation of a researcher from his or her research subject. Such separation is indeed jeopardized by becoming a member (even partially) of the group that you are studying. However, some knowledge may only be accessible as a member of a group. This is not limited to cases where a group is actively concealing some part of their behavior (like a group that carefully avoids using racist language around researchers—though the language is common when left to themselves). It may also be the case that certain behaviors are only understandable with the deep familiarity that comes with group membership. Proponents of such an approach suggest that where you stand may influence what you can know or understand. Separation and objectivity, then, prevents you from understanding some subjects that are only understandable from a specific standpoint. This argument is known as **STANDPOINT EPISTEMOLOGY**. Your willingness to blend into a group and become a member should depend on whether you adopt a standpoint epistemological perspective and believe that such membership is crucial to understanding what certain behavior means at your site.

Conducting Site-Based Research

Once you have access to your site, you need to have a strategy for collecting data. In this, field research can take on a variety of different forms. What you do when you are at the site will depend on this decision over the type of data you hope to collect.

On-Site Field Notes

The type of data most often associated with field research is observation. Of course, just watching what is going on at the site does not guarantee that you will generate useful data for purposes of answering research questions. How you observe and how you document what you observe are critical factors in effective field research.

The most common strategy for site observation is the writing of **FIELD NOTES**. Simply put, field notes are the field researcher's written record of his or her observations. These written notes become the data for future analysis. The purpose of field notes is clear. You cannot possibly remember all of what you observe. You need to take notes to remind yourself of the wide range of activities or remnants that you have seen in the field.

There are very few rules about how you write field notes. The content of the notes can range widely. You may include lists of items (e.g., the organizations identified on the clothing of people working at a disaster recovery site) or even draw pictures of what you see. You may even draw the arrangement of how people stand around in the train station. All of these sorts of notes are valid observations for inclusion in field notes.

It is natural to ask what you should observe at the site and what you should record from these observations. There are trivial answers to both questions. You should observe anything that is relevant to your research question. I doubt that is very helpful. Similarly, you should record anything and everything that is relevant to your research question. Of course, the relevance of anything you observe may not be obvious at the time. The best practice is to write down everything you can. Of course, if there are specific behaviors or phenomena that you know to look for based on your research question, you should record anything related. Trained and experienced field researchers will have both a repertoire of phenomena they like to look for and the practice to make extensive notes of their observations. An organizational field researcher will have experience in organizational settings and will emphasize a specific set of observations (possibly, cubicle decorations or office postings) while an anthropological ethnographer may emphasize social gatherings and interpersonal exchanges. Given the uncertainty over what may be relevant, it is generally in your interest to record as much and as varied information as possible.

The ability to record a wide range of observations comes with practice. As a novice field researcher, it is in your interest to practice observation and recording skills. You can turn everyday activities into opportunities to practice. You can ask yourself to observe what is going on as you wait for a table at a restaurant or at a party. Force yourself to observe the things that would normally pass below your attention. You might not normally observe which people are moving out of the way to let other people in the door or who is holding the door for whom. Look for opportunities to observe patterns that you have never questioned before. If, as many field researchers do, you have a small notebook, you can practice recording by writing down these notes. You can sprinkle these practice exercises in your notebook alongside incidental thoughts that come to you related to any ongoing research project.

The strongest recommendation for the formatting of research notes is to document the context of your notes extensively. Of course, you will need to indicate which site you are at when you take the notes. You will also want to indicate who you are (especially when part of a research team) and when you visited the site. These notes are critical to the later process of analyzing your notes. Remember, you will want to return to these notes later. If you have not carefully noted where and when you took any set of notes, it will be hard to put your notes in context. If you do document your notes, it is not clear when and where that was observed (or by whom). Without careful documentation of the researcher, time, and location, the notes are often useless. You should go so far as to repeat your indications of time, place, and researcher on each page of the field notes—just in case your pages of field notes are eventually separated.

Recent innovations in technology have made the process of creating field notes easier. Tablets, in particular, have made the recording and collection of field notes much easier. It is no longer the case that you have to carry large notebooks with you.

> **Class Exercise:** Take notes at some location where you sit for a time between classes. What challenges did you encounter in taking these field notes? Did people who took notes at different locations encounter different difficulties? Look at other students' notes. How easily can you interpret the notes they took?

You can have all of your notes with you in an easily portable tablet. You can then add to your notes with a stylus or any other favored form of input. If using an electronic device for recording your observations, you will want to develop a careful backup strategy. Regardless of this complication, tablets and voice recorders provide great opportunities for field note collection.

It is important to keep in mind that your strategy for taking notes may make you stand out at the research site. Taking notes on a notepad, talking into a voice recorder, or taking pictures can all seem peculiar to the people at the research site. As discussed earlier, people at a research site who know that they are being observed may change their behavior. At the very least, they may be less relaxed or candid with their actions and conversations. Some take the extreme measure of not writing any field notes or any obvious form of recordings (and take extensive notes as soon as they leave the research site). This approach runs the risk of the researcher forgetting a number of important observations—but it may be the only way to avoid sticking out too much. Others choose to use small and relatively unobtrusive methods for taking notes (small notepads or small tablets that are easily concealed). Your choice of field note recording strategy will depend on your skill set as a researcher as well as the nature of the location (and what sorts of behavior will seem peculiar).

On-Site Document Collection

In addition to taking notes of what you observe, you can collect documents and other evidence from the research site. Returning to our analogy of field research as tracking, many public affairs research projects involve locations containing documents. We are more likely to study administrative offices than distant villages. If public affairs locations are likely to contain many remnants in the form of documents, it behooves us to develop skills in the collection and analysis of these documents.

You can look for documents in a wide variety of locations. Memos sent to all or some members of an office represent an obvious example of a potentially interesting observation. The memo provides insight into what issues warrant attention within the office. If there is a memo to establish (or reinforce) the office dress code, it is clear that the dress code is the subject of some discussion and, potentially, conflict. If the memo has been targeted to a specific group within the office, the targeting choices may tell you something about the discussion of the dress code. Collecting these documents can provide important insight into the dynamics of the research location and can elaborate on what you noticed in your field notes.

It is important to take a broad view of what constitutes a document. You are likely to first think of paper documents like memos, manuals of standard operating procedures, or other sorts of formal paper documents. The transition to electronic documentation and the paperless office has moved some of these documents out of paper form but into electronic versions that mimic their previous paper analogues. Those are easy examples of documents. You should think more broadly, though. Posters on the walls are documents. Handwritten notes are documents. One can even consider decorations of an office or house as documents. Just about anything you can see (including photos taken from a location) can be considered documents.

Just as with field notes, you want to document the nature of each piece of evidence that you collect. You will want to collect similar information on your documents that you do with your field notes, but the nature of documents will make this tricky. You will want to record the location of the document (possibly including where, specifically, at a site that you found or were given the document), the date the document was received (which may be different than a date indicating when the document was created), the researcher who collected the document, and any other pertinent information. Adding "date collected" information may seem like overkill, but consider this example. Imagine that you are collecting an operating manual from one of the responding organizations during the NHH research project. If the manual is dated 2000, and the director gave you a copy of the manual in 2011, the discrepancy in dates could be informative. This may be an important document, but it has not been updated often. That is only obvious if you know that the manual was in force in 2011 (implied by being provided to you in 2011 by the manager of the site) while the document was dated a decade earlier. If you had not recorded the date received (and the context in which you received the manual), you might not have noticed this discrepancy. The manual might just end up in a pile of "old documents" that do not receive much attention.

To ensure that you have proper notes on documents (be they paper documents, pictures, etc.), you should create a standardized field note form for your documents. You can simply create a form that has space for you to write down your name (as researcher), location, date/time, any details on how you received or found the document, and the title or description of the document. This will allow you to consistently document your documents—as strange as that sounds. You should take care to ensure that these document descriptions remain attached to the physical document. Electronic documents are more of a challenge to document—though you can use **META-DATA** for this purpose in many document formats. Meta-data consist of the descriptions of data often embedded within electronic files. For example, the information about a band and song title embedded within an mp3 file is meta-data. Similarly, you can embed information about where documents were collected inside a file—possibly in locations like where the author information is stored (without changing the text of the document itself). A document found without a description of where, when, and by whom it was found will be of limited use.

Post-Visit Documentation

When you leave a research location, your work as a field researcher is not complete. There are a variety of tasks you will need to complete to make sure that your field work will be useful once you get to the analysis stage. For the most part, these tasks involve transforming your notes into a form that will make later analysis possible. We will also discuss some of the challenges to field research documentation that make the process fundamentally difficult.

Off-Site Field Summaries

The very phrase "field note" implies that these notes are taken in the field. It is hasty to conclude, though, that field notes only come from the location of a research project. However, it is often essential to review and summarize your notes from the field. These secondary review notes are **FIELD SUMMARIES**. The field summaries represent your integration of thoughts inspired by the observations of the day and your review of the notes you quickly took on site.

In some cases (say, if you were trying to conceal that you were taking notes on site at all), you will have only limited notes from the actual site. These limited notes are known as **JOT NOTES**. Quick notes like jot notes are likely hard to interpret—even by their original author. You will likely resort to forms of shorthand notation and abbreviations, rushed through barely legible writing, and the like. As a result, interpreting your jot notes later will be exceedingly difficult. In the extreme case, you will only have your memory. It should be obvious that you do not want to rely on your memory of a visit days, weeks, or months in the past. Instead you can record and synthesize your memory or jot notes into an off-site field note. The field summaries are a reliable means to record and systematize any site-based notes. These summaries also have the advantage of being sharable among a research team whereas jot notes (and, obviously, memory) will be difficult for research team members who were not at the site to understand.

Field summaries require documentation just as do the notes you have taken while in the field. The documentation of field summaries will help to define the context of the summaries. You will want to be able to reconstruct the context if you, or some other researcher, looks back at your summary at a later date. With a significant research project, you may need to look back at summaries from weeks or months earlier. Detailed notes will help you put the summaries in order (which visit occurred when) as well as organize the summaries of multiple locations or researchers. The summaries may even include initial themes that you see emerging from your own field notes (though we will take up the topic of analyzing themes from notes and summaries in a later chapter).

The summary of field notes is an important part of the field research process and should involve a significant investment of time. Accounts vary, but many field researchers recommend devoting three or more hours to summarizing field notes for every hour that you are actually in the field. This means that a full day in the field can require the rest of the week just to work on summaries and initial analysis. While this investment of time may seem like overkill at this point in the analysis, time invested in field summaries will pay off later in the analysis stage. While you may want to get back into the field immediately to take more notes, notes without summaries or summaries that you only get to days later can result in lost opportunities to clarify your notes—and, thus, lost opportunities for important observations.

In the immediate hours following a site visit, writing field summaries should focus largely on making sure that your notes are comprehensible to yourself and others (if on a team research project). At a trivial level, you will want to transcribe sloppily written notes into easily legible language. You can think about the words you used in the moment of jotting notes to consider whether a more appropriate term is available. If you summarize your notes quickly after you conduct the site visit, you will be able to recall the context of the notes and choose the language in your summary carefully—more carefully than you can in the heat of the moment while on site. You will likely start to notice themes emerging from your notes. You may observe behaviors or documents that represent groups or classes of objects that you want to give a general name. While your field observation of the train station may simply report on the people that you see, you may start to create categories in which you will place the people you observe. This is the point at which you move from data collection to data analysis. You need not hesitate to record your reactions to what you observe in your summary, but we will take up strategies for structured analysis of these types of data in a later chapter.

Challenges in Field Research Documentation

It may strike you as odd that this book spends so much space on the documentation of field research. We chose to devote almost as much space to documenting your notes as we do in providing guidance in how to conduct field research and write notes in the first place. This choice is quite deliberate. While the process of observation resembles an art developed through practice and defying simple description in a textbook, the process of documenting field research is an essential part of the process on which we can provide more definite guidelines. All of the practice and artistry in conducting field observations will be useless if you do not take care to document your notes carefully.

Careful documentation of field notes also serves to address one of the chief criticisms of field research—difficulties in replication and validation. Recall that the ability to replicate an analysis is often seen as a core component of social scientific research. If your research is reliable, anyone could follow your protocol and generate the same research results. Field research is particularly difficult to repeat—and, hence, to replicate. Conducting field research happens at a particular place at a particular time. Replication efforts may not have access to the same location and can't possibly occur at the same time. Multiple field researchers at a single site on a given day may give some amount of contemporaneous replication, but it is impossible for researchers to read your results and truly replicate them. At best, they can try to replicate the process elsewhere (or at a different time) to see if they degenerate consistent data. Careful documentation confirms the procedures followed on site and eases this replication, even if true replication is impossible.

> **Class Exercise:** Imagine that you read a paper whose results were based on field research in college classrooms. Of course you cannot observe the same classes at the same time as those observed as the basis for the article. However, you could replicate the observations at your own school. What sort of information would you need to see in the documentation of the original field notes to replicate the study on your campus?

Carefully documented field notes also help with the validation of the contents of the notes. Validation, confirmation that what you observe in the field happened as you observed it, is easier when you can be specific about where and when you recorded field notes. Detailed notes allow you to collate the field notes most easily with other sources of data to confirm events and provide additional information that may not have been observable at the time. For example, if field notes of the disaster recovery site included the names of all of the organizations represented on the site on a given day, carefully noting the date and location of the field notes would allow you to compare the field notes to other sources of data (like after-action reports) that may further confirm who was involved on a given day. Sloppy documentation may make it difficult to tell whether the external reports confirm or contradict what you observed on the site.

In brief, field research is vulnerable to accusations that observations are arbitrary and idiosyncratic. Extensive documentation helps to ensure that the conduct of observation is as systematic as possible. With careful documentation, other researchers can tell exactly what the field research process consisted of and how it was conducted. This allows the researchers greater opportunity to replicate the protocol and test the reliability of your findings. Careful documentation, then, is vital to confirming to basic scientific research principles and comes at no cost in flexibility for field observation.

Ethics and Field Research

Conducting field research raises important issues regarding the ethical treatment of research subjects. Recall from the previous chapter that two key components of the ethical treatment subjects are privacy (in terms of confidentiality or anonymity) and informed consent. Both of these norms of ethical research are problematic in field research and require great care.

Confidentiality and Anonymity in the Field

A chief advantage of field research is the involvement of the research in the field of practice or the actual social process under investigation. However, the personal nature of field research complicates the treatment of confidentiality and anonymity. As with in-person interview research, anonymity may be impossible. If you are familiar with the site (and if you aren't, the advantage of field research is lost), you are likely familiar with the people on the site. While you may carefully avoid recording identifying information on any person in your field notes, you will know who said and did what within your view. The identity of the actor will be known, at least, to you.

Confidentiality is less problematic in a field research setting but still requires great care. With confidentiality, the researcher's knowledge of the identity of people at the research site is not a problem. Problems can only arise if the identity of individuals at the research sites are released beyond the research team. The difficulty is in ensuring this secondary release of identifying data does not happen.

The personal nature of field notes predisposes field researchers to include identifying information in their field notes. It is often easier to refer to people by name with notes such as "Mr. Hernandez spoke to Mrs. Jones about training their volunteers to assist with shelter management" when observing the disaster recovery site. However, the release of this note will violate the confidentiality of these two actors on the disaster site.

Ensuring confidentiality requires careful handling of these field notes. A first step is to eliminate references to specific individuals when writing field summaries. Once you are off site, it will be much easier to summarize the notes in a way that scrubs out identifying information. It is possible, then, for you to release your field summaries without compromising the identities of the research subjects at the research location. The original field notes then have to be protected from release through protective storage (storage in some way that prevents anyone not on the research team from getting access to the notes) or destruction of the original notes that include identifying references.

The potential to destroy field notes possessing identifying information raises strong reactions from many field researchers. Our instinct is to preserve as much data as possible. Data, once destroyed, can never be re-created exactly. Furthermore, field summaries may lose important information if they are truly scrubbed of all identifying information. Once people at the site are reduced to "person #1312," you will never be able to reread the notes and think about how the person's identity influences behavior on the site. If Mr. Hernandez is a representative of the local Red Cross office asking Mrs. Jones, the local emergency manager, about training shelter volunteers, you may learn something about the relationships between nonprofit representative and government representatives. Once you have de-identified the notes in the summaries, the interactions between two unidentified people will not provide you the same information to notice important patterns. De-identification works against the richness of field data. However, strict IRBs will require exactly this treatment. Under such circumstances, it is essential that you analyze your field notes as carefully as possible before you have to destroy them or the identifying references.

Informed Consent in the Field

In some situations, you may not be too concerned about confidentiality because you never learn the identities of the people at your research site. The train station research project is an example of just this situation. You may never ask any person you see at the site for identifying information, avoiding problems related to confidentiality. However, the lack of contact raises thorny issues. If you do not have contact with each person on the site, they never have an opportunity to offer (or withhold) their consent to be a part of the research study. While public places provide no expectation of privacy, the legal restrictions of privacy do not necessarily override the responsibility of any scientific researcher to get the informed consent of all people involved in the study. Recall that the fundamental principle of informed consent is that it is not the researcher but the research subject who decides what constitutes risk. Without contacting each member of the research site, you are assuming that what you are doing represents no risk to the subject without her consultation. Frankly, most field research represents only minimal risk to research subjects (equivalent to the risks they face in the absence of the field researcher). Technically, though, we cannot assume this.

A related problem common to all field research is the difficulty of evaluating field research that uses a flexible protocol. One of the great strengths of field research is its flexibility. Field researchers do not know what they will observe or what they will collect from the research site. It is fair to ask then, is it possible to get informed consent to participate in a protocol without clear definitions of what will be observed or collected? Again, field research general presents minimal risk to the participants on the site (with the notable exception of the possibility of collecting potentially embarrassing information). However, it is not for the researcher to decide. Instead, the researcher must provide an accurate (but encompassing) definition of the protocol, the limits of what will be observed, and when and how the data will be protected to prevent embarrassment. This remains a thorny and unsettled issue for many IRBs.

Obligations to Other Actors

Research at a specific research site will also raise difficult questions about the obligations researchers have to people other than the subjects of our projects. The core question is this: what obligation do you have to report illegal or dangerous activities you observe while conducting research? The ethnographic literature is rife with (admittedly rare) cases of observing behaviors that are held to be moral unconscionable to the researcher and the home culture of the researcher. When studying in one village, a researcher observed a gang of men dragging a woman from a neighboring village out to the street. To the researcher, the gang's intention to rape the woman was clear. The researcher knew that to say or do anything would jeopardize her role as an unobtrusive observer of the culture. However, passively allowing such violence was morally suspect. To complicate matters, the researcher knew that such behavior was common before her arrival and would likely continue after she left. What good would she do by interfering in just this case?

The rape case is an extreme one and one you are unlikely to face in public affairs research. However, variations on the theme are common in field research. What should you do if you observe biased handling of cases at the disaster recovery site with people of color being treated differently than others? If you report it immediately, you are not likely to have the sort of access to the research site you hope for after it gets out that you blew a whistle. On the other hand, what moral obligation do you have to confront racism and report abusive behaviors? In the train station research, you may notice that a large number of people are coming from a direction where there is no legal parking. Are you obligated to report this behavior and in doing so open your research subjects to risks of being ticketed? These examples are not as extreme as the rape case, but they are the sort of moral quandaries you may very well confront in public affairs field research. As important as it is to consider our obligations to research subjects, we must also consider our obligations to all of those people affected by our research subjects as well.

Conclusion: Field Research in Evidence-Based Public Management

Field research is a subject that few public affairs research textbooks actually cover. It may be unfamiliar to you or your colleagues in public affairs organizations. However, this tool provides important opportunities for public affairs research and evaluation. Collecting data from a specific location provides an important grounded perspective to your research project.

The grounded nature of field research helps ensure that you do not miss important sources of information that are present in the practical experience of people at the research location. With other research tools, there is a physical distance between the data collector and the actual processes under investigation. Doing a survey of transportation location, users still leave the survey writer removed from the experiences of traveling on the train and the day-to-day experiences of the train users. Field research facilities and organizes the collection of data where the researcher can make sure that his or her research has a strong connection to the practical nature of whatever it is that he or she is studying.

Field research also provides a nice check against research findings that wander too far from practical experience later in the research process. The experiences of field researchers can inform the later analysis of data from a variety of data collection techniques. You are less likely to make unrealistic or grossly counterproductive recommendations based on research if some of that research involves a familiarity with the experiences at a research location.

The mantra for field research for evidence-based public management may simply be "keep it real."

Vocabulary

ETHNOGRAPHY—The application of field research techniques to study cultures, often cultures quite different than that of the researcher him- or herself.
FIELD NOTES—The field researcher's written record of his or her observations.
FIELD SUMMARIES—Summaries of field notes a researcher writes after leaving the site.
GATEKEEPER—A person who can allow access to a research site.
JOT NOTES—Minimalist field notes in situations where the researcher has decided that detailed note taking is inappropriate for the research setting.
META-DATA—Descriptions of data often included within electronic versions of the data themselves.
PARTICIPANT OBSERVATION—A research technique in which the investigator collects observational data about a research site while participating in the activities of the site.
RAPPORT—Sense of connection a researcher may develop with the people at the research site.
STANDPOINT EPISTEMOLOGY—the argument that some forms of knowledge are only understandable from a specific standpoint, typically as a member of a social group.

Suggested Readings

There is a large literature on field research—with most focusing on ethnographic techniques. This large literature offers a great deal of detailed advice and many examples of excellent field research practice. The challenge is often applying lessons from ethnographic techniques focused on the study of foreign cultures to issues more common in public affairs research.

DeWalt and DeWalt's *Participant Observation: A Guide for Fieldworkers* represents a superb introduction to field research for a general audience. This book focuses on the sorts of practices that you can apply in a broad range of settings, including those of concern to public managers. While, like the larger literature, the book does provide many exotic examples, the book also provides a strong foundation on which to build knowledge of fundamental field research skills.

Flashcards
& MCQs

Other more specific books provide insight into field research in organization settings—settings that are more likely to come up for public affairs researchers than remote villages. A good place to start is Neyland's *Organizational Ethnography*.

Useful
Websites

Some support exists of the analysis of specific sorts of field data as well. Prior's *Using Documents in Social Research* provides some tools for understanding the complexity of analyzing books. The focus of Prior's book is on the nature of documents and authorship at a rather abstract level, but the book raises important questions for field researchers.

Review Questions

- What distinguishes jot notes from other forms of field notes?
- Provide three examples of research sites and potential gatekeepers for each site.
- What is rapport, and why is it important for field researchers?

Discussion Questions

- Imagine that you were conducting field research at the housing department discussed in other chapters. You are using the waiting room of the housing office as your research site. What might you do to establish rapport with people in the waiting area? What mistakes would you want to avoid that would set you apart from the research subjects?

- What sort of guidelines would you use to decide whether your field research represented only minimal risk to research subjects in the case that you did not seek individual informed consent?

- Consider the syllabus for your current course. What does your class syllabus tell you about the nature of the class and the relationship between the instructor and the students? What limitations exist on the design of the syllabus? Is it fair to say that the instructor is the single author of the syllabus and that the book represents his or her attitudes about the class?

CHAPTER 11

Survey Data

Learning Objectives

✓ Identify the different types of questions used in survey research
✓ Be aware of the many threats to validity inherent to the survey research process
✓ Identify how the sampling strategy should be represented in the resulting data
✓ Identify factors to reduce sample attrition
✓ List benefits and weaknesses of each type of survey medium

Cases in Research

Case A—National Helping Hands

Ron and Jeremy are senior administrators with nonprofit organizations delivering goods and services to individuals in the flood-affected regions of the Yukon River Basin. They are interested in improving the routing of supplies by mapping demands. To do this, they team up with a renowned geographer named Jenna. Together they want to position their organizations to provide a happy ending for all the of the floods.

Case B—Dewey Independent School District

Ken and Larry are school principals of separate organizations in the Dewey Independent School District. After reading a good deal of organizational research, they come to the conclusion that the way schools are staffed might have an impact on student success. Together they are interested in identifying how they can improve student success through the human resources branch of their organizations.

Survey Data

Surveys are easily the dominant source of data for social science research. These range from the very complex instruments used in psychology to the simple comment cards that may be found on the tables of most dining establishments. From consumer feedback on the World Wide Web, to employment screening—it is difficult to get through a week these days without encountering some sort of survey. Often, these are undertaken in a haphazard fashion, and the resulting data—and the conclusions drawn from it—suffer as a result.

It should be noted at the outset of this chapter that one chapter in this book is not sufficient to prepare you to employ surveys as a valid tool in research—quite the opposite. This chapter is designed to acquaint the reader with a taste of the promise and peril that survey research provides.

To begin, survey research must begin with the development of research questions and measurable operationalizations of the concepts identified in the research questions. If you are not comfortable with these concepts at this point, we would urge you to review chapters 5 and 6 before proceeding. Once you have identified what you want to investigate and how you want to measure it, it is time to develop a survey and a survey administration plan. The distribution of a survey must be based on a sampling technique that provides adequate coverage of the phenomenon to be explored. Earlier in this textbook we discussed the concept of sample populations and frames, so we will not review that here. But it is important to note that, in order to draw reliable inference from an unknown population, rigorous sampling processes need to be developed and adhered to during the administration of a survey instrument.

Why to Survey

Survey research is primarily used to gather data from either participants in a system or consumers of a product that either does not exist in another form or are data that are not easily available. For example:

Federal and state agencies use electronic surveys to judge the level of customer satisfaction with services and information provided on the World Wide Web. In this case, the agency is able to compare the satisfaction data to changes in information and services to evaluate changes in the websites. The data collected through the electronic survey gives near real-time capacity for website evaluation and enhanced the value provided to the users. While there may be other measures the agency could use (perhaps counts of "hits" on the website or interviews), few offer the convenience or timeliness of the survey.

In June of 2011, a nonprofit organization sponsored a needs assessment survey of the Katanga slum in Kampala, Uganda. In this case, no data existed on the number of residents, population densities, gender distributions, or the like. Surveys were used to collect both descriptive data and to identify the importance of different types of community support. The nonprofit organization then used this information to draw a strategic plan to meet the needs of the residents in the area.

In 2001, a nonprofit organization was trying to identify promising practices to reduce violence in schools in the United States. While the researcher could find information about antiviolence programs from the Department of Education, all the violence data in the United States were collected by state agencies so the measures were different for each state. The organization surveyed school districts to create a measure of school violence that could be used to examine the effects of the various antiviolence programs.

Example 11.1—Getting the Information Necessary for a Decision

Jeremy has made note of the extremely high cost of shipping goods through the Yukon River Basin area and has been disappointed with the amount of goods coming back on the trucks. It has become obvious that they need a better management system to allocate resources to different areas based on need; however, the lack of reliable communications make it difficult to employ some of the newer "just-in-time" (JIT) material management principles. For the first part of the recovery effort, Jeremy and Ron have just been loading trucks with the same goods and sending them to the response sites. One of the volunteers, Jenna, happens to be a geographer and mentions to them that it would be easy to estimate the needs of the regions based on photographic records widely available through Google Maps™ if they had an idea of what the demand per household was for each area.

Armed with this information, Ron begins to develop a household level survey to identify the needs for the areas that have been affected by the flooding.

As you can see, there are many places where going straight to the source and asking a question is the best or only way to collect some data that may be very important in evaluating systems or organization outputs. While surveys are a good way to collect data, far too often they are undertaken without giving thought to the process or costs associated with this data collection technique. In this chapter, we present some general rules for question development, important things to remember for survey deployment, some techniques for collecting data, and general strengths and weaknesses of the process.

General Survey Rules

Survey question design is a complex subject that can have as many exceptions as there are rules. We are beginning this chapter talking about a few general rules of thumb, but remember that for every rule, there may be some good reasons to break them. Notwithstanding, we are going to go through a couple that remain sound advice and to help get you in the mindset of survey research.

Avoid Value-Laden Questions

One of the easiest ways to get into trouble with survey research is to make the mistake of using questions that have value statements in them. Look at the questions in Figure 11.1:

Healthy drinks like milk are better for children than empty. . .

A1) Calories provided by soda

O	O	O	O	O
Strongly Disagree	Disagree	Neutral	Agree	Strongly Agree

B1) Milk is a healthy drink for children

O	O	O	O	O
Strongly Disagree	Disagree	Neutral	Agree	Strongly Agree

B2) Soda is a healthy drink for children

O	O	O	O	O
Strongly Disagree	Disagree	Neutral	Agree	Strongly Agree

Question A1 asks the question: given that milk is good and soda is bad, is soda good? In contrast, Questions B1 and B2 simply ask if each is good. In the first question we have primed the respondent to provide an answer that is what we want while the second two capture the concept with somewhat less bias. This example leads to our second general rule.

No Double-Barreled Questions

In Figure 11.1, question 1A asks the reader to provide information about two different items in the same question. A question that asks about two different items but provides for only one answer is a double-barreled question and can skew the question results. Far better are the second and third questions that ask about each question separately.

Watch Out for Loaded Language

All words have meanings, and sometimes words can be used to frame issues. One obvious example in the United States is the policy debate about abortion. Supporters of legalized abortion frame the issue as women's rights, while opponents of legalized abortion frame the debate as one about the right to life. Each framing is powerful and if used inappropriately in a survey could easily bias results.

Avoid Jargon

Often, individuals who are collecting data about a given subject have far more expertise in the subject area than the general public. Using jargon in survey questions can serve to confuse or sometimes alienate respondents. If they cannot understand the question, they will either not respond to the survey or provide unreliable information. For example, The State of Texas uses a standardized test now called the STAAR test. If we were interested in how taxpayers felt about the use of this test to evaluate school districts, we would most likely want to use the term "standardized test" instead of STAAR test as the taxpayers who do not have children may not be familiar with this term.

> **Class Exercise:**
> Consider the survey statement to which respondents were asked to rank their agreement: "Guns kill people and should be banned." In what ways is this question "double barreled?" Nations ban firearms of all sorts but allow air rifles. Similarly, some limit all but double shot shotguns, while a few like the United States have private ownership of numerous types of firearms. How might this affect your evaluation of the question?
>
> If your discussion is limited to only the statement that they kill people and should be banned, you missed an earlier mistake. The word "gun" itself refers to several different classes of firearms that are readily distinguished around the globe. Many nations ban firearms of all sorts, but allow air rifles. Similarly, some limit all but double shot shotguns, while a few like the US have private ownership of numerous types of firearms. How might this effect your evaluation of the question?

> **Class Exercise:**
> Consider some of the more pressing issues in the news as of late (the economy, murder, religion, political parties), and identify some of the value-laden language that is presented in the news. Discuss how these statements might bias survey results.

Types of Survey Data

The basic components of any survey instrument—and the resulting data—are the questions used to gather the data. Before discussing the design of these questions, we will first review some of the more common elements of a survey instrument.

Indicator Variables

In order to make sense of the data during the analysis process, it is important to make sure that every factor of the survey design and data collection is reflected in the survey data. This is done by creating indicator variables that reflect each aspect. When this is done, we would encourage the reader to make sure that the identifiers are numeric, as unnecessarily mixing numbers and characters may cause problems with manipulating the data during analysis. Additionally, the inclusion of these indicators should be built into the data collection process so as to not take up respondent time that is better spent on collecting data. For example, surveys can be produced with unique numbers on them. Dates, locations, and the like can either be automated into the software or completed by the surveyor before or after the survey is completed.

The first and most important is a unique case identifier. This is simply the process of issuing a unique identification code to each case in the data set. If you are collecting data from individuals, each individual should have a unique identification number. It may be tempting to use some available number for this, but this practice may cause problems down the road, so it is better to simply use consecutive numbering as you go.

Next, each layer of the sample needs to have a unique identifier. So if the survey is being deployed across different organizations, you will need a separate code for each. Similarly, if you are sampling across jurisdictions such as States of Counties in the United States, the FIPS code (Federal Information Processing Standard—a unique code issued by the U.S. government that identifies every region in the country) should be included with each observation. Also, surveys that span time through multiple waves need to have a code for that as well. When spatial distribution is important for the data application, coding for the spatial locations should be included. Often, GIS codes are great for this.

In addition to indicators for data analysis, surveys should include indicators used for diagnostics. Each observation in the data set should have a unique number that will link it to the physical survey used for data collection. This is paramount when cleansing the data before analysis. If you do not have a way to link observations back to the physical instrument, there is no way to double check suspicious values in the data.

Also for diagnostic purposes, survey data should include a code to represent the individuals who collected the data if survey teams are used, or for mode of deployment for surveys that use combinations of electronic, phone, mail, and live distribution.

Example 11.2—Ensuring the Indicator Variables Work with the Deployment Plan

Ron and Jenna have decided that if they could see where the areas of demand were for goods and services throughout the affected area, it would be easier to deliver goods in the most efficient manner. Jenna suggests that the easiest way to do this is to stratify the sample by geographic blocks, then plot the mean demand for services across those blocks. "This approach bares it all," she claims. To do this, they decide exactly what this survey will need in terms of indicator variables. Jenna argues that collecting the exact GPS coordinates would provide the greatest flexibility for later analysis. Ron suggests that this will require too much work. For each survey, the surveyor will need to log both the latitude and longitude. To start, this means that they will have to be able to use equipment that will provide such information, and then the resulting data will have to be collapsed in the analysis phase on two dimensions. Can you think of a way to improve upon this method?

Your answer should be that they could use unique codes for each "block" of the grid and simply use this indicator to identify the stratification in the sample. By carefully developing the grid system, they can avoid a great deal of work in the collection and analysis portion of the survey process.

Open-Ended Questions

The most popular, yet often least useful, question in survey research is the open-ended question. These are questions that ask a question and do not impart any structure on how the question is answered. Probably the most often used open-ended question is *why*. While open-ended questions offer the greatest promise for variance in responses, the open-ended nature of the question complicates the process of coding the data and using it later on. Often, open-ended questions are a signal of a poorly designed survey instrument.

Example 11.3—Using Standard Identifiers

Larry and Ken want to collect data from all the schools they can so they can match the information they find about administrative structure with some commonly available outcome variables for the schools and with census information to provide statistical control. Ken suggests that one thing they must do is include the FIPS code since the unit of analysis will be the school. By doing this, the data they collect may be matched to a host of available governmental data.

If an open-ended question is used, it means that an individual is going to have to iteratively recode all the answers until some sort of usable data are the result. While many statistical packages offer functions that will aid in this process, the long and short of the matter is that the more handling the data require, the greater the risk of error in the data.

Likert-Type Questions

Surveys often contain sets of questions that ask for the respondent's agreement or feeling for a statement. These are commonly (and incorrectly) referred to as Likert Scale Questions. For example, a researcher may be interested in a respondent's agreement with a policy or position. In this case, she may employ a question such as in Figure 11.2:

Research Methodology is the best course in our

1) Program's curriculum.

O	O	O	O	O
Strongly Disagree	Disagree	Neutral	Agree	Strongly Agree

While this type of question may yield some valuable information, the researcher has neglected to include some options in the response. For example, it may be that the respondent has not taken the course so they have no opinion or not enough information on which to base a response. By neglecting a category for "not applicable," the respondent is left to either (a) respond neutral, (b) not answer the question, or (c) guess. Often, when the researcher limits the options for response in an effort to force an opinion, he unintentionally obscures the meaning of the responses obtained. When evaluating a question of this sort, it is important to not only think about the question wording and the options for response, but to also think about what a nonresponse is going to mean. Additionally, nonresponse means that the observation is useless. Survey research is an expensive endeavor, and it is important to not drive up the cost of viable observations through poor questions. More importantly, it is critical to not create response bias in the sample by doing the same. Similarly, some researchers will exclude the neutral category on this type of scale to "force" a position. This practice can be both good and bad, and it is important to evaluate a priori what effects this might have on the resulting data.

At the outset, we referred to this as a Likert-type question as a true Likert item in a scale is designed as an additive scale built to capture some underlying question. Thinking back to Figure 11.1, if the intent is to capture feelings about the subject of Research Methodology, we could design a series of questions and use the sum value of the responses to represent the value for that concept. This sort of scale design is a field of practice itself, and the psychometric literature is replete with research about scaling, numbers of response categories, and the like. A great benefit to the voluminous research in this particular field is that banks of questions that have been tested for validity exist across a diverse array of topics. Many survey companies have these readily available, and there are volumes available in every university library that will provide these types of scales.

Grouped Data Questions

Because there are types of information that are difficult to put an exact figure to, or that respondents might be reluctant to report, surveys often ask questions that require the respondent to choose answers that correspond to grouped data. Most frequently, these questions deal with matters of money but may also be used for age, education, or counts (for example, number of sexual partners or individuals living in a household).

Grouped response questions can enhance question **RESPONSE RATES** as often, individuals may not want to divulge exactly how old they are or how much money they make. Conversely, they may also artificially truncate data so as to limit the utility of the resulting data. Income is a very good example of this. Many surveys are developed that look like the one in Figure 11.3:

21) How much money do you make each year?

O	$1,000	to	$10,000
O	$11,000	to	$20,000
O	$21,000	to	$30,000
O	$31,000	to	$40,000
O	$41,000	to	$50,000
O	$51,000	to	$60,000
O	$61,000	to	$70,000
O	$71,000	to	$80,000
O	$81,000	to	$90,000
O	$91,000	to	$100,000
O		>	$100,000

The question above might be suitable *if* we are sure that those individuals who make over $100,000 a year do not make significantly more and do not represent a majority of the population. Similarly, this question could create several challenges if the $10,000 interval is not sufficiently small enough to create meaningful variation in the data. It is important to ensure that the groupings used in the questionnaire are compatible with both the hypotheses you intend to answer with the data and with the distribution of the variable in the sample population.

A similar problem can be created if the intervals are appropriate, yet the cut points for the groupings are not compatible with the phenomenon being investigated. Such an example is evidenced in the literature about private handgun ownership in the United States. A well-published set of papers and books have examined the effect of laws regulating private citizens carrying firearms. To accomplish this, the seminal authors in the debate employ U.S. Census data. The Census groups age categories in 10-year blocks (e.g., 11–20, 21–30), yet the highest rate of firearm homicide occurs in males ages 18 to 24. By splitting this population in the data, the control effect of having the variable in the model is compromised. Logically, grouping half of the "prime suspects" with children ages 10 to 18, and the other half with those 25 to 30, the researchers cannot really "control" for the age effect because the effect to be controlled for is created by males 18–24.

While this section has focused on numerical groupings, any survey data that uses grouped data for reporting purposes must be thoroughly scrutinized to ensure the assumptions of the research are suitable to the data obtained.

Single and Multiple Response Questions

Almost every survey has some set of questions where the respondent is asked to "check the box," or "mark all that apply." These questions are typically used to record categorical data but may also be used to record ordinal data and continuous data. Typical applications are for nominal variables such as gender, race, ethnicity, sexual preference, religious beliefs, or the like. While some of these types of questions seem straightforward (such as gender), often they can create as many problems in response as they might solve in time.

Collecting data on national race can be problematic in countries with diverse populations like the United States, while in more homogeneous populations like Canada it presents less of a problem. On a national level in the United States, it may not be problematic to lump Hawaiians, Filipinos, and individuals from places like Guam and Micronesia into one category as together they comprise such a small percentage of the population. Conversely, if a study were being performed in the Philippine Islands, it would be important to break down the options to include many of the more typical ethnicities within that diverse population. In the United States, there are similar problems with the Hispanic ethnicity, which often includes several groups with remarkably diverse cultures and preferences.

Continuous Data Questions

By this point in the book, it should be obvious that continuous data always provide a researcher with the greatest latitude in approach for analysis. While this is generally true, the collection of accurate continuous data in survey research has a few problems that make it sometimes more difficult than it is worth. Paramount in this is that respondents often do not know the number you may be asking.

It is usually easy for an individual to remember her age with precision; however, the more the developed world moves to e-commerce, the less easy it is for an individual to give an exact figure to personal revenues and expenditures. Similarly, questions that inquire about quantities that change quickly, like customers in a store or cars parked on a street, may suffer from unintentional bias. For example, if you were asked on the street how old a family member was, would you be able to provide an exact age? Or if you were asked how many times you visited a business that you frequent over the last six months, could you be accurate? There are many times where when presented with questions like this, responses will be skewed toward respondent bias. Frequently, by providing ranges, a researcher can trade precision for accuracy. That is not to say that continuous data cannot be collected through survey research. And as survey research transitions toward electronic media, respondents can more frequently locate accurate answers as they have the luxury to take surveys in home, the office, and even on handheld devices.

Survey Techniques

As we mentioned earlier, survey research is a vast and complex field. While most individuals who employ surveys for data collection will never master all of the intricacies of the endeavor, there are some common applications of advanced techniques that are pretty handy to keep in mind.

Embedded Experiments

One way to increase the usefulness of survey research is to move beyond the parochial question and answer approach by embedding tests of knowledge about subjects or creating variance in questions to test the change in response.

There are two ways to use a survey to find out how knowledgeable a respondent is on a subject: you can ask, or you can test. Sometimes there is value in doing both as the difference in these measures can reveal a great deal about an individual's perceptions. Because people do not want to feel unintelligent or uninformed, often they will report a greater expertise of knowledge about subjects they feel is important. In this case, it can be prudent to test what the actual knowledge is with a set of questions of increasing difficulty on the subject. With this in hand, the researcher is able to identify the bias. In a different vein, veiled knowledge tests in a survey can be useful tools to test the effects of media campaigns surrounding policy issues.

Example 11.4—Measuring Item Worth

Jeremy is interested in how to prioritize services for the flood-affected region. To assess this, he creates a bank of questions to tack on the end of the survey that aids him in the process. These questions are a bank of Likert Scale questions that ask the respondent if he would sell something for a given dollar amount. On each survey, the dollar amounts will vary. The questions are the following:

1. I would prefer the government give me $X instead of rebuilding my home
2. I would be willing to sell my land for $X

3. I would be willing to relocate for $X
4. I would be willing to sell my dog team for $X

    By varying the price for each item (X) to the willingness to sell the item, Jeremy is hoping to be able to do a cost analysis of providing support in these areas to simply relocating or compensating individuals for losses. When Jenna asks why he just doesn't ask how much they would take for each, Jeremy replies that he believes that her approach would lead to grossly inflated costs.

Second, we can create actual tests within a survey by using questions with embedded variables that vary across test forms. This approach is born out of the economics choice modeling literature and has become a standard technique for many survey designers. The basic concept is that a question is poised with some variable X embedded, and the respondent is asked to agree or disagree with the statement. It may be something as simple as asking the question "would you be willing to pay $X monthly for clean drinking water?" Then the surveys would have values from a range randomly inserted into the question. The resulting data provides variance on the cost and a dichotomous outcome for the response. While this technique is routinely used to put a value on nonmarket commodities, it can also be used to test any number of hypotheses.

Validity and Bias Tests

By this point, we would hope that the idea of collecting survey research data would give you pause as the first three sections were replete with the inherent problems associated with surveys. Fortunately, there are ways that a good survey designer can overcome some of these obstacles. The first approach to this was mentioned earlier. That is to use questions and batteries of questions that have had extensive validity testing done by other scholars. The second was to include multiple measures of constructs and compare the results of the multiple measurements.

Beyond that, the researcher may also use different versions of the same question across the survey sample to verify that question wording is not affecting the survey results. Let's return to question 1B from Figure 11.1 for a moment and examine this further.

The question asked the respondent to mark her level of agreement with the following statement: *Soda is a healthy drink for children*. While this question may seem innocuous at first glance, we are making a positive statement about soda and asking for agreement. We are able to examine if this wording is affecting the responses by simply splitting the sample into two groups and maintaining the wording on one group, while changing the wording to a negative statement in the second group. See Figure 11.4 for an example.

2v1) Soda is a healthy drink for children

O	O	O	O	O
Strongly Disagree	Disagree	Neutral	Agree	Strongly Agree

Coding	1	2	3	4	5

2v2) Soda is not a healthy drink for children

O	O	O	O	O
Strongly Disagree	Disagree	Neutral	Agree	Strongly Agree

Coding	1	2	3	4	5

Using these two questions and coding the data with a reverse coding system (as displayed in the figure) allows us to directly test the hypothesis that there is no bias resulting from the question wording. That is, with all else held constant, we would expect the median of question 2v1 to be equal to the median of question 2v2.

Question Location

Where a question is located in a survey is an often overlooked part of survey design, but it is not only very important in terms of response rate, it can also aid in validating measures in the survey.

Many surveys ask about information that is considered somewhat sensitive to the respondent. This might be asking about opinions on company management practices, opinions about superiors, or divulging personal information like salary, presence of functional or cognitive disabilities, status of infectious disease, or sexual and religious practices, to name just a few. Often, questions like these can lead a respondent to stop answering survey questions, and for that reason it is good practice to put information or questions that may cause consternation toward the back of the survey. This has two effects. First, it means that the survey will not create concern for the entire duration of the questionnaire. If the question is asked early, the respondent may stop responding early, or she may be vacillating on the question throughout the rest of the survey wondering how that information relates to the other questions and how the other questions might allow them to identify the respondent. By waiting until the end of the survey, the items answered before the troublesome question will not be answered under duress. Second, if the subject is sensitive enough to make the respondent quit answering questions, the researcher will at least have collected a majority of the data and it still may prove to be useful. In fact, the researcher may be able to glean information about all the people who quit responding at that question using the data collected earlier in the instrument.

Another aspect to question location is using location to test item responses. Often there are times where valid and reliable survey items to measure a concept of interest do not exist. In this case, there is no choice but to create some measures of this concept. One technique to help assess the veracity of the measure is to generate multiple measures of the concept and put them in different locations throughout the survey. When all the data have been collected, the researcher can use correlation analysis to assess the quality of the measures.

Survey Mediums

Most typically, surveys take one of four forms: in-person, telephone, mail, or electronic. Each of these mediums offer different advantages and disadvantages, and each should be weighed when considering how to implement a survey.

In-person surveys tend to be very expensive, time consuming, and may require training personnel on survey techniques. In-person surveys are very good when you know the location and availability of the survey sample, and those locations are not accessible by other techniques. Thus, if we wanted to collect data on individual attitudes of individuals in a given profession, we could deploy surveyors at an annual conference. Similarly, if we needed to collect data in Port-au-Prince, Haiti, we could not depend on phone, mail, or web service and would have to resort to using individuals. Using individuals also allows us to collect data like gender and race/ethnicity without having to ask about them. For surveys that have a locational component, having surveyors collect location information is far more accurate than asking a respondent to provide it.

Telephone surveys were at one time the gold standard of survey research in the United States. Because telephone directories provided convenient sample frames, developing the sample and implementing the survey was rather easy. In fact, numerous companies and universities have survey research centers that have call centers and trained operators who, for a price, will implement telephone surveys. Trends in landline ownership in the United States show a decrease in the number of households who have standard telephone service, and so the possibility of bias is being generated in the sample. Similarly, many of the developing nations in the world that are on the rise will never have universal landline ownership. Because cellular service is remarkably less expensive than building the infrastructure for landline phones, telephone surveys may never be an option in places like the Middle East, Africa, South America, and many island nations.

Mail surveys do not share the same potential for bias as do phone surveys; however, they are expensive, time consuming, and typically have a lower response rate than in-person or telephone surveys. One of the largest challenges with a mail survey is the time delay that results as a function of having to mail the survey. Typically, a researcher generates numbered surveys, records which number survey went to whom, and then can perform follow-up surveys to nonrespondents. This process is complex and can easily fall apart.

Electronic surveys are becoming more and more popular and can provide the benefits of a mail survey while greatly reducing the lag time caused by the postal service. Currently, electronic surveys take three forms. The first is where a survey is e-mailed to a respondent, and she completes a form and returns it. The second is where a unique link is sent to each respondent, and she enters her responses while the software codes who she is based on the unique link. Finally, there are electronic surveys that are simply web-hosted surveys where anyone may respond. Each of these formats provides strengths and weaknesses. In general, the major concern with electronic surveying is that it automatically excludes individuals who do not own personal computers from the sample. Advances are being made in this area with new software that is doing surveying via smart phone. Additionally, a number of studies on public opinion data indicate that this bias is not as problematic in general as it might seem at face. Similarly, when managers are employing surveys of organizational members, they will have knowledge of whether the organization provides electronic web access to the employees.

When choosing the medium for survey deployment, it is critical to evaluate the sample frame and think about who is going to be able to respond to the question based on how the question was asked. Obviously, the homeless are going to have problems with many of the indirect survey techniques. One might suspect that low income families may also have problems with electronic survey techniques.

Incentives

One technique for combating attrition in surveys is to provide a benefit to the respondents for completing the survey. This may take the form of money; however, it usually occurs as discounts, gift cards, or something similar. While these may improve the response rate, this practice can become very expensive. Additionally, at some value (and it is not easy to generalize where this pint is for everyone), you may begin to enter some ethical challenges. By offering an incentive to complete surveys, you are inherently affecting the mindset of the respondent. If the incentive becomes large enough, you may actually influence the responses given. For example, a $5 gift card to college students for responses on a public health survey may seem innocuous enough; however, there are places where that small sum of money can be a month's salary for the respondent. In this case, the respondent may be inclined to reveal information that is not in her best interest, or may be inclined to provide positive reports for the organization providing the money. There is a fine line between incentive and bribe, and this line represents the difference between objective data and purchased responses. A second alternative to incentives that has been pioneered by several private companies is engineered samples. Some companies have pools of respondents from which

> **Class Exercise:**
> As a group, identify two government agencies and two nonprofit organizations that provide services in your town. For each, think about which medium would be best for surveying 1) employees and 2) service recipients.

they can generate a population with most any required demographics. These organizations provide incentive structures that are separate for the surveys, so the instrument can have attached incentives without the exposure to some of the possible consequences.

Strengths of Survey Data

While there are several threats to the use of survey data, there are also almost as many ways to avert or nullify those threats. While ensuring the veracity of survey data may be difficult at times, it is also the only technique that allows the collection of certain types of data. For example, opinion data is very difficult to collect from observation or data generated from the process—and these types of data are critical to provide feedback to service delivery organizations.

Surveys may also be used to create "bridge data." That is to say, there are many data generating processes that exist in general, but often data that result from a project or process may not always be sufficient to reliably test hypotheses. Survey data can be used to supplement or even connect existing data through the use of indicator variables that link the two data sets.

Surveys are also a very quick way of collecting data. While this statement may seem contradictory at first blush, it is possible to deploy surveys to get real-time data far more quickly that a researcher can collect institutional data or interview data. A good example of this is in disaster research performed in post-event disaster affected areas. At one point, it was at least possible to get institutional data from Port au Prince, Haiti; however, the earthquake that hit the region destroyed most all of the areas that hosted such data. Immediately following the disaster—and even now—data collection by survey is by far the most efficient way to collect data from this area.

Weaknesses of Survey Data Collection

In previous sections, we have discussed the problems that are associated with individual parts of survey instruments; but beyond sample design and item development, there are still problems that are inherent to survey data collection. While these are not fatal flaws, without attention to them, the utility of survey data can be greatly diminished.

Response Rates

A good survey is administered with a plan for distribution based on some logic to collect a representative sample. In most cases, surveys are deployed to selected respondents based on a probabilistic design meant to ensure that the sample values generated from the instrument are reflexive of the underlying population parameters. Even with great care in the planning process, nonresponse can greatly affect the validity of the data in terms of the relationship to the underlying population. We always expect some degree of non-response to a survey questionnaire, and current literature on the subject demonstrate that response rates as low as 25% may still yield reliable results; but the validity of the data is only one of the major problems associated with low response rates.

In addition to affecting the validity of the sample parameters, survey response rates may have a huge impact on the utility of the data and the costs associated with generating the data. Even to produce a mail survey by hand, a researcher is going to spend at least a dollar a survey for postage and supplies. A 25% response rate means that the actual cost of each observation is going to quadruple, so for a sample of n = 100, instead of costing $100, the researcher will have to expend $400.

Response rates also affect what can be done with the data. While small samples are fine for generating descriptive statistics, the more complex the hypotheses that underlie the data collection process, the more degrees of freedom that are required to address them. There are many factors that can affect the response rate of a survey. It is important to balance these factors when developing a survey research process. These include survey length, subject, sample frame, deployment medium, and incentives for completion.

Obviously, the longer a survey is (in terms of time for completion), the lower the response rate will be. For this reason, researchers are very careful about what and how many questions are added to any survey. The length in reference to the number of variables is not an absolute figure, though, as the deployment medium can also affect response.

Generally, the level of intimacy of contact between the respondent and survey administrator will play a role in the response rate. When there is no direct connection between the two (such as in Internet or mail surveys), the response rate will drop. Conversely, the response rate will improve somewhat when the survey is administered over the phone and even more so when the survey is done in person. Response rate may also be improved by using captive samples and subjects that are more salient to the respondent.

Surveys done in the workplace or that concern a subject of interest to the respondent will typically yield a higher response rate than general interest surveys done in the population at large. Salience and location can also be a double-edged sword, though, as some individuals will be hesitant to complete a survey that deals with sensitive subjects in a place where they perceive the answers may negatively impact them. Thus, a survey in an organization dealing with the use of illicit substances may not yield the most valid results or highest response rates.

Item Nonresponse

When a respondent does not answer a question on a survey, the entire observation may be useless depending on how important that item was to the larger research. Additionally, respondents often will stop answering survey questions altogether if they perceive that the material is too sensitive. For this reason, survey design needs to also account for the effect each individual question may have on a respondent. More sensitive subjects are typically reserved for the end of a questionnaire to provide the greatest likelihood that the respondent will answer as many of the items as possible. Specifically, questions about income, illicit activities, or shunned preferences should be reserved for the last sections of a survey. In this way it is possible to garner the most information about even those individuals who choose to avoid answering these questions.

Attrition

Often, research is interested in effects over time. Using survey research to investigate these types of questions involves administering surveys to fixed panels of respondents over time, but time can change many things in addition to individual perception. Individuals may relocate, pass away, or simply lose interest in participating in the project. It is important to take the natural attrition into account when panel survey designs are going to be employed.

Test Effect

Simply asking someone a question about something will have some effect on her response to that question. If the respondent has had no opinion on a subject, asking her about the subject signals that the importance of the subject may be greater than she had first considered. This may, in turn, prompt her to reevaluate her prior beliefs. In application, this small bit of bias in imperfect measures may not be of consequence; however, in cases where repeated measures are collected, there is the possibility for the effect to be compounded. A classic example of this is the Hawthorne effect discussed earlier in this book.

Ethical Considerations in Survey Research

No discussion of survey research is complete without a discussion about the ethical implications of collecting such data. First, many nations require training any time data is collected from individuals. This law does not just apply to university-based research, but to any office of government in the country where the law exists. In the United States, laws concerning human subjects experimentation is governed by an Institutional Review Board (IRB) within the organization. Even in places where IRB oversight is not required by law (such as with nonprofit organizations) it is good practice to familiarize yourself with IRB requirements by taking the free trainings offered online. Human subjects training not only help to prevent any legal ramifications that may result from unethical data collection or use, but it can also help to improve the quality of the data collected.

Often, respondents can be wary of providing information they perceive to be risky in some capacity. This may include revealing sensitive information about health or the use of illicit substances, but it may also simply be due to shirking behaviors in the workplace.

By following standard research practices of properly securing data, and building in mechanisms to the data collection processes that ensure either anonymity or confidentiality (these two are mutually exclusive) and clearly explaining these as part of an informed consent process, researchers will be able to get more accurate data. In organizations that are not governed by laws that pertain to human subjects data collection, these practices can ameliorate the likelihood of civil repercussions if the research has an unintentional negative impact on the respondent.

Similarly, there are times when deception must be used to measure an underlying concept on which respondents simply will not provide reliable data. Doing so can put a researcher in a position where he has a great deal of legal exposure should something go awry. For these reasons, it is a good practice to make sure that when deception is employed, the data collection process be followed by a debriefing that explains this to the respondent—offering the respondent a second opportunity to withdraw from the project.

Example 11.5—Who Can We Tell What?

Larry and Ken are pretty pleased with their findings in relation to organizational structure and student achievement in primary education, and want to share the results. Larry suggests making the data public so that anyone interested can also examine what they have found and have the opportunity to expand on it.

Ken disagrees. He points out that they have collected a great deal of sensitive data from school principals and that it would be easy for anyone who looked at the data to identify exactly who said what. He contends that making the data public could cost people their jobs and prevent them from being able to collect such data in the future.

Finally, the use of incentives is often employed in survey research to increase response rates. This practice has been demonstrated to reduce panel attrition and increase the response rate; however, it comes with a price. The use of incentives must be employed judiciously to ensure that the reward for participation does not exceed a material value to the respondent that would entice him to act in a manner that is in conflict with his self-interest. Importantly, this hypothetical value will vary in reference to the nature of the study (how much risk is involved) and the nature of the sample population (how vulnerable the population may be). Special care is necessary when the risks of divulging information are great, or when the sample population is compromised either cognitively or socially. When dealing with economically disadvantaged groups it can be difficult for a researcher to fully understand the value of goods to the respondent. Similarly, respondents that have not fully matured or have impairments to their cognitive abilities may not be able to competently weigh the relative benefits of incentives to the risks involved with participation. Researchers have an ethical responsibility to the subjects in research, and it is imperative not just for individual researchers but for all researchers that this trust be carefully guarded.

Flashcards
& MCQs

Useful
Websites

Vocabulary

RESPONSE RATE—The ratio of the number of surveys completed to those issued.
LIKERT-TYPE QUESTION—Survey questions that seek a respondent's concurrence with an objective or subjective statement using a multi-point scale. Most typically, the scale is based on five or seven points.
SURVEY ITEM—A measure of a single variable on a survey instrument.
SCALE—Data that result from a bank of questions that takes multiple measures on a complex concept.
SAMPLE FRAME—The operationalization of the hypothetical population being sampled.

Review Questions

- How can asking double-barreled questions bias survey data?
- Is it possible to test a question for wording to see if it is affecting responses?
- What are some disadvantages to collecting continuous data with a survey instrument?
- List thee concerns when collecting grouped data with a survey.

Discussion Questions

- How might the survey location impact the responses to question items?
- Identify four ways to overcome low survey response rates with an excessively long survey.
- In what circumstances would using excessive incentives with a vulnerable population be justified?
- What are some potential outcomes of violating respondent trust when doing survey research?

CHAPTER 12

Coding and Data Display

Learning Objectives

✓ Define coding as a strategy for data analysis
✓ Describe strategies for coding including individual and group coding
✓ Understand different strategies for data display including temporal, site, and theoretical displays

Cases in Research

Case A—National Helping Hands

Following the interviews and field research, the research project leader for National Helping Hands (NHH) finds herself with a great deal of data. Each interview has produced pages and pages of text on a wide range of subjects. Each site visit team brought back a wide range of information including documents collected from the locations and notes taken during their stay. In all, it looks like there are close to a thousand pages of notes for this research project. What she needs now is a strategy for analyzing these vast sources of data to provide insight into the role of nonprofit organizations in disaster recovery.

Case B—Springfield Housing Department

The Springfield Housing Department has conducted a series of interviews with its clients at four sites across the city. With little idea of what to look for, the department manager wants to address his core research question: "What barriers do our clients face when applying for housing assistance?" He wants to investigate this general question while also looking for patterns that may emerge from specific sites. What he needs now is a way to analyze the numerous interview responses to facilitate the comparison of the housing department sites and the challenges reported by clients at each location.

Coding Texts

It is often the case that after data collection, you will find yourself overwhelmed with the volume of material that you have collected. One researcher has called this the "10,000 page problem." The very purpose of data analysis is to reduce the complexity of the real world into usable information. If one simply reproduces the complexity of the real world, you have not actually done any useful work. To analyze data means to reduce the complexity of information to produce simple (or at least simpler) conclusions or answers to your research questions. One starting point to the process of reducing the complexity of your data is to use established coding strategies. This chapter will provide an introduction to coding procedures along with some strategies for analyzing coded data using data display techniques.

What Are Codes?

The goal of coding your data is to identify general patterns that emerge from the vast volumes of information you have generated. You can think of this process much like taking notes in a class lecture. Most of us are not capable of writing down every word that a lecturer utters. Instead, you take notes that select key phrases and information from the lecture. You may write down a key word or phrase that you want to remember. At times you may write down extended passages including formal definitions—but these tend to be rare in lecture. You may also draw small pictures to represent relationships between key concepts in a lecture. What one seldom does is simply transcribe the lecture verbatim.

Active note takers will even write down reactions and inspirations to the lecture. If a lecture introduces a concept like selection bias, an active lecturer might write down reactions such as "How often does this apply in the research that I conduct?" or "What can I do about this?" These comments inject your interests and perspectives into the material to which you are listening. The purpose is to go back to your notes, possibly as you study for an exam, and have a shorter, simpler representation of the lecture that boils down to what is most essential for you to remember.

The process of coding your data is much like taking notes on a lecture. You will take notes (with the notes called codes) on sources of data so that you can review your data quickly and search for the areas of the data on which you want to focus on at any given time, etc.

A **CODE** is a meaning or characteristic that you assign to a piece of data. The process of assigning meaning or defining the characteristics of a piece of data—**CODING**—is the essential starting point to data analysis.

What Types of Data Call for Coding?

In some sense, just about any data calls for coding. A survey with closed-response options requires respondents to code their own responses. The purpose of these closed-response options are the same as any other coding strategy—to create comparable and easily interpreted response options. Open-ended response questions in surveys do not interpret themselves, though. If you ask people to identify the most important problem the city faces, you will get a wide variety of responses, and many of these responses may be similar enough to group together. One respondent may say "jobs" while another says "unemployment." Chances are you want to count these two responses as equivalent. If you had used a closed-ended survey question, you may have even had a single option labeled "jobs/unemployment." Everyone who marked that single option would be assigned the same numerical code. With an open-ended survey question, you will have to group responses together on your own. This exercise is a classic example of coding.

Other types of data more obviously call for coding. In some interviews, people provide answers in natural language. Like with open-ended survey questions, you will have to assign meaning and characteristics to these responses. You will have to decide whether discussing "jobs" as a problem is equivalent to "unemployment." The richness of responses when people are allowed to speak for themselves provides many opportunities for attributing meaning and assigning characteristics. Rather than simply lumping terms like "jobs" and "unemployment" together, you may read the surrounding discussion to investigate whether respondents have subtly different meaning to these two terms. While the terms in isolation could be difficult to distinguish, in context you may see differences emerge. It could be that people who refer to "jobs" tend to discuss the problem in reference to specific friends and family who are having difficulty finding jobs while those who refer to "unemployment" discuss the problem in abstract and depersonalized terms. It could be that friends and families lose jobs while faceless other people experience unemployment.

The process of coding is not limited to interview texts. One could code meaning and descriptions to just about any source of data. If during a field visit one were to collect documents from the research site, one could code these documents. One could analyze photos or videos taken from the site in a similar way. The world is full of potential meanings that can reveal an underlying process of relevance to public managers in a variety of ways. Coding is the process of extracting or imposing meaning on the world around us.

Codes and the Unit of Analysis

With the diversity of potential types of media for coding, it is important to consider what it is, exactly, that one is coding. The correct answer depends on the nature of the research question one seeks to answer. If you have a photo of a number of people, one may study the photo as a whole ("How many people are waiting for the train?", "Where are people sitting while they wait for the train?"), or on each specific individual in the photo ("What did each person bring with him or her to the train station?").

Similarly, one could focus on different units for interviews. One could argue that every word is deliberately chosen and thus code individual words. Alternatively, one could focus on entire sentences as wholes. In written documents, one can focus on paragraphs, sections, or entire documents. Your choice of the unit of analysis will depend on your research question. Some researchers will focus on incredibly precise units of analysis—even counting the number of seconds one waits to respond to a question. If one's theoretical approach suggests that the answer to your research question operates on so small a scale, this may be appropriate. If, however, your research question and theoretical approach directs you to focus on the context of words or meanings that only emerge as part of entire sentences, then you will want to focus on that larger unit of analysis. In the end, you have to choose a unit of analysis that has the meanings and characteristics that you want to investigate. Some researchers refer to the basic units that they are studying as **CHUNKS**.

Types of Codes

We can start with two general phases of coding, each representing a different relationship between the code and the data source. Understanding the types of codes is essential to understanding how coding can be a tool for answering research questions in public affairs. Initial efforts to analyze the data will rely on descriptions of the text. Later analysis may start to group these descriptions together to identify patterns between the described elements. These coding approaches are known as descriptive and pattern coding, respectively.

Descriptive Coding

The first type of code is a **DESCRIPTIVE CODE**. Descriptive codes are uniform descriptive terms that a researcher assigns to material he or she is coding. One could describe many aspects of a chunk. As an initial part of your research, you will need to define the codes that you will use. We will discuss the development of this list in the next section. For now, just imagine that you have such a list at hand. Your purpose is to assign short descriptive terms to each chunk for easy reference later. Your aspiration is to later be able to gather all of the chunks that include similar topics.

Putting Knowledge into Practice: Descriptive Coding Partner Identification in Recovery Operations

The director of National Helping Hands has collected a wide variety of documents related to disaster recovery operations following some recent floods. These documents include news reports of recovery efforts, official documents related to these efforts, and follow-up reports called "after-action reports." She wants to know which nonprofits (and which types of nonprofits) are active in these recovery efforts. This requires coding this diverse set of documents to identify all the nonprofit participants. She reads through each document marking each mention of a nonprofit organization (possibly keeping a separate list of her own). For each document, she creates a roster of nonprofit actors involved. She also creates an overall list of all actors mentioned in any document. This reveals the diversity of nonprofit organizations in these recovery activities (within the limitations of the available sample of documents).

Description can be a complicated process. The key is using descriptions that are relevant to your research project. Sometimes descriptive codes are easy to implement. It is not too hard to identify the actor's names within a document (though you may sometimes find sources referring to actors by different names and will have to develop a strategy for reconciling these differences). Other descriptions may be more subjective. If you were studying public opinion related to a proposed local ordinance, you could conduct a series of interviews. You could then code the transcripts for positive, negative, or neutral statements related to the ordinance. If a respondent mentioned that the ordinance was potentially costly to the city, you could mark the passage with a negative code. However, there may be some uncertainty as to whether a statement is positive or negative. We will later discuss some techniques for assessing the subjectivity in codes.

One strict approach to descriptive coding, **IN VIVO CODING**, requires limiting codes to the specific language used within the original data source. If a respondent refers to "jobs" as a public problem, the code would need to be "jobs" and not combined under a general heading like "economics" or even "unemployment." This disciplined approach limits the potential for coders to read meaning into the original data that may not be there. On the other hand, in vivo coding may artificially distinguish codes that refer to what is best treated as a single subject. In vivo coding also limits the ability to link codes to the language of research questions because you are limited to the language of respondents—which may be less formal or less precise than a good research question.

The context of your codes will depend entirely on your substantive research question. While we cannot define all of the different types of codes that you may use, consider these examples of types of codes.

Attribute Codes: These codes refer to the attributes of the source of the data you are coding. You may have many basic attributes from the data collection sheets you generated for data management. For example, you may have recorded the name, position title, gender, age, site, or other attributes of interview subjects. These become attribute codes for data analysis purposes. If you wanted to look at all interview transcripts from people at a given site, the attribute code would allow you to quickly reference all of the relevant data.

Descriptive Codes: These codes refer to the topic raised within a data source. If an interview respondent discussed the challenges of getting reimbursed for disaster recovery activities, you may code that chunk as "financial" or "reimbursement" (or some other code motivated by your research question). This type of code is not limited to interview data. You could also code notes taken by field researchers based on the subject they are describing in their notes. If they describe the behavior of people in the waiting room at the housing office (are people sitting or pacing, etc.), you can code these notes as well. You could potentially code the field researcher's observations on the layout of the room or any other description that seems relevant. Within an audio, video, or photographic recording, you could use codes to describe the content of the record.

Valence/Magnitude Codes: You can step beyond descriptive coding to attribute meaning to aspects of the record. You could assign a value to statements as being positive or negative in relation to a subject. For example, if interview subjects from the housing office complain about their long waits in the lobby, you could code this as a negative report. A statement about the politeness of the people with whom the interview subject interacted in the office would be a positive report. You could go further to code the degree of positivity of negativity as the magnitude of a report. One could separately code mildly positive and negative responses ("The people at the front desk were helpful to me.") and strongly positive and negative responses ("I have never been treated so rudely in my life."). Magnitude codes can be as precise as you want—though you want to ensure reliable coding of magnitudes. We will discuss reliability of codes in the next section.

Pattern Coding

The second type of coding is **PATTERN CODING**. Pattern coding involves identifying relationships between elements within the coded data. This requires reading beyond the immediate data to inferences about these relationships. In some ways, pattern coding represents the coding of descriptive codes. Pattern codes can look for two different patterns within the (description) coded text. First, you can look for clusters of description codes. Clusters of codes are a method for collecting similar codes together for further analysis. Of course, what counts as similar depends on your research project.

Putting Knowledge into Practice: Pattern Coding Barriers to Housing Application Descriptive Code Clusters

After initial descriptive coding of the interviews with housing applicants, the manager wants to define the types of barriers that respondents report. The first step is to create a list of hypothesized clusters. The manager decides to focus on three initial clusters: (1) transportation barriers, (2) administrative barriers, and (3) personal barriers. The first barrier includes all references to difficulty traveling to or from the housing office. The second barrier involves complaints regarding the paperwork and procedures related to housing assistance. The final barrier involves statements regarding personal conflicts that make getting to the housing office difficult. Examples of the latter may include difficulties securing child care or getting off of work. The manager considers a fourth cluster—psychological barriers. The manager is concerned that people may be reluctant to apply for housing assistance out a sense of shame. Instead of including this as a fourth code, the manager includes an "uncategorized" code. The manager plans to go back following the pattern coding exercise to look at all of the "uncategorized" codes to look for clusters within this group—including psychological barriers or something completely unanticipated.

The second type of pattern code is a relationship code. These codes look for relationships between descriptive codes. This type of codes can accommodate a wide range of relationships. While clusters codes look for descriptions that are all of one type of phenomenon, relationship codes look for connections between different codes. For example, if you see an example of what you think may be a cause and effect, you may code it as such. These codes are considered preliminary and suggestive. These codes represent your reactions to the descriptive codes and the accounts included in the chunks you are coding.

Developing Codes

The examples of coding in the previous section took for granted that the research already has a set of codes ready to apply in a research project. Of course, one has to develop a list of codes just as one would develop a sample of interview subjects, write survey questions, or decide what documents to collect from a site. There are two predominant approaches to this process. This section will focus on theoretically directed processes for generating codes. This approach parallels deductive reasoning.

The starting point for developing codes is in the language of one's hypotheses or research questions. What are the key concepts that your research questions involve?

Putting Knowledge into Practice: Developing Codes Related to Types of Nonprofits in Disaster Recovery

The director of National Helping Hands is interested by the results of her initial assessment of nonprofit organizations active in disaster recovery. However, she feels that a long list of names is of limited use. She wants to look for patterns in the types of nonprofits that are active in the disaster recovery event. This requires identifying the types of nonprofit actors that interest her. In her previous work, she knows that there are nonprofits with primary affiliations to religious institutions such as Lutheran Disaster Response. One code that interests her, then, is religiously affiliated disaster nonprofits. Further brainstorming provides some other potentially interesting codes: local/nonlocal, disaster-focused nonprofits, service provided (housing, feeding/nutrition, employment, health, education, etc.). She notes that these codes are not mutually exclusive but will enable her to quickly find references to nonprofit organizations of specific types rather than having to look for specific nonprofit organizations.

Coding Strategies

The work of coding involves analyzing data sources and applying codes where they are appropriate. While this is a relatively simple operation, care and attention are vital to produce useful research. A well-designed process for coding your data will provide more consistent data. This data will then be more amenable to analysis. This section will discuss some specific strategies to ensure consistent codes amenable to later analysis.

Individual Coding Strategies

The first set of strategies involves individual coding. These are the approaches one can employ to ensure effective and consistent coding. The goal is to set up your coding procedure to ensure that you read every chunk in the same way, with the same care, and employing the same potential codes. The key is consistency. You want to code every piece of data with consistent rules.

A good coding process may start before you actually look at the data. Consistency in coding requires, at the very least, a consistent understanding of the codes themselves. If you change the meaning of the codes as you are reading, you will treat later chunks in a different manner. This compromises the consistency of coding. Of course, achieving perfect consistency in the meaning of codes is often difficult and may be impossible. We often use coding techniques when we want to understand concepts better (or the meaning of concepts in certain contexts). In these situations, it is natural that our understanding of concepts and the meaning of codes changes over time. Our goal though is to minimize these changes in most situations—especially avoidable changes.

To promote consistency in codes, it is best to invest a great deal of thought into defining your codes in as much detail as possible. This requires developing a set of codes along with a formal definition. It is best if you take the time to write out the definitions of each code. This exercise will force you to confront ambiguities in the codes and to take a stand on specific meanings. This process can supplement your brainstorming efforts. Where you identify incompatible definitions of a candidate code, you can split the code into two mutually exclusive codes. This exercise will both promote consistency in your codes and provide a more detailed set of codes from which to choose.

Once you have a code list with clear definitions, you can begin the actual coding process. How you code is largely a matter of individual style and workflow as well as the nature of the chunks you are coding. We will discuss some basic procedures for coding for three common types of chunks: interview transcripts, documents, and video. This discussion will provide simple strategies that one can implement with standard software or no software at all. The final section of this chapter will discuss how to use specially designed software for coding and data analysis.

Coding interview transcripts can use strategies similar to taking notes in a class. We recommend a split-page note-taking framework. In such a framework, you only print the data source on one side of the page. Typically, the right side of the page is left blank—possibly because of the preponderance of right handedness. It does not really matter which side you leave free, though. You can then number the chunks along the edge of your free space. Next to each chunk, you can list the codes that you feel apply (if any). The setup of the page should resemble Exhibit 12.1

Exhibit 12.1—Coding Interview Transcripts

Questioner—How did you get to the housing office to apply for assistance?

Respondent—I took the bus . . . and walked some of the way. [1]

Chunk [1]

Codes: mode (bus), mode (walk-in)

Questioner—Was it difficult to get to the office?

Respondent—Getting to the office was kinda' hard. I had to find care for my kids. I did not want to drag them along and then wait in the lobby. The office is in an odd place. The buses do not run near there. I had to catch two buses and then still walk to get here. [2]

Chunk [2]

Codes: barrier (child care), barrier (waiting time), barrier (bus stops), barrier (walking distance)

Notice in Exhibit 12.1 that you can apply multiple codes to a given chunk of data. In this case, the answer to a direct question about the difficulty of getting to the office generated four different codes. This raises the question of what the actual chunk size should be. In interviews, people rarely answer questions in easily identifiable paragraphs. The exhibit uses the entire response as a chunk. For some purposes, you may want to look at each sentence or even each word. The choice of chunk all depends on your theory and hypothesis. If you think that the choice of specific words is informative to your study, the word could be a good chunk size. If you think that sentences are the natural unit for your study, you can use sentences. It is always easier to aggregate up from codes applied to smaller chunks to larger chunks (say, from words to sentences) than it is to do the reverse. We have found it difficult to attribute meaning to words and sentences in isolation, so we tend to use clusters of sentences (responses) as the chunk. In other fields, other chunk sizes may be more common. Some scholars of psychology, for example, are intensely interested in the time (in seconds or smaller units) that people pause between answers or when they interrupt each other. In these studies, chunks may be much smaller units. The choice depends entirely on the questions you seek to answer.

The basic ideas behind coding interview transcripts are instructive for coding other types of media. The clearest analogue to interview transcripts is a formal document. This set would include any documents you collect on site or that you otherwise feel are relevant to your research. You may not want to change the format of documents to force them into a split-page format similar to what we recommend for coding interview transcripts. If you want to use a process as similar a possible, it may be possible to rotate the document 90 degrees and print it on one half of a printed page. Alternatively, you may create shorthand for your codes. For each chunk, you can write a small number indexing the chunk along with a brief notation indicating codes. If the margins of the document are generous, you can write a word or words in the margins themselves. If the margins are thin or you have many codes, you may need to number your codes or create alphanumeric representation code (e.g., "7" or BAR-CHLD to represent the barrier of child care needs). Such shorthand is easy to use but may make the codes harder to interpret later (especially by people who were not involved in coding earlier).

Coding videos has a number of differences. As a form of media that does not have a space you can reserve for written codes (even shorthand), you will need to create a separate document for storing your codes. The trick to coding video data is to create a correspondence between the specific code and a video chunk. Most often, this is done through the use of time codes. A time code is simply an indication of the starting time and ending time for a segment of the video. You can use these time codes to create chunks in what would otherwise be one continuous stream of video. These chunks do not need to be of uniform length or spaced uniformly through the video. Think of this strategy as defining scenes (as in a movie). Some scenes may be shorter or longer. The key is having the scenes be discrete units. In movies, this may involve having scenes broken up by the location of the events. For other types of videos, you can separate the chunks however you like. You can define the chunk (say, "from the 30 second mark to the 48 second mark") and then associate codes with this chunk. Typically, you will create a separate document that lists all of the chunks and any associated codes. The same logic holds for photos. While photos do not require time codes, they require some unique identifier for each photo (presuming each photo is a chunk) and a separate sheet linking the unique identifier to codes.

It is generally a good idea to set aside time when you have completed coding the specific series of chunks to write a summary memo. Memos provide a quick reference to the content of the data. You can include a summary list of the codes from the specific data source. You may move beyond a simple summary to include your reactions to the data overall, comparisons between this data source and other data sources, and thoughts about future research. The memos provide a nice starting point if you need to look back at the data without reading through each of the data sources themselves.

Group Coding Strategies

Larger projects will require the use of entire teams of coders for data analysis. Spreading the work over a number of people allows you to code a great deal more data in a shorter period of time than would otherwise be possible. However, having an entire team of coders requires taking special precautions. Again, the focus of the process is ensuring consistent coding across all of the data. The last section discussed steps to ensure consistency when just one person is coding the data. The challenge grows when trying to ensure consistency across multiple coders.

The basics of coding remain the same. Each coder acts as an individual coder. However, there are two steps you can take to promote consistency in a team coding environment: training and mid-stream team meetings.

Coder training is essential for group coding processes. In the case of individual coders, we recommended that you take great pains to define your codes. The team training exercises are the equivalent of group coding processes. Of course, defining the codes will still be essential. However, you now need to ensure that your code definitions are clearly and consistently understood by all of your coders. In addition to clear definitions, it is useful to provide as many examples as possible as well as training passages to test whether coders are employing the codes as you expect. It is best if you keep these training passages as similar as possible to the material you are coding without drawing them from your sample itself (because your training passage would get far more scrutiny than any other passages if they were singled out for use in training).

The need to gather all of the coders does not end following training and the beginning of actual coding activities. To ensure that your team of coders continues to use the same definition and to deal with problems that emerge in the coding process, it is best to have coding team meetings throughout the process. At these coding team meetings you can ask for problems that the coders are encountering. These problems may be in the coding management process (time management, paperwork, etc.) or ambiguities in the meaning of codes. This is a great time to listen to the coders to hear what difficulties they are having assigning codes to chunks. They can tell you whether they feel that there are important concepts for which they do not have a code or if they are using generic or miscellaneous codes where they feel new, specific codes are in order. The coders can also tell you if they are having difficulty deciding between two codes where both seem to apply to a given situation. This can help you update your definitions to clarify the meaning and use of codes. It helps that these meetings are also a time where you can disseminate any changes to coding procedures, code lists, or code definitions to all of your coders.

Reliability Assessment

The previous sections have discussed steps you can take to promote consistency in the coding process. While you should implement such strategies, they are no guarantee of consistency. Instead, you should also check the consistency of coding once the process is complete. This process is referred to as reliability assessment. For the most part, people use reliability assessment in group coding situations. They can assess inter-coder reliability—that is, whether different coders are identifying the same codes from the same passages.

There are many approaches to assessing inter-coder reliability. The simplest approach is percent agreement. The starting point is to have two coders analyze an identical passage or series of chunks. After each coder analyzes each chunk, you compare the codes they have assigned. For each coder, count the number of codes they applied that were also applied by the other coder. Each of these is an agreement. Then, count the number of codes applied by each that were not matched by the other coder. Each of these is a disagreement. You can calculate percent agreement with the following simple equation:

Percent Agreement = Agreements / Agreements + Disagreements

This approach to calculating reliability is simple but has some serious limitations. The approach works best when there are a small number of potential codes to apply. In the simplest case where you have one code to apply (or not) to every paragraph, the measure provides a nice summary of the agreement between two coders. This is the case with most codes that will eventually be part of a quantitative assessment—as discussed in future chapters. Typically, people want to see reliability in the 80–90% range with these conditions. However, as the number of codes increases, the number of potential disagreements increases. Sets of codes with fine distinctions make disagreement much more likely. The standards for such research are not lower (people still want close to 80% agreement), but these situations will likely require extensive training to prepare for consistent coding.

With projects in which there are sufficient resources, one can have two coders analyze every chunk and only retain those codes on which there is agreement. You should still conduct reliability assessments to see how many disagreements are present, but this approach provides a great deal of confidence in the codes you do use. If it is not possible to allocate two coders to every chunk, you should still choose a small sample on which to conduct such an assessment. This can represent only a small number of chunks or even 10% of the sample. You need to select enough to ensure confidence that the codes are applied reliably—or to redesign the process and retrain the coders until you can be confident.

Data Display Strategies

Fundamentals of Data Display

You can think of codes as an essential bridge between raw data (even 10,000 pages of raw data) and hypotheses. The real world is messy and confusing. It only reveals itself to researchers slowly and seldom directly. Instead, we have to look for meaning in messy data. Your hypotheses should be stated precisely and clearly. Coding translates raw data into a format in which you can compare your expectations to what you actually observe.

The resulting coded passages are useful as a means to test hypotheses. Each chunk is an observation and an opportunity to falsify your predictions about relationships. Even thoroughly coded texts are not easy to analyze. You still find yourself with pages and pages of text and associated codes. With codes in place, you can begin analysis of the data. The actual analysis should begin with an exploratory display of the data. This section will discuss a variety of strategies to display your codes in a way to facilitate hypothesis testing.

Summary Display

The starting point is to summarize your codes. You have a list of codes with which you have analyzed text. It is natural to first ask which, if any, of the codes were used in the analysis and with what frequency. You can start with summaries of text characteristics. If you have conducted interviews, you can provide simple summaries of the number of interviews with people with various characteristics. How many were men and how many were women? How many interviews did you conduct at each site? These are characteristics that you did not have to code chunk by chunk but are characteristics of entire interviews.

Exhibit 12.2—Summary of Housing Interviews

Total: 22 Interviews

Gender:

Female Interview Subject   17 Interviews
Male Interview Subject   5 Interviews

Site:

Site A   9 Interviews
Site B   6 Interviews
Site C   7 Interviews

Barriers mentioned:

Transportation	16 Interviews
Waiting time	4 Interviews
Paperwork difficulties	7 Interviews
Child care	14 Interviews
Time off of work	5 Interviews

The resulting summary can provide some insight into the subjects under study and provides the foundation on which many of the other data display techniques will be built.

It is important to note that there are serious limitations on what you can learn from these basic descriptions of the data. A sample of 22 interviews is small. If you had chosen 22 people off the street for questions about their political opinions, the answers would not provide a great deal of insight into the proportion of the greater public that holds specific opinions. Even if 11 people had said they supported increasing spending on education, you should be hesitant to suggest that 50% of the general public support the same. The proportions and frequencies of responses within such small samples should not be taken to provide clear evidence of proportions and frequencies in the general population.

However, there are some conclusions you can reach from even small samples. The most obvious is the existence of some opinion. For example, if a respondent mentions that he had a problem getting time off work to get to the agency, it is safe to conclude that this is a problem within the general population. You can't infer how frequently this problem occurs or whether it is more common than other problems. The results provide a view of the existence and range of responses. More detailed research questions about frequencies and ratios should be left to other research tools.

Site Display

Basic summaries can be useful, but there are other tools that can provide insight into more nuanced patterns within the data. In these cases, use displays to organize responses and visualize patterns. There are a wide variety of potential display strategies, but we will focus on a few that are particularly useful for public management research.

Public management research often involves the comparison of different offices or locations. If you want to compare different neighborhood offices or school buildings, you can break up the display of information along the lines of the sites you want to compare. The pattern of responses you discover when you consider responses site by site may reveal information suggestive of hypotheses and warrant further investigation.

Putting Knowledge into Practice: A Site Comparison of Housing Office Site

The housing manager wonders if the barriers that people encounter when applying for housing assistance vary based on the location of the offices themselves.

She wonders, specifically, if there are some offices where applicants face more barriers to transportation. Based on the basic summary of interview responses, she knows that there were between 6 and 9 interviews at each site. She decides to break down the barrier responses by site to see how many specific barriers are mentioned in interviews with clients at specific sites.

Site A	9 Interviews

Barriers mentioned:

Transportation	8 Interviews
Waiting time	4 Interviews
Paperwork difficulties	3 Interviews
Child care	5 Interviews
Time off of work	2 Interviews

Site B	6 Interviews

Barriers mentioned:

Transportation	1 Interview
Waiting Time	0 Interviews
Paperwork difficulties	2 Interviews
Child care	4 Interviews
Time off of work	2 Interviews

Site C	7 Interviews

Barriers mentioned:

Transportation	6 Interviews
Waiting time	0 Interviews
Paperwork difficulties	2 Interviews
Child care	5 Interviews
Time off of work	1 Interview

There are a couple of interesting patterns. First note that waiting time was only mentioned as a barrier in one of the sites. This is an indication that further investigation into the waiting time at that location is in order. Something seems to be setting site A apart—though these data are far from definitive in that they are based on a small sample of interviews. The results are more inspiring than conclusive. Notice also that only one respondent mentions transportation barriers at site B. This also warrants further investigation. What is it about this location that seems to be easier to reach than the other sites?

As the example illustrates, reporting codes based on different sites can be revealing. You can see patterns in the differences in codes appearing in different sites. The results are not conclusive or definitive. However, they can be inspiring.

Patterns that emerge even from these small samples can justify more detailed investigation—often justifying more attention. Maybe more importantly, such displays can help you prioritize investigations by identifying patterns that stand out most obviously. In the case of site displays, they can help you target sites for more detailed investigation (possibly more interviews or an entirely different data collection strategy).

Time Display

There are a variety of other simple data display strategies that have proven useful for public management research. It may be that you are not interested in diversity across different sites but across different time periods. When your theory suggests that conditions may change over time, displaying codes across time is a potentially useful tool. This may be the case where you expect phenomenon to develop over time. It could be that the implementation of a new program will only slowly reveal problems. It may be that you want to compare responses at different points in the calendar year. This could be particularly important in situations like education management where the nature of work changes dramatically in the summer.

These two theoretical inspirations undergird two types of time displays: calendar displays and duration displays. In a calendar display, you break up codes by the calendar day, week, or month of the data source. When your research question involves the relationship between calendar date and a code, these displays can be useful. Duration displays involve arbitrary starting dates and then durations removed from these starting dates. You could, for example, look at codes one month or six months following the implementation of new software in an office. It does not matter whether the first month was January or July. What matters is the separation of the data source from the start date of the program.

Putting Knowledge into Practice: Disaster Recovery Partners by Time

The manager of National Helping Hands is curious as to whether the nonprofit organizations that help with disaster recovery change over time. Are the organizations that help out in the first month following a disaster the same ones that continue to work in the community six to nine months later? Here the specific calendar month is not the central concern (though that could be interesting to look at later). The central concern is the change in the roster of nonprofit partners at different points in time after a disaster event. Previous efforts coded documents describing disaster response and recovery efforts following a flood. The manager has decided to use a time display to compare the organizations named in the reports immediately following event (the first 30 days) to those who were mentioned as acting two or more months after the event. The resulting display may look like the following:

Month 1	Month 2	Months 3–6	Months 6–12
Red Cross	Local Church A	Local Synagogue A	Local Church A
Salvation Army	Local Synagogue A	Local Temple A	Local Temple A
Local Temple A			

The manager notices that as time passes, the number of active organizations drops off. This supports her hypothesis that the composition of nonprofit groups changes as time passes in the response and recovery phase. While not definitive, this evidence suggests further investigation may be warranted.

Theoretical Display

The logic of data displays is not limited to the previous examples of summaries, site displays, and time displays. These types of displays are motivated by specific theoretical concerns. Any theoretical concern that inspires a hypothesis about how different types of units may exhibit different coded characteristics can be the basis of a theoretically tailored display strategy. The key is having some independent variables that you suspect explain some of the variation in some dependent variable—a very general condition. Whatever the independent variable is, you can use that as a dimension in your data display. In the past two examples of display techniques, the independent variables were site and time. You can use many other potential factors. If you believe gender affects the barriers to housing applications, you can simply separate barrier codes by gender. You could alternatively use age, race, level of education, or any of a variety of other characteristics. The logic of data display with codes arrayed and ordered based on an independent variable is fully generalizable to just about any theory.

Putting Knowledge into Practice: Disaster Recovery Partners by Role and Time

The manager of National Helping Hands was encouraged by her initial display of nonprofit partners across time. Clearly there are differences across time. To more formally display some of the potential differences, the manager wants to combine a display across time with a display separated by role. This adds a new dimension to the prior display. Now the arrangement is time by role:

	Month 1	Month 2	Months 3–6	Months 6–12
Evacuation	2	4	1	0
Health Care	8	2	2	2
Counseling	0	1	1	0
Economic Support	1	2	3	4

The pattern the manager finds is not entirely surprising but may be useful for planning purposes. The quick exit of health care organizations may inspire efforts to keep those organizations involved for a longer duration. The slow build-up of economic support organizations may be exactly as planned. The delayed introduction of counseling organizations may inspire efforts to recruit more of these organizations and to bring them into recovery efforts faster.

Software for Coding and Data Display

The preceding discussion has not assumed anything about the technology you have available for data analysis and display. You could perform any of the analytic techniques described earlier with paper and a pencil. This section will introduce the basics of software that can assist with coding and these basic data display techniques.

It is natural to ask why one would bother using software to assist in coding and data display. If you can accomplish your goals without sometimes expensive software that requires additional training, why adopt the software at all? The answer is simple. The software, while requiring some additional efforts, facilitates the process and makes some advanced techniques much simpler. Software suited to these tasks is known as computer-assisted qualitative data analysis software (**CAQDAS**).

There are two general types of computer software packages for coding and basic data display. There are freely available open-source packages that provide a limited set of options. For researchers that need a more robust toolset, commercial packages are also available. This section will conclude by describing the most common features of these two types of software packages and the most prominent representatives of each. You should note that the world of software is constantly changing. Some of the packages most popular today were not even in existence five years ago. The descriptions of the merits of each type of software, the options available in each, and the names of specific software packages may all change rapidly. The general features in CAQDAS, however, are likely to be of persistent interest to those using techniques like those described in this chapter.

CAQDAS software generally includes the following: search tools, coding tools, note-taking tools, and query tools. Other tools are available in some packages, but these functions represent the core. The basic operations of the software involves, first, loading a data source into the software. If you have interview transcripts or documents, this will create searchable text. If you have photographs or video, searching the media directly is not generally a concern (or an option). Search functionality is useful for finding segments of texts but is not itself an analytic technique or particularly unique to CAQDAS software. You can load documents into just about any viewer or word processor to accomplish the same goals. CAQDAS software does a lot more than this, though.

The first unique software function of CAQDAS software is the development and management of codes. CAQDAS software is designed to facilitate the cataloging of these codes as well as, in many cases, the clustering and hierarchical arrangement of the codes. The software lets you keep track of formal definitions of codes along with the relationships between codes. The software keeps track of such relations as having a set of codes for barriers to applying for housing assistance where each is distinct (child care, transportation, etc.) while also being a type of barrier. This software generally also helps the development and elaboration of codes throughout the analysis process.

The second unique function is assistance in coding. The specifics of coding vary from package to package, but the basics are consistent. The software allows you to read through and assign codes to the various chunks of your data. This operation typically involves processes like you might find in "track changes" operations in word processing software. In fact, many "track changes" visualization styles look just like codes attached in CAQDAS. The differences are vital, though. CAQDAS software knows that what you are doing is assigning codes rather than attaching generic annotations. In fact, many CAQDAS software packages allow either notes or codes. Codes are something special, though. The software keeps track of which codes are assigned to which chunks. It knows that codes are going to be used repeatedly through the analysis.

Some CAQDAS software provides key stroke substitutions to make coding easier. The goal is to make coding fast and reliable. To this end, some of the software lets you assign keys to specific codes. You can read rapidly through the chunks and assign codes with a single keystroke. The result is faster coding once you are familiar with the keystrokes. This is particularly important for projects that involve a great deal of coding. Such automation can also help with team coding efforts. The software also facilitates the application of multiple codes to a single chunk.

The assignment of codes and the software recognition of codes are essential to the central distinguishing function of CAQDAS. Up to this point, the functionality of CAQDAS software largely overlaps with what you can do with basic word processing software using a combination of search and annotation functions. CAQDAS, however, allows for complex searches of the codes rather than searching the text itself. You can search for all references to a specific code indicating a reference to child care as a barrier to housing applications. The structured query will return all chunks with this code. This is the point where CAQDAS pays off uniquely. Once the coding is done, you can now do a variety of comparisons of the coded text with ease. You could reproduce the tables and data displays in the previous sections with ease. Instead of just listing counts of references, you could include entire chunks organized by site, time, gender, or topic. This is the function that justifies all of the start-up costs in formalizing codes development, defining the hierarchy of codes, and using this specific software for analysis.

This basic functionality is available in a wide variety of software packages. You can find open-source software to serve many of these functions. Attractive options include WeftQDA and RQDA. There is also an online program to facilitate group coding— Coding Analysis Toolkit (CAT). These open-source packages offer basic annotation, coding, and queries. Their chief limitations are with the sorts of media that the software can analyze and the complexity of the queries that one can use on the data. Open-source packages typically allow for simple text format (.txt files) and open document standards (like .pdf files). They typically do not allow proprietary document standards (like .docx files), video, or graphic data sources. For these more complicated data sources (or more complicated queries), you will need more complex, commercial software.

There are a variety of commercial QACDAS packages, but the most popular are NVIVO and Atlas.ti. These packages provide an ever-expanding set of functions including complex queries, rich text integration, and options to output quantitative queries (like those that one would use to create the tables in earlier parts of the chapter) to standard statistical packages. These statistical packages can cost thousands of dollars. In the end, you will have to assess whether the cost of the commercial packages is worth the investment for your specific project.

Conclusion

One of the challenges of conducting thorough research is that you end up with a great deal of data. Rather than being frustrated, you need a strategy to use the data to inform your decisions. This chapter has provided some initial strategies for organizing the data you collect in ways that will help reveal patterns. These strategies will be particularly useful for data like open-ended questions from interviews or field notes. Future chapters will expand your strategies for analyzing a broad range of data.

Suggested Readings

Coding and data displays are techniques on which fewer books have been written (compared to other topics like conducting interviews, writing surveys, etc.). These are often techniques that people learn by doing them. We find two texts to be most helpful for the development of coding strategies and data displays. Each of these books go far beyond the material discussed here and would be excellent material to consult as you embark on coding and data display exercise.

First, Johnny Saldaña's excellent *Coding Manual for Qualitative Researchers* provides dozens of potential types of codes appropriate at various stages of analysis. While the book draws from a field somewhat distant from much public affairs research (theater and education pedagogy), the diversity of coding strategies discussed is superb and inspirational.

Second, Miles and Huberman's *Qualitative Data Analysis: An Expanded Sourcebook (Second Edition)* provides a strong overview of qualitative coding and data analysis. While the text is starting to show its age, it provides diverse examples of data displays on a wide range of research topics—many of which will be comfortable to students in public affairs with their focus on education reform implementation and education management.

Those interested in CAQDAS software could begin by looking into the CAQDAS Networking Project (caqdas.soc.surrey.ac.uk). This group of researchers at the University of Surrey provides a number of resources to help explain and compare CAQDAS software. This is also a useful site to keep up with new software releases and training opportunities.

Vocabulary

Flashcards
& MCQs

CAQDAS—Computer-Assisted Qualitative Data Analysis Software.
CHUNKS—The basic unit of analysis of coding.
CODE—A meaning or characteristic that you assign to a piece of data.
CODING—The process of assigning codes to segments of text.
DESCRIPTIVE CODE—A code based on the specific meaning or characteristic of a chunk.
IN VIVO CODING—Coding that only uses language used within the original chunk.
PATTERN CODING—Identifying relationships between elements within the coded data.

Useful
Websites

Review Questions

■ What distinguishes descriptive coding and pattern coding? Which occurs first?

■ Identify four different types of chunks and when they may be appropriate.

■ Under what conditions would a site display be most appropriate?

Discussion Questions

■ Develop a list of descriptive codes for a project in which a public manager interviews teachers following the implementation of a new accountability system in their schools. The goal of the project is to explain why the program seems much more popular in some schools than others.

■ Under what circumstances might you want to limit yourself to in vivo coding?

■ Imagine that you have transcripts of a series of focus groups conducted with representative of a local neighborhood where Walmart is considering a new location. Each focus group was conducted at a different location and consisted of different representatives. What sorts of displays would you want to use to analyze the data?

CHAPTER 13

Descriptive Statistics

Learning Objectives

✓ Understand how descriptive statistics are used to simplify large quantities of information
✓ Identify and calculate the appropriate measure of central tendency
✓ Identify and calculate the appropriate measure of dispersion
✓ Identify ethical issues with the selection of statistical tools

Cases in Research

Case A—National Helping Hands

As one step in evaluating the contribution of the nonprofit community in national disaster recovery, Roshawna was asked to provide an estimation, for the board meeting next week, of the typical cost for nonprofit groups to repair storm damaged homes. To this end, she has collected from the member organizations, the amount of money they have spent on materials repairing damaged homes for the first quarter of 2011. Her mission is to find a way to present this information in a meaningful way to the governing board.

Case B—Amity Department of Homeland Security

In Amity, emergency responses that involve animals are handled by a volunteer community group, the County Animal Response Team (CART) that is led by the

County Animal Control Officer and local Livestock Extension Agent. Because there is a sizable animal population in the county, Colton, the training director for Amity HLS, is considering a new training program to improve the time it takes the Emergency Operations Center (EOC) to activate the CART team. Before doing so, Colton wants to make sure the resources he will devote to this program are really necessary and decides to first evaluate on average, how long it currently takes to get the CART team deployed. Colton has collected data from the months of January and February about the time (in minutes) it takes his county to have a CART team deployed from the initial request.

Descriptive Statistics

The sole purpose of data analysis is to apply parsimony to large quantities of information. That is, we seek to find ways to simplify the information provided by the world around us into understandable and usable bits of information. People do this naturally and very regularly. What statistics offers us is a standardized process by which to do this. In this chapter, we will explore the first step in making sense of data—applying descriptive statistics.

When we collect information (data) about a single phenomenon (variable), it becomes important to find ways to summarize this information for later use in our decision-making processes. For example, every day we typically have to be somewhere at a specified time. This may be to work, school, a sporting event, or some other similar engagement. To make this happen, we must get up at a time that allows sufficient enough time to (1) get cleaned up (variable 1), and (2) commute to the required location (variable 2). Consciously or unconsciously, we combine the usual time it takes us to get ready and the usual time it takes us to commute and add them together to provide adequate time to arrive at our event at the desired time. While this may sound simple, when most people think about statistics, they are not contemplating the use of these simple, yet powerful, descriptive statistics.

Descriptive statistics are the statistical tools we use to represent what we know about information on any given variable. They are used to inform decision making, illustrate operations, to *describe* the information in a simple way. We do this by identifying the typical values or outcomes and the amount of variance in those outcomes. We refer to these two major dimensions of descriptive statistics as Central Tendency and Dispersion.

Before proceeding to the individual measures, we first need to clarify terminology that will be used throughout the chapter. One of the goals of statistics is to add precision to the communication of data-based information. In this spirit it is important to have a common vocabulary. For the purposes of this text, we will call any group data that is collected on a single construct/idea/activity a **VARIABLE**. Similarly, we shall refer to any individual observation within that variable as an **ELEMENT**. So if we are interested in

travel time to work as our variable, each day's travel time will comprise an element in the variable. The group of elements will be the variable.

Variables are abbreviated using letters in the alphabet. Most commonly, X is used to indicate any given variable. The elements are abbreviated using a subscript to the variable abbreviation. Thus, the first element in a variable is abbreviated, while the fifth element would be abbreviated x_5 (note the use of lowercase when referring to individual elements). If capital letters were used instead (X_1, X_2, X_3), we would be referring to individual variables (variable 1, variable 2, and variable 3).

In addition, many of the important calculations in statistics require us to use the number of elements in a variable in the computation. Because this number is so frequently used, there is a common convention for abbreviating the number of observations of events. In most cases we use "N" to symbolize the number of observations of events in a variable.

Measures of Central Tendency

Either explicitly or implicitly, we all use measures of central tendency every day. We couch our language with words like "usually," "on average," "typically," and a plethora of other terms that provide a hazy reference to central tendency. We do this because we inherently seek to simplify the great amount of information we encounter daily. However, because our thought patterns are so complex, this intuitive approach becomes problematic when we need to communicate our interpretations or expectations of the world. Additionally, different approaches to identifying the "typical" occurrence of an event may relay very different impressions of what is actually happening in the underlying data. In statistics, we rely on three primary measures of central tendency to provide a common framework: mean, median, and mode.

Mean

By far, the most widely used expression of central tendency is the mean. This is the arithmetic average of the values of the variable observed. This is commonly seen as averages (test grades, batting averages, etc.). In statistics, this measure is represented many ways. It may expressed as E[X]—the expected value of X, μ—the arithmetic mean of a population X, or $\bar{X}$—the arithmetic mean of a sample variable X. Because we rarely if ever deal with true populations, defined as all possible observations of a variable across all units in the population, we will stick with the notation $\bar{X}$ (pronounced "X bar").

Calculating the Mean of a Variable

Calculating the mean of a variable is straightforward. We simply add up each of the elements (observations of the variable), then divide the total by the number of elements. Thus, if variable X1 has the elements 12, 14, 10, 8, 9, 13, and 11, we would find the mean by adding the seven elements (12+14+10+8+9+13+ 11 = 77) then divide the result by the number of observations (N = 7). Thus, summing all elements and dividing by the number of observations (N) yields $\bar{X}$ = 11. This is summarized by Formula 13.1

Formula 13.1

$$\bar{X} = \frac{\sum X_i}{N}$$

mean = Sum of elements / # of elements

Read as, "x-bar is equal to the sum of all x's divided by N." Recall, $\bar{X}$ is the sample mean, $\sum x_i$ tells us to sum (sigma is the symbol for summations) all the values of X, and N is the number of observations.

Example 13.1: Case B—Amity DHS

Colton has the following data for the months of January and February. There were ten (10) calls each month, and each element represents the time in minutes it took from when a call for CART assistance came in to the 911 call center to the time the CART team rolled out the door to head to the scene of the call.

Table 13.1

CART Team response times (in minutes)

January	1	5	6	6	6	6	6	6	5	10
February	1	2	4	10	9	1	9	3	10	8

To calculate the mean, Colton first sums up all the individual elements ($\sum x_i$) and gets the total response time (114), then divides that number by the number of observations (N = 20). This results in an average call-to-roll time of 5.7 minutes.

Calculating the Mean in Grouped Data

Sometimes, it becomes necessary to calculate a mean from grouped data. This occurs for many reasons. First, we may have collected information in a "grouped" fashion. That is, we may have put out a survey that asked for individuals to report their age in categories, or we could have asked about income in brackets. Also, it is common for organizations to have subunits report to a central office. In this case, it may be that information has been grouped before it is available for analysis. In either case, it is possible to calculate a mean from grouped data; there are simply a few steps that need to be added to the process.

Class Exercise: Many governmental and nonprofit agencies generally report averages as organizational output measures. This can reflect the number of customers served, arrests made, or potholes filled. Compile a list of average rates of service delivery that would be helpful to evaluate nonprofit agencies in your area.

To calculate a mean home repair cost from this grouped data there are four steps:

Step 1. Calculate the midpoint of each group. In this case, we have six groups that are evenly spaced. For the lowest cost group, the midpoint is the number half way between 1 and 5—which is 3. For the next group, it would be 8.

Step 2. Multiply the midpoint by the frequency. In this case, the frequency is the number of affected units.

Step 3. Find the sum of all the frequency X midpoint values.

Step 4. Divide the sum of all frequency X midpoints by the total number of observations (N). In this case, it would be the sum of all the frequencies.

Example 13.2: Case A—Identifying Average Home Repair Costs for NHH

Roshawna has taken the 500 observations that the NHH affiliate organizations have provided and put each element in a "cost category" as a first step to understanding all the numbers. Consider the following data on housing repair costs:

Housing Repair Costs

Cost (in hundreds of dollars)	Number of effected units
1–5	133
6–10	196
11–15	95
16–20	54
20–25	13
26–30	5
31–35	3
36–40	1

Housing Repair Costs

Cost (in hundreds of dollars)	Number of effected units	Midpoints (M)	Frequency (f) x midpoints (M)
1–5	133	3	399
6–10	196	8	1568
11–15	95	13	1235
16–20	54	18	972
21–25	13	23	299
26–30	5	28	140
31–35	3	33	99
36–40	1	38	38
N = 500			$\Sigma(fxM)$ = 4750

$$\frac{\Sigma(fxM)}{N} = 9.50$$

Formula 13.2

$$\overline{X} \text{ for grouped data} = \frac{\Sigma(f \times M)}{N}$$

The sigma tells us to sum, so we are to sum the values of the frequency times the sum for each group, then divide by the number of observations.

The mean is by far the most used measure of central tendency. It is an intuitive and easily calculated statistic. Further, because it can be derived through simple mathematics, it lends itself well to use in advanced statistical techniques. This is not to say that the mean is the be-all end-all measure. One very important shortcoming of the mean in representing a set of elements occurs when the elements are not evenly distributed throughout the set of possible outcomes for the variable. In this case, we refer to the variable as being **SKEWED**. Look at the histogram in Figure 13.1.

In Roshawna's data on home repair seen above, the mean takes into account all of the data points including the tale of higher values that string out to the right, providing a representation of the "average" cost when we consider all the values, but in cases like this where there are a small number of relatively larger values, that "average" does not represent what is happening for "most" of the cases. In these cases we have other options for representing the data, and the most common of these are the median and the mode.

> **Class Exercise**: Identify some reasons a manager may only have grouped data available. What are the benefits to grouped data, and what are the costs?

Median

The **MEDIAN** describes the central tendency of a variable by identifying the middle value of the elements. So, for instance, if we have a variable X with the elements [1, 7, 4, 9, 11, 2, 3, 5, 1, 6, 41], then we would simply order these elements from lowest to highest and identify the middle number. As we have 11 elements (N = 11), the sixth element in

Figure 13.1 Housing Repair Costs

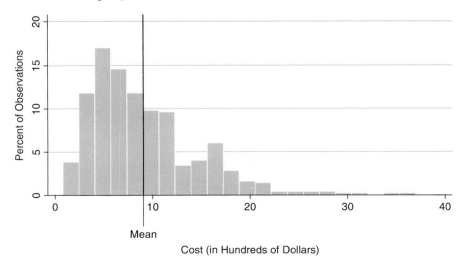

the sorted data will be the median. Thus, if X = [1, 1, 2, 3, 4, 5, 6, 7, 9, 11, 41], the median is equal to 5 (while the mean would be 8.18). We formalize this process in the following formula:

Formula 13.3

$$Median = \left(\frac{N+1}{2}\right) th \text{ item in a sorted list.}$$

In cases where N is odd, this application is straightforward; however, in cases where there are even numbers of elements in the variable, we have to take one more step to identify the median. If we eliminate one of the observations from the variable X above, we would need to identify the (10+1)/2 or 5.5th element. In this case, we would take the average of the 5th and 6th element. So if X = [1, 2, 3, 4, 5, 6, 7, 9, 11, 41] the median would be equal to $(x_5 + x_6)/2$, or (5+6)/2=5.5.

Notice that when the elements of the variable are mainly small numbers with just a few large numbers, what is referred to as positive skew, the median tends to be smaller than the mean. In cases where the elements are predominantly large numbers with a few smaller numbers, or a negative skew, the median will tend to be larger than the mean. This is the reason variables that have noticeable skew tend to be reported in terms of medians instead of means.

Example 13.3: Case A—Choosing a Statistic to Illustrate the Typical Case

After creating a histogram of housing costs, Roshawna sees that her data have a large skew. This is confirmed when she calculates the median for the data and sees that it is less than her mean. If she reports the mean, it will lead people to believe that storm damage will be more costly than it actually is to the "average" victim, but the mean multiplied by the number of occurrences will provide an accurate total cost; however, if she reports the median, the portrayal of the "average" case will more closely mirror what individuals will face if they incur storm damage, but the median times the number of occurrences will not be an accurate measure of total cost. Thus, for reporting purposes, she has decided to present the median value; however, she notes in her report the total costs as well.

It is important that the results of statistical analysis reflect the question being answered with the data. When calculating a representation of the average, the measure of central tendency, it is important to identify the most likely outcome on average.

Mode

A final approach to representing the central tendency of a variable is the **MODE**. This is simply the most frequently reported element. So if we have the variable X with the elements [1, 2, 3, 3, 4, 5, 5, 5, 6, 7, 7, 8], the mode would equal 5. This measure of central tendency is most commonly seen when reporting ordinal data such as survey questions that have categorical responses and is particularly useful for presenting the results of dichotomous outcome variables (such as yes/no or true/false questions).

An important difference between the mode and the other measures of central tendency discussed here is that while a variable can have only one mean or median, it may have multiple modes. At times, this may present very important information, and other times it may simply be an indicator that the mode is a poor choice of tool to simplify the data at hand. For example, if we survey an area and ask about memberships to civic organizations, it may be that there are two or three that stand out from the rest—our data may be bi-modal or tri-modal. In this case, it might be interesting to have an idea of who the "big players" are in an area. Conversely, if 15 out of 20 organizations are reporting similarly large memberships, reporting the modal values will not serve to differentiate the groups.

Example 13.4: Case B—Amity DHS

When we looked at Colton's data in Example 13.1 we calculated a mean time of 5.7 minutes. Now we will calculate the two other measures for his data.

CART Team response times (in minutes)

January	1	5	6	6	6	6	6	6	5	10
February	1	2	4	10	9	1	9	3	10	8

Sorting the data and tallying up the frequencies of each value gives us the following:

The median is the 10.5th element in the list, and the mode is the most reported. In this case, the average of the 10th and 11th values (both sixes) is 6, and the most frequent value is also 6.

Value	10	9	8	6	5	4	3	2	1
Frequency	2	2	1	6	2	1	1	1	3

Choosing the Appropriate Measure of Central Tendency

Each of the three measures of central tendency has unique strengths and weaknesses, and choosing which to tool to use to describe your data is a matter of deciding which *best* represents the true center of the distribution. The appropriate measure is the one that gives the superior representation of the center of mass of all the observations.

The mean is the most used measure of central tendency, in part, because of the ease of calculation but also because this ease of calculation makes it convenient to embed in more complex statistical tools (this will become more evident in later chapters). It is most appropriate when the observations are evenly distributed around one center point. In cases where there are extreme values to one side or the other of the center of the distribution, the mean tends to be skewed away from the center in the direction of the extreme values. Means are best when the differences in the values of the observations are a function of random effects (such as the height of all students in the eighth grade, the number of people in an office at any given moment, or scores on a test).

STATA

SPSS

Putting Knowledge into Practice: Calculating Measures of Central Tendency Using Excel

Many spreadsheet programs offer a host of tools that make data analysis very simple. Learning how to use formulas and cell references will provide the ability to make template documents that will update regularly and provide instant feedback about data.

To use a formula in Excel, one simply types the equals sign and then types the formula. For example, if we want to add cell A1 and B2, we would enter " = A1+B2" in the cell where we wanted the calculation to appear. Other functions allow for more complex calculations to take place. For instance, if we wanted to sum up the contents of column A from row 1 to row 15, we would use the sum function. To do so, simply type " = sum (A1:A15)" where you wish to have the results displayed. This tells Excel to add the contents of all the cells between A1 and A15.

There are two ways to calculate the mean in Excel. One can either add the contents and divide them by N, or we can use the built-in function for calculating the mean.

	A	B	C	D
1	Observation		Value	
2	1		8	
3	2		6	
4	3		9	
5	4		4	
6	5		6	
7		$\sum X$	=SUM(C2:C6) ⟶	33
8	Number of Observations		=COUNT(C2:C6) ⟶	5
9	mean		=C7/C8 ⟶	6.6
10			=AVERAGE(C2:C6) ⟶	
11				

The picture shows the contents of each cell, and the arrows indicate the values that would actually be displayed from each cell entry.

The median is less often used because it requires some manual manipulation of the data to identify, but as a measure of central tendency it is far more robust to extreme values than the mean. In cases where the observations are evenly distributed, the mean and median will provide similar if not identical values; however, when the observations contain elements that have values that are extremely different from the majority of the other observations, the median provides a superior representation of the "typical" observation. One example of when the median is a better choice to represent the typical case in a set of observations is when we examine income in a capitalistic society. Wage earners in the United States, for the most part, receive income across a set range of values, but a small subgroup of this population earns income that is exponentially higher than the majority. If we calculate the mean income for wage earners in the United States, we would arrive at a value that is significantly higher than what most wage earners in this country actually receive. In this case, the median is a far better representation of what is happening for the typical worker. This phenomenon also occurs with housing prices. Many naturally occurring events lend themselves to the possibility of extreme values. When the possible values for observations are limited (such as income or housing cost not being able to be negative), the possibility of extreme values grows, and care should be taken when representing the typical case.

When the possible values of observations are limited to a very few choices (such as the case with nominal and ordinal data), both the mean and median fail to provide intuitive information about the typical observation; the mode is the best choice to represent central tendency. If we are interested in gender, and of 10 observations 6 are female, a mean or median is not going to be of much help. To demonstrate the utility of modes further, consider the case of describing the distribution of religious beliefs among a group of individuals.

Percentages and Proportions

While percentages and proportions are not classically thought of as measures of central tendency, they do convey the same notion and are akin to the mode in that they represent the most likely value for a variable. Additionally, percentages and proportions are by far the most used—and most abused—statistical technique.

> **Class Exercise**: Identify three variables where either the median or mode would be better representations of the "typical" outcome. What would happen if the mean were reported instead of the more appropriate statistic?

Percentages

Percentages are a popular way to convey how often an event occurs. For example, Alcoholalert.com reports that in 2008, 37% of all motor vehicle fatalities were alcohol related. This statement is meant to convey the dangers of alcohol by relaying that such a large percentage of the accidents involved drinking. What we really should infer from this is simply that 37 out of every hundred 100 people who die in a vehicle accident had a blood alcohol content equal to or greater than .08 (or interestingly, that their blood had 8% or greater alcohol content). A long discussion of whether or not the alcohol actually impaired the driver, or how many drunk drivers *did not* wreck, or how many drunks are on the road at any given time is important; however, it just serves to cloud the point the author wished to make. The number is easy to understand, meaningful, and compelling. This is the reason so many "facts" are presented in terms of percentages.

Percentages are also so widely used because they are so easy to generate. To calculate a percentage, we simply divide the number of occurrences of an outcome of interest (say number of dead drivers with a blood alcohol content equal or greater than .08) by the total number of outcomes observed (total number of fatalities).

Formula 13.4

$$Percentage\% = \left(\frac{f}{N}\right) \times 100$$

Example 13.5: Case A—Identifying Average Home Repair Costs for NHH

Returning to Roshawna's data on housing, let's say we want to know how many of the home repairs cost more than $2,000. In that case, we can look at the frequencies and see that of the 500 elements (N = 500), that only 22 homes cost more than $2,000 to repair (that is: 13 + 5 + 3 + 1 = 22). We divide 22 by 500 and multiply by 100 to find that only 4.4% of the home repairs cost more than $2,000.

Proportions

Nine out of 10 dentists who chew gum chew Sparkly brand chewing gum.[1] While this statement is interesting for a number of reasons, it interests us now because it is a raw proportion. That is, 9 out of 10 is the same as 9/10 or .9 (notice this is the same form as the blood alcohol content was presented in the previous section). The proportion is simply a representation of percentages in decimal format.

Formula 13.5

$$Proportion\, p = \left(\frac{f}{N}\right)$$

Much like the percentage, the proportion is a great way to display information quickly and simply, but the context does matter. For instance, the proportion in the opening sentence of this paragraph qualifies the statement with "dentists *who chew gum*." We could probably do an informal survey and out of the some 150,000 dentists in the country find 10 who chew tobacco. If 9 of these 10 chose Beechnut™ chewing tobacco, we could make the same powerful claim.

Measures of Dispersion

Understanding the average value of a variable, that is, describing the central tendency, is a very powerful tool, but it is only the first step in understanding what data have to teach us. The next step is to understand the amount of variance in the outcomes. This is important because average values give us an idea of what will likely happen, but they do not give us an idea of all the things that could happen. For example, suppose you wanted to become a community service professional because you heard it paid above-average wages. It is quite possible that you may know someone in the field who makes $68,000 annually. But after checking the Bureau of Labor Statistics for median wages in the area, you learn that you will most likely make around $38,970 (the median wage—after all, you are at least average, right?). After applying for a job in the field, you are pleased to get an offer of employment—that is, until you hear the starting salary is a mere $22,000 annually. Why is this? It is because while the measure of central tendency tells us what is most typical, you are not typical as you have no job experience. Therefore, your potential employer has offered you a wage from the bottom of the salary range.

All kidding aside, measures of dispersion are important because they let us know about the breadth of possible outcomes, and they allow us a way to quantify the variance in a variable. As we move on in this book, you will come to see that variance is more than just an important concept in statistics: it is more the *reason* for statistics. Think about it: if outcomes did not change, statistics would be pointless. Since they do change, we use statistics to glean information about that change and present it in a way that aids us in decision making. Statistics offer us four important tools to express the variance of possible outcomes: the range, variance, standard deviation, and interquartile range (IQR).

Range

The **RANGE** is simply the difference between the highest and lowest value of elements in a variable. This provides some information about how much change occurs within the variable in the variable's unit of measure. So, if the variable is measured in minutes, the range will represent the difference in minutes from the longest time to the shortest time measured. Similarly, if the variable is measured in dollars, the range would tell us how much larger the maximum value is from the minimum in dollars.

Formula 13.6

Range = highest score − lowest score

The range is a good statistic for cursory evaluation, but it gives little information about the real variance within the variable. While it provides a distance between the floor and ceiling, it conveys little information about what goes on in between. For this, we turn to some more robust measures.

Variance

The first step in creating a measure that provides information about all the change within a variable is to generate a measure of **VARIANCE**. Consider the following two months of data from Colton's work (Table 13.1):

CART Team response times (in minutes)

January	1	5	6	6	6	6	6	6	5	10
February	1	2	4	10	9	1	9	3	10	8

If each of these were considered a variable, we would see that both January and February have $\bar{X} = 5.7$, and $R = 9$. In this case, the range statistic is not able to differentiate the levels of variance occurring for each element in the two groups. To do this, we construct a statistic that sums the distance of each element from the center of the group, squaring the sum, and then dividing it by N.

Step 1

We take the distance of each element from the center (mean) and square them. Remember, the mean is the exact center of all the data points, so there will be just as many negative values as there are positive values. If we did not square the numbers, the sum would have to equal zero. The graph below shows the elements of February plotted with a horizontal marker for the mean and bars representing how far each element deviates from the mean.

Figure 13.2

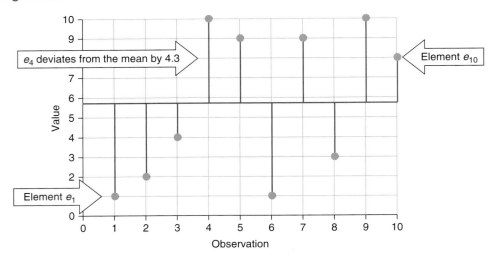

Step 2

We sum the squared deviations—the squared distances from each element to the mean.

Step 3

We divide the sum squared deviations by the number of observations. If we did not do this, the variance would grow with each additional observation, and the measure would be rather useless. The table below shows the calculation for January response times.

January	$\bar{X}$	$x_i - \bar{X}$	$(x_i - \bar{X})^2$
1	5.7	−4.7	22.09
5	5.7	−.07	.49
6	5.7	.03	.09
6	5.7	.03	.09
6	5.7	.03	.09
6	5.7	.03	.09
6	5.7	.03	.09
6	5.7	.03	.09
5	5.7	−.07	.49
10	5.7	4.3	18.49

$$\sum x_i - \bar{X} = 0$$

Notice the sum of the deviations is equal to zero

$$\sum (x_i - \bar{X})^2 = 42.1$$

$$\frac{\sum (x_i - \bar{X})^2}{N} = 4.21$$

Formula 13.7

$$Variance\left(S^2\right) = \sum \frac{x_i - (\bar{X})^2}{N}$$

The result is that for January, we get a variance (s^2) = 4.21. If we would repeat the calculations for February, the result would be s^2 = 13.21. Notice that even with identical means and ranges, the month with the most *change* has the higher value variance statistic.

Variance is a preferred statistic for use in the computation of more advanced comparisons of multiple variables and will be used liberally in later chapters. The greatest problem with variance is that because we squared the values, it has the potential to become quite large very quickly. More common when examining variance for descriptive purposes is the standard deviation.

Standard Deviation

The **STANDARD DEVIATION** is simply the square root of the variance.[2] This relieves the measure of some of the value inflation from squaring the deviations, and leaves us with a parsimonious statistic that is comparable across groups. Formally, this is expressed in Formula 13.8.

Putting Knowledge into Practice: Giving Meaning to Variance

Managers need to pay attention to more than just the average output of their organization. When Colton was evaluating response times we only looked at that average times for the entire team, but what if we could break that down into response groups? If Colton has two response groups in his team, we can assume that both have the same average response time of 5.7 minutes; however, one has a much larger variance in the response time. What might this indicate to Colton?

Discussion: What this indicates is that one team has much more variance in their work than the other. This could be the result of environmental factors (the calls came from vastly different locations requiring disparate travel times) or varying levels of skills of the team. Both of these possibilities identify areas where the performance of the organization could be improved.

Formula 13.8

$$Standard\ deviation\left(\sigma\right)=\sqrt{s^2}=\sqrt{\sum \frac{x_i-(\bar{X})^2}{N}}$$

Recall from our discussion on variance: January had a variance of 4.21, and February had a variance of 13.21. To compute the standard deviations for these two months, we would simply take the square root of the variance for January: $\sigma=\sqrt{4.21}=2.05$ and for February: $\sigma=\sqrt{13.21}=3.63$.

As you can see, the month with the largest amount of change also has the largest standard deviation. When we interpret the standard deviation, we can say that lower values mean that the individual observations do not deviate much from the mean, while larger values tell us that the individual observations largely deviate from the mean.

Interquartile Range (IQR)

The **INTERQUARTILE RANGE (IQR)** reports the difference between the 25th and 50th percentile of the variable. This statistic is very similar to the range; however, it avoids the problem of having extreme outliers influence the size as it reports only on the 50% of elements closest to the mean. Figure 13.3 assumes a well-behaved variable whose elements have a mean of 5 and are evenly distributed between 0 and 10.

Figure 13.3

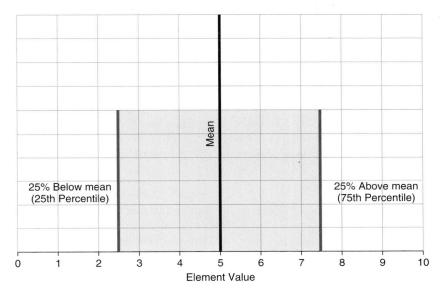

The IQR is identified in four simple steps:
Step 1
Order the elements from lowest to highest.
Step 2
Multiply the number of elements (N) by .25 (recall, this is the proportion for the lower 25%) to identify the element representing the 25% bound. If the result is not even, round off to the nearest whole number.
Step 3
Multiply N by .75 to identify the element representing the 75% bound, again rounding to the nearest whole number if necessary.
Step 4
Subtract the value of the element identified as the lower (25%) bound from the element identified as the upper (75%) bound. The resulting number is the IQR.

Much like the median, the IQR is a good statistic to use when distributions have a few elements with values way outside the norm. In statistics, we say that the IQR (much like the median) is robust to extreme outliers. Because the IQR and median are both robust to extreme outliers, it is typical to report the IQR when reporting the median just as it is typical to report a standard deviation when reporting a mean. Also, while Figure 13.3 shows a symmetrical distribution of the IQR around the mean, this is rarely the case. More typically a graph of the IQR will be asymmetrical around the center of the elements. This makes it very useful for visually representing skew in data.

Example 13.6: Case A—Using Dispersion to Aid in Management

Reflecting on Figure 13.1, Roshawna knows that the data on home repair costs are skewed. To avoid misrepresenting her data, she has used the median as a measure of central tendency and now she plans to use her data to identify cases that are of interest for further investigation. She knows that there will be some average variance in costs; however, she believes that some observations are either far too inexpensive or far too expensive to be random, and she has decided to evaluate some of the cases to (1) identify best practices to reduce costs, and (2) identify factors that might lead to higher repair costs. To do this, she wants to look at all the extremely inexpensive cases to find out what went right with these, and identify all the extremely expensive cases to see if there are any common elements that lead to the high cost. Because the data are skewed, she decides to calculate the IQR and examine all the cases that fall above the 75th percentile and below the 25th percentile to identify commonalities.

Class Exercise: Identify three functions of your local government (for example, arresting burglars, educating students, maintaining streets and walkways). For each of these functions, what are some of the possible causes of variance in each? Which of the causes of variance can be addressed by management and how?

Figure 13.4 uses a box and whisker graph to display the median and IQR of the Home Repair Cost data. Notice how both the box and the whiskers are much longer on the right side of the median. This demonstrates how far the data extend in that direction in comparison to how compressed the elements are on the left side.

Figure 13.4

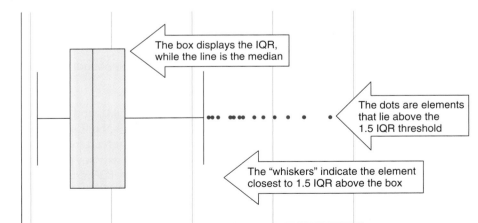

The box displays the IQR, while the line is the median

The dots are elements that lie above the 1.5 IQR threshold

The "whiskers" indicate the element closest to 1.5 IQR above the box

Housing Repair Cost

Putting Knowledge into Practice: Calculating Descriptive Statistics Using Excel

In an earlier section, we described how to calculate the mean using Excel. This software can also be used easily to calculate descriptive statistics. Assume we have a spreadsheet with 20 observations in cells H2 to cell H21. The formulas to calculate the descriptive statistics are the following:

	J	K	L	M	N
1					
2					
3	Mean (population)	=AVERAGE(H2:H21)		Smallest Value	=MIN(H2:H21)
4	Median	=MEDIAN(H2:H21)		Largest Value	=MAX(H2:H21)
5	Mode	=MODE(H2:H21)		IQR	=N4-N3
6					
7	Standard Deviation (population)	=STDEVP(H2:H21)		75th Percentile number	=COUNT(H2:H21)*0.25
8				25th percentile number	=COUNT(H2:H21)*0.75
9					
10				75th Percentile value	=LARGE(H2:H21,N7)
11				25th percentile value	=LARGE(H2:H21,N8)
12				IQR	=N10-N11
13					
14					

The formulas for most of the statistics are rather straightforward. For the IQR and Range, we have to do a few calculations. Notice that for the range, we first calculate the maximum and minimum values and then subtract them. For the IQR, we have to calculate which numbers would represent the cutoff for the 25th and 75th percentile, and then we have to identify those values. Finally, we can subtract the value for the 25th percentile from the value for the 75th percentile.

Ethics and Descriptive Statistics

Throughout this chapter, we have tried to demonstrate the many tools available to illustrate information gathered on a specific variable. At times we have made light of some of the differences; however, these differences have serious consequences. In textbooks, data are pretty and behave "as expected." In the real world, this is not the case. Data are not clean and very often are skewed for one reason or another. The tools we choose have a great effect on the way those data are understood and acted upon. While this may be of little consequence in the business world, decision makers in the public and non-profit sectors have an ethical (and in some cases legal) obligation to present data in a true light as opposed to a beneficial one.

Recall the discussion about percentages, and think about the public service notices you have heard about drunk driving. What if the federal government changed the statistic from "37% of traffic fatalities are alcohol related," to say "63% of all traffic fatalities are sobriety related." This would not necessarily be true (these would comprise cell phone use, eating/smoking while driving, and the like), but it would be technically correct given the data. Similarly, we could grossly inflate the valuation of the housing industry simply by changing reporting from median to mean home values.

Vocabulary

Flashcards
& MCQs

Useful
Websites

ELEMENT—Value for a single observation in a variable.
IQR—Value between the 25th percentile and 75th percentile of a variable.
MEAN—The arithmetic center of a variable.
MEDIAN—Middle element value in a sorted variable.
MODE—The most reported element value in a variable.
STANDARD DEVIATION—A measure of dispersion of elements in a variable about the mean.
VARIABLE—The collection of elements (data) representing observations for one phenomenon of interest.
VARIANCE—A measure of how spread out a set of numbers are.

Review Questions

- If a variable contains elements with values well above or below the rest of the observations, what would be the appropriate measure of central tendency? Why?
- If a variable contains elements with values well above or below the rest of the observations, what would be the appropriate measure of dispersion? Why?
- Explain the relationship between proportions and percentages.
- What measure of dispersion should be reported in conjunction with the mean?
- For the following variable, calculate the mean, median, and mode: X = [1, 5, 16, 20, 31, 11, 14, 17, 23, 28].
- In the question above, which measure of central tendency provides the "best" representation of the variable?
- If two variables have the same mean but different standard deviations, what is the difference between the two?
- If you calculate $s^2 = 47$ for a variable, what is the standard deviation?

Discussion Questions

- Look at a news report website and identify a story that utilized descriptive statistics as evidence. Setting aside what these statistics are supposed to say, what are the authors intentionally not saying with this story [hint—think about the Sparkly brand gum example]?

■ Why might it be important to describe data using the "center mass" of the elements instead of the actual arithmetic mean? What ethical challenges might this pose?

■ Bearing in mind that the standard deviation measures change within a variable, in what cases might a manager be concerned with minimizing or maximizing the standard deviation of a variable?

■ Thinking back on your week, what instances of informally using descriptive statistics stick out in your mind? Are there times when you chose medians or modes over means? Are there times that you considered variance in your decision-making process?

Demographics
Data Set -
Excel, STATA &
SPSS

Data Set
exercises

Notes

1 Sparkly brand chewing gum is not a real brand of gum and is used here simply to avoid involving lawyers unnecessarily.
2 More accurately, standard deviations for populations are the square root of variance. The standard deviation calculation for samples also accounts for the degrees of freedom, which will be addressed in the chapter about distributions and again in sampling.

CHAPTER 14

Introduction to Probability and Distributions

Learning Objectives

✓ Understand the basic concepts of probability including mutual exclusivity and event independence

✓ Utilize the generalized theories of probability to answer questions in social science

✓ Utilize the Gaussian Distribution to map continuous variables to a standardized distribution

✓ Apply combinations to address Bernoulli Processes

Cases in Research

Case A—National Helping Hands (NHH)

Maria is a regional coordinator for National Helping Hands. Recently, NHH supported a disaster recovery effort funded by the United States Federal Emergency Management Agency along the banks of the Ohio River in West Virginia. As the organization's efforts wind down, she knows it is important to be able to quantify the work her agency has provided for the community.

Case B—Amity Department of Homeland Security

Ping is in charge of policy research for the Amity Department of Homeland Security. In her capacity, she evaluates the effectiveness of proposed and current policies. She is currently reviewing a number of tax incentives that were passed locally to try to reduce the cost resulting from structural fires in the town.

Probability

Probability is arguably one of the most important quantitative tools available and is the foundation of most of the statistical techniques used in social science. This powerful tool provides the ability to quantify outcomes and base decisions on the likelihood of events. In reality, the subject of probability is merely a rudimentary formalization of how individuals make decisions; unfortunately, many people do not see this because the simplicity of probability is typically hidden in Greek letters and mathematical symbols.

For example, at some point you had to make a number of decisions that led you to taking this course in research methods. Similarly, on a weekly (or more frequent) basis, you have to make the decision to attend this class. Thinking about your decision to attend this class, you probably weighed a number of the following considerations: if attendance was mandatory; if attendance would improve your knowledge of the material; if attendance would increase your course grade; or even if you would get the opportunity to have an engaging discussion of ethical presentation of data. All these discreet factors required you to think about how each one would affect the outcome you desire from the course. If attendance is mandatory, then there is a 100% chance that missing a class will affect your final grade. If attendance is strongly recommended, then the likelihood of your grade being affected by skipping class is somewhere below 100% but also above zero. Probability allows us to formalize these decisions—and, through formalization, greatly improve the accuracy.

Basic Concepts of Probability

Probability is expressed as a number ranging from zero to one with one being the equivalent of a 100% chance of occurrence of the event and zero being no chance of the event occurring. Going back to the case of mandatory attendance, we could say that the probability of missing class affecting your grade is equal to one. We can further formalize this: (1) let the variable x represent if the class grade is negatively affected by missing class; (2) we will code the variable 1 = yes, and 0 = no. Now we can express the probability of the event x being coded yes (1) by writing:

Equation 14.1

$$P[x=1]=1$$

Now, in all actuality, we know that this is not true. First, class being mandatory means only that your instructor *can* lower your grade for nonattendance; however, the instructor still has the discretion to not do so. Next, educational institutions typically have a grade appeal process, thus further reducing the probability. In actuality, the probability is probably still pretty high but not quite a one. For the sake of argument, let's call it. Pr $[x = 1]$ = .89. This would mean that there is an 89% chance that your grade would suffer if you missed class under a mandatory attendance policy (we can actually calculate the effects of each stage in the process, but we will save that for later in the chapter).

Think of probability in terms of area, and that all the possible outcomes are the entirety of the area. So if we were to think about the flip of a coin, there are two possible outcomes: heads or tails. Given a fair coin (one that has exactly equal chances of coming up heads or tails), we know that the probability of heads is .5 (similarly, we know the probability of tails is also .5). We will define the entire **SAMPLE SPACE** (100% of the possible outcomes) as a square and the probability of the coin coming up tails as a subset of this space.

Similarly, we could represent the probability of two flips of a coin using the same type of diagram. In two flips of a fair coin, the sample space would be [H-H, H-T, T-H, T-T]. That is, we could have two heads, a heads on the first and a tails on the second, a tails on the first and a heads on the second, or two tails. Representing two of the four possible outcomes yields the following:

Figure 14.1

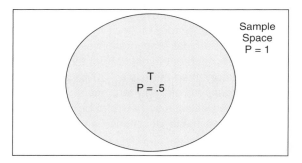

Figure 14.2

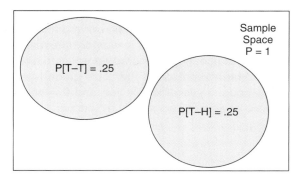

Notice that both outcomes lie completely within the sample space and that they do not overlap. This is because the sample space represents all the possible outcomes, but there is no way that both these events could occur at the same time. Because these events cannot both occur, we call them **MUTUALLY EXCLUSIVE**. We do not overlap them in the diagram because overlap would indicate that they could both occur.

Also notice that we have assigned the probability of .25 to each possible outcome. This is because we have 4 equally likely outcomes, so our total sample space of 1 is divided equally into 4 outcomes of .25 a piece. Anytime we can logically deduce the probability of an event, we refer to that as an **a PRIORI PROBABILITY**. The other way to generate probabilities is through multiple trials. When probabilities are generated by trials, we refer to them as **POSTERIOR PROBABILITIES**.

Example 14.1: Case A—Calculating the Probability of Events

Maria knows one of the major benefits of the U.S. government allowing NHH to participate in rebuilding efforts is that NHH is not a contractor for the U.S. government and therefore is not bound by many of the same rules. One of the most important differences for NHH is that while contractors are all required to use new materials, NHH is able to use salvage material. This means that NHH has the ability to provide more services for the same costs.

During the recent West Virginia flooding event, NHH rebuilt 35 homes on the banks of the Ohio River. These homes all sit on a small island in the middle of the river, which is just 3 meters above the river level. The specifications for the replacement homes called for the homes to be elevated 2 meters above ground level—which equates to just 2.5 meters above flood stage.

During the construction phase, Gary pointed out to Maria that there was enough good salvageable material that the construction crews could actually raise the homes to 3.5 meters above ground level with no additional costs. Maria quickly looked at the record books kept by the Tennessee Valley Authority and saw that in the last 100 years, the river had crested above 2.5 meters above flood stage 32 times at that location, but only 2 times above 3.5 meters above flood stage in any given year.

She quickly realized that if the builders stuck to the specifications, the homeowners would have a 32% chance of being flooded in any given year, but that because NHH could incorporate the salvage material, they could reduce that probability to just 2% in any year.

Calculating Probabilities for Independent Events

In Figures 14.1 and 14.2, we used simple math to identify the probability of the given events. This was uncomplicated because the numbers were obvious; however, this is not always the case. In cases where the probability is not easily known, we can calculate the probability of any given outcome by simply dividing the number of times a specific outcome occurs by the total number of times the event is repeated. Thinking of the coin flip again, if we define tails as our outcome of interest and flip a coin a set number of times, the posterior probability of this experiment will equal the number of tails divided by the total number of flips. We can generalize this formula as:

Formula 14.1

$$P[X] = \frac{r}{n}$$

Where:
r = the number of desired outcomes
n = the total number of trials

Using this formula, if we flipped a coin 10 times and got tails 4 of the 10 times, then the posterior probability would be .4.

At this point, you should be asking yourself why the example above does not have a posterior probability that is equal to the a priori probability listed earlier. The answer is quite simply because in 10 flips of a coin, you may not get exactly 5 tails. Posterior probabilities are very sensitive to the number of trials. The more trials, the better the posterior probability will be, and it will more closely approximate the theoretic (a priori) probability. Thus, if we were to repeat this experiment 1,000 times, we would expect the number of tails to approach 500.

Once we have probabilities for events, we can combine events to produce probabilities for outcomes of complex events. This is easiest when the events in question are **INDEPENDENT EVENTS**—that is, the outcomes of each event have no bearing on the other.

Let's return to the example of the probability of getting two tails on two flips of a fair coin. First, we will begin by illustrating this using a probability tree:

Figure 14.3

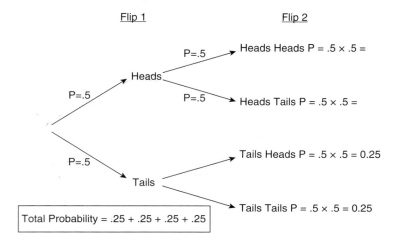

Figure 14.3 demonstrates two important rules for combining probabilities for independent events. First is calculating the **JOINT PROBABILITY**. This is the probability of two specific outcomes over two independent events. So if our two independent events are two flips of a coin, and we want to know the probability of getting two tails, we multiply the probability of the first event outcome (A) by the probability of the second event outcome (B). We call this the intersection of A and B and represent it symbolically as $P(A \cap B)$. Thus, the probability of getting a tails on the first flip of a coin *and* getting a tails on the second flip is $P = .5 \times .5 = .25$

Formula 14.2

$P(A \cap B) = P(A) \times P(B)$ *for independent events*

Using Venn diagrams, the intersection is represented by the area where the two event probabilities overlap.

Figure 14.4

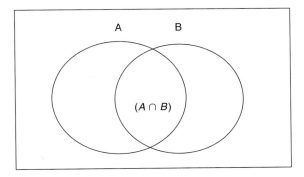

Compare Figure 14.4 to Figure 14.2. Can you guess what the intersection of two tails and tails-heads would be $P(TT \cap TH) =$??? **(HINT:** What effect does being mutually exclusive have on the *intersection* of two events?)

The second important rule demonstrated in Figure 14.3 is that the probability of any combination of mutually exclusive outcomes occurring is the sum of the probabilities of those outcomes. Each of the four outcomes listed on the right side of Figure 14.3 is mutually exclusive of the other three. That is, if we get a heads-tails outcome, we cannot have a heads-heads outcome as well. Each of the four possibilities occurs to the exclusion of the other three. There are times, though, when we might want to consider more than one of the outcomes. Perhaps we are interested in the probability of getting one heads and one tails in any order. In that case, we can calculate the probability of getting either a heads-tails or a tails-heads outcome by simply adding the probabilities of these two mutually exclusive outcomes. This is referred to as the union of the two probabilities. So if we were to label each outcome so that A (heads-heads), B (heads-tails),

C (tails-heads), and D (tails-tails), we can say that the union of B and C is equal to .25+.25 = .5 or:

Formula 14.3

$P(B \cup C) = P(B) + P(C)$ for mutually exclusive events

A concept similar to mutually exclusivity is that of **COLLECTIVELY EXHAUSTIVE** events. When a set of events comprises the entire sample space, the events are said to be jointly or collectively exhaustive. If we were interested in the outcome of the role of a single die, and our events were odds (rolling 1, 3, or 5) or even (2, 4, or 6), these events would be collectively exhaustive because $P(ODD) + P(EVEN) = S = 1$. Events may be both mutually exclusive and collectively exhaustive as is true in this case; however, they need not be.

Unfortunately, events are rarely independent and often, things are not mutually exclusive. In such cases, calculating probabilities becomes a bit more complicated (but only a bit). In the next section, we expand the concepts used here and provide some general rules of probability.

> **Class Exercise**: Identify three sets of events that are collectively exhaustive and mutually exclusive and three sets of events that are collectively exhaustive but not mutually exclusive.

General Rules of Probability

Example 14.2: Case B

Ping has been tasked with gathering and evaluating data for the Amity fire mitigation tax incentive program. She has gathered information for all of the structural fires since the program went into effect and has broken the data down by the type of incentive in place at the structure and the general amount of damage that the structure suffered. The data are as follows:

Incentive	Structure Damage			
	Total Loss	Severe Damage	Minor Damage	Total
None	13	2	0	15
Water reserves on site	5	4	1	10
Residential sprinklers	5	0	9	14
	23	6	10	39

Using Formula 14.1, Amelia is able to provide a great deal of information about structure fires since the program has taken affect. For example, she knows that the probability that a structure fire will result in a total loss is .59 ($r = 23$, $n = 39$); that the probability of severe damage is .15; and using Formula 14.3 she knows that the probability of total loss or severe damage is .74 (alternatively, she could have calculated the probability of only minor damage and subtracted it from 1).

Additionally, she is also able to calculate **CONDITIONAL PROBABILITIES.** That is, she can calculate the probability of an event given that another has already occurred. For example, she knows that if a given structure has residential sprinklers, the probability of a fire resulting in a total loss is only .36 ($r = 5$, $n = 14$). We symbolize the probability of an event (B) given that another event (A) has already occurred as $P(B\backslash A)$, which is read "the probability of B given A."

She can also quickly tabulate the **JOINT PROBABILITY** of events. So if she wanted to know the probability that a structure received severe damage and had water reserves on site, the probability would be .10 ($r = 4$, $n = 39$). Notice that if she were to try to use Formula 14.3 to find the joint probability, she would have grossly underestimated the probability (try this). This is because 14.3 only works in cases where the events are independent. In this case, the damage to the structure (or lack thereof) is in part a function of the incentive in place. To find the joint probability in this case, we would have to use the General Rule of Multiplication.

General Rule of Multiplication

Formula 14.4

General Rule of Multiplication

$$P(A \cap B) = P(A) \times P(B \backslash A) = P(B) \times P(A \backslash B)$$

So while we easily calculated the joint probability using Formula 14.1, let's give it a shot using Formula 14.4. We define (A) as the probability structure received severe damage ($r = 6$, $n = 39$); (B) as water reserves on site ($r = 10$, $n = 39$); and we will use the probability that water reserves were on site, given the structure received severe damage ($P(B\backslash A) = r = 4$, $n = 6$). This yields $P(A) = .15$ x $P(B\backslash A) = .67$ or .10. Now try verifying this number using $P(B)$ x $P(A\backslash B)$.

General Rule of Addition

Amelia is also able to quickly calculate the probability of one of a number of events occurring. In this case, she would be calculating the union of some events. For example, if she wanted to know the probability that a location had either (A) severe water damage or (B) water reserves on site, she could apply Figure 14.1 to calculate the posterior probability. This would be a bit tricky though, because these events are not mutually exclusive (note that there are four observations that overlap both the events in question—these four represent the intersection of A and B or ($A \cap B$)) and therefore would get "double counted" if we tried to simply use Formula 14.3. We can, however, generalize 14.3 so that it will work in situations where events are not mutually exclusive. To do so, we simply must subtract out any double counting that results from the intersection of any variables.

Formula 14.5

General Rule of Addition

$$P(A \cup B) = P(A) + P(B) - P(A \cap B)$$

Using the General Rule of Addition, we can easily calculate the probability of (A) severe damage or (B) water reserves on site. Given, $P(A) = .15$, $P(B) = .26$, and $P(A \cap B) = .10$, then $P(A \cup B) = .31$ then, if we were to use Formula 14.1, we would have to calculate the probability as $r = 12$ (that is 6 + 10 minus the cases that are counted twice or -4) and $n = 39$. It is possible to extend this formula to calculate the union of any number of events, but it becomes an increasingly complex task to ensure that areas are only counted once in the calculation.

Distributions

The utility of probability is not limited to the examples here where we examine the likelihood of discreet events. Probability can also be employed to discern useful information from large groups of data. For any roughly normal distribution of continuous data, we can apply what we know about the normal or Gaussian distribution to identify the probability of outcomes from a known population.

Gaussian

The Gaussian distribution, commonly referred to as the normal distribution, is the workhorse of statistics throughout the sciences. This distribution is named after Carl Friedrich Gauss, who was one of the great mathematicians in history and the individual most credited with the discovery and application of the normal curve. Over the last couple centuries, mathematicians have come to identify many useful properties of the normal distribution, and the first that we will explore here is the utility in understanding the probability associated with distributions of a continuous variable.

The normal curve represents a process that is very common: a distribution with heavy concentrations around the average (mean) value with decreasing density as values move away from this center. Think of throwing a mud ball against a wall. In the center there will be a big splotch of mud, with less and less mud as we move concentrically away from the center. Alternatively, you might also try a little experiment on your own. If you had a jar full of nuts (actually, any type of snack will do), and you reach your hand in and grab a handful, you could count the number of nuts in your hand. Repeating this multiple times will yield a data set that represents the number of nuts per handful. After many repetitions, you will find an average amount in a handful; however, you will most likely not have very many draws with exactly the same number of nuts (except for the most proficient snackers out there). You have just generated a data set that will have a mean, standard deviation, and also some known probabilistic characteristics.

In research, this sort of variation can be created through natural randomness (think of seasonal temperatures, income, age of respondents), or through measurement error, or as a function of the sampling strategy used in the data collection process (more on this in a later chapter). No matter the source of the variance in the distribution, what is known about the normal distribution allows us to glean a great deal of information from these data.

In the last chapter, we learned how to calculate the mean and standard deviation for a variable. Using these two bits of information, we can map most variables onto a normal curve. In chapter 13, Roshawna collected some data on home repair costs for use in her organization. With just 500 responses, the data were a bit skewed; however, as she collected more observations, the data appear to become more normal in distribution. Let's revisit these data and see what additional information she can provide about them by applying what we know about probability distributions.

Example 14.3

After collecting N = 1,000 observations on the cost of home repairs after being damaged in a disaster, Roshawna has the following data:

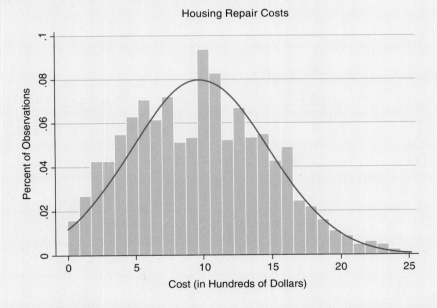

Housing Repair Costs

Notice that while these data are not perfectly normal, they do reasonably approximate a normal distribution. Given this, she feels comfortable reporting a mean of 9.73 and a standard deviation of 4.99. So what can she do with this beyond telling us that on average, home repairs will cost roughly one thousand dollars?

Well, we know that in a normal distribution that exactly half of all the observations will fall on either side of the mean. Second, we can calculate the probability of any given area under that curve in standard deviations.

The shaded area of Figure 14.6 shows the area to the left of the mean and represents 50% of the observations. The X-axis of this figure is scaled in standard deviations. That is, the -3 represents three standard deviations to the left of the mean. When dealing with the normal distribution, we refer to the scale across the X-axis (the standard deviations across the bottom) as Z-scores. Throughout the years, mathematicians have calculated the exact percentage of observations under a normal curve by standard deviations. So we know that by moving from the mean, 34.13% of all the observations will fall between the mean and one standard deviation (see Figure 14.7)

Figure 14.6

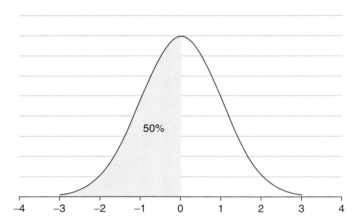

Figure 14.7

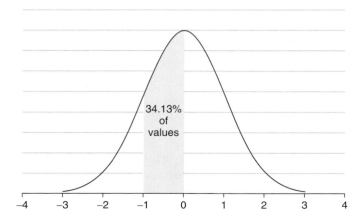

Because the normal distribution is symmetrical, it is also true that 34.13% of the observations would fall between the mean and one standard deviation above the mean as well. Thus, 68.26% of all the observations in a normal distribution lie from one standard deviation below to one standard deviation above the mean.

Knowing the descriptive statistics of the distribution of home repair costs, Roshawna can calculate pretty quickly the values for one standard deviation above and below the mean. In this case, (μ = 9.73 *and* σ = 4.99) roughly 68% of home repairs cost between 4.74 and 14.82 hundred dollars (that is, 9.73+/- 4.99) to repair. In fact, because the properties of the normal distribution is so well known, she can map her housing cost distribution onto the normal distribution by converting any value into Z-scores. Likewise, she can calculate values for her distribution that represent given percentages by converting known Z-scores into values for her distribution. This is done using the Z-score formula.

Formula 14.6

Z-Scores

$$z = \frac{X - \mu}{\sigma}$$

So to find out where a value lies in the normal distribution, we simply plug it into our formula for X, and the resulting Z-score tells us where it lies in terms of standard deviations from the mean. For example, to calculate the Z-score for $600 we would do the following:

Step 1: Subtract the mean from 6 ($X - \mu = 6 - 9.73 = -3.73$)

Step 2: Divide the result by the standard deviation to obtain the Z-score $\left(\dfrac{3.73}{\sigma} = \dfrac{3.73}{4.99} = -.75 \right)$

Thus, we know that 600 is .75 standard deviations below the mean for the distribution. Using the Z-score table in the back of the book (or alternatively we can use

Figure 14.8

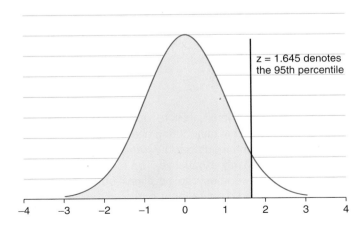

z = 1.645 denotes the 95th percentile

computer programs like Excel or Stata to convert Z-scores into probabilities), we know that 27.34 percent of the observations will fall between .75 standard deviations and the mean. Put in terms of our data, 27.34% of home damage ranged from $600 to $973.

It is more typical to calculate set percentages of a distribution. For example, we may want to know about the 95% of cases around the mean, or the top 5% of the distribution or the like. Let's look at each of these examples. First, we will calculate the top 5% of observations.

Step 1: Identify the Z-score that marks the 95th percentile of the distribution.

Step 2: Calculate the X value for the given Z-score $1.645 = \dfrac{X - 9.73}{4.99}$

Step 2a: The point is 1.645 standard deviations above the mean, and a standard deviation = 4.99 so first we multiply 4.99 by 1.645 and obtain 8.21 (remember, when moving constants from one side of the equals sign to the other, they change sides. So the standard deviation that divides on the right, multiplies on the left).

Step 2b: As we said, the value is above the mean, so we must add the *calculated value of 8.21 to* the mean of 9.73 to get an X value of 17.94.

We can now say that 95% of all home damage costs are below $1,794.

Working with the normal distribution is very straightforward; however, it is important to remember that the calculations rely on the symmetry of the distribution, and that the point of reference is always the mean. That means that when we make calculations about areas under the curve, we always have to think of each side as 50% and base our calculations for each side separately. Until this point, we have only looked at calculations involving one tail of the distribution, but if we wanted to look at a calculation that involved both tails we would have to perform two sets of calculations. For example, what if we wanted to find the range of the middle 50% of observations? That is, what if we want to identify the values that represent the 25% above and below the mean? In this case, we would want to find 25% above and 25% below or from our Z-table the .68 standard deviations above and below. In this case, we would multiply the standard deviation by .68, and then add it to the mean to find the upper bound and subtract it from the mean to find the lower bound. Try this for yourself.

Binomial Distribution

A second distribution that lends itself well to applying probability to events is the Binomial Probability Distribution. This distribution allows managers to estimate the probability of discreet events (noncontinuous data) when the process generates outcomes that are mutually exclusive and jointly exhaustive. The most typical example of this is the flip of a coin; however, many outcomes can be classified in this manner. In the public sector, we can classify policy and management outcomes as either a success or not a success, services rendered or not rendered, and equipment serviceable or not service-able. Each of these outcome classification schemas will lend itself to this application of the binomial distribution, and we refer to these as **BERNOULLI PROCESSES.**

When we have a Bernoulli Process in action, we need only know three pieces of information to be able to calculate probabilities for these events using a statistical tool called a **COMBINATION.**

Formula 14.7

Combination

$$C_r^n p^r q^{n-r}$$

Where:

n = the number of trials
r = the number of desired outcomes
p = the probability of the desired outcome
q = $1 - p$ (the inverse probability of the desired outcome or conversely, the probability of the undesired outcome

Demonstrating this with a coin toss, let's consider again the discussion on posterior probabilities. We noted earlier that in 10 flips of a coin we only got tails 4 times. We can calculate the probability of only getting 4 tails given the true probability of .50. To do so, we estimate the following:

$$C_4^{10} 0.5^4 0.5^{10-4}$$

Step 1: The first stage is to calculate the combination. This is done by the following:

$$C_r^n = \frac{n!}{r!(n-r)!}$$

In this formula, the exclamation points mean factorial, so we would read the above as "n factorial divided by r factorial times n minus r factorial." The factorial means that we multiply the number by every whole number below it to zero.

$$C_4^{10} = \frac{10!}{4!(10-4)!} = \frac{10 \times 9 \times 8 \times 7 \times 6 \times 5 \times 4 \times 3 \times 2 \times 1}{(4 \times 3 \times 2 \times 1) \times (6 \times 5 \times 4 \times 3 \times 2 \times 1)} = \frac{10 \times 9 \times 8 \times 7}{4 \times 3 \times 2 \times 1} = \frac{5040}{24} = 210$$

Step 2: Now we simply complete the rest of the formula so we know that .5 raised to the fourth power is .0625, and .5 raised to the sixth power is .0156 as the formula is now 210 × .0625 × .0156 = .2051. So we could say that the probability of getting exactly 4 tails on 10 flips of a coin is .205 or that this should happen by random chance 20.5% of the time. If we wanted to know what the probability is that we would get 4 or less, we would have to calculate the probability for each possible outcome (4 tails, 3 tails, 2 tails, 1 tails, and 0 tails) and then add them together (Table 14.1).

$$C_4^{10} 0.5^4 0.5^{10-4} + C_3^{10} 0.5^3 0.5^{10-3} + C_2^{10} 0.5^2 0.5^{10-2} + C_1^{10} 0.5^1 0.5^{10-1} + C_0^{10} 0.5^0 0.5^{10-0}$$

Table 14.1

# of Tails	Exact Probability
4	0.2051
3	0.1172
2	0.0439
1	0.0098
0	0.0010
Total	0.3770

Thus, the probability of getting 4 or fewer tails on 10 flips of a fair coin is .377, or there is a 38% chance that you will get 4 or fewer tails on 10 flips of a fair coin. Try calculating each of these outcomes for yourself.

Example 14.4: Case B—Using the Binomial Distribution to Assess Likeliness of Outcomes

Ping knows that nationally, only 3 in every 100 homes have sprinkler systems, yet of the 7 homes she visited recently, 3 of them had residential sprinklers. Ping wants to know what the probability is that this would be the case given the national average. To solve this, she calculates uses the binomial distribution where:

$n = 7, r = 3, p = .03, q = .97$

She finds the probability of this happening by random chance is .0008. What reasons might cause this to have happened?

Probability is the foundation of statistical methods, sampling, and game theory methods used in the social and physical sciences. This chapter presents a brief introduction, but there are far more resources available. Certainly, if you are comfortable with the techniques in this chapter, then you have a good foundation for further learning in empirical methodology. Subsequent chapters will provide further applications of probabilistic techniques for addressing social phenomena, as well as more distributions that cover more specialized areas of inquiry; however, we strongly suggest that any students that are serious about quantitative evaluations of social sciences continue to develop analytical skills that provide a greater coverage of this particular topic.

Putting Knowledge into Practice: Using Excel to Calculate Exact Probabilities

Calculating the probabilities using the binomial distribution can get to be a bit complex by hand, however, Excel has some handy tools that will let you produce a spreadsheet to do this for you.

	A	B	C	L
1		Binomial Probability		
2				
3		n =	7	
4		r =	3	
5		p =	0.03	
6		q =	=1-C5	
7	C^n_r	=	=COMBIN(C3,C4)	
8	$C^n_r\, p^r q^{n-r}$	=	=(C7)*(C5^C4)*(C6^(C3-C4))	
9				
10				

Vocabulary

A PRIORI PROBABILITY—The probability of an event outcome that can be logically deduced before it occurs.

BERNOULLI PROCESS—A discreet process that results in a dichotomous outcome.

COLLECTIVELY EXHAUSTIVE—A set of events whose joint probability is equal to 1.

COMBINATION—a mathematical process that identifies the number of ways a group of items can be taken from a larger group.

CONDITIONAL PROBABILITY—The probability of an event outcome given that another related event has already occurred.

GAUSSIAN DISTRIBUTION—The normal distribution.

INDEPENDENT EVENTS—Events whose outcome probabilities do not affect one another.

JOINT PROBABILITY—The probability of two events both occurring. This is referred to as the intersection of two probabilities.

MUTUALLY EXCLUSIVE EVENTS—Two or more events that the occurrence of one prevents the occurrence of any other. With mutually exclusive events, the occurrence of any given outcome precludes the occurrence of any other.

Flashcards & MCQs

POSTERIOR PROBABILITY—The probability of event outcomes that is calculated from repeated trials.

SAMPLE SPACE—All possible outcomes of a process under examination.

Z-SCORE—A standardized scale in standard deviations that identify locations on a normal distribution.

Review Questions

- What is the intersection of two mutually exclusive events?
- Is it possible to use the General Rule of Addition to calculate the union of two independent events?
- How can income be classified as a Bernoulli Process? Education?
- List five typical events in Public Management for which you can identify a priori probabilities.
- Where in Public Management do we tend to use posterior probabilities?

Discussion Questions

- The expression "curving grades" comes from fitting the outcomes of student examinations to a normal curve to produce variance across all the possible grades. Is this practice "good" or "bad?"
- How could the normal distribution be used to prioritize organizational goals?
- Are there times when Public Management should not base decisions on probabilities of outcomes? If so, when and why?

CHAPTER 15

Hypothesis Testing

Learning Objectives

✓ Use appropriate statistical tests to determine the probability that two samples are from the same distribution

✓ Use appropriate statistical tests to test for sample independence

✓ Understand the concepts of statistical power and significance

✓ Understand the concept of a standard error

Cases in Research

Case A—Amity Department of Homeland Security

Amity is in the process of hiring a new batch of employees to enhance organizational capacity. Frank, the human resources director, has implemented a hiring process that conforms to the area's Equal Opportunity hiring laws. This process includes broad advertising in a variety of mediums, physical- and skill-based testing, and a background test. Frank is concerned that although this process seems unbiased on the surface, some of the screening tools may be inadvertently disadvantaging specific segments of the population.

Case B—Springfield Housing Department (SHD)

Hakeem, an analyst with SHD, has been tasked with evaluating the distribution of minority versus nonminority applications to identify any possible bias in the program.

The Concept of Hypothesis Testing

In the previous chapter, we discussed the concept of probability and ways to use it to understand the likelihood of events. This chapter focuses on using what we know about probability to answer specific questions that we want to ask of our data. Classically, hypothesis testing is a formalized process to ask our data if two groups are fundamentally different based on an a priori (developed before the test) criterion. To do this, we fall back on what is known about the probabilistic distribution of events.

Recall from chapter 3 that we defined a hypothesis as a proposition proposed as an explanation of a phenomenon. The key to a good hypothesis is that it asserts a quality about one specific variable or set of events. A hypothesis may state that workers on flextime are more productive than workers on set shifts, or it could state that nonprofit organizations are able to implement new programs more rapidly than governmental organizations. The first hypothesis makes a statement about employee efficiency, while the second one is about program implementation speed. When we use statistical techniques to test hypotheses, it is important that we can express the hypothesis in terms of quantifiable measures and express our assumption about the effect of the proposition on the phenomenon with a mathematical operator. We want to be able to say that group A will be less than group B, or that group C will be equal to group D. Whatever the proposition, as long as we can measure the constructs and express our expectations with a logical operator, we can apply statistical tools to evaluate the probability associated with our proposition.

To express these hypotheses in mathematical terms, we will have to introduce another symbol. In chapter 13 we identified the symbol for the mean of a **SAMPLE** as $\bar{x}$ (x-bar). To indicate the different samples in our hypotheses, we will include a numeric subscript, so instead of writing $\bar{x}_{flextime}$ we will let flextime be sample 1 and shift work be sample 2. Then we can state our **WORKING HYPOTHESIS** as $\bar{x}_1 > \bar{x}_2$. In the second hypothesis, we can let 1 represent implementation times for nonprofit organizations and 2 represent implementation times for government organizations. We could then write this working hypothesis as $\bar{x}_1 \cong \bar{x}_2$. In the following sections, we will discuss how to critically evaluate hypotheses such as these in Nominal, Ordinal, and Continuous data.

Hypothesis Testing: The Process

Before we can test our hypothesis, we must have a couple things in place first: (1) we must have operationalized our hypothesis into a statement (or statements) of expectations for the variables in question; (2) we must have identified quantifiable measures of the variables; and (3) we must identify the level of measurement for each variable. The concept of hypothesis testing itself consists of two steps.

First we need to establish a probability threshold that we consider to be rare enough to make the event noteworthy. Seeing a bird in the sky is not much of an event as it happens pretty frequently. The probability that you will see a bird on any given day is probably pretty close to one. Conversely, if you would see a penguin fly overhead, you might be encouraged to tell everyone you saw. This is because penguins do not fly, so the probability of this event happening is pretty close to zero. Subconsciously, we all have some probabilistic threshold that renders events important. Hypothesis testing formalizes this process by establishing this threshold before we observe the event. This probabilistic threshold allows us to identify events that are deemed **STATISTICALLY SIGNIFICANT**, and we represent this threshold with the symbol α (alpha). Typically, .05 is used as a rule of thumb in hypothesis testing. This means that if the probability of an event happening by random chance is .05 or less, we deem the event to be statistically significant. It is very important to understand what statistical significance means, though, as a decision rule.

The probability of an event happening through random chance is a statement about how certain we feel we need to be about an event to make a decision based on its occurrence. For example, if we use $P \leq .05$ as our threshold for statistical significance, this means we are comfortable with the event happening 1 out of every 20 times by pure chance. Picture yourself as a hospital director. In this position, you have many decisions to sign off on; among these today will be two new pieces of equipment. The first is an industrial oven for the cafeteria, and the second is a dialysis machine. If the first burns food once in every 20 times by random chance, there may not be much consequence; however, if the second fails once every 20 times, you could be putting patients' lives at risk. In the field of public and nonprofit administration, we are faced with decisions every day that affect large numbers of people; the decision criteria we use are critical in this respect.

Example 15.1: Case A—Deciding What Constitutes Important

Hakeem is beginning to investigate whether the application rate for minorities is significantly less than what would be expected given the percentage of minorities that live in Springfield. Before running any tests, he knows that deciding on α, his threshold for significance, is going to be critical in defending his findings to his superiors. Hakeem has collected continuous level data on applications, and is certain that his measures are reasonably free of error. Because he has a great deal of confidence in the accuracy, reliability, and validity of his data, Hakeem decided that the traditional $\alpha = .05$ is a reasonable threshold for statistical significance in this case.

In his final report, he justifies this decision by stating that if the data were not direct measures, he would have chosen a level for alpha that was much smaller.

The second step in establishing statistical significance is to identify the proper statistical test to assess the probability of the event in question. This decision is made based on the level of measurement of the data.

Class Exercise: In Example 15.1, Hakeem states that if the measures were not direct measures, he would have chosen a smaller value for alpha. How could having more or less objective measures influence outcomes, and why might he choose a higher threshold with more subjective data?

Hypothesis Testing with Nominal and Ordinal Data

The most basic form of hypothesis testing involves differentiating two items. We ask our data the very simple question, "Is A different from B?" While simple, this is the seminal question in statistics. Probably the most frequently used statistic to evaluate this is the X^2 test for independence. A very common application of the Chi-Square test is in evaluating contingency tables.

Contingency Tables

Contingency tables are a convenient way to display information from nominal and ordinal data that contrasts the data by a second variable. Returning to our discussion of probability, consider a variable in a sample space where that sample space is partitioned by another variable. Such is the case in the following example:

Example 15.2

Frank has administered a screening exam to a batch of new recruits. As expected, about a quarter of the applicants are eliminated from the candidate pool by the screening tool. Unfortunately, he realizes that all of the exam failures are female. The results of the examination are in the Table 15.1:

Table 15.1

Test Results	Gender Female	Male	Total
Fail	35	0	35
Pass	28	60	88
Total	63	60	123

While this contingency table looks like a simple table, there are a few important items to note. First, the dependent variable is the row variable. This is the same as being on the Y-axis of a graph. The dependent variable is always on the Y-axis of a graph or contingency table. Second, the values of the variables (in this case, only the dependent variable has rank order, so this does not apply to the independent variable) go from lowest to highest. For the purpose of the Chi-Square test, this is unimportant; however, this will become important in later chapters. Third, gender is an independent variable. Except in cases in biomedical sciences, gender usually cannot be a dependent variable because it is not affected by other things. Here is a case in point: failing the exam cannot change an individual's gender, therefore the test cannot be an independent variable affecting the dependent variable gender. And fourth, because gender is a nominal variable, the order in which the categories are presented in the table has no meaning. It would seem that there is a difference between the outcomes of the exam for males and females; however, raw data can be deceiving. To examine the results for these two groups, Frank has to take a couple more steps. The first is to standardize the data so that he is comparing outcomes on the same metric. The easiest way to do this with a contingency table is to calculate the frequencies of the independent variable. In other words, he can simply calculate the percentages for each column. This produces the following, as shown in Table 15.2:

Table 15.2

Test Results	Gender		
	Female	Male	Total
Fail	55.56%	0.00%	28.46%
Pass	44.44%	100.00%	71.54%
Total	100.00%	100.00%	100.00%

Table 15.3

Test Results	Gender					
	Female		Male		Total	
Fail	63	100%	57	95%	120	98%
Pass	0	0%	3	5%	3	2%
Total	63	100%	60	100%	123	100%

The total column represents what we know about the distribution of grades, absent the information from the independent variable. Thus, in a fair world, we would expect the failure rate for both men and women to be about 28%. Similarly, we would expect the pass rate to be about 72%. As we can see in the columns for each gender category, this is not the case. In this case, we see that there is about a 56 percentage point difference in the performance of females and males, so the biased outcomes are pretty clear. But consider the following distribution of the same data in Table 15.3:

In this case, there is only a 5 percentage point difference in the outcomes of the two groups. Can we tell if there is gender-related bias in this case? When the results are not as clear, the Chi-Square statistic can be employed to calculate the probability that these two groups are the same.

Calculating the Chi-Square Statistic

The Chi-Square statistic evaluates the difference between the information provided by the independent variable and what we would expect to have if we did not know the actual outcomes of the independent variable. If we only knew the outcome distribution from the exam in Table 15.3, we would know that 97.56% of all applicants who took the exam failed it. Thus, since we know that 63 of the applicants were female, we would expect that 61 of the 63 female applicants would fail (that is 97.56% x 63 = 61.46. The number is rounded off to the nearest whole person as we should always present statistics in logical scales, and because working with fractions of people can become quite messy). The Chi-Square statistic uses these expected frequencies to assess the probability of the differences between the two groups. Calculating the Chi-Square statistic is a straightforward process and is done with the following steps:

1. Calculate the expected frequencies for each of the cells in Table 15.4.

Table 15.4

Expected Frequencies

Test Results	Gender	
	Female	Male
Fail	61.46	58.54
Pass	1.54	1.46

2. Calculate the difference between the observed and expected frequencies (Table 15.5).

Table 15.5

Cell	Observed	Expected	Difference
Female Fail	63	61	2
Female Pass	0	2	−2
Male Fail	57	59	−2
Male Pass	3	1	2

3. Next we square the difference and divide it by the expected value. This is done to get rid of the negative signs (or else the differences would add up to zero). Remember, you must square the values, and divide each squared value by the expected value before moving on to the next step (Table 15.6).

Table 15.6

Cell	Observed	Expected	Difference	Difference Squared	Difference Squared/ Expected
Female Fail	63	61	2	4	0.07
Female Pass	0	2	−2	4	2
Male Fail	57	59	−2	4	0.07
Male Pass	3	1	2	4	4

4. The final step is to sum the values, and the result is the value for the Chi-Square statistic. In the example, our value would be 6.14.

The Chi-Square statistic is summarized in the following formula:

Formula 15.1

$$X^2 = \sum \frac{(observed - expected)^2}{expected}$$

This test gets its name because numerous scholars have demonstrated that this particular ratio (among many others you will encounter in the field of statistics) is Chi-Square distributed with degrees of freedom equal to the number of rows minus one times the number of columns minus one.

Formula 15.2

—Degrees of Freedom (d.f.) for the Chi-Square test for independence

$$d.f. = (r-1) \times (c-1)$$

DEGREES OF FREEDOM is a concept in statistics that identifies the effects of the constraints placed on data through calculations in reference to how much data we have. This is important because the degrees of freedom affect the probability (as demonstrated by Table 15.1), and because we cannot impose more constraints on the data than we have pieces of data. In the case of contingency tables, each cell of the table represents a piece of data, so there are degrees of freedom in a contingency table. When we perform the Chi-Square test, each division of the data beyond the first cell becomes a restriction on the data so we impose $r + c - 1$ restrictions on the data. The degrees of freedom for the test are simply the degrees of freedom remaining after we impose the restrictions associated with the calculations. Technically, the degrees of freedom are equal to the degrees of freedom minus the restrictions, $(r \times c) - (r + c - 1)$, or this can be reduced to Formula 15.2.

Figure 15.1 illustrates the Chi-Square distribution ranging from one to seven degrees of freedom.

Notice how the distribution changes, given the different degrees of freedom. Using Excel (alternatively, you may also use the table in the back of the book), we find that a Chi-Square statistic of 6.14 with 1 degree of freedom has a probability of .013. We can say that there is a 1.3% probability that these two groups have the same distribution, or that the chances of this outcome happening by random chance are less than 1 out of 50.

The Chi-Square test is a powerful tool in statistics, and as you can see from above, it can make evaluating data much easier. In fact, there are many ways the Chi-Square distribution can be applied. The case above is one where continuous data have been compressed to make them ordinal (the actual test scores were dichotomized by coding everything above a 95 to a pass and all the other values to fail). In practice, giving up variance is not a good practice. While the compression has enhanced the presentation of the data and we have used logical coding for the compression, there are tools that exist that will allow us to evaluate the probability that two samples of continuous data are drawn from the same distribution. This is done using a t-test.

Figure 15.1

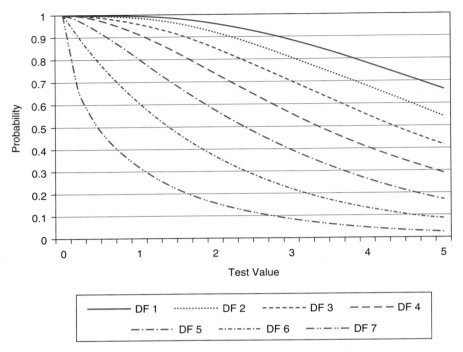

Putting Knowledge into Practice: Using Excel to Calculate a Chi-Square Statistic

You can calculate the Chi-Square statistic several ways in Excel. First, if you make a table of observed and expected frequencies, Excel will calculate the probability of Chi-Square directly. Excel provides three tools:

1. CHITEST—this will calculate the probability from tables of the observed and expected frequencies
2. CHIINV—this will calculate the value of the Chi-Square statistic given the probability and degrees of freedom. This is a great way to identify the Chi-Square critical value from a desired alpha
3. CHIDIST—this calculates the probability of a Chi-Square value for given degrees of freedom

	A	B	C	D	E
19			Observed		Expected
20	Results	Female	Male	Female	Male
21	Fail	63	57	61	59
22	Pass	0	3	2	1
23					
24			Formula	Result	
25		d.f.	1		
26		Chi Square (P)	=CHITEST(B21:C22,D21:E22)	0.013265	
27		Inverse Chi-square	=CHIINV(C26,C25)	6.13337	
28		Calculate (P) from Chi-square	=CHIDIST(C27,C25)	0.013265	
29					

SPSS

STATA

Hypothesis Testing in Continuous Data

The t-distribution or student's t-distribution is very similar to the Gaussian distribution in shape. In fact, as the number of observations increases, the t-distribution converges with the normal distribution. You may think of the t-distribution as a distribution for use in finite (small) samples.

Before we get into calculating the t-statistic, first we need to understand a little about how samples relate to the population from which they are drawn.

The Distribution of Samples in a Population

Recall our discussion of standard deviations in a distribution from chapter 13, where we examined how points in a Gaussian distribution cluster around the mean. When we sample from a distribution, the means of those samples will cluster around the mean of the population. Thus, if our sample is large enough, we can approximate the mean of the population with some degree of accuracy. Just how accurate our estimate is can be distinguished by calculating the standard error (s.e.). The **STANDARD ERROR** is simply the standard deviation of sample means in a population. Now you might be thinking that to calculate a standard deviation of sample means, we would need a large number of samples. Fortunately, mathematicians that have come before us have done this laborious task for us and have demonstrated that the standard error of the sample means can be calculated as the following:

Formula 15.3

$$s.e. = \frac{\sigma}{\sqrt{n}}$$

That is, the standard error is the standard deviation of the population divided by the square root of the number of observations. Unfortunately, if we only have a sample, we will have to approximate the standard deviation of the population with the standard deviation of the sample. The standard deviation of the sample is calculated the same way as the standard deviation of the population except that instead of dividing by N, we divide by (n-1). Thus, when dealing with samples, here is the standard deviation:

Formula 15.4

$$s = \sqrt{\frac{\sum \left(X_i - \overline{X} \right)^2}{n-1}}$$

Bear in mind that because we are dealing with both populations and samples, we have slightly different notations to represent the statistics for each. These are summarized in Table 15.7:

Table 15.7

Statistic	Population Symbol	Sample Symbol
Mean	μ	$\overline{X}$
Standard Deviation	σ	s
Number of Observations	N	n

Calculating the T-Statistic

One interesting quality of the t-distribution is that it is important to specify whether your hypothesis has a direction or not. This is because when using a t-distribution, we can specify how we want to test the sample in relation to the mean. So if we are interested in if the sample mean is below the hypothesized mean, we would only use a one-tailed test. In this case where the hypothesis is $\overline{X} < \mu$, the value of t would be negative. Similarly, if we wanted to test $\overline{X} < \mu$, we would expect t to be positive. These are examples of one-tailed tests. Conversely, if we are only interested to know if $\overline{X} \neq \mu$, this is a two-tailed test. In the following examples, we apply a one-tailed t-test.

The basic t-statistic is quite simple to calculate. It is just the difference between the two means divided by the standard error.

Formula 15.5

$$t = \frac{\overline{X} - \mu}{s.e.}$$

So if we want to compare the mean of a sample to some hypothesized mean, we would simply divide the difference by the standard error. For example, let's return to Frank's testing data.

The One-Sample T-Statistic

Example 15.3

Frank wants to know if the mean score of the test is different from 85. Put differently, Frank wants to know the probability that the sample (his test data) comes from a population with $\mu = 85$. Currently he knows the following (Table 15.8):

Table 15.8

Grouping	Test Grades		
	Mean	s	n
Overall	78.59	10.68	123
Males	85.12	5.97	60
Females	72.38	10.50	63

To test if the overall mean is different than 85, he calculates: $(78.59 - 85)/(10.68/\sqrt{123}) - 6.41/.963$.

This yields the result t = 6.66. In this case, the t-statistic has d.f. of n-1, or d.f. = 122. Looking this up on a t-table provides a probability less than .0001 (in fact, the probability is so small that Excel will not calculate it). What this means is that if this sample was drawn from a population with a true mean of 85, this sample would lie more than 6.6 standard deviations away from the true mean. The probability that this sample is drawn from a population with a mean of 85, which is less than .01%.

The Two Sample T-Statistic

The t-statistic is also useful for comparing two samples for equivalence. This only requires a bit of adjustment to the calculation of the standard error and the degrees of freedom. Let's return to the data in Table 15.8 and calculate the probability that the sample of females and the sample of males are drawn from the same population (that there is no statistical difference between the two).

To calculate the t-statistic, we will insert the second sample mean in place of the hypothesized mean. Also, instead of using

Class Exercise: Using Example 15.3, try testing whether the overall sample could have come from a population with a mean of 77. You should find that the probability of the overall sample coming from a population of 77 is a little greater than 10%.

the standard error, we will have to use the standard error of the difference. The pooled standard error is calculated as follows:

Formula 15.6

$$s.e._d = \sqrt{s.e._{females}^2 + s.e._{males}^2}$$

Step 1: Calculate the s.e. for each group. For males it would be .77, and for females it would be 1.32.

Step 2: Square each of the standard errors. For males this would be .59, and for females it would be 1.75

Step 3: Add the two values. This yields 2.34

Step 4: Take the square root of the result. In this case, the $s.e._d = 1.53$.

Now we can calculate the t-statistic substituting the $s.e._d$ in place of the standard error. Calculating $\overline{X}_{females} - \overline{X}_{males}/s.e._d$ provides a t-score of (72.38–85.12)/1.53 or -4.41. So there is a 4.41 standard deviation difference between these two means if they were drawn from the same population. This particular t-statistic has $df = (n_{females} + n_{males}) - 2$. Or, the d.f. = 121. For a one-tailed test, the associated probability is again well below .0001.

As you can see, the t-test is a useful tool for understanding how samples relate to populations. This chapter provided a brief introduction to two of the most prolific tests used in statistics, and as you will see in the coming chapters, both have numerous applications throughout statistics. The important thing to remember is that no matter where these test statistics are applied, the basic logic of each remains constant, and the basic question these two tests pose to data remain the same. We use the t-test and Chi Square to identify if two groups of data are different.

Putting Knowledge into Practice: Using Excel to Calculate t-tests

Excel offers a number of options for calculating values for t-tests. The TTEST function will let you compare one list of values to another, but you must identify the values, decide on the number of tails for the test, the degrees of freedom, and which particular t-test you want it to perform. Excel has three options: (1) is the paired t-test, (2) assumes equal variance between the two groups of values, and (3) assumes different values. In relation to the tests described above, the 3rd option—the heteroskedastic model—is the equivalent of the two sample t-test we present. The second option—the homoskedastic—may be used to approximate the one-sample t-test value. The inverse function (TINV) returns the critical value of t for a given value of alpha and degrees of freedom. Importantly, this function only reports one-tailed probabilities. The distribution function (TDIST) will return the probability associated with a value of t, and requires the degrees of freedom and number of tails.

SPSS

STATA

	A	B	C	D	E
				E12	f_x
1					
2	A	B		Type of test	3
3	1	9		# Tails	2
4	2	8		d.f.	18
5	3	6		t-test function	=TTEST(A3:A7,B3:B7,E3,E2)
6	4	7		Inverse	=TINV(E5,E4)
7	5	1		Distribution	=TDIST(E6,E4,E3)
8					
9					
10					
11					
12					

This chapter has demonstrated how to evaluate hypotheses based on the probability that observed events could come from distributions of interest. Specifically, we used the Chi-Square statistic to evaluate contingency tables to see if the information we gain by knowing the independent variable provides better predictive power in reference to the dependent variable than the mean of the dependent variable. In sum, Chi-Square test simply tells us if the observed distribution (the data in the table) provides a better estimate of the value of the dependent variable than we would guess only knowing the distribution of the dependent variable. This test can be performed on data at any level of measurement, but because tools exist that provide more flexibility for continuous level data, the Chi-Square test of contingency tables is typically reserved for nominal and ordinal levels of measurement.

When dealing with continuous level data, the t-test is the significant test de jour. The t-test reveals the probability that some distribution of data came from some other distribution of data, either real or hypothetical. Stated differently, the t-test tells the difference between a distribution, and a mean is significantly different (either larger or smaller) from zero. Table 15.9 provides a handy reference to guide the choice of statistical test.

Table 15.9

Level of Measurement	Significance test
Nominal	Chi-square
Ordinal	Chi-square
Continuous	t-test

Statistical significance is a specific term with a specific meaning. Up to this point, we have applied it as a level of probability below which we find an event interesting. Thus, if we specify alpha = .03, we would interpret any hypothesis test with a probability at or below this to be statistically significant. Using the functions in Excel, we are able to calculate values for t- or Chi-Square that identifies this critical threshold. While this approach may seem a bit arbitrary, the basis of it lays in the scientific method.

Errors, Power, and Significance

In research, our hypothesis of interest is referred to as the **ALTERNATE HYPOTHESIS**. The act of hypothesis testing does not directly test the alternate hypothesis, but it actually tests for all other possibilities. These other possibilities are known as the null hypothesis. For example, if we are interested in comparing the productivity in customer service between two agencies, we might hypothesize that Organization 1 processes more claims than Organization 2. We would represent this alternate hypothesis as $H_a : \overline{X}_1 > \overline{X}_2$. In this case, the **NULL HYPOTHESIS** would be that the output of Organization 1 was the same or less than that of Organization 2, and write it as $H_o : \overline{X}_1 \leq \overline{X}_2$. Thus, we evaluate the alternate hypothesis by either rejecting the null hypothesis (this indicates evidence in support of the alternate hypothesis) or failing to reject the null hypothesis (providing evidence that the alternate hypothesis is not correct). This approach to hypothesis testing leads to four possible outcomes: we can correctly reject the null hypothesis, incorrectly reject the null hypothesis, correctly fail to reject the null hypothesis, or incorrectly fail to reject the null hypothesis.

If we reject a null hypothesis that is actually correct, we are committing what is known as **TYPE I ERROR**. That is, we are accepting evidence for our alternate hypothesis that is incorrect. The probability of committing type I error is the statistical significance. In contrast, **TYPE II ERROR** is when we fail to reject an incorrect null hypothesis and type II error is represented by the symbol β. The **STATISTICAL POWER** of a hypothesis test is simply $(1-\beta)$ (see Table 15.10).

In practice, it is rare to see analysis couched in terms of the null hypothesis, so Table 15.11 reiterates the previous table framed in terms of the alternate hypothesis.

Table 15.10

		Null Hypothesis is:	
		Incorrect	Correct
But we:	Reject	OK	Type I Error
	Fail to Reject	Type II Error	OK

Table 15.11

		Alternate Hypothesis is:	
		Incorrect	Correct
But we:	Reject it	OK	Type II Error
	Accept it	Type I Error	OK

Statistical Power

The statistical power $(1-\beta)$ provides information as to how strong the test is. That is, a test that has very low statistical power is very likely to reject a hypothesis that is, in fact, correct. Conversely, a test with very high statistical power is less likely to do so. Unfortunately, very little research tends to include power tests. Often this will be considered when sample sizes are drawn (for more on this, see chapter 11 about surveying), and statistical power will also be discussed infrequently in academic literature in the field of public health; however, this is very rare in the fields of public administration and public policy. This is problematic as rejecting a correct hypothesis in academic work has little cost (and in fact, it provides others the opportunity to publish); in applied work in management and evaluation, it could mean the end of a productive program.

Statistical Significance

The probability of type I error, the statistical significance of a test, is represented as α. Alpha is probably the most used and most misunderstood statistic used in research. It tells us what the probability is that the information we accept as true is true. Academics rely heavily on this as there is a high cost to accepting false information into the body of academic work. In practice, the consequences can be much higher.

Proper hypothesis testing requires the researcher to specify the threshold of α, which will be used for acceptance of information. That is, when we select alpha, we make a statement about how often we are willing to be wrong. For instance, if we select $\alpha < .01$ as our threshold for accepting a hypothesis, we are saying that we are comfortable being wrong 1% of the time. Stated differently, $\alpha < .01$ means that there is a 1 in 100 chance that we are accepting false information as being true. In statistics, $\alpha < .05$ is the "rule of thumb" for statistical significance. The problem with this is that this "rule of thumb" means that we are accepting a 1 in 20 chance that the information is incorrect. This threshold is probably alright as the cost of including false information in the general academic literature is low (although some of our colleagues may disagree). But because many students of statistical methods leave the course only remembering .05 as an important threshold, application of this threshold without *understanding* what it means to the evaluation may be highly problematic.

Remember, .05 means that 1 in 20 times the information you derive from your hypothesis test will be wrong. There are times when this is probably alright. For example, if you are trying to identify optimal stocking for an ice cream novelty vending machine at the public pool, then under- or overestimating the necessary reserves is probably alright. If the concession area runs out of product or has excess product, then the result will simply be a reduction in net revenue. If on the other hand you are estimating staffing at a suicide hotline, underestimating staffing levels might have much more dire consequences. It is very important to weigh the importance of the decision with the threshold selected for alpha. In day-to-day life, we adjust our thresholds instantaneously; however, in statistics classes we tend to stick to an arbitrary rule because it is easier. In application it is important to make sure that your decision rule makes sense. To these ends, many researchers have moved away from the practice of putting asterisks by numbers indicating significance in favor or actually reporting the probability itself. To us, this seems like a more fair practice, but it requires that consumers of statistics understand what significance really signifies.

Vocabulary

Flashcards
& MCQs

DEGREES OF FREEDOM—The number of values in the final calculation of the statistic which are free to vary.

NULL HYPOTHESIS—The counterfactual statements to the working hypothesis.

SAMPLE—Some subgroup of a defined population.

STANDARD ERROR—The standard deviation of a sample means around the true population mean.

STATISTICAL POWER—A probabilistic statement about the leverage a statistical test provides.

STATISTICAL SIGNIFICANCE—A probabilistic statement about the reliability of a statistical test.

TYPE I ERROR—Rejecting a correct null hypothesis (accepting an incorrect alternate hypothesis).

TYPE II ERROR—Failing to reject an incorrect null hypothesis (rejecting a correct alternate hypothesis).

WORKING (ALTERNATE) HYPOTHESIS—A proposition proposed as an explanation of a phenomenon.

Data Set
tables - Excel,
STATA & SPSS

Review Questions

Data Set
exercises

- How do statistical tests assist in interpreting data?
- Why would collapsing continuous data not be a good practice?
- Why might you want to collapse continuous data?

CHAPTER 16

Measures of Association

Learning Objectives

✓ Understand how to apply appropriate measures of association to different types of data
✓ Understand the similarities between each measure of association
✓ Identify the three underlying questions to association evaluation
✓ Apply appropriate statistic in nominal, ordinal, or continuous data

Cases in Research

Case A—Grover's Corner Department of Transportation

Grover's Corner is considering a mixed application of light rail systems incorporating the traditional "street car" approach in areas where creating more separation between the rail and surface traffic is difficult; and an enhanced system with dedicated crossings, elevated sections, and dedicated stations with large-scale parking where resources allow. Bituin Masipag, the section head of planning, has received complaints that the distribution of rail locations and system types appeared to be biased by the ethnicity of the area residents. To examine this problem, she has started a series of assessments of the planned light rail system.

Case B—Springfield Housing Department

Effie Hawthorne has been tasked with substantiating and identifying some possible causes for why residents qualifying for housing assistance might not be applying for these benefits. She has several "working" hypotheses including the length of the application process, distance from application centers, and the variance in housing costs throughout the city.

Measures of Association

Statistics concerns itself with understanding variation in data. If there were no variation, using statistics to summarize the data would be pointless. In earlier chapters, we have examined how we can summarize the variance in a single variable using measures of central tendency and dispersion. We have also learned how to tell if two distributions are different as defined by a predetermined threshold. These tools provided not only the ability to describe change within a single variable, but also laid the groundwork for the work we will begin in this chapter.

Measures of association give us an indication of how closely two variables are related in the sense of how the individual variables change together. This chapter on association will be the beginning of our exploration of how variables influence each other. Take, for example, Figures 16.1 and 16.2

Figure 16.1 represents two normally distributed random variables Y and X, graphed in a standard scatter plot. Notice that the graph shows no distinct pattern. In fact, the

Figure 16.1

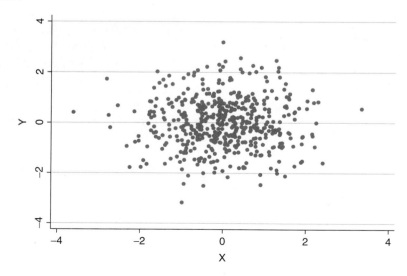

Figure 16.2

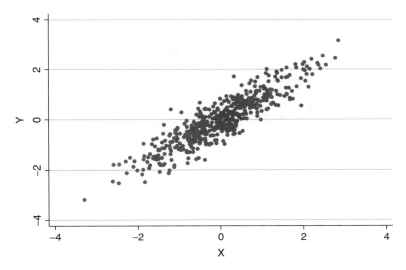

two variables here are completely unrelated. Conversely, Figure 16.2 tells a different story.

In Figure 16.2 we have a second set of normally distributed random variables. In this case, notice that as X increases in value, so does Y. It would appear that there is some sort of relationship between the variables; however, we do not know if the relationship we observe is more than random chance. We also do not know the actual strength of the relationship. Measures of association provide us with uniform tools to assess these important qualities of variables that change together.

Before we undertake the evaluation of variance shared between two variables, there are a few things we must keep in mind as we move forward. First is that each level of data (nominal, ordinal, and continuous) require specific tools for assessing the strength of the correlation between the two variables. Second is that each level of data provide different amounts of information about the relationships. Third, and perhaps the most important, is that measures of association **do not** imply causality. Remember our discussion earlier about the requirements for causality (that is, time order, non-spuriousness, and covariance). Our evaluation of association will provide empirical evidence addressing the covariance; however, this is not synonymous with causation.

When we examine the association between two variables, we intend to answer three important questions about the relationship between these variables. First, we want to identify that the covariance at hand is not simply random chance. Second, we want to identify the strength of the relationship. Finally, we want to address the directionality. Each step in this process is distinct, and not all the steps are available with each type of data. What is important in the application of these assessments of association is that we begin our discussion of the likelihood that the association is more than random chance— or as we have referred to it in the past, statistically significant.

Measures of Association in Nominal Data

Nominal data are frequently encountered in public and nonprofit management and provide a bit of trouble in higher level analysis. This is simply because as these types of data have no rank order or set interval, they are very difficult to include in mathematical analysis. Fortunately, there are several techniques for dealing with these data that allow us to garner some useful information. For evaluating the association between two measures, we will employ the use of contingency tables.

To evaluate the three dimensions of association in nominal data, we use the following steps:

Step 1: Significance: first we identify if the association between the two variables is statistically significant. To do this, we use the Chi-Square test from chapter 15.

Step 2: Strength: next we assess the strength of the relationship between the two variables. While there are several statistics available for this, it is most commonly done with Phi coefficient, Cramer's V, or Lambda.

Example 16.1

Bituin has had multiple complaints that the proposed plan for the new light rail system provides disparate benefits between three of the region's racial/ethnic groups. To evaluate this claim, she has broken the region down into three areas: one where they will use a traditional light rail program, one where the plan calls for enhanced light rail service, and the third where no mass transit will be offered. She then had 300 families randomly selected from each area and collected information on the race/ethnicity of each family. The results of this data collection are displayed in Table 16.1.

Table 16.1

	Hispanic	Pacific Islander	Asian	Total
No Service	261	60	27	348
Traditional System	24	186	36	246
Enhanced System	15	54	237	306
Total	300	300	300	900

Step 3: Direction: because nominal level data has no rank order, it is not possible for us to talk about directionality of association.

Before we evaluate the levels of association between the race/ethnicity of the families and the light rail service proposed, let's review a few important aspects of the contingency table presented in Table 16.1.

First, note that the Y-axis of the table (what is traditionally the dependent variable) is the transit system. This is because it is not possible for the current race/ethnicity of the population to be a function of the proposed rail system, and the theory is that the race/ethnicity is what is driving the system type.

Second, the Y-axis variable is listed in a temporal order from least to most. When possible (with ordinal and higher data), it is important to always set up contingency tables in this manner. While it makes no difference with nominal data, consistency in presentation is always good, and reinforcing good habits will help prevent mistakes when the data at hand do have rank order.

Third, because one of these variables is nominal and the other is ordinal, we treat this table as nominal for analysis purposes. Any contingency table analysis is limited by the lowest form of data included in the table.

In assessing the table, Bituin first must make sure that any correlation between these two variables is more than just random chance. Certainly there are some differences, but it is important for her to first identify that the covariance in these variables is systematic and not random. To do this, she employs the Chi-Square statistic introduced in chapter 15.

Formula 16.1

$$X^2 = \sum \frac{(observed - expected)^2}{expected}$$

Calculating this for the data in Table 16.2 yields the following:

With d.f. = 4 (remember, we defined the degrees of freedom for Chi Square as the number of rows minus 1 times the number of columns minus 1), the table in the back of the book shows that this is well above our critical value for a .05 significance level.

Table 16.2

Y	X	Observed	Expected	O-E Squared/E
Hispanic	None	261	117	177.2307692
PI	None	60	117	27.76923077
Asian	None	27	117	69.23076923
Hispanic	Traditional	24	81	40.11111111
PI	Traditional	186	81	136.1111111
Asian	Traditional	36	81	25
Hispanic	Enhanced	15	102	74.20588235
PI	Enhanced	54	102	22.58823529
Asian	Enhanced	237	102	178.6764706
	Chi Square			750.92

Alternatively, suing the Chi-Square distribution function in Excel will provide an exact probability. In the case at hand, that probability is well below .0001.

At this point, we can tell that the planned distribution of the light rail system differs significantly by the race/ethnicity of the local population. The next step is to identify how strong the association is between race/ethnicity and the rail distribution. To do this we can use a number of easily available statistics. Each of these is expected to be bound by zero at the low end and one at the high end, and provide a statistic that can be compared to other associations. The first is the Phi coefficient

Phi Coefficient

The Phi coefficient is the easiest of all the measures of association for nominal level data. It is simply equal to the square root of Chi Square divided by the number of observations.

Formula 16.2

$$\phi = \sqrt{\frac{\chi^2}{N}}$$

In our case above, the Phi coefficient would be equal to .91 (that is equal to the square root of 750.92/900). We can interpret this using Table 16.3 as a strong relationship; however, the Phi coefficient statistic is generally known for being unreliable in tables larger than 2 × 2, and therefore is **NOT INDICATED** for use in the case above.

A better statistic to use for the data in Table 16.1 is Cramer's V.

Table 16.3

Nominal Level Measures	
Value	Strength
0 to .10	Weak
.11 to .30	Moderate
> .30	Strong

Cramer's V

Cramer's V is a similar statistic to the Phi coefficient; however, it has controls built in to deal with tables that are larger than 2 x 2. The statistic is calculated as follows:

Formula 16.3

$$v = \sqrt{\frac{\chi^2}{(N)(\textbf{min}\, r - 1\, or\, c\, -1)}}$$

Cramer's V is simply the square root of Chi Square divided by the number of observations times either the number of rows minus one or the number of columns minus one (whichever is lower). So for the data in Table 16.1, we would calculate it as 750.92/

(900)(2) or roughly .65. Notice that while the statistic is much smaller, the relationship can still be characterized as strong using Table 16.3.

Also note the relationship between Cramer's V and the Phi coefficient. While the two values were very different in the example here, what would be the difference in the two values if we were to use a 2 x 2 table (Try this using the data in Table 16.3)?

The two measures of association above both relied on "scaling" the Chi-Square statistic to give it the feel of a proportion. A second approach to assessing the association between two variables does so by providing a measure of impact of how the independent variable improves our understanding of the dependent variable. The general approach of this measure is a consistent theme throughout statistics.

Lambda

Lambda is a statistic based on the idea of proportional reduction in error. The logic is pretty simple insomuch as Lambda tells us how much more we know about the dependent variable when we have information about the independent variable.

Returning to Example 16.1, let's review what we have. First, the dependent variable is the race/ethnicity of the families in the region. Second, the type of light rail service proposed is the independent variable. If all we knew about the 900 families surveyed in terms of race/ethnicity, we would have the following:

Table 16.4

	Total
No Service	348
Traditional	246
Enhanced	306
Total	900

With only the information in Table 16.4, if I told you to guess the type of service available to any single family in the sample, you would have three options. If you guessed none, you would be correct 34% of the time; if you guessed traditional, you would be correct 27% of the time; and if you guessed enhanced, you would be correct 39% of the time. Hence, knowing only the distribution of the dependent variable, your best guess would be to guess the modal category, and then you would have the least possible errors with the information at hand. In this case, you would be incorrect 61% of the time, or you would make 552 incorrect guesses.

Now, bring back the information about the independent variable (race/ethnicity), and you will be able to guess a little better (Table 16.5).

Table 16.5

	Hispanic	Pacific Islander	Asian
No Service	**261**	60	27
Traditional System	24	186	36
Enhanced system	15	54	**237**
Total	300	300	300
errors in guessing	39	114	63

For Hispanics, we would guess the rail system for the column and would only guess incorrectly 39 times (the number who has access to traditional and enhanced systems). In areas where Pacific Islanders resided, we would guess traditional rail and would only be incorrect 114 times (those who have access to enhanced systems or no access). Finally, in areas where the Asian families live, we would guess enhanced rail and only be incorrect 63 times. All in all, we would only be incorrect a total of 216 times out of the total 900 population when we have information about the independent variable. Thus, we have reduced the error in our guessing by 336 mistakes by having information about the independent variable.

The Lambda statistic is simply a proportion of the amount of error reduction by the total amount of error. This formula is specified as the following:

Formula 16.4

$$\lambda = \frac{E_1 - E_2}{E_2}$$

So with the example above, Lambda would be equal to (552–216)/552 or .608.

Measures of Association in Ordinal Data

Dealing with ordinal level data is very similar to dealing with nominal level data in that we will employ the use of contingency tables, and that our first step in analysis will be to establish significance using the Chi-Square test. The advantage to having ordinal level data is that now we can speak to the directionality of the relationship as well as to the strength. Test statistics for use in ordinal level data are similar to those for nominal data in that they are bound by zero and one; however, with ordinal data the statistic may be either positive or negative, depending on the relationship between the variables. In cases where the value of X increases as Y gets larger, the relationship between the variables is referred to as a positive relationship. Conversely, if the values of X decrease as Y gets larger, we refer to the relationship as a negative relationship. Figure 16.2 (seen earlier in this chapter) illustrates a positive relationship. Figure 16.3 demonstrates a negative relationship:

Figure 16.3

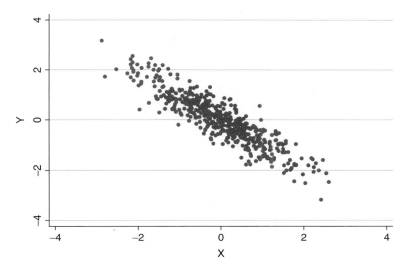

There are several measures of association available, but the one that is most demonstrated in textbooks by far is Gamma. This is due largely to the ease of calculation.

Gamma

Gamma uses the difference between concordant pairs and discordant pairs to estimate the strength and direction of a relationship. **CONCORDANT PAIRS** are the number of pairs of observations that reflect a positive relationship, while **DISCORDANT PAIRS** are the pairs of observations that reflect a negative relationship. The difference is then divided by the total possible number of pairs to produce a ratio of excess pairs that are either negative or positive to the total possible pairs. Table 16.6a shows a fictitious contingency table with ordinal level data.

> **Class Exercise:** Make a list of five qualities that are most often used as nominal data, and make note of the unit of analysis for each. Are there ways to gain more precision in measurement (use a higher order level of measurement) for these by changing the unit of analysis?

Table 16.6a

	Low	High
Low	6	2
High	7	8

In this example, the concordant pairs (shared in table 16.6b) would be the pairs where the values are the same (low-low, high-high) and a positive relationship is one where the value of X increases as the value of Y increases.

Table 16.6b

	Low	High
Low	6	
High		8

The concordant pairs for this table would be all the possible pairings between the 6 observations in the top left cell and the 8 observations in the lower right. For Table 16.6, the total number of concordant pairs is 48. The discordant pairs (shared in table 16.6c) will be the pairs from the cells representing a negative relationship. These are the cells where one variable is low and the other is high. For example, see Table 16.8.

Table 16.6c

	Low	High
Low		2
High	7	

Thus, we have 7 x 2 or 14 discordant pairs in Table 16.6. To calculate Gamma for this table, we take the difference between the number of concordant and discordant pairs (34), and divide that by the total number of possible pairs. In this case it would be the sum of the concordant and discordant pairs (62). For Table 16.6, Gamma would = .55. So assuming we had a significant Chi-Square test for this table, we could then interpret Gamma as being a strong positive relationship between X and Y.

Formula 16.5

$$Gamma = \frac{(Concordant\ pairs - Discordant\ pairs)}{(Concordant\ pairs + Discordant\ pairs)}$$

While Gamma is pretty simple to calculate in a 2 x 2 table, it becomes more complicated as the size of the table grows. To identify the possible concordant pairs, we simply multiply the contents of each cell by the sum of all the cells below and to the right of it. In a 3 x 3 table, that means we would have to calculate four different sets of concordant pairs. Look at Table 16.7:

Table 16.7a

	Low	Medium	High
Low	a	b	c
Medium	d	e	f
High	g	h	i

In this table, we identify the first group of concordant pairs as the low-low cell (cell a) and all the cells below and to the right of it (cells e, f, h, and i).

Table 16.7b

	Low	Medium	High
Low	a	b	c
Medium	d	e	f
High	g	h	i

Next, we move to the medium-low cell (cell b) and all the cells below and to the right of it (cells f and i).

Table 16.7c

	Low	Medium	High
Low	a	b	c
Medium	d	e	f
High	g	h	i

We repeat this for the medium-low and medium-medium cells as well:

Tables 16.7 d and e

	Low	Medium	High
Low	a	b	c
Medium	d	e	f
High	g	h	i

	Low	Medium	High
Low	a	b	c
Medium	d	e	f
High	g	h	i

Notice that we do not repeat this starting in any of the high column or row cells. We then calculate the total number of concordant pairs:

Concordant pairs = $[a \times (e + f + h + i)] + [b \times (f + i)] + [d \times (h + i)] + [e \times i]$

Class Exercise: By this point in your studies, it should be obvious that you should always try to get the most detail possible in any data collection effort. Try to list five reasons why having nominal or ordinal level measures for continuous level data might happen.

If you have assumed at this point that the discordant pairs are calculated in the exact opposite manner, you are correct.

Example 16.2

Effie has been told that one possible cause for the low number of applications for housing assistance is that the forms for the program are entirely too long. To test this hypothesis, she has devised two new application forms. The standard form is now classified as the long form, and she has created a medium length and short form as well. She then assigns one form type to each of the city's 100 districts. When an applicant comes in to apply, she is asked where she lives and is given the appropriate form to complete and return by mail. Effie then classifies the return rates as high, medium, or low. Her data appears in Table 16.8:

Table 16.8

Number of applications

	Low	Medium	High	Total
Short	2	11	26	39
Medium	6	18	7	31
Long	25	4	1	30
Total	33	33	34	100

(Application Length)

Calculating the Chi-Square statistic for these data, Effie obtains a value of 722.22, well above the critical value for alpha < .05 for d.f. = 2, so she knows that there is a statistically significant relationship between the application length and the number of returned applications. Next she calculates Gamma by calculating the number of concordant and discordant pairs. Her work appears in Table 16.9.

Table 16.9

		Concordant pairs			
Low	Short	$2 \times (18 + 7 + 4 + 1)$	=		60
Medium	Short	$11 \times (7 + 1)$	=		88
Low	Medium	$6 \times (4 + 1)$	=		30
Medium	Medium	18×1	=		18
				Total	**196**
		Discordant Pairs			
High	Short	$26 \times (18 + 4 + 6 + 25)$	=		1378
High	Medium	$7 \times (4 + 25)$	=		203
Medium	Short	$11 \times (6 + 25)$	=		341
Medium	Medium	18×25	=		450
				Total	**2372**

In addition to Gamma, several other measures of association exist for ordinal data that are computationally difficult, but readily produced on most commercial software programs. Two of the most prevalent warrant mention here. Kendal's tau-b and tau-c are much akin to Gamma in computation; however, they impose more restrictions on the pairs that are assessed to identify the strength and direction of the relationship. For the purposes of this text, you need only remember that these measures are more conservative estimates and that tau-b is used for square tables (2 x 2, 3 x 3) while tau-c is used for rectangular tables (2 x 3, 3 x 4).

Similarly, Somer's d offers the user preference to one variable or another in the evaluation of the underlying relationship.

Measures of Association in Continuous Data

In continuous level data, the association between two variables is measured using correlations. More specifically, the comparison is made using Pearson's *r*. In practice, correlations are not used very often as they are the precursor to more advanced analysis; however, they are used frequently for cursory scans of data and for diagnostics in regression models. You may recall in chapter 13 we discussed the idea of variance. Calculating correlations is simply a matter of expanding on that concept.

To calculate the correlation coefficient, we simply divide the covariance of the two variables (that is the variance they share) by the combined variance of the two variables separately. If you want to think of this as a Venn diagram, we are dividing the intersection of X and Y by the union of X and Y. Consider the following example:

Example 16.3

Effie has been considering other sources of reluctance in filing for housing assistance, and hypothesizes that young residents may be more reluctant to apply than the more seasoned residents. To test this hypothesis, she gathers a small sample of data from 10 districts in the city. She collects information about the median age in the district and the percentage of the district currently collecting housing assistance. Her first step in evaluating these data is to calculate a correlation coefficient to quickly assess the relationship between these two variables.

Formula 16.6

$$Pearson's \ r = \frac{\Sigma(X - \overline{X})(Y - \overline{Y})}{\sqrt{[\Sigma(X - \overline{X})^2][\Sigma(Y - \overline{Y})^2]}}$$

Step 1: Calculate the covariance of X and Y. To do this, we have to compute the deviations of X and Y about their means and then multiply them together. After doing this we simply sum all the values (Table 16.10a).

Table 16.10a

Mean Age (X)	% Population Receiving Assistance (Y)	Deviations of X about the mean	Deviations of Y about the mean	DX x DY
30	5	−18	−2.9	52.2
28	7	−20	−0.9	18
41	8	−7	0.1	−0.7
55	8	7	0.1	0.7
53	7	5	−0.9	−4.5
67	10	19	2.1	39.9
81	15	33	7.1	234.3
29	7	−19	−0.9	17.1
52	8	4	0.1	0.4
44	4	−4	−3.9	15.6
			Σ DX x DY =	373

Step 2: Square the deviations of X about its mean and the deviations of Y about its mean. Multiply these values together and take the square root (as in Table 16.10b).

Table 16.10b

Mean Age (X)	% Population Receiving Assistance (Y)	Deviations of X about the mean	Deviations of Y about the mean	DX Square	DY Square
30	5	−18	−2.9	324	8.41
28	7	−20	−0.9	400	0.81
41	8	−7	0.1	49	0.01
55	8	7	0.1	49	0.01
53	7	5	−0.9	25	0.81
67	10	19	2.1	361	4.41
81	15	33	7.1	1089	50.41
29	7	−19	−0.9	361	0.81
52	8	4	0.1	16	0.01
44	4	−4	−3.9	16	15.21
			$\Sigma =$	2690	80.9
				Product	217621
				SQRT	466.50

Step 3: Divide the numerator (the covariance of X and Y) by the denominator (the combined variance of X and Y) to obtain the correlation coefficient. In this case, $r =$ 373/466.50 or .799.

From this, Effie could simply characterize the relationship between age and the percent of the population receiving assistance as a strong positive relationship. Pearson's r has a better interpretation though. If we simply square the correlation coefficient we obtain the r squared, also known as the coefficient of determination. This statistic reports the variance of the dependent variable (Y) explained by the independent variable (X). In this case, .799 squared is .6393, so we should report that 63.93% of the variance in the population receiving housing assistance can be explained by the median age of the population.

To test the significance of the correlation coefficient is straightforward, and the formula is as follows:

Formula 16.7

$$t = \frac{r}{\sqrt{[(1-r^2)/(N-2)]}}$$

Table 16.11

Step 1	Step 2		Step 3		
Weakest Level of Data Measurment	Significance Test	Question Answered	Measure of Association	Question(s)Answered	Test strengths / weaknesses / limitations
Nominal	Chi-Square	Is there a significant effect of X on Y	Phi Coefficient	Relationship strength	Only for use with 2x2 tables
			Creamer's V	Relationship strength	
			Lambda	Relationship strength	
Ordinal	Chi-Square	Is there a significant effect of X on Y	Gamma	Strength and directionality	Least conservative
			Tau-b	Strength and directionality	for square tables (r=c)
			Tau-c	Strength and directionality	for rectangular tables (r#c)
			Sommer's-d	Strength and directionality	Most conservative
Continuous	t-test	Is there a significant effect of X on Y	Pearson's r	Strength and directionality and magnitude	

Recall from chapter 15, we said that a t-test was simply an estimated value minus some hypothesized value. In the case above, our hypothesized value for rho is zero. This is because rho = 0 would mean no relationship; thus, if we use a t-test to show that rho is significantly different from zero, we are providing support for the idea that the relationship is valid. For the correlation coefficient, t is distributed with d.f. = N-2. Calculating the t value for the example above provides a t value = 3.766 with d.f. = 8.

One word of caution is due to the correlation coefficient. This statistic *only* identifies linear relationships between the two variables. In the case of a curvilinear relationship, the correlation coefficient may not reveal the underlying relationship. This is why it is imperative that all data analysis is accompanied by visual confirmation of what the statistical tests report. Far too often, students, researchers, and scholars alike skip the step to visually examine the data, and this simple oversight has and will continue to hinder the proper application of data analysis (Table 16.11).

Putting Knowledge into Practice: Using Excel to Perform Correlations

To calculate the correlation coefficient, simply use the function CORREL and designate the two arrays in the parentheses.

	A	B	C	D	E
1	**A**	**B**			
2	2	1		Pearson's r	=CORREL(A2:A9,B2:B9)
3	2	3			
4	4	5			
5	5	7			
6	4	4			
7	6	6			
8	8	4			
9	5	6			

SPSS

STATA

Vocabulary

CONCORDANT PAIRS—Pairs of observations that indicate a positive relationship.
CORRELATION—An analysis of the covariance shared by two variables.
DISCORDANT PAIRS—Pairs of observations that indicate a negative relationship.
NEGATIVE RELATIONSHIP—A relationship between two variables where the values of X decrease while the values of Y increase.
POSITIVE RELATIONSHIP—A relationship between two variables where the values of X increase as the values of Y increase.

Flashcards & MCQs

Useful Websites

Review Questions

■ What is an appropriate test of association for ordinal level data?

■ If a contingency table contains both nominal and ordinal data, what measure of association should be used?

Discussion Questions

■ Is the coefficient of determination a better measure of association than the correlation coefficient?

■ How does Phi coefficient differ from Cramer's V?

■ In what circumstances might a researcher want to collapse continuous data into ordinal data?

■ Is gender always nominal data?

■ Why is Gamma not used for nominal data?

■ Is it possible to use the t-test to see if a relationship between two variables is significantly different from rho = .5?

Data Set
exercises

■ How could you use contingency tables to test for the effect of a third partitioning variable?

CHAPTER 17

Simple Linear Regression

Learning Objectives

✓ Understand the limitations of the least squares methodology
✓ Be able to apply least squares techniques to common data problems
✓ Describe the basic assumptions of least squares analysis

Cases in Research

Case A—National Helping Hands

Rockwell is a FEMA regional analyst and has been tasked with evaluating the relative costs of some of the reconstruction efforts sponsored by FEMA and NHH member organizations in the Yukon River Valley. Specifically, he is interested in the cost differentials between work done in the remote area of Eagle Pass and the somewhat more accessible Stevens Village. To these ends, he has collected data on the number of completed projects by worker on each site. His data includes a dichotomous variable for the location of the worker, the number of projects the worker completed per day during the two-month effort, and the average cost per construction project the worker completed.

The Concept of Least Squares

Probably the most used of the advanced statistical techniques is what is commonly referred to as regression analysis. This approach seeks to identify a linear relationship between a dependent variable (also called the outcome variable and symbolized y) and one or more independent variables (or variables of interest and denoted as x). This is done by using a little simple algebra to calculate the equation for a line through the data points on a plane. Regression is a well-known technique; however, what it represents about the data at hand is often not well understood. This is because many discussions of regression focus on the line it produces as opposed to how that line is produced.

A regression line represents a series of estimated means (one for every possible value of the x variable), estimated in a way that reduces the squared **ERROR** of each mean. Recall the discussion of means in chapter 13. We introduced the concept as the center point of a distribution of a variable. This can also be thought of as the best estimate for the value of that variable when examined in isolation. For the sake of parsimony though, we skipped a step in demonstrating why this was the estimator we applied most readily. This missing step was demonstrating that the arithmetic mean is also the least squared estimator of the distribution.

The Method of Least Squares

The term **LEAST SQUARES** implies that the test statistic we are offering is one that minimizes the amount of squared error in our estimate of the parameter. Take for instance, the following data in Table 17.1.

Table 17.1

Ages of 10 Female Employees

44	51
54	46
47	35
34	45
35	36

Table 17.1 lists the ages of 10 female employees of an organization. We could quickly compute the mean or average age as $\sum x_i / n = 42.7$; however, why is this the best estimator? Why do we take this instead of the minimum or maximum value? If the range is consistent, then either of these two figures might be equally as valid for computational purposes. The answer is because the mean provides the least amount of error in our guess about the likely value of any point in the distribution.

When we say error, we speak of the difference between the mean and each value in the distribution. In past chapters we referred to this as the deviations from the mean. So if we were asked to guess every value in the distribution, and we guessed the mean every time, the difference between our guesses and the actual values squared would be to what we refer. Table 17.2 shows this calculation for the data in Table 17.1:

Table 17.2

Age	Mean	Error	Squared Error
44	42.7	−1.3	1.69
54	42.7	−11.3	127.69
47	42.7	−4.3	18.49
34	42.7	8.7	75.69
35	42.7	7.7	59.29
51	42.7	−8.3	68.89
46	42.7	−3.3	10.89
35	42.7	7.7	59.29
45	42.7	−2.3	5.29
36	42.7	6.7	44.89
Sums		0	472.1

Table 17.2 displays the sum of both the error and the squared error. Notice that the sum of the error is zero. We should have expected this since the distance of all the points from the arithmetic mean should equal zero. The squared error column, on the other hand, is significantly larger as squaring the errors makes all the values positive.

The sum squared deviations of each point around the mean, the error, is the heart of linear regression and all of the techniques in the least squares family. We use a mean because not only because it is the center of the data (and sometimes it is not), but because it is actually the single value that is closer to all the points in the distribution than any other. For example, in the data above we know that 42.7 is the arithmetic center of all the observations, but it is also closer to all the values than any other number. We can demonstrate this by calculating the sum squared deviations for a number of other points and picking the one with the lowest value for the sum squared error. In Figure 17.1 we have selected a number of values ranging from 32 to 52 to substitute for the mean in the computations in Table 17.2. The values for the substitute means are along the X-axis, and the sum squared deviations from that point are on the y-axis.

Notice that the farther we get away from the mean of 42.7 in either direction, the values for the sum squared deviations increase. Thus, the mean is not only the arithmetic center of these data, but it is also the point that is simultaneously closest to all the other values; it is the value that provides the least sum squared deviations.

Figure 17.1

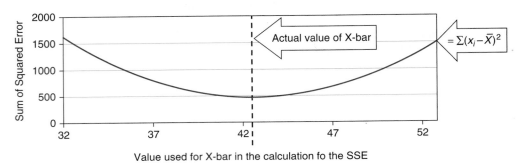

At this point, there should be two questions that enter your mind. First is, "Why not just use the value that produces a zero for the summed error?" The answer to this is twofold. First, the concept of squared error is pervasive in the field of statistics, and there are times when there will be multiple values that will produce a summed error of zero (as we will demonstrate later). Second is that often the error is used in later calculations, and a value of zero can often prove to be problematic, thus the squared error—the absolute measure—has greater utility.

Using Least Squares Techniques

The preceding section demonstrated *why* investigators use squared error to produce reliable estimates of statistical parameters, but we did not show how they are used. Some time ago, mathematicians demonstrated that the covariance (variance shared by two variables) of two continuous distributions could be standardized using the variance of the dependent variable to produce a single line that best represented all the data simultaneously. That is, this line was closer to all the data points in the distribution than any other straight line.

Class Exercise: Visualizing Lines to Represent Data

Take a look at the following scatter plots and, reflecting on what we learned in chapter 13, think about what a single straight line through the data would look like.

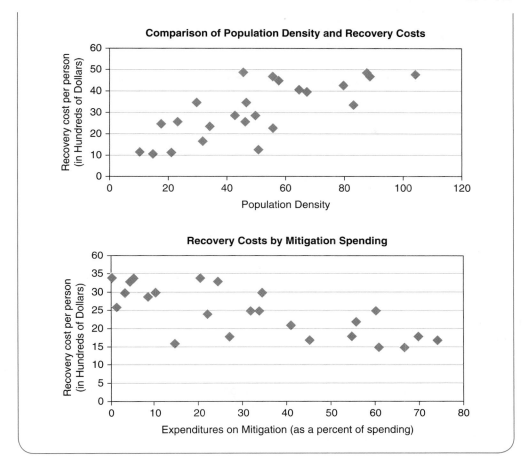

In the class exercise above, you should have identified a positive relationship in the first graph and a negative relationship in the second. Recall in chapter 16, we compared similar pairs of variables using a correlation **COEFFICIENT**; that technique is very similar to what we will do in **SIMPLE REGRESSION**. The correlation coefficient provided information about the covariance between two variables and was scaled from -1 to 1 to give a proportional measure. In linear regression, we estimate coefficients that allow us to estimate the value of the dependent variable using any value of the independent variable. Herein lies a major difference between correlation and simple regression—where the correlation is evaluating the covariance shared by two variables, simple regression is evaluating the effect of the independent variable (x) on the dependent variable (y).

We evaluate the effect of the independent variable (x) on the dependent variable (y) by creating a mathematical model of the dependent variable. Simple regression assumes that the dependent variable (y) is some function of the independent variable (x) and random error. You may recall from a geometry class that we can express a line on a graph in terms of an equation that has two terms, a **Y-INTERCEPT** and a **SLOPE COEFFICIENT**. The y-intercept is the value where the line crosses the y-axis, and the slope is the change in the y value for each unit change in x. If we have a y-intercept of 2.5, and a slope of 5, we know that the first data point in the line will be at x = 0, y = 2.5; and the second point will be at x = 1, y = 7.5. With these two points we could easily draw a straight line (or we could continue to calculate values of X for the values of Y.

Class Exercise: For the table below, fill in the missing Y values.

y-intercept = 2.5 slope = 5	
X	**Y**
0	2.5
1	7.5
2	12.5
3	17.5
4	?
5	?
6	?

To abbreviate this in somewhat more parsimonious terms, we represent the y-intercept with the symbol, β_0, and we represent the slope coefficient with the term β_1. If we use the symbol $\hat{Y}$ to represent the line that summarizes the relationship between the independent variable (x) and the dependent variable (y) we can write the equation for this line as shown in Formula 17.1

Formula 17.1

$\hat{Y} = \beta_0 + \beta_1 X_1$ read y-hat is equal to beta naught plus beta one times X one.

The equation for the class exercise above is $\hat{Y} = 2.5 + 5 \times X$, and with this, we can calculate the value of y-hat for any given value of X. The difference between this line and the scatter plots we looked at earlier is that with the line, all the data points fall on a single line where with the data they all fall around a line. To compensate for the variance around the line that occurs with data in simple regression, we include an error term to account for the variance of the data points around the line y-hat. So while the equation for a regression line (y-hat) is displayed in Formula 17.1, the formula for simple regression can be found in Formula 17.2.

Formula 17.2

$Y = \beta_0 + \beta_1 X_1 + \varepsilon$

Notice the difference between the equation that represents the regression line (y-hat) and the equation that represents the actual values of the dependent variable (y) is simply the term ε. ε is called the error term because it represents the error of the regression line in predicting the actual values of the dependent variable (y). For simplicity, we call the two betas in the simple regression model **PARAMETERS**.

Figure 17.2 shows a scatter plot of the income (y) and age (x) of 21 employees in an organization. The line through the center of these points represents the single line that is simultaneously closest to **ALL** the data points in the plot. This line is the regression line y-hat for the regression, estimating income as a function of age.

Figure 17.2

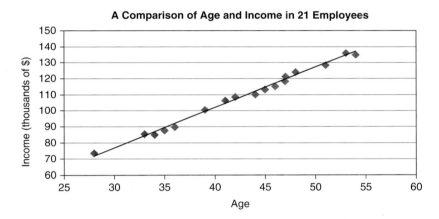

It is obvious in the graph above that the regression line (y-hat) does a very good job of representing the data points as they are tightly clustered around the line. Even still, it is hard to tell what the y-intercept and slope are for this line. One method to finding these values would be to try a variety of values for each, then we could calculate the squared error. If we graphed the squared error for each slope coefficient, we could then select the one that produced the lowest squared error (similar to Figure 17.1), but this would be time consuming. An easier approach is to use formulas to calculate the slope and intercept as they are both rather straightforward and rely on formulas we have already used. The slope of this line (B_1) is calculated simply as the covariance of x and y divided by the variance in x (if you do not remember these formulas, review chapter 16 where we calculated the correlation coefficient). The y-intercept (B_0) of this line is calculated simply as $B_0 = \bar{y} - B_1\bar{x}$.

Formula 17.3

(17.3.a) Slope

$$B_1 = \Sigma(y_i - \bar{y})(x_i - \bar{x}) / \Sigma(x_i - \bar{x})$$

(17.3.b) Y-Intercept

$$B_0 = \bar{y} - B_1\bar{x}$$

Notice, that if we apply Formulas 17.3a and 17.3b to calculate just a mean as in the previous example, the result is the same. Because there is no independent variable (x), we see that the second term in 17.3b falls out and that $B_0 = \bar{y}$. In the case of calculating a single mean, using the least squares approach seems a bit like make-work; however, there are advantages when we want to calculate multiple means within a single distribution.

Using OLS to Compare Means (ANOVA)

In Table 17.1 we introduced data that represented the ages of some of the female employees of the organization. In Table 17.3, we now include the ages of both the females and the males in the organization. For computational purposes, we have coded the gender of each observation as either 0 for female or 1 for male.

Table 17.3

Gender	Age	Gender	Age
1	28	0	44
1	53	0	54
1	33	0	47
1	48	0	34
1	47	0	35
1	47	0	51
1	39	0	46
1	41	0	35
1	42	0	45
1	42	0	36
1	48		

Class Exercise: Verify the statistics for these two groups presented in Table 17.4.

We already know that the mean of age for females = 42.7. Some simple computation would identify the mean for males as 42.55 (verify this on your own). We could quickly compare these two by falling back on what we learned about t-tests in chapter 15 by calculating the standard errors for each group and performing a two-sample t-statistic. Recall also that in the calculation of the standard error, the number of observations is used as a denominator. This means that the larger the number of observations, the smaller the standard error will be. In the example above, we have n = 10 and n = 11—representing very small samples. Figure 17.3 displays a box and whisker plot of the employee age by gender:

Figure 17.3

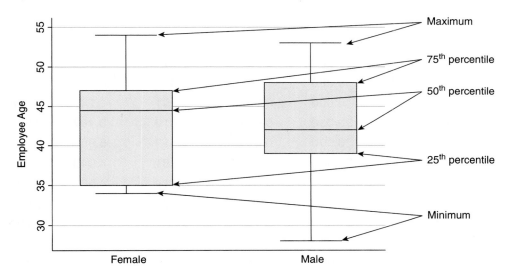

As you can see, there is a difference in the median age between genders; however, it is difficult to find meaning in this result. Similarly, we could calculate the appropriate test statistics for the two-sample t-test and evaluate these groups empirically (Table 17.4).

Table 17.4

Group	n	Mean	Std. Dev.	s.e.
Females	10	42.70	7.24	2.29
Males	11	42.55	7.26	2.19
combined	21	42.62	7.07	1.54
Difference		0.15		3.17

We can easily re-create these findings using the least squares approach. First, we must calculate the values for B_0 and B_1 from Formula 17.1. Table 17.5 displays these calculations.

Table 17.5

Gender (x)	Age (y)	x-xbar	y-ybar	Cov(x,y)	Var(x)
0.000	44.000	−0.524	1.381	−0.723	0.274
0.000	54.000	−0.524	11.381	−5.961	0.274
0.000	47.000	−0.524	4.381	−2.295	0.274
0.000	34.000	−0.524	−8.619	4.515	0.274
0.000	35.000	−0.524	−7.619	3.991	0.274
0.000	51.000	−0.524	8.381	−4.390	0.274
0.000	46.000	−0.524	3.381	−1.771	0.274
0.000	35.000	−0.524	−7.619	3.991	0.274
0.000	45.000	−0.524	2.381	−1.247	0.274
0.000	36.000	−0.524	−6.619	3.467	0.274
1.000	28.000	0.476	−14.619	−6.961	0.227
1.000	53.000	0.476	10.381	4.943	0.227
1.000	33.000	0.476	−9.619	−4.580	0.227
1.000	48.000	0.476	5.381	2.562	0.227
1.000	47.000	0.476	4.381	2.086	0.227
1.000	47.000	0.476	4.381	2.086	0.227
1.000	39.000	0.476	−3.619	−1.723	0.227
1.000	41.000	0.476	−1.619	−0.771	0.227
1.000	42.000	0.476	−0.619	−0.295	0.227
1.000	42.000	0.476	−0.619	−0.295	0.227
1.000	48.000	0.476	5.381	2.562	0.227
Mean 0.524	42.619				
Sum				−0.810	5.238
			B1	−0.155	
			B0	42.700	

According to the formulas, the line that best represents the relationship between age (y) and gender (x) can be represented as $y = 42.7 − .155x$. In the case where x is a **DICHOTOMOUS VARIABLE**, that means when $x = 0$ (as in the case of females), the estimated value of y is 42.7, and when $x = 1$ (as in the case with males), $y = 34.7−.155$ or 42.55. Notice that the values are exactly the same as if we had calculated the two means separately. This is because in the case of our x variable, we have precisely two possible values. If we were to add a third category, this technique would not work as our model is estimating a straight line (although there are other approaches we will explore in the next chapter).

Example 17.1: Case A—Location Matters

Rockwell has used least squares regression to model the average cost of home construction as a function of the location of the build. He assumes that construction in Eagle Pass (coded as zero in the data) is going to have lower average expenses than the constructions in Stevens Village (coded as one in the data). He calculates the model $\hat{Y} = \beta_0 + \beta_1 X_1$ where X_1 is the location variable and gets the following: $\beta_0 = 213$ and $\beta_1 = 79$. Based on this, he sees that his assumption is correct as the mean for Stevens Village (coded as one in the data) is higher than that for Eagle Pass.

For Eagle Pass $X_1 = 0$ and for Stevens Village $X_1 = 1$, so:

Y-hat for Eagle Pass = $\hat{Y} = 213 + 79 \times 0 = 213$

Y-hat for Stevens Village = $\hat{Y} = 213 + 79 \times 1 = 292$

Putting Knowledge into Practice: Using Excel to Calculate a Simple Regression

SPSS

STATA

Excel has a number of add-ins that can be downloaded. One of these is the VBA analysis toolkit. It you enable this software package, Excel will calculate regressions for you. To do this, select the **data** tab, and on the far right side of the toolbar should be a button marked **data analysis**. Selecting this will open a scroll-down menu where you can select **regression.** Doing so will open a dialogue box that looks like Figure 17.4:

Figure 17.4.

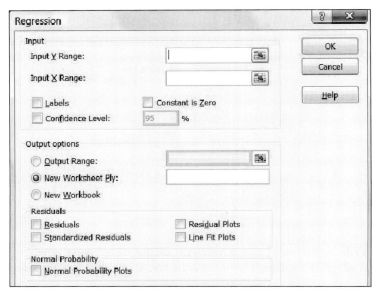

This dialogue box allows you to indicate the y variable and x variable by high-lighting them in the sheet.

For demonstrations of this software and other popular software packages, visit the companion website for this book.

Model Fit

To test model fit, we examine the variance in the dependent variable (y) explained by the variance in the independent variable (x). That is, we look to see if the covariance between the two variables represents a significant portion of the variance of the dependent variable.

Recall from chapter 14, variance is defined as:

Formula 17.4

$$Variance(s^2) = \frac{\sum(x_i - \bar{x})^2}{N}$$

Using the data from Table 17.3, we can calculate the variance of the dependent variable, age, as 998.952 (try this on your own). In least squares parlance, we refer to the variance of the dependent variable as the Total Sum Squared Variance, or SST. The SST is equal to the amount of squared variance explained by the model (SSM) plus the sum squared error (SSE). Or more simply SST = SSM + SSE.

Figure 17.5

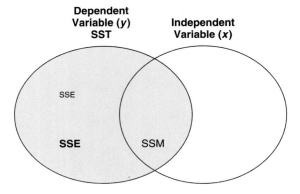

Figure 17.5 illustrates how the variance of the dependent variable is partitioned between that which is explained by the model and that which is unexplained—the error

in the model. To calculate the error in the model forecast, we simply calculate the difference between the model estimates, $(\hat{y})$, and the actual values of y. To do this for the data in Table 17.3, we simply calculate the estimated value of (y) and subtract it from at actual value of (y), square it, and sum over all the observations. More formally:

Formula 17.5

$$SSE = \sum (y_i - \hat{y})^2$$

Try calculating the SSE on your own for the data in Table 17.3 (hint, you should only have two values for y-hat).

Alternatively, the SSM may be calculated as the variation the estimates of y-hat around the mean of y, or:

Formula 17.6

$$SSM = \sum (\hat{y} - \bar{y})^2$$

You should arrive at the number 998.827. This is the amount of variance in the dependent variable **not** explained by the model, leaving the SSM, or variance in the dependent variable explained by the model as SSM = .125. The most typical way to describe the model fit is to use a simple proportion where the variance explained by the model (SSM) is divided by the total variance (SST). This can be directly interpreted as the variance in the dependent variable explained by the model and is represented as R^2 (note—this statistic is the same as the R-squared presented in the section on correlations).

Formula 17.7

$$R^2 = \frac{SSM}{SST} \text{ or } 1 - \frac{SSE}{SST}$$

The R-squared statistic provides a pretty concise way to visualize how good a job the model does in explaining the variance in the dependent variable (in this case, a pretty poor job), but it does not provide a threshold test based on probability for us to judge the statistical significance. The value of R-squared can theoretically range from zero to one and is commonly interpreted as the percentage of the variance in the dependent variable explained by the regression model. More specifically, the R-squared tells us how much of the variance in the dependent variable uniquely covaries with the variance of the independent variables. Because a simple regression has only one independent variable, it is acceptable to interpret the R-squared statistic as the percent of the variance in the dependent variable that covaries with the independent variable. Importantly, the R-squared only tells us about the strength of the relationship, to test if the likelihood of this relationship exceeds some specific threshold (level of alpha) mathematicians have deduced that a proportion of the SSM and SSE are F-distributed. To test model significance, we calculate the F-value for the model as the proportion of the SSM divided by its degrees of freedom to the SSE divided by its degrees of freedom.

Formula 17.8

$$F \ statistic = \frac{SSM / df_{SSM}}{SSE / df_{SSE}}$$

Where the degrees of freedom for the SSM is defined as the number of parameters in the model (in this case, two), minus one, and the degrees of freedom for the SSE is defined as the number of observations minus the number of parameters in the model.

Using this, the F-statistic for this model is equal to $\dfrac{SSM / 1}{SSE / 19}$ or $\dfrac{.1251}{52.57}$ or .0023

To determine if the model is significant, one need only look this number up on an F-statistic table with degrees of freedom of (1, 19).

Formally, the F-test tests if all the estimated parameters in the model are equal to zero. This is often a heroic hurdle (although not in this case). For interpretation purposes, it is sufficient to think of the F-test as asking whether the model (both parameters simultaneously) provide more information about the dependent variable than the mean of the dependent variable.

As well as testing the entire model for fit, a second utility of the least squares approach is that we may also test each estimated coefficient in the model alone. In cases where there is only one parameter, this is a bit redundant; you will notice greater utility to this practice in the next chapter where we will examine multiple covariates simultaneously.

Simple Linear Regression

Simple regression is nothing more than applying the least squares model to two continuous variables (as seen in Figure 17.2). In the previous section, we discussed the implication of the parameters B_0 and B_1 in the context of a dichotomous independent variable. In this case, the coefficients represented the conditional mean of the dependent variable for the given value of the independent variable. That is to say, the regression line (y-hat) is simply the mean of y if we were to calculate the mean at any single value of X.

In the last section, we demonstrated how when X only had two possible values, the least squares regression equation provided the mean of Y for each of those values. When the independent variable (x) is continuous, the same thing holds, only because X is continuous there is an infinite number of values of X, and therefore y-hat represents the infinite number of means.

For the sake of consistency, we will add another variable to the example data we have used thus far. Now we will look also at the income of the individuals. The updated data are displayed in Table 17.6:

At this point, you should easily be able to calculate the values for the model coefficients, (B_0 and B_1), as well as the model goodness of fit statistics (R-square and the

Table 17.6

Gender	Age	Income
1	28	73.885
1	53	136.066
1	33	85.838
1	48	123.908
1	47	121.27
1	47	120.675
1	39	100.526
1	41	106.456
1	42	108.862
1	42	108.57
1	48	123.82
0	44	110.388
0	54	135.013
0	47	118.219
0	34	85.144
0	35	87.98
0	51	128.347
0	46	115.28
0	35	87.807
0	45	113.217
0	36	90.09

F-statistic), and you should be able to perform a number of hypothesis tests on the coefficients. Let's start by calculating these statistics by modeling income as a function of age. You can check your answers against the figures in Table 17.7.

Table 17.7

Source	SS	df			
			Number of obs	=	21
Model	6263.072	1	$F(1, 19)$	=	2114.27
Error	56.283	19	Prob > F	<	.000001
Total	6319.356	20	R-squared	=	0.99

(Continued)

Table 17.7 (*Continued*)

	Coef.	Std. Err.	t	P>|t|
$\beta 1$	2.504	0.0545	45.98	0
$\beta 0$	1.921	2.3510	0.82	0.424

Interpreting Models and Coefficients

In the last chapter we discussed the importance of order when we interpret statistics. With least squares models, the rules are much the same. We will always first interpret the significance and then interpret the meaning, as an insignificant statistic is statistically no different than zero. In addition, we should always be in the habit of discussing the model before interpreting the components (the coefficients) of the model. Bearing this in mind, we interpret the above model in the following manner:

(1) **Interpret the F-statistic**—The model fits as the probability of F is less than the traditional alpha of .05.
(2) **Interpret the R-square statistic**—The model explains 99% of the variance of the dependent variable (income).
(3) **Examine the significance of the coefficient t-tests**—The y-intercept is not statistically different from zero; however, the slope coefficient is significantly different from zero.
(4) **Interpret the significant coefficients**—The model indicates that for each additional year of age, the employee salary increases by $2,504.

Remember, the slope coefficient is always a one unit shift in the *x* variable (in this case, age in years) resulting in a coefficient change in the dependent variable (in this case, thousands of dollars). Sometimes it is helpful to interpret the coefficients by creating a number of ideal cases and calculating the values of the dependent variable for each case. For example, there might be interest in comparing the average age of starting employee income and average age after 10 years of employment. One of the worst things that an analyst can do is to simply regurgitate numbers without giving some sort of contextual meaning to those numbers. Interpreting them is a start, and in later chapters we will examine some graphical approaches to interpretation.

Example 17.2: Case A—Productivity Matters

Rockwell continues his evaluation of the construction costs by modeling construction costs as a function of worker productivity. He assumes that the more houses a worker builds, the more efficient he is. After calculating the coefficients for the model, he finds $\beta 0 = 237$ and $\beta 1 = -7$.

At first blush this does not make much sense to him, as clearly more productive workers should be more efficient as well. Knowing that it is important to test model fit before interpreting the coefficients, Rockwell finds the probability of $F = .078$. Because the model is insignificant, he knows that while the value of the coefficient is negative, because the model is insignificant, it has no explanatory power so the value of the coefficient is moot.

On the subject of graphical approaches, it is important to note that regression should never be performed on data that have not been examined visually. This is because the premise of simple regression rests in the concept of estimating a straight line of conditional means of the dependent variable. Moreover, least squared regression not only requires a straight line to provide the best fit, but it also assumes that the errors will be random and normally distributed around the regression line.

Assumption 17.1

The relationship between the y variable and the x variable must be linear in the parameters.—Essentially, this means that a straight line is an appropriate way to generalize the relationship between the two variables. If the relationship is curvilinear, quadratic, or the like, the simple regression is not an appropriate way to estimate this relationship.

Next, we also need the distribution of y for each category of x to be roughly equivalent. Just as the mean becomes a poor measure of central tendency in the presence of outliers, heavily skewed distributions of the y variable for the different values of x may mean that the least squares estimates are also not the best statistic.

Assumption 17.2

Homoskedasticity—The variance in the errors will be consistent across all the values of x.

To this point we have not talked much about the errors that are the namesake of this family of estimators. Recall, we are defining the errors in our estimators as the difference between each actual value and the estimated value given our computations. Together, the formulas in 17.1 provide us with a linear equation that represents a *model* of the relationship between the dependent variable (y) and the independent variable (x).

This model, $y = B_0 + B_1 x$, is the line that approximates the relationship between the variables, and differs from the actual data points by the error (ε). Formally, we refer to the model of the data as $y_i = B_0 + B_1 x + \varepsilon$, and the line it represents as $\hat{y} = B_0 + B_1 x$ (read as y-hat equals beta naught plus beta one times x). Y-hat is the actual line estimated by the equation, while y_i are the actual values of y for the data.

When we refer to the model, we mean the equation as a whole, including both estimated betas; but remember that each model includes two parameters. Because of this, we can test the fit of the entire model, and perform specific hypothesis tests of each parameter in the model.

Evaluating Model Coefficients

Earlier, we defined B_0 as the Y-intercept and B_1 as the slope of the line ($\hat{y}$) that represents the relationship between the independent and dependent variables. The value of each of these coefficients is important, but for different reasons. The value of the y-intercept identifies the estimated value of the dependent variable when the independent variable is equal to zero. In the case of the example that has run throughout this chapter, this would be the average employee age for female employees. The slope, B_1, identifies how much change there is in the estimated value of the dependent variable for each one unit change in the independent variable. Again, in the case of our example, this would be how the average age of the employee changes as we move from the female employees to the male employees. We could say that the average age of female employees = B_0, while the average age of male employees = $B_0 + B_1$.

It is important to remember that we are now examining covariance, the variance shared between two different variables. Thus, if one or the other variables does not change, there is no covariance. If all the employees were female, then there could be no change between the two groups. Similarly (and perhaps better stated), if all the employees were exactly the same age then there could not be any shared variance because one of the variables has no variance to share. Thinking about this, what would a graph of age and gender look like if all the employees were 50 years old?

When there is no relationship between the two variables in a regression equation, one of two things will happen. The first is that there will be a zero for the variance in x, and the equations will collapse to the mean of y (as in the first example in the book), or there will be no change in the mean value of y for a unit change in x and the slope will equal zero. The latter proposition can easily be tested using the t-test from chapter 15.

Recall, the basic t-test is simply, $t = \dfrac{\bar{x} - \mu}{s.e}$

x-bar is the estimated mean we wish to test and mu is the hypothetical test value. To construct the t-test then we simply need to calculate standard errors for the parameters in the model. To do this, we will need to calculate three values: the Mean Square Error (MSE), the variance in x (Var(x)), and the standard error of the estimate ($\bar{\sigma}$).

Formula 17.9

$MSE = SSE / df$ where the degrees of freedom is equal to n—the number of parameters in the model.

Formula 17.10

$$\sigma = \sqrt{MSE}$$

Formula 17.11

$$Var(x) = \Sigma(x_i - \bar{x})^2$$

Formula 17.12

$$s.e.(B_0) = \sigma\sqrt{\frac{1}{n} + \frac{\bar{x}^2}{Var(x)}}$$

Formula 17.13

$$s.e.(B_1) = \sigma \Big/ \sqrt{Var(x)}$$

For the data presented in Table 17.3, calculate the coefficients, appropriate standard errors, and t-statistics using the formulas provided. You should obtain the following (Table 17.7b) for an answer:

	B	s.e.	t
1	-0.155	3.168	-0.05
0	42.7	2.293	18.62

To evaluate the resulting t-statistics, simply use the *Student's* t table with (n–2) degrees of freedom. As you can see, the results of the significance test are not much different from what we saw with the model goodness of fit. Clearly we can identify the mean age of males and females, but the t-test reveals that the difference between the males and females (-.155) is not statistically different from zero. Interestingly, we can apply this test to evaluate a multitude of hypotheses. Say, for instance there was reason to believe that the average age of men in this organization was five years older than females. We could simply test this hypothesis by changing our test value from zero to five. Thus the t-test would change from: $t = \dfrac{\bar{x} - 0}{s.e.}$ to $t = \dfrac{\bar{x} - 5}{s.e.}$.

Frequently, this application of the least squares model is used in the natural sciences. Often it is referred to as ANOVA (analysis of variance) because it is being applied to examine how the variance of an outcome variable is partitioned by groups. This method is very useful in true experiments where there is an actual control or baseline group. While the social sciences also has good applications for the ANOVA model (for example, program evaluations, comparisons between states, or organizations), more frequently the regression model is the area workhorse.

Understanding the Data behind the Model

Earlier in this chapter we mentioned two assumptions: that the model must be linear in the parameters and that the error variance must be constant. Additionally, we also have subtly mentioned that to be able to evaluate covariance, there must be variance on both variables. The best way to ensure these assumptions are met is through visual inspection. For a demonstration of this, we will fall back on data first propagated by Anscombe (1973; Table 17.8).

Take some time and consider the models displayed above. Perhaps you will note that it is very difficult to tell one from another. To help illuminate the differences, the following set of figures will display the scatter plot associated with each model.

Table 17.8

				Model 1		
Source	SS	df	MS	Number of obs	=	21
				F (2, 18)	=	33000.69
Model	6317.63	2	3158.82	Prob > F	=	0
Residual	1.72	18	0.10	R-squared	=	0.9997
Total	6319.36	20	315.97			
	Coef.	**Std. Err.**	**t**	**P>|t|**		
$\beta 1$	0.5001	0.1179	4.24	0.002		
$\beta 0$	3.0001	1.1247	2.67	0.026		
				Model 2		
Source	SS	df	MS	Number of obs	=	21
				F (1, 19)	=	2114.27
Model	6263.07	1	6263.07	Prob > F	=	0
Residual	56.28	19	2.96	R-squared	=	0.9911
Total	6319.36	20	315.97			
	Coef.	**Std. Err.**	**t**	**P>|t|**		
$\beta 1$	0.5	0.118	4.24	0.002		
$\beta 0$	3.0009	1.1253	2.67	0.026		

Model 3

Source	SS	df	MS			
				Number of obs	=	11
				F (1, 9)	=	17.99
Model	27.51	1	27.51	Prob > F	=	0.0022
Residual	13.76	9	1.53	R-squared	=	0.6665
Total	41.27	10	4.13			
	Coef.	**Std. Err.**	**t**	**P>|t|**		
$\beta 1$	0.4997	0.1179	4.24	0.002		
$\beta 0$	3.0025	1.1245	2.67	0.026		

Model 4

Source	SS	df	MS			
				Number of obs	=	11
				F (1, 9)	=	17.97
Model	27.50	1	27.50	Prob > F	=	0.0022
Residual	13.78	9	1.53	R-squared	=	0.6662
Total	41.28	10	4.13			
	Coef.	**Std. Err.**	**t**	**P>|t|**		
$\beta 1$	0.4999	0.1178	4.24	0.002		
$\beta 0$	3.0017	1.1239	2.67	0.026		

Figure 17.8

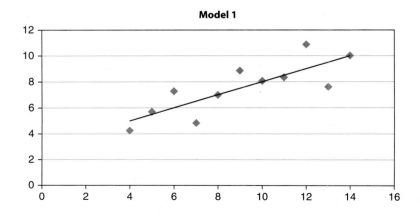

Note that the regression line superimposed on the scatter plot does a good job of representing the data at hand. While one might think that a curve would better represent these data, the linear model is a perfectly adequate representation. Now look at the second model:

Figure 17.9

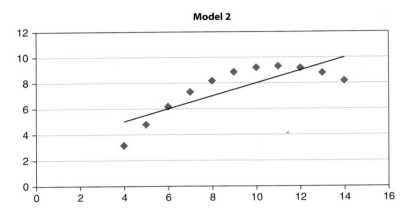

Notice that in the second model, the regression line clearly does not represent the relationship between the two variables. Even though the model fit statistics indicate that the model provides a good fit, the relationship between these two variables is clearly curvilinear, and thus the regression is not linear in the parameters. In later chapters we will discuss how least squares can be applied in this situation, but the model at hand clearly does not fit the data.

Figure 17.10

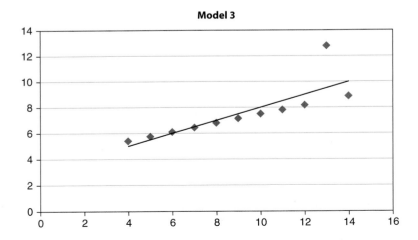

In Model three, we can see that there is one observation that is skewing the fit of the regression line. If not for the one stray observation in the upper right hand quadrant, the slope of the line would be more shallow, and the fit statistics would be stronger. In a case like this, it is important to identify the case that is an outlier and try to understand what makes it different. In later chapters we will examine some advanced approaches to dealing with this type of problem.

Figure 17.11

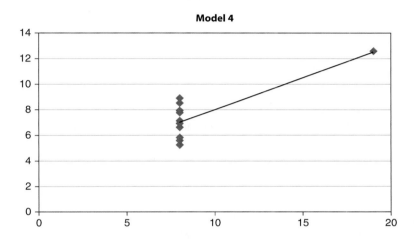

Again, in Model 4 we see one case that is entirely responsible for the slope of the regression line. In fact, without that one point the model would collapse to the mean of *y*.

General Considerations for the Application of Least Squares

As we move further in the book, it will become clear just how robust the method of least squares estimation is in helping managers and analysts make sense of large volumes of information. That said, it is important that the application of least squares is done purposively. As statistical tools become more complex (and as more of them become automated in computer programs), the costs of inattention to the modeling process becomes extremely high. There is a common misnomer that it is easy to "lie" with statistics, or that a good statistician can "make numbers say anything."

For the record, statistics do not lie, and a good statistician cannot make numbers say whatever they want. Properly modeled data can only reveal the underlying patterns within the given data. It is possible to misrepresent these relationships, and it is possible to have too few observations to get a true understanding of the phenomenon at hand—but it is not possible to make numbers say anything.

Good data analysis requires an understanding of the data that comprise the sample the researcher is working with. The analyst should examine the distributions of each variable before using them for more advanced statistical applications. It is easy for an observation to be coded improperly, or for a variable to have too little variance to be of much analytical use. The only way to catch this problem is to visualize the data. Similarly, and as the last section illustrated, all applications of least squares require the researcher to actually look at the data and not just the numbers a computer program spits out. Only this way can you be confident that you have truthfully represented what the data have to say.

Vocabulary

COEFFICIENT—The term used to describe the parameters estimated by least squares.

DICHOTOMOUS VARIABLE—A variable that has only two values and may be referred to as a "dummy" variable.

ERROR—Distance from an individual observation to the mean of the observations (or to y-hat). When this value is calculated for every observation in a variable and the resulting values are squared and summed, it is called the Sum Squared Total variance (SST). Typically this term is used in reference to least squares models.

PARAMETER—A term used to describe the estimated values in a least squares model.

SIMPLE REGRESSION—A least squares model with only one independent (x) variable.

SLOPE COEFFICIENT—The value of the beta-one coefficient that tells the change in the value of the dependent variable for every one unit change in the independent variable (x).

Y-INTERCEPT—The value of the beta-naught coefficient that indicates the value of the dependent variable (y) when the independent variable (x) is equal to zero (where the regression line y-hat crosses the y-axis).

Flashcards
& MCQs

Useful
Websites

Review Questions

Education
Data Set -
Excel,
STATA &
SPSS

■ Why can you not use the simple OLS model to test means of data with more than two groupings?

■ Under what circumstances might you want to test if a model coefficient is significantly different from some value other than zero?

■ What do we mean by the term "model"?

■ What information do you need to calculate the SSM?

■ What test is used to evaluate the significance of model coefficients?

■ What test is used to assess model significance?

■ What statistic is used to display the model fit?

Discussion Questions

- What do we mean by least squares?
- Explain why the R-square can be interpreted as a percentage.
- How are the coefficients different from the model?
- How can a model with an R-square of .03 be important (hint: Think about the difference between statistical and substantive significance)?

Non-Profit
Data Set -
Excel,
STATA &
SPSS

Protected
Data Set -
Excel,
STATA &
SPSS

Data Set
exercises

CHAPTER **18**

Multiple Least Squares Regression Analysis

Learning Objectives

✓ Apply the least squares method with multiple independent variables
✓ Describe what is meant by unique covariance
✓ Define the difference between regression coefficients and partial regression coefficients
✓ Identify common violations of OLS Assumptions

Cases in Research

Case A—National Helping Hands

Rockwell is a FEMA regional analyst and has been tasked with evaluating the relative costs of some of the reconstruction efforts sponsored by FEMA and NHH member organizations in the Yukon River Valley. Specifically, he is interested in the cost differentials between work done in the remote area of Eagle Pass and the somewhat more accessible Stevens Village. To these ends, he has collected data on the number of completed projects by worker on each site. His data includes a dichotomous variable for the location of the worker, the number of projects the worker completed per day during the two-month effort, and the average cost per construction project the worker completed.

The Foundations of Multiple Least Squares

In the previous chapter, we stated that the least squared family is the most used technique in social sciences research. To be more specific, multiple least squares—commonly referred to as linear regression—is the tool that dominates research in the field. Due to the relative ease of application and coefficient interpretation, multiple regression has proven to be a powerful tool for individuals investigating social science phenomenon. Unfortunately, because this technique has become so easy to apply, it is often used incorrectly. In this chapter, we intend to assist the reader in acquiring a basic understanding of the concepts that underlie the use of least squares in the multivariate environment.

The Method of Multiple Least Squares

Much like bivariate least squares, multiple least squares summarize linear relationships between independent variables and a single dependent variable. The major difference that occurs when multiple X variables are introduced into the equation is that in the multivariate environment, the regression coefficients reflect only the correlation between each X variable and the Y variable that is unique to those two variables. Thus, regression coefficients for a multivariate model will not be identical to those produced in bivariate regression models unless there is absolutely no correlation between the X variables. Look at Figure 18.1 to understand this concept better.

Because the regression coefficients in the multivariate model do not reflect all of the shared covariance between each variable and the dependent variable, they are called **PARTIAL REGRESSION COEFFICIENTS**. Starting with the data set containing 200 observations with a known correlation structure listed in Table 18.1. The table lists a matrix of the correlation coefficients (rho) for each variable combination.

If we run the bivariate regressions for each X variable on Y, we get the following (Table 18.2).

Based on the bivariate regressions, we would describe the relationship between Y and each X variable as follows: For X1, the mean value of Y would be 1.7 if X1 equals zero; and for every one-unit increase in X1, the mean value of Y increases by .1. For X2, the mean value of Y is .38; and for each one-unit increase of X2, the mean value of Y increases by .23. Notice that we are careful to say "the mean value" of Y. As we pointed out in the last chapter, the Y values predicted by least squares regression are estimates—the values are what we would expect on average, not true point estimates.

Now we will produce partial regression coefficients using a multivariate model (Table 18.3).

Comparing the two tables, we see that while both approaches produce positive coefficients, the slopes in the multivariate model are both less steep when compared to the bivariate models. This happens because the variance shared by the two X variables is not considered in the calculation of the coefficients in the multivariate model.

Figure 18.1

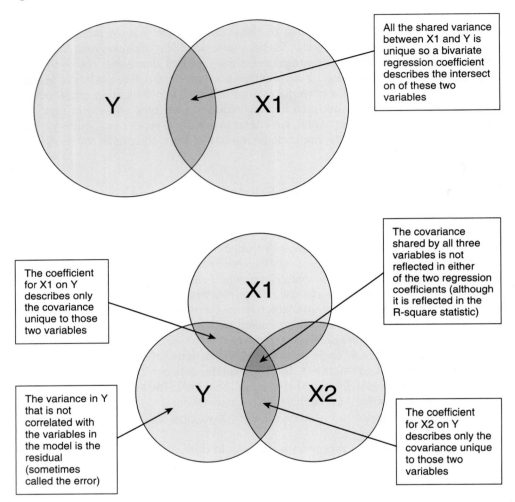

Table 18.1

	Y	X1	X2
Y	1		
X1	0.4	1	
X2	0.6	0.2	1

Table 18.2

Model	X1	X2
Constant	1.7	0.38
Coefficient	0.1	0.23

Table 18.3

Constant	0.32
Coefficient X1	0.07
Coefficient X2	0.21

We could correct the regression coefficients in the bivariate models to match the partial regression coefficients by applying a little ingenuity. Because the partial regression coefficients reflect the relationship between each X variable and the dependent variable, we are able to use regression to purge each X variable of the correlation with the other X, then use these new variables in bivariate regressions that will produce coefficients identical to the partial coefficients in the multivariate model.

Thus, if we had the multivariate model $Y = b_0 + b_1 x_1 + b_2 x_2 + \varepsilon_y$, we could replicate the coefficient b_1 by estimating the model $X_1 = b_0 + b_2 x_2 + \varepsilon_1$, then running the bivariate regression $Y = b_0 + b_2 \varepsilon_1$. By using the residuals of the regression of X2 on X1 as a variable in the regression on Y, we are using the variance in X1 that is not correlated with X2.

Figure 18.2

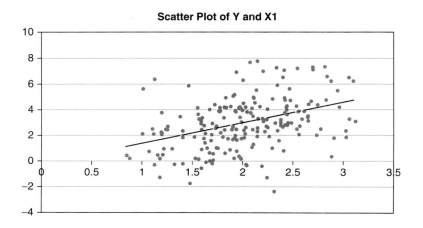

Scatter Plot of Y and X1

Figure 18.3

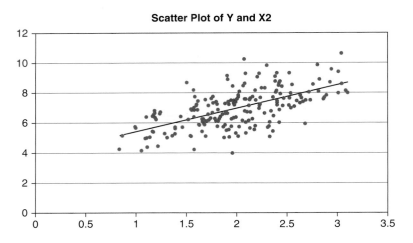

Scatter Plot of Y and X2

Thinking about it another way, when we estimate the bivariate model, we are estimating a straight line through a scatter plot of points.

In contrast, when we perform the multiple regression with two independent variables, we are projecting a plane through a three-dimensional cloud of data points.

In fact, every multiple regression is an expression of an n dimensional plot of the data where n is equivalent to the number of X (independent) variables.

Figure 18.4

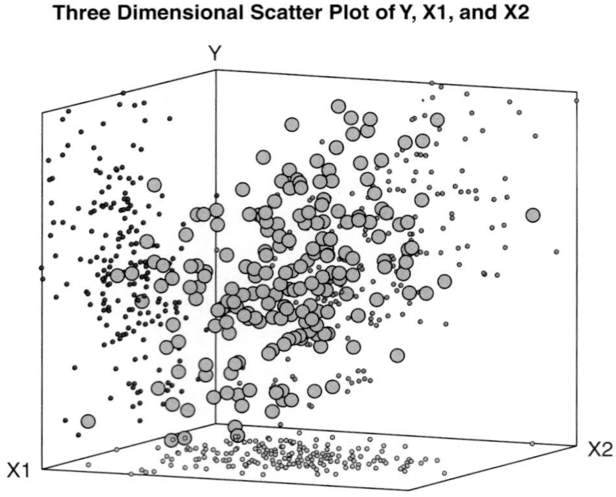

Three Dimensional Scatter Plot of Y, X1, and X2

Assumptions of the Multiple Least Squares Model

We have stated repeatedly that the least squares model is an incredibly robust framework for data analysis, and this is true; however, this does not mean that there are not assumptions that we need to worry about. In the previous chapter, we talked about two of them. We will review those here in the multivariate environment and add a few more to keep in mind.

Regressors Must Be Linear in the Parameters

The assumption that the relationship between the dependent variable and each independent variable described in the previous chapter (see Assumption 17.1) holds true in the multivariate environment. In the bivariate model, we had the option to transpose variables to make the relationship "linear in the parameters." This could be done by using logs of variables in place of the variable. We also could use exponential transpositions of the variables. One of the major benefits of the multivariate model is that we have the ability to model complex relationships through the use of additional variables.

For example, look at the data in Figure 18.5.

These data could be modified by transforming the variable X. Generating the new variable X-squared and graphing it against the dependent variable produces Figure 18.6.

Notice that while the relationship between Y and X now appears linear, we have created a second problem. Do you see it? If not, refer back to Assumption 17.2 in the last chapter.

A second approach to modeling the relationship in Figure 18.5 is to model a quadratic equation. To do so, we would create a new variable that was equal to the

Figure 18.5

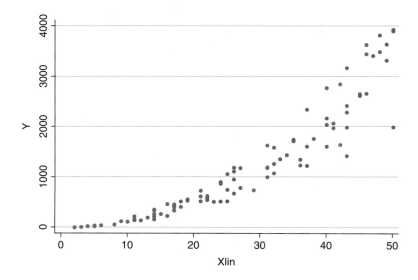

square of X and put them both in the regression equation. This yields the model, $Y = b_0 + b_1 x_1 + b_2 x_1^2 + \varepsilon_1$.

Look at the difference between the linear model of $Y = b_0 + b_1 x_1 + \varepsilon$ and the equation for the quadratic model above in Figure 18.7.

Figure 18.6

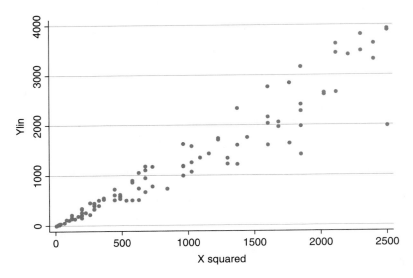

Figure 18.7

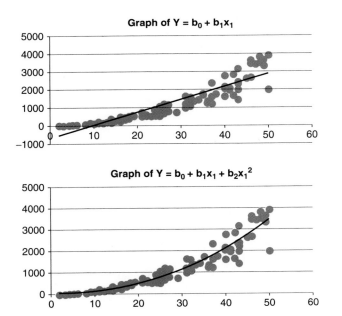

Putting Knowledge into Practice: Creating Residual Plots with Excel

If you use Excel's Analysis Tools to perform a regression, there are two ways to generate a residual scatter plot. The first is to calculate the residuals (or select the option in the dialogue box that does so for you) and simply create a scatter plot. The second technique is to check the residual plot option in the dialogue box identified with the arrow in the picture below.

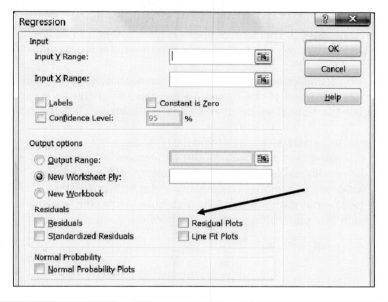

STATA

SPSS

Clearly, the second model is a far better fit, and even when modeling the curve we have not violated the assumption that the model be linear in the parameters.

No Heteroskedasticity

This assumption that first appeared in the last chapter holds true here as well. The reason for this is based in the probabilistic assumptions we make when using the t-test to evaluate the model parameters. Recall in chapter 15, we said that we test the beta estimates (the slope coefficients) using a t-test. If you think back to when we discussed t-tests, you will remember that the t-test uses a measure of variance in the equation. Given this, if our regression model has uneven variance in the residuals, then we cannot be sure that the estimate of the variance we are using in the t-test is correct.

While there are statistical tests to detect heteroskedasticity, none of them are as good as simply looking at the data. In the bivariate model, this was simple because we could simply graph X and Y and see the variance in the relationship. In multivariate models where we are dealing with nth dimensional relationships, we have to use a surrogate to evaluate heteroskedasticity. That surrogate is a plot of the residuals.

Recall, the residuals are simply the difference between our estimated values of Y (Y-hat) and the actual values of Y. Mathematically, $\varepsilon=(\hat{Y}-Y)$. The residuals can either be plotted against one of the predictor variables (one of the independent variables), or more generically against the fitted values of the Dependent Variable (Y-hat). Figure 18.8 displays the **RESIDUAL PLOT** for the homoskedastic data from Figures 18.2–18.4.

Notice that the residuals are nicely distributed around the mean (the residuals are on the Y-axis in this figure). This type of figure is often referred to as a "sneeze plot."

Figure 18.9 displays the residual plot resulting from the regression of X^2 on Y displayed in Figure 18.6.

In this graph you will notice that the residual variance around its mean changes significantly from lower values of the estimated dependent variable to larger values. This produces the tell-tale "funnel shape" that we look for to identify heteroskedasticity in the regression.

Unlike nonlinear relationships, heteroskedasticity does not affect the parameter estimates. What the regression produces for the parameters is correct. Heteroskedasticity only nullifies the hypothesis tests of those coefficients. The downside to heteroskedasticity is that while we can model nonlinearity, heteroskedasticity is a function of the data—that is to say that data are naturally distributed with uneven variance, and often there is not much that can be done about it. There are several solutions to addressing

Figure 18.8

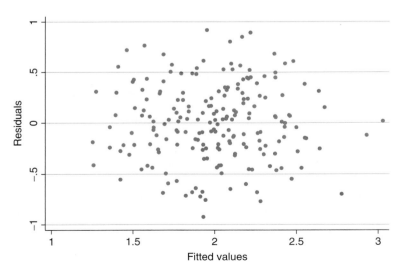

Figure 18.9

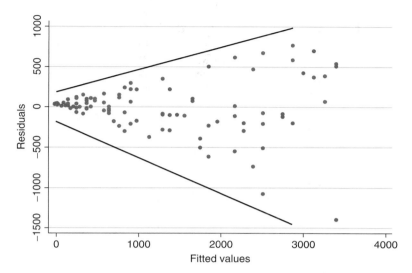

these in research. Most common is the use of a robust standard estimator, while others address this issue through the use of weighting. We leave addressing this issue to the discretion of your instructor.

One assumption not mentioned in the last chapter, but equally valid there is the problem of autocorrelation.

Autocorrelation

AUTOCORRELATION is when the residuals are correlated with the dependent variable. This most commonly occurs in data that are collected across time as opposed to cross-sectional data; however, it may also occur in a spatial distribution as well.

The quickest way to identify autocorrelation is to plot the residuals against the time intervals in a scatter plot. Figure 18.10 displays the residual vs. time plot for data that are positively and negatively autocorrelated.

Most often, autocorrelation is a function of events happening over time (serial auto-correlation), and as such, can be corrected for using some advanced modeling. Sometimes autocorrelation can be the result of diffusion across areas (spatial autocor-relation) generated by trends in policy or program adoption or the like. In either event, autocorrelation is much like heteroskedasticity in that it affects the estimate of dispersion used in the hypothesis tests.

Moving from the bivariate to the multivariate environment introduces additional con-cerns that we did not have to deal with in the previous chapter. The main one is the problem of multicollinearity.

Figure 18.10

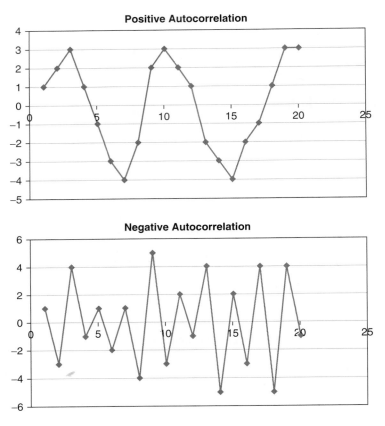

No Perfect Multicollinearity

Think back to our opening discussion about partial regression coefficients and the effect that correlation between the X variables had on the coefficients. This correlation between the X variables is what is called **MULTICOLLINEARITY**. Perfect multicollinearity is when two X variables are correlated at a rho = 1. In practice, perfect multicollinearity is not as big a problem as near-perfect multicollinearity as there is no way to calculate whether regression coefficients are identical. This is simply because if the two X variables are the same, there is no unique solution to the regression equation. Look at the three diagrams in Figure 18.11

In the first diagram (a), there is no multicollinearity between the two variables. In the second diagram (b), there is a small amount of multicollinearity between the variables; and in (c), the third diagram, we see near-perfect multicollinearity. The first step in identifying whether multicollinearity may be a problem in a multiple least squares regression is to produce a correlation matrix of the variables to be used in the regression. A clean

Figure 18.11

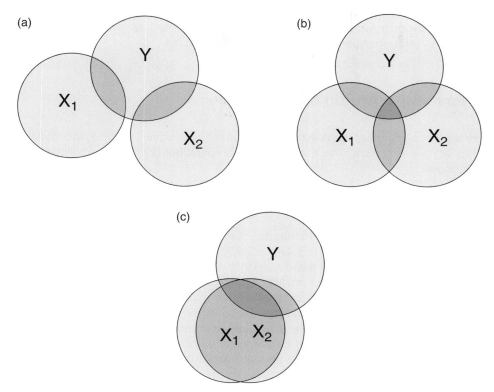

(a)

(b)

(c)

correlation matrix is not a guarantee that multicollinearity will not be a problem (as combinations of variables may also create a problem), but it is a good first step.

The second way to identify if multicollinearity is a problem is to look at the coefficients and compare the t-tests to the F-statistic. Because the partial regression coefficients are calculated using only the unique covariance between the dependent variable and the independent variables, multicollinearity can cause coefficients to change signs between bivariate and multivariate models. Additionally, because the t-tests are also based on the unique covariance, models that suffer from problems with multicollinearity will often have a number of insignificant t-tests but a very high R-square statistic. This is because the F-statistic and the R-square are calculated from the ratio of the intersection of the dependent variable with all the independent variables (not just the unique covariance).

Multicollinearity may be addressed in several ways. First, if two X variables are measuring the same thing (as evidenced by a high correlation), we can simply eliminate one of the variables and discuss why the variable was eliminated. We can purge the

X variables of multicollinearity (as described in the first section) and perform the regression with the transformed variables. It is important to note though that this will not address the problem with the coefficient values or directionality. Finally, we can collect more data or get better operationalizations of our variables.

Performing a Multiple Regression

There are three important steps in running a multiple least squares regression model, and each is equally important. These are (1) data preparation, (2) model specification, and (3) diagnostics.

Data Preparation

It is crucial in data analysis to understand your data, and an important step in this is to thoroughly examine the data prior to any statistical modeling. First, you must *ensure the veracity of your data*, and then make sure that you have sufficient variation to examine within the data. When doing this, you also want to see if there may be any problems with how you think the data are going to behave in the multivariate model.

Start by running descriptive statistics on all of the variables you are going to use. While this may seem silly to say, many scholars and practitioners alike have been bitten by not making sure that the data were what they thought they were. First, make sure that the variables do not have values that are outside the bounds of what is possible. There have been data used in refereed publications and for policy analysis in the United States that had school superintendants listed as being 126 years old. In another case, a top journal published research performed on data that had a number of erroneous −99 values in the data (−99 is a value often used to mark "Don't Know" or "Refused" answers on survey data). While you are looking at the descriptive statistics, also ensure that the variables have variance. After all, least squares regression is an analysis of covariance between variables. It is impossible to have covariance when one of the variables has no variance.

The second step in evaluating your data before modeling it is to run a covariance matrix and bivariate scatter plots of the dependent variable against each of the independent variables. The correlation matrix will identify most potential problems with multicollinearity, while the bivariate scatter plots will help identify the functional forms (linear, curvilinear, quadratic) of the relationships between the dependent variable and independent variables.

Model Specification

Once you have ensured that the data are appropriate for modeling, the next step is to build your model. If you have problems with multicollinearity, or nonlinear relationships, this is the time to take remedial action. This process really starts when you are evaluating the data. Create any new variables necessary to model a curve or perhaps to deal with discreet data. You will also find it nice to think about how you want to order the data going into the model to help with the interpretation later. Typically, it is helpful to put like variables next to one another in the model to ease reading and to facilitate quicker copy and pastes.

You will also want to make sure that you have working hypotheses for all of the variables you are including in the model—even if some of the variables are only there for statistical control. You should never just put in all the variables and see what comes out. Similarly, stepwise regressions and other iterative data mining are a strict no-no. Along with your hypotheses, you are going to want to have already identified your thresholds for significance for each model. We will not repeat our discussion on the concept of statistical significance now, but you do need to develop some sort of criteria for variable importance before you run the model. Having these decision rules set up in advance will help you retain your integrity in data analysis.

Diagnostics

After performing the regression calculations, the first thing that must be done is to check for indications that the model violates one of the four assumptions listed above. To do this, first it is important to compare the R-square statistic to the t-values in the model output. Having a large R-square and insignificant t-values is a clear indicator that multicollinearity is a problem. Next, compare the individual coefficients to the a priori hypotheses for each variable and to the coefficients of bivariate regressions. Are there values that seem to be counterintuitive? Do the coefficient signs change from the bivariate environment to the multivariate model? Again, these are clear signs of multicollinearity.

Next, the residuals from the regression must be assessed by plotting the residuals against the predicted values of the dependent variable (the fitted values of Y). Abnormal patterns in distribution indicate that the functional form of the model may not suit the data. Similarly, asymmetric residual distributions may also indicate a problem with heteroskedasticity. In data that are across time, it is vital to check for problems with autocorrelation. To do this, plot the residuals against the variable in the data set that represents time, and look for trends in the residuals. It may also be important to check for serial correlation in cross-sectional data, but to do this is a bit more complex. Checking for serial correlation will require some sort of idea of *how* the data would be spatially oriented and then ordering the data so that a scatter plot of the residuals vs. the distribution can be created.

Discreet Variables in Multiple Regression

Regression is typically applied to continuous data; however, it is possible to use discreet variables as independent variables in a regression model. Occasionally, you may see researchers using discreet variables such as what might result from a Likert Scale question on a survey; however, this is a bad practice. Recall from the last chapter that we interpret the coefficient from a regression analysis as a slope change. The coefficient is the change in the estimate of the mean of Y given a one-unit change in X. Because nominal and ordinal data do not have a fixed unit interval (the difference between strongly disagree and disagree may not be the same as the difference between neutral and agree), it is unrealistic to believe that we can confidently talk about unit changes in discreet variables. This problem can be addressed by creating a series of dichotomous variables to represent the categories of the discreet variable.

Recall in the previous chapter, we talked about a variable for a dichotomous variable representing the change in the estimated mean of Y from the constant in a regression. Thus, if we have a dependent variable Y that was income, and an independent variable X that was gender coded 0 for males and 1 for females, we could interpret the following regression: $Y = b_0 + b_1(gender) + \varepsilon$ as the constant (b_0) being equal to the mean income of males, and the coefficient for gender (b_1) as the change in the mean of income for females. So if we wanted to know the mean income for females, we could easily calculate it as $\hat{Y}(female) = b_0 + b_1(gender)$. The t-test for the coefficient b_1 will test if the coefficient is different from zero. In other words, we are testing to see if the change in the mean income is significantly different from the constant (which is the mean income for men).

Using this same approach, we can address multiple category discreet variables by including a dichotomous variable for each category.

Example 18.1

Assume we have survey data covering attitudes about education that we combined with income data. We are interested in whether there is a relationship between regard for education and a person's actual education. In the original data, we have a variable for annual income, and we have one that came from the following survey question:

I believe that education is vital for success later in life:
    0 Strongly disagree   0 disagree   0 neutral   0 agree   0 strongly agree

The first step in analyzing these data is to create five new variables from the current data on educational importance. We would create a variable SD that is coded 1 if the individual strongly disagreed and 0 for all others. We would create a variable D coded 1 if the individual disagreed and 0 otherwise. We create a variable N coded 1 if the respondent was neutral and 0 otherwise. We create a variable A coded 1 if the individual agreed with the statement and 0 otherwise, and finally we create a variable SA that is coded 1 if the respondent strongly agreed and 0 otherwise.

The next step is to decide which category will be our baseline. Recall in the example with gender, we only included a variable for females, and the mean of Y for males was the constant (y-intercept). This is because we controlled for the effect of being female by including the dichotomous variable coded 1 for female. The selection of the excluded category is very important as all the t-tests will be comparing the coefficients to this baseline category. So returning to our example, it might be good to use those respondents who were neutral on the subject as a baseline. This implies two hypotheses: **H1**: individuals who disagree with the statement will make significantly less than those who are neutral, and **H2**: those who agree will make significantly more than those who are neutral.

We can then calculate the coefficients for the model $Y = b_0 + b_1 x_{sd} + b_2 x_d + b_3 x_a + b_4 x_{sa}$. We would expect that the coefficients for b_1 and b_2 would be negative and have significant t-tests indicating that they were significantly less than b_0 (the mean value of Y for those individuals who were neutral on the subject). We would also expect that the coefficients b_3 and b_4 would be positive and significant indicating that those who agreed with the statement made significantly more on average than those who were neutral on the subject.

Notice that the t-tests only tell us about the relationship between each category and the omitted category—they do not provide information about how they relate to each other. A t-test is only able to test one relationship; however, there are versions of the t-test that will allow for multiple comparisons. These approaches are beyond the scope of this introduction to regression, but the reader may easily find information on multiple comparison tests in an introductory text on ANOVA applications.

A second approach to dealing with these data would be to include all the variables but not estimate the constant. By removing the constant and putting all five variables in the equation, we simply change the model from a comparison to a baseline to a model that compares each category to zero. So if we were to model the same data with the equation, $Y = b_1 x_{sa} + b_2 x_d + b_3 x_n + b_4 x_a + b_5 x_{sa}$, each coefficient would tell us if the coefficient is different from zero. This approach is a nice way to gain some insight about what the intervals of a Likert variable look like. In the case where the estimated coefficients are somewhat even, it may not be too problematic to use the original variable as a continuous variable in a regression.

Interpreting a Multiple Regression

Coefficients from a multiple regression are interpreted largely in the same manner as those in a bivariate regression. That is, each coefficient represents a change in the mean value of Y for a one-unit change in X. What the multivariate model offers above this is twofold. First, we are able to interpret the unique effect of some variable X while holding all others constant. Take for example the model: $Y = b_0 + b_1 x_1 + b_2 x_2 + b_3 x_3 + b_4 x_4$. If we wanted to calculate the mean values of Y for different values of $x1$, we could easily do so by assuming all the other values are zero and just calculating the values of Y using the following formula: $Y = b_0 + b_1 x_1$. This is because if we allow the values of x_2, x_3, and x_4 to be zero, they drop out of the equation. Similarly, we could hold them constant at any other value, and the results would be the same in terms of the slope of x_1. This is true for all the individual coefficients in the model. The second advantage is that we can interpret multiple coefficients simultaneously.

There are two cases where interpreting coefficients simultaneously are typically used. The first is when a single variable has been used in different forms in the regression to model a nonlinear relationship. A good example of this is seen earlier in this chapter. In this example, the value of Y was a curvilinear function of X and was modeled as $Y = b_0 + b_1 x_1 + b_2 x_1^2 + \varepsilon$. There are two ways to evaluate these data. The first is to use a little calculus to define the curve (this is probably the easiest but also the least transparent). The second is to set up a simple Excel spreadsheet that has a column for X and one for Y. Let the X values vary from the minimum value in the data set to the maximum value in the data set. Now enter the regression formula into the column for the Y values. When this is done, simply produce a scatter plot with a connecting line that will illustrate the estimated values of Y for any given value of X. While this graph may not provide the same detail as calculating the critical values for the curve, it will be a much better tool for communicating the results of the analysis. The second case where coefficients should be used simultaneously is when we use categorical variables in the regression.

There are two ways to use categorical variables in a regression model. They can be used alone or interacted with some other continuous variable. Each of these implies certain assumptions about the relationship of the categorical variable. Used alone in a regression, a dichotomous variable represents a change in the mean value of Y related to that condition. Thus, if we regress gender (coded 0 for males and 1 for females) on income, the constant would be the mean income of males, and the constant plus the coefficient would be the mean income for females, while the coefficient would be the difference in mean income between males and females. This is because if the respondent is male, the value of X is zero, and zero times the coefficient equals zero—thus, when the respondent is male, the equation reduce to the constant (b_0). When the respondent is female, the value of X is one, and one times the coefficient equals the coefficient. Thus, the dichotomous variable is simply a step change to the y-intercept (the constant) in the presence of the condition represented by the coefficient (in this case, being female).

When we combine a dichotomous variable with a continuous variable in a regression, the effect of the coefficient for the dichotomous variable is the same. So if we regress, $Y_{income} = b_0 + b_1 x_{gender} + b_2 x_{education}$, the slope of the continuous variable education does not change because of gender—only the Y-intercept changes. Assume that we ran the model and obtained the following significant coefficients: $b_0 = 5$, $b_1 = -2.89$, and $b_2 = 1.13$. If we were to calculate some values of Y based on this entire equation and graph it, we get the following (Figure 18.12):

Notice that the slope reflecting the relationship between Education and Income does not change for either males or females. The slope of both lines is 1.13. The y-intercept for males is 5, while the y-intercept for females is $b_0 + b_1$ or 2.11. The difference between any female value of X and corresponding male value for X is −2.89. In this case, the dichotomous regressor in the model creates a step change for the cases that have the quality indicated by the variable. Unfortunately, this assumption is not always tenable. When we modeled this data, we implicitly assumed that the effect of education would not change between genders, but that there was simply a different baseline between the

Figure 18.12

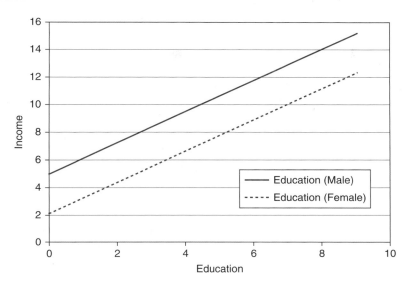

two groups. We can change this to assume that the dichotomous variable will also affect the slope of the relationship by interacting it with the education variable.

To test for interaction effects, we simply create an interaction variable by multiplying the dichotomous variable of interest by the continuous variable of interest. This results in a new variable that is equal to the continuous variable when the dichotomous variable is equal to one, and zero otherwise. Using the example above, if we thought that the slope of the relationship between education and income changes for males and females, we would simply make a new interaction variable that was equal to education times gender (so that the resulting variable equals zero for males and the value of education for females). We include the new variable in the regression so it is now $Y_{income} = b_0 + b_1 x_{gender} + b_2 x_{education} + b_3 x_{gender \times education}$. Running this regression produces the coefficients: $b_0 = 4$, $b_1 = -1.89$, $b_2 = 1.33$, and $b_3 = -.51$. The resulting graph of this regression would look like Figure 18.13.

As we can see, the regression line for males is $Y = b_0 + b_2 x_{education}$. The regression line for females is $Y = (b_0 + b_1) + (b_2 + b_3) x_{education}$. That is, the y-intercept for females is 2.11, and the slope of the relationship for females is .82. The difference between the y-intercept for males and females is equal to b_1, and the difference in the slope is the coefficient for the interaction variable b_3. Furthermore, the t-test for b_1 tells us if the difference in the y-intercepts is significant, and the t-test for b_3 tells if the difference in the slopes is significant.

Dichotomous variables and interactions are a powerful tool for examining effects of some characteristic. In the example, we used it to examine gender, but it is also handy for looking at anything that can be grouped. These can be used to test policy effects, location differences, time differences, and pretty much anything a crafty researcher can devise.

Figure 18.13

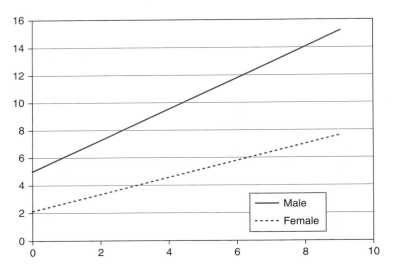

Conclusion

Multiple least squares is a powerful tool for assessing the effects of variables in a multitude of ways. This chapter has introduced you to some basic concepts in modeling and diagnostics, but it was just that—an introduction. The least squares family has been around for a long time because of its great utility and simplicity in application. Important to the application of least squares is understanding the assumptions that underlie the models. Least squares regression is actually a very robust approach, and even though we have identified several assumptions, violating these assumptions is not always a fatal flaw. Advanced texts provide numerous techniques for dealing with some of the flaws that may plague a regression model.

Vocabulary

Flashcards
& MCQs

AUTOCORRELATION—A condition where the residuals have a time-dependent trend in values. This can be either negative autocorrelation or positive autocorrelation.

HETEROSKEDASTICITY—A condition where the variance or the residuals from a regression have variance that changes for different values of the independent variables.

HOMOSKEDASTICITY—A condition where the variance of the residuals from a multiple regression is constant. This is the desired condition.

MULTICOLLINEARITY—Correlation shared between independent variables in a multiple regression model that affect the calculations for the partial regression coefficients.

PARTIAL REGRESSION COEFFICIENTS—The coefficients produced by multiple regression. These coefficients are referred to as partial because they do not represent all the shared covariance between an individual independent variable and the dependent variable, but only the covariance that is unique to the two of them.

RESIDUAL PLOT—A scatter plot with the residuals on the y-axis and either one of the x variables or the predicted values of y (y-hat) along the x-axis used for diagnosing violations of regression assumptions.

Sequencing

Useful
Websites

Review Questions

■ Why can you not use the simple OLS model to test means of data with more than two groupings?

■ Under what circumstances might you want to test if a model coefficient is significantly different from some value other than zero?

■ What do we mean by the term "model"?

■ What information do you need to calculate the SSM?

■ What test is used to evaluate the significance of model coefficients?

■ What test is used to assess model significance?

■ What statistic is used to display the model fit?

Education
Data Set -
Excel,
STATA &
SPSS

Discussion Questions

■ What do we mean by least squares?

■ Explain why the R-square can be interpreted as a percentage?

■ How are the coefficients different from the model?

■ How can a model with an R-square of .03 be important (hint: think about the difference between statistical and substantive significance)?

Data Set
exercises

CHAPTER **19**

Mixing Research Methods

Learning Objectives

✓ Understand the circumstances in which mixing methods can improve research projects
✓ Identify the difficulties present in mixing research methods
✓ Develop alternative models of mixing methods, including concurrent and sequential designs

Cases in Research

Case A—National Helping Hands

The work on nonprofit participation in disaster recovery has included a wide variety of data collection and analysis techniques. Interview data along with the formal analysis of after-action reports and on-site data collection provide many different views of disaster recovery. The results of the various studies were quite interesting, but many questions remain and the director of National Helping Hands (NHH) would like to continue research into how to integrate nonprofit organizations—this time into emergency planning. Given the success of the various methods, the director would like to mix various research methods again—but this time with a planned mixing approach.

Case B—Springfield Housing Department

The case for collecting both user survey data and on-site observational data made a great deal of sense. The director of the housing department is encouraged by the volume of data generated in these processes. Many of the office's clients participated in the survey, and the memos from the site visits are detailed and intriguing. Now, though, the director is left with a challenge. How does one compare data from such disparate research techniques?

The Logic of Mixing Research Methods

There are many different strategies for collecting and analyzing data to address public affairs questions. A public manager faces important choices at the outset of any research project about what research approach to use, as each approach has its own strengths and weaknesses. Rather than settling for the strengths and weaknesses of any one approach, you could instead choose to pair multiple research methods together. One could use both interviews and surveys to address a research question. Alternatively, one could use budgetary data combined with on-site observation and document collection. The combination of the methods may provide a more compelling strategy than any one method in isolation. This chapter will present a variety of strategies for combining different research methods into a single research project.

Advantages of Mixing Research Methods

Mixing research methods can serve a number of purposes and present a number of advantages over using a single research approach. Most broadly, each research approach has its own strengths and weaknesses. If you rely on a single research method, your results may be limited by the method's strengths and weaknesses. You may find it useful to do a survey of a large number of nonprofit organizations to see what they list as the primary barriers to their participation in emergency planning activities. Of course, this approach would have its limitations. You may have to use short questions with few options if you hope to reach a large number of people. These short questions may limit your ability to identify truly innovative ideas because you have to list the options in advance. Mixing in some in-depth interviews or other methods may allow you to complement the survey with a deeper understanding of the barriers to nonprofit participation. Of course, the in-depth interviews would be limited by themselves—only able to include a small number of people relative to the survey. The best approach may be to use both the survey and the interviews to offset the weaknesses of each.

> **Class Exercise:** What methods do you think could be most fruitfully combined? What weaknesses does each method offset in the other?

One popular metaphor to describe the advantage of mixing methods is **TRIANGULATION**. Triangulation involves the estimation of some unknown point by reference to two or more known points. The geometry of formal triangulation is less important than the basic idea. If you do know where a specific point is (or the answer to a specific research question), you may be able to deduce the answer from the answers to related points (or the results of related research). In mixing research methods, this means that the information you are looking for may not be discoverable through one method. Instead, you can use multiple methods to get at partial answers (limited by the weakness of a specific research method) which when combined reveal the full answer. The goal is to select methods where the strengths of one research method offset the weaknesses of another.

A second justification for mixing methods is **CORROBORATION**. Corroboration involves the comparison of the results of studies using different methods to find similar answers that emerge from studies using different methods. The process of corroboration is like getting a second opinion from a doctor. If the first doctor tells you that you need surgery, you would not seek a second opinion by asking the same doctor the next day. You know what he or she is going to say. You want to ask a separate doctor—preferably without telling him or her about the original opinion. If both doctors recommend surgery, you can be more comfortable with the conclusion that surgery is the best option. In mixing research methods, corroboration involves using different data collection or analytic techniques to answer the same research question and accepting the answer if the techniques agree.

A third justification is the opposite of corroboration: **COMPREHENSIVENESS**. Comprehensiveness combines the results of various research methods to chart all of the various possible answers to a research question. With corroboration, your goal was to eliminate potential answers that were the product of one research method but not the others. With comprehensiveness, the goal is to make as long a list as possible of potential answers. The best analogue to comprehensiveness may be the search for vacation plane flights. You may want to use various search engines and websites to look for inexpensive flights for your vacation. You would not eliminate search results that appeared in one search engine but not another. In this case, you are using different search engines because they may find flights that others miss. If you want to catalog all nonprofit organizations active in emergency planning, you may similarly want to employ different methods. You could combine interviews, surveys, document analysis, and news reports to make as comprehensive a list as possible. Each of these techniques is likely to miss some participants. Combining the various techniques may give you the most comprehensive list possible.

In the end, the reason for using a mixed methods strategy is simple. You would want to investigate a mixed methods strategy when it would allow you to answer questions that you can't answer otherwise. This may be the case where the individual tools you have available are limited in important ways but can be combined. This may also be the case where you need to have a great deal of confidence in any results you find.

Disadvantages of Mixing Research Methods

Mixing methods offers a number of advantages over the use of individual research methods. However, combining research methods creates complexities and costs in a variety of ways.

Most obviously, mixing research methods requires completing multiple research projects. In the parlance of mixed research methods, these are known as **STREAMS**. To mix a survey and an interview protocol will require completing two full research protocols—or streams. The intent to mix research methods does not free you to do a poor job with any component of the project. A project that mixes interviews and surveys should seek to do an excellent survey and excellent interviews and to combine them to answer questions better than the excellent projects would have separately. This means that a mixed methods project may take as much time as each of the components combined (though there are some opportunities to economize on time).

Similarly, mixing methods can be an expensive proposition. Each research method has its own source of expenses. Surveys may cost money to write, duplicate, distribute, and collect. Interviews require hiring interviewers and, possibly, compensating interviewees. Site research requires paying observers and the time associated with memoing. All of these approaches require time (and time is money) to analyze data. As you combine research methods within a study, you also accumulate expenses related to data collection and analysis. While one might ideally want to combine a variety of methods, you may not have the money in practice to accomplish this mixture.

There are also intellectual challenges peculiar to the mixture of research methods. While we have emphasized a pragmatic approach to research, scholars and practitioners often associate specific research methods with specific philosophical assumptions about research. Survey research typically assumes that there is a single answer to a research question—often one that you can represent with a number (a quantitative orientation). In-depth interviews and some types of ethnographic site research often assume that there is no single answer to a research question and that the answer depends on the researcher him- or herself. You could combine these methods, but you cannot simultaneously assume an objective and a subjective view of reality. The strongest critics of mixing methods argue that many methods are incommensurable—that is, a researcher ought not to combine research methods because of incompatibility between the foundational assumptions in each method. Proponents of mixing methods counter with a **COMMENSURABILITY ASSUMPTION**—the assumption that one can combine methods historically associated with specific, competing paradigms, possibly under an umbrella like a pragmatic paradigm.

Mixed research strategies can provide a great deal of confidence in your findings. However, they are not easy to manage. Each stream adds to the costs of the project as well as complicating the management of the project. You should only embark on a mixed methods project if you are convinced that the strengths of the approach exceed that of the costs.

Designing Mixed Methods Research

Once you have decided to embark on a mixed methods study, you will have to make a number of decisions about how to structure and combine your chosen methods. The real advantage of mixed methods research comes in the skillful combination of methods rather than two (or more) entirely separate research projects. It is essential that you plan for the mixture of methods from the very beginning rather than waiting until you have started and then combine the methods ad hoc. To assist in the design of mixed methods studies, proponents of mixing research methodologies have adopted a specific notation system to describe potential systems. The notational system allows authors to summarize their approach quickly as well as being clear about the relationship between the components of their study. Recall that a chief challenge of mixed methods research is the management of the various streams. A notational system allows a manager to define clearly the relationships between the streams and makes management easier. Furthermore, the clarity of the notation system allows one to discuss and debate various designs at the research design stage to make sure that you end up with the best mixed design for your project needs.

Notational System for Mixing Methods

The notational system starts with a shorthand term to describe each research stream. Recall, a research stream is a component of a mixed methods project that includes a single research strategy. The survey component of a larger mixed methods project (that may also include such elements as site-based investigation or in-depth interviews) would be a single stream.

By convention, the notation system for mixed methods research refers to two types of streams: quantitative (quant) and qualitative (qual) research. You should not take this to mean that a proper mixed methods study includes exactly one quantitative component and exactly one qualitative component. You could combine two qualitative or two quantitative components or more than two components. The assignment of research streams as either quantitative or qualitative is itself controversial. For these reasons, the shorthand is merely a placeholder to describe specific streams of research but should not be taken as limiting. You can substitute your own shorthand for specific streams (maybe "surv" for a survey stream or "budg" for the analysis of budgetary data), but we will present the favored quan/qual terminology out of respect for the tradition of mixed methods research.

If one of the research streams is primary within your study, you represent priority by using all capital letters for the primary stream's shorthand. In a study where the qualitative strand is primary, you should represent this by referring to the stream as QUAL. What constitutes a primary stream depends on your own interests and design of the project. If you think of your project as primarily a quantitative survey with a qualitative interview component that simply serves to validate or contextualize findings, you might decide this project has a QUANT and a qual stream. In a research project where both streams are equally important, you can represent each stream with the same priority—either in capital letters or not.

> **Class Exercise:** How would you represent a mixed research project that includes an initial series of in-depth interviews and on-site observations (conducted separately) to inform the design of a large sample survey followed by a (separate) analysis of official documents? Is there more than one way to represent this project? What would the differences in representation mean in practice?

notation system minimizes complexities in management

Once you had decided on the number and type of streams that you have and their relative priority, you need to decide on a sequence of the streams. This is where planning mixed methods research starts to impact your research project. There are two general strategies for sequencing. A **CONCURRENT DESIGN** is one in which two (or more) research streams occur simultaneously without reference to each other. In the NHH case, you might want to explore the role of nonprofits in emergency planning using a research strategy that mixes a survey of nonprofit organizations with in-depth interviews of specific nonprofit leaders. A concurrent design would keep these streams separate with any integration of the findings coming at the very end of the project. You can represent a concurrent design by connecting two shorthand stream names with a plus (+) sign. The concurrent project described above, a concurrent survey (quant) and in-depth interviews (qual) with equal priority, is represented as: quant + qual.

A **SEQUENTIAL DESIGN** involves one stream feeding information into the design and conduct of a second stream. For one stream to feed into another, the first stream has to be at some stage of completion. The second stream builds on the results of the first. A common example of a sequential design is qualitative survey instrument design. For the NHH case, you could use this approach by conducting in-depth interviews (qual) to inform an initial investigation of the role of nonprofit organization in emergency planning with the goal of creating valid categories and concepts for use in a broad survey amenable to quantitative analysis (QUANT). Note that in this case the interviews are intended to support the primary stream of the survey; so the survey stream is listed in all capital letters. You should represent a sequence of streams with an arrow (→) such that the example discussed in this paragraph would be qual → QUANT.

Uses of Concurrent Research Designs

Concurrent designs rely on each component stream being largely separate. This separation can be advantageous in a number of situations. If you are using different methods to ensure that any answers are consistent across research methods, you do not want the various streams to mix too much. For example, if the purpose of the interviews is to confirm the patterns that you see in a large survey, you do not want the interview subjects or the interviewers to have seen the survey results. Knowing what the survey results suggest may bias the interview subjects toward confirmation of the patterns in the survey. Keeping the streams separate reduces the impact of these sorts of bias.

In the Springfield Housing study, you may want to pursue a concurrent survey and interview protocol. Interviews may be vulnerable to interviewer bias—in this case, involving interviewers influencing the respondents' statements about their experiences at the housing office. In this case, one would not want the interviewers to have access to the survey results for fear that they would simply lead the interview respondents to repeat back the findings of the survey. You may want each of those studies to be independent. The easiest way to do this is to run the studies concurrently with different teams of researchers.

Concurrent designs are particularly useful when you have separate research teams assigned to each research stream. Because the teams assigned to each research stream do not need to communicate, you do not have to manage the interactions of the teams. Instead, the teams operate more or less independently, and their individual success and failure does not depend on anything done by the other team.

> **Class Exercise:** If you were studying why some students drop out of college, how might you design a concurrent mixed research study? What methods would you use in the streams? Why would the streams be concurrent?

Corroboration approaches are ideally suited for concurrent designs. In corroboration approaches, you want to assess whether the answer to a research question depends on the particular research method you use. Independence of the streams is vital to useful corroboration testing. If the two members of each stream are constantly communicating with each other any bias present in one stream may contaminate the other stream. In the housing department study, you may create a concurrent design using interviews and surveys. Your hope would be to see if the same barriers to housing applications that your clients identify in your surveys show up in the interviews. If the two methods—operating independently and concurrently—reach the same conclusion, you can have a great deal of confidence in the results. For example, if the survey results and the interviews both point to the "bank hours" of the housing department as the primary barrier to clients, you can have greater confidence than if the result came from just one of the methods.

If the interviewers are reading the initial survey results, they may ask questions that guide respondents to make similar statements in the interviews. It could be that interviewers had seen initial results about the hours of the department office and asked specifically about them. This could lead the interviewees to talk about the hours as a barrier to applications when they would not have if the interviewer had not brought up the subject. The survey results created an echo in the interview results, and the interview results should not be seen as corroborating the survey results. The two streams being connected limit their usefulness as a check on each other.

Uses of Sequential Research Designs

Sequential designs involve using one research stream to feed into another research stream. The goal is to use one stream to allow you to better carry out a second, generally primary, stream. There are two most popular types of sequential designs: **EXPLORATORY SEQUENTIAL DESIGN** and **EXPLANATORY SEQUENTIAL DESIGN**.

In an exploratory sequential design, you start with a qualitative method followed by a quantitative method (qual → QUAN). In this design, the initial qualitative work serves to discover the appropriate categories and concepts that you will investigate more thoroughly (and primarily) with the quantitative method. This is the case in an area where one does not have strong prior information about the subject under study or the purpose of the research. The first phase may serve to explore the subject—typically in depth but with a small and nonrandomized sample. This may involve a case study of a specific organization, in-depth interviews of a few people, or ethnographic site observation. The purpose is to identify candidate explanations or concepts that are important for your study. A key limitation of this approach, if conducted without mixing in the second stream, is that such small and nonrandom samples cannot tell you much about the prevalence of attitudes or conditions in the world as a whole. The incorporation of the quantitative stream addresses these limitations. The initial explorations of the qualitative methods are confirmed (or not) by the second, quantitative component. The large, randomly selected sample can serve to illustrate whether the attitudes or conditions observed in the smaller, nonrandom samples were representative of the world as a whole.

We can take a different approach to the Springfield Housing Department example. If we were primarily worried about contamination or bias crossing over the research streams, we would want a concurrent design that kept the streams separate for later corroboration. On the other hand, we could focus on exploration rather than corroboration. In this case, we may decide that we know so little about the barriers to applying for housing assistance that we need to conduct interviews as a pretest of our survey protocol. The interviews, then, are not intended as a separate research project whose results we will compare to the survey later for corroboration. Instead, the interviews would take place before the survey, and the results of the interviews would help design the survey. The interviews may help identify the specific barriers that warrant investigation and the wording for questions in the survey instrument. If the interviews revealed that the hours of the housing office are important, you can design a battery of questions investigating this issue. A concurrent design would not allow for this sort of interactivity and learning between the streams.

It is not just the qualitative component that would have weaknesses on its own. If one went straight to the quantitative component without careful consideration of the concepts important to the study, you may leave out something important or conflate two concepts that should be carefully distinguished. The early qualitative component supports a stronger and more valid quantitative research design. The mixed research method is made stronger by combining the strengths of the two methods and by avoiding the limitations of each.

In the housing department case, the initial qualitative work (say, a series of in-depth interviews) could serve to populate a list of potential barriers to applications. The in-depth interviews could clarify which barriers are specific examples of some broader class of barriers (different types of transportation problems) or which barriers should be treated as independent barriers. This method would be particularly useful in investigating the role of individual clients' emotional reactions to the application process. The result of this stream could be a series of potential barriers but little information about the relative proportion of clients that actually experience each barrier or their relative importance.

The quantitative survey could provide specific answers to the prevalence of transportation barriers (that is, the proportion of clients who report that transportation has been a problem for them when trying to apply for housing assistance). With careful design of the sample and the use of the right statistical tests, you could see whether the proportion of clients who report transportation problems is different than the proportion who report child care-related problems. The usefulness of these comparisons depends critically on having presented the survey respondents with a good list of options. If you had left a key potential barrier off the list, your proportions may not be valid anymore. The previous qualitative phase should give you much more confidence that your survey instrument is thorough and valid.

The explanatory sequential method reverses the order of the qualitative and quantitative components. In the explanatory sequential design, the quantitative stream precedes the qualitative stream (quan → qual). The priority of the two phases depends on the goals of the research project. The quantitative phase typically involves a large sample exploration of the proportions or various attitudes or conditions as well as the correlations between these. However, the correlations and proportions do not interpret themselves. The quantitative sample may point to specific units that warrant more careful investigation—possibly though a case study. The second, qualitative stream serves to explain what you observe in the first, quantitative stream.

Consider an explanatory sequential study of the barriers to applications in our housing department. If a quantitative comparison of the application rates at various housing department offices revealed that one office was doing a particularly good job, an on-site observational study may be warranted. **BEST PRACTICES RESEARCH** involves the investigation of a high-performing organization with the hope that you can learn lessons that can be generalized to help other organizations. More generally, one can use an explanatory sequential design to conduct **OUTLIER ANALYSIS**—an assessment of a specific unit that is an outlier (either positively or negatively) in a large sample quantitative study. Outlier analysis generally allows you to investigate whether organizations in the most extreme cases reflect the patterns you have seen on average. For example, are the highest performing housing offices the ones where the purported barriers are absent? Are the lowest performing housing offices those in which the barriers are present?

More Complex Mixed Designs

Class Exercise: What would this study look like if the shorthand were: news + intv → docs

The preceding sections have presented some of the most popular mixed methods designs. However, these designs are quite simple, and one can elaborate upon them in a variety of ways.

First, you can represent research streams with more specific designations and mix more than two methods. In the NHH case, you may want to identify all of the actors that are involved in emergency planning activities within a specific community. With the goal of comprehensiveness in mind, you would seek a mixed methods approach with each method potentially capturing actors that the other methods mixed. You could mix interviews with emergency management officials (intv) with a collection of news reports (news) and assessment of specific emergency planning documents (docs). Now you can decide whether to combine the methods concurrently (intv + news + docs) or in some kind of sequence. You could use the news reports to identify potential interview subjects and the interviews to identify the documents you should consult (news → intv → docs). More complex combinations are possible if some of the methods are pursued concurrently while others are pursued sequentially.

Second, you can break apart specific streams into individual phases with sequences and connection between streams at different phases of each stream. The result is a **MULTI-PHASE DESIGN**. You can break a particular stream into multiple phases with opportunities to revise the research method between each phase. For example, you can break a large survey into two (or more phases) so that you can revisit the sampling strategy or the survey instrument itself. In a mixed methods design, you can introduce points where the streams intersect at the gaps between the streams. For example, a gap between two phases of a survey (surv1 and surv2) can allow for the consultation of in-depth interviews (intv1) on the subject to consider whether to add, drop, or revise questions in the survey. Of course, revising a survey instrument should not be done lightly. You may introduce comparability problems between the phases. However, having comparable phases with a bad instrument can be worse. Such a design could be represented as surv1 → intv1 → surv2.

You can create break points for the phases at many different points within streams. With the NHH case in-depth interviews, you may use the initial handful of surveys to inform the sampling decisions for a survey while still continuing to conduct interviews. That is, you can create connections between streams (here the interviews and the surveys) with-

> **Class Exercise:** How can you describe the previous shorthand description of a mixed project in words?

out having completed even the data collection phase of one of the streams. Similarly, you can connect streams in the middle of data analysis. If the NHH interviews were intended to create insight into the barriers to participation by local nonprofit organizations, you could connect the data analysis of the interviews to other methods by initially simply listing the actors mentioned in interviews (possibly to supplement a survey sample) while later analyzing the interviews in more detail for barriers to participation. Such a design could be represented as intv.analy1 → surv.sample3 → intv.analy2.

Such complex projects can result in complex representations. Adding the previous two designs together (involving mixing at the early data collection states as well as later in the analysis phase) could be part of a larger project represented here.

surv1 + intv1 → surv2 + intv2 → intv.analy1 → surv3 + intv.analy2 → surv.analysis

Analysis of Data in Mixed Methods Research

Analysis in mixed methods studies can take many forms. As with data collection, mixed methods studies do not so much introduce new techniques as provide a variety of strategies for integrating different techniques into a unified whole. Mixed methods data analysis involves the use of traditional methods of data analysis (data display, statistical analysis, etc.) but with connections between analysis taking place in separate streams. The statistical analysis of a survey, for example, may involve consultation with the results of a data display analysis of official documents. The art (and the challenge) of mixing analytic techniques is pulling different analytic techniques together to provide a unified answer to your research question.

Intermediate Analysis

If one of your streams is clearly the primary component of your research plan, you may use other research streams in a supporting role. You can break up the primary research stream into a series of phases to provide opportunities to revise the methods in the stream. The previous section illustrated how you might represent this process in formal mixed methods notation. It is important to also know why you would want to do this.

In an intermediate analysis, your goal is to ensure that your primary stream of research has the greatest probability of generating useful answers to your research questions. The secondary research streams fulfill this role by filling gaps that exist in the primary research technique. This has become quite common in survey research.

Survey research is a powerful tool, but many have come to recognize that it also has a number of important limitations. Survey results can be sensitive to question wording and other design elements of the survey instrument. In some cases, it is hard to tell whether the survey instrument design is creating misleading results if you only have recourse to the survey instrument itself. If you use a mixed methods design, you can employ other research strategies to check the survey along the way.

> **Class Exercise:** When might intermediate analysis introduce biases into your research project?

Before you send out the survey at all, you may pretest the survey using formal interviewing techniques using the survey questions. The survey instrument questions can be directly included in the survey protocol followed by questions to test whether the respondent understood the question and the response options. A full interview protocol would be a sequential exploratory study that uses the interviews as the primary basis for survey questions and response options. Even in a subordinate role in an intermediate analysis, the interviews can help prevent you from making key mistakes in the survey instrument design by including terms with which the respondents are unfamiliar.

You can also break up the survey into phases after the initial results are in. You could repeat a similar wording assessment by taking the instrument back out for testing with interviews. After the initial survey is in the field, though, you can start to ask interview subjects new questions related to initial results. If there are surprising patterns that are emerging in the early survey results, an intermediate interview phase can serve to test whether the pattern represents some process as understood by the respondents and what that process means to the respondents. After the final survey results are in, you can take the emerging patterns back to your interview subjects to get their reactions. While the results may be a surprise to them, there may also be simple explanations for the patterns. Such a final interview phase can provide additional confirmation that any patterns you observe are operating as you interpret them and helps to avoid relying too much on patterns that may be misleading if understood from the side of the respondents—possibly because you are interpreting survey questions or answers in a way different than your respondents.

In the NHH case, survey instrument design could be quite tricky. The goal of the survey is to better understand the role of nonprofit organizations in emergency planning.

However, the term "emergency planning" is not entirely clear. You would want to spend some time considering how best to define the term and include these thoughts in the survey itself. You could do a presurvey series of interviews that focus on identifying the meaning of emergency planning and the role that nonprofits can play. You may also include questions about whom you should include in the survey protocol to supplement your survey sampling efforts. After the initial survey begins, you can continue interviews to check whether emergency management practitioners have simple explanations for the patterns emerging from the survey and to expand the sample. Your final set of interviews, following analysis of your survey data, can solicit reactions to your initial inferences from the survey to see if any of the interviewees can see a problem with the inferences or if they believe the inferences are illusions created by poor question wording, a poor sample, or any other flaws in the research project.

Corroboration and Comprehensive Analysis

Mixed methods research strategies can be particularly useful when your research involves making a list of potential answers to a research question—rather than a single best answer. There are two strategies for using mixed methods for building lists of answers; which one you want to use depends on your goals with the research project. If your reason for adopting a mixed methods approach is corroboration, you can conduct a specific corroboration analysis approach. The easiest way to understand a corroboration analysis strategy is to envision a Venn diagram (see Figure 19.1). Each circle represents a specific research stream. The contents of each circle include the answers supplied by each method. The answers in the intersecting portion of the circles are the corroborated research answers.

In the housing department case, you may be concerned that surveys and interviews each possess the potential for leading the respondents to providing answers (about barriers to applying for housing assistance) that may not be reliable. You don't want to base

Figure 19.1 The Logic of Corroboration

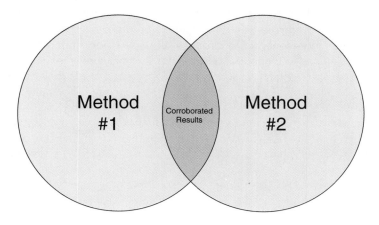

your housing policy development on responses that are an artifact of the specific research methodology. If this is the case, you only want to focus on the barriers that emerge from both a survey and interview research streams.

The resulting Venn diagram may look something like Figure 19.2:

In this simple case of corroboration analysis, you would note that "child care concerns" and "office hours" only emerge from one of the methods—not both. In this case, you would discount the importance of these concerns. "Access to transportation" is a concern that emerges from both of the research streams and is thus a corroborated result.

A comprehensive analysis takes the opposite approach. With a comprehensive analysis, your goal is to document as broad a set of potential answers to your research question as possible. You are not as concerned about results emerging as artifacts of a specific research method than you are that specific research methods may miss potential answers. You want as many potential answers as possible so you do not want to miss the answers that specific methods may neglect. Instead of eliminating potential answers that emerge from only one method, you would accept all answers that emerge from at least one research stream.

> **Class Exercise:** How might you use classifications such as partially corroborated and fully corroborated in later analysis?

In the Venn diagram above, you would accept all three potential barriers emerging from the survey and the interview streams. You may give some amount of priority to "access to transportation" given that the barrier emerged from both methods. However, you would continue to investigate "child care concerns" and "office hours" because their omission in one method is taken as a potential limitation of the method. All of the emerging barriers become potential answers within the comprehensive set.

Figure 19.2   An Example of Corroborated and Contrasting Research Findings

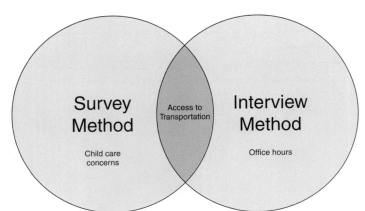

To preserve as much information as possible from your research, you can employ and document both approaches simultaneously and mark each emerging patterns as corro-borated or not. In the NHH case, you may want to document all of the nonprofit organizations active in emergency planning within some community. Your primary goal is comprehensiveness—though you have some interest in seeing which participant's role is corroborated. You could combine three streams (document analysis, interviews, and media accounts) to generate a comprehensive list of all actors mentioned in at least one of the streams. If you were using this list as the basis of a survey, the comprehensive list would be quite valuable. However, you can also note which participants were listed in only one or two of the streams (with being mentioned in two of three streams being partial corroboration). You may later decide to focus attention on those organizations fully or partially corroborated. The degree of corroboration becomes information you may (or may not) choose to use later in the study.

Data Transformation: Qual to Quan Transformation

It is also possible to transform information from one type of study for analysis in other types of studies. In the mixed methods literature, the focus is on distinguishing qualitative and quantitative methods. We will adopt this distinction as well and discuss how to transform data from one of these types of methods to the other (though each type includes a variety of potential specific methods). For the sake of this comparison, qualitative methods are taken to result in some form of textual data. This may be a series of quotes from interviews, images from pictures or documents taken from a study site, or a site observer's notes. Quantitative studies produce data in the form of numbers.

Qualitative to quantitative transformations involve the transformation of words and images to numbers. Typically, such a transformation starts by counting incidences of some characteristic or event within the qualitative data. In the housing department case, you may be interested not simply in which barriers that respondents mention but also in the frequency with which the respondents mention each barrier. You could simply read through the interview transcripts to identify each mention of a barrier. The result could be two lists: one list of the count of the number of mentions each barrier receives (some respondents may mention some barriers more than once) and the proportion of respondents that mention each specific barrier.

Proponents of qualitative research are often quite uncomfortable with such transformations. From a qualitative paradigm, the move from text to counts or proportions is a significant loss of information. In the interviews related to barriers to housing assistance applications, the respondents may provide nuanced explanations of the various barriers they have faced and their own experiences of these barriers. Transforming the data into counts loses much of this nuance by lumping various specific experiences into counts of broad categories. Of course, any textual or visual information still exists. Transforming the initial qualitative work does not destroy the original. It may, though, allow for the comparison of qualitative results to other quantitative results. Counts of mentions of barriers, for example, may be compared to survey data that is natively in quantitative form.

Data Transformation: Quan to Qual Transformation

It is also possible to transform quantitative information into qualitative groupings. In this case, the transformation takes a slightly different approach. You cannot add meaning to data by translating a numerical rating to a textual account. Any transformation of data involves the reduction of information (as with the qual to quan transformation, this is an exercise in lumping). Instead, a quantitative to qualitative transformation breaks up quantitative data into a small number of categories representing qualitative types.

It is common in medical research to use such a transformation. Consider measures of systolic blood pressure. The full information measure is on a scale that goes from 0 to 200 (or more in really bad cases). You could treat this fairly as a continuous variable and utilize the fine distinctions between readings of 120 and 122. However, many health researchers don't think that such fine distinctions really make much of a difference. They are more concerned about looking at the differences between broad levels of blood pressure like mild hypertension (between 140 and 160). They lump all of the patients with systolic blood pressure between 140 and 160 together into a qualitative group called mild hypertension. They are throwing away information (because two different levels, say 145 and 159, are now treated the same as mild hypertension), but the result may be more easily analyzed.

These transformations are less common in public affairs research but can come in handy. In the housing department case, you may have collected quantitative information on the number of housing assistance applications processed at each location. If there were a large number of departments, you could plot the number of applications per department to see if there were any natural groupings. If such a plot (a simple histogram) revealed a bi-modal distribution where one cluster of agencies had a low number and another cluster had a large number, you could transform the data to simply describe agencies as either being in the "low rate" group or the "high rate" group.

Conclusion: How Mixed Methods Research Affects Evidence-Based Public Management

The quality of evidence-based public management depends, in the end, on the quality of the evidence that one can use to make decisions. The tendency for most researchers is to look for the best tool for a specific task. In the process of home repair, one decides whether one needs a screwdriver or a hammer. If you need to drive a nail into a piece of wood, you would choose a hammer. You probably could drive a nail with a screwdriver, but it would be difficult. It is the notion of having multiple tools that motivates people to develop skills with many research skills—as you have through this textbook.

This chapter emphasizes that research questions may be sufficiently complex to warrant the application of multiple tools at the same time (or on the same project). Public affairs research projects are not as simple as driving a nail. They are more like the process of building an entire house. For building a house, you need to have both a screwdriver and a hammer—among many more tools. You must carefully sequence which tools you use at which time to build something as complex as a house. Public affairs research projects can be similarly complex. You may need multiple research streams using different research tools arranged carefully. Mixed methods approaches allow you to tackle a broader range of more complex public affairs research tools. This chapter has made it clear, though, that the process of designing and managing mixed methods research projects requires a great deal of care and attention.

Suggested Readings

Mixed methods research methods have experienced an explosion in coverage over the past decade. This explosion has led to the release of a number of superb books and a great deal of material to help get you started.

The best of the current textbooks on mixed methods research is Creswell and Plano-Clark's *Designing and Collecting Mixed Methods Research*—now in its second edition. This introductory textbook provides a superb introduction to the various components of a mixed methods study and includes examples of high quality mixed methods research reports. These examples illustrate excellent mixed methods research in ways that are difficult to communicate in more traditional textbook chapters.

Teddlie and Tashakkori's *Foundations of Mixed Methods Research* is also a strong textbook to introduce mixed methods. The strength of this book is in its coverage of the philosophical foundations (and controversies) related to mixing research methods. The textbook also includes an engaging history of mixed methods research to illustrate the evolution of approaches that have led to the current state of the field.

The explosion of interest in mixed methods research has led to the creation of a journal dedicated to mixed method studies—the *Journal of Mixed Methods Research*. This journal provides a number of examples of mixed methods research in every issue along with articles on how to conduct and report on mixed methods research. A good entryway into the contemporary scholarship on mixed methods research, like that reported on in the journal, is Plano-Clark and Creswell's *The Mixed Methods Reader*.

Vocabulary

BEST PRACTICES RESEARCH—The investigation of a high-performing organization with the hope that you can learn lessons that can be generalized to help other organizations.

COMMENSURABILITY ASSUMPTION—The assumption that one can combine methods historically associated with specific, competing paradigms.

COMPREHENSIVENESS—The goal of combining the results of various research methods to chart all of the various possible answers to a research question.

CONCURRENT DESIGN—A mixing strategy in which two (or more) research streams occur simultaneously without reference to each other,

CORROBORATION—The comparison of the results of studies using different methods to find similar answers that emerge from studies using different methods.

EXPLANATORY SEQUENTIAL DESIGN—A mixed methods research design where a quantitative stream precedes the qualitative stream.

EXPLORATORY SEQUENTIAL DESIGN—A mixed methods research design where a qualitative stream precedes a quantitative method.

MULTI-PHASE DESIGN—A research strategy where one breaks apart specific streams into individual phases with sequences and connections between streams at different phases of each stream.

OUTLIER ANALYSIS—An assessment of a specific unit that is an outlier (either positively or negatively) in a large sample quantitative study.

SEQUENTIAL DESIGN—A mixing strategy that involves one stream feeding information into the design and conduct of a second stream.

STREAMS—Specific components of a research project, generally consisting of a single research strategy. Separate streams are brought together to make a mixed methods research project.

TRIANGULATION—The estimation of some unknown point by reference to two or more known points

Flashcards
& MCQs

Useful
Websites

Review Questions

- Identify two potential reasons one would consider mixed methods research.
- Translate the following shorthand notation into words: QUAN → qual.
- Under what conditions might you want to use a corroboration analysis?

Discussion Questions

- How might a mixed methods approach be useful in forecasting retirement rates in a school district?
- What strategies would be the easiest to mix? Hardest?

CHAPTER 20

Managing Research and Evaluation Projects

Learning Objectives

✓ Understand the core concepts related to project management
✓ Understand key issues in applying for and administering an award
✓ Identify key issues in working with project clients
✓ Identify ethical issues associated with managing a project and working with clients

Cases in Research

Case A—National Helping Hands

As noted in earlier discussions of the National Helping Hands (NHH) case, assessment of member organizations' activities, processes, and contribution value presents a range of measurement challenges, data collection challenges, and analytic challenges. Our university researcher, Melanie, has approached research challenges in several different ways, including case study work and survey work. Thinking about these efforts in total is not just a challenge for measurement and assessment, but these various activities also present a considerable project management challenge. We can ask: How will Melanie proceed in terms of setting up a plan to design, manage, monitor, and ensure ongoing feedback for her work? How are her various project activities all linked together?

Case B—Amity Department of Homeland Security

A group of three analysts at the Amity Department of Homeland Security have been tasked with conducting an evaluative assessment of the effectiveness of National Incident Management System (NIMS) training among relevant Amity government personnel. The purpose of that assessment work was to determine the level of training effectiveness associated with the city's current approach. Therefore, the team doing the analysis for the department set up a project approach that will be able to permit inferences as to whether the existing training system produces benefits to employee knowledge of NIMS. Because there was a group working collaboratively on this assessment, an initial question for the team to tackle is, how will they set up a plan to implement the project?

Managing a Research or Evaluation Project

While we have covered a variety of analytic tools and provided guidance for conducting research and evaluation, one topic that we have yet to touch on is the matter of project management. **PROJECT MANAGEMENT** in the context of research and evaluation can be defined this way: it is the process used to structure a set of research or evaluation tasks that are undertaken within a specific time frame and within a defined budget in order to ensure the efficient and effective completion of the project's stated goals and objectives. In other words, project management is the plan for the means by which a research or evaluation project is set up and implemented to make sure it gets done on time (ideally), that it is done within the targeted budget (ideally), and that the stated goals and objectives are met (again—at least ideally!).

Understanding some basic principles of project management is very important for several reasons. First, while a researcher or evaluator might have an excellent idea for pursuing analysis of some public question, if he or she does not have a well-defined plan for how to execute the project work, it is not uncommon for the project to be unsuccessful—simply due to ineffective follow-through from poor planning and structure of effort. Second, while some research and evaluation work is done strictly by an individual investigator, more common is the case where project work is completed by a team of investigators. As a result, critical to effective project implementation is how work is distributed throughout the team, how task responsibilities are assigned and monitored, and how overall work is coordinated. As a result, a key part of project management is working through those very issues. Finally, if a researcher or evaluator is relatively new in his or her career, following basic principles in setting up a project's work will help establish a set of proper and effective practices that will serve them well in the future— especially as they become responsible for more complex projects and have greater responsibilities in supervising and directing such work efforts.

Many research methods textbooks ignore the topic of project management, but that is unfortunate because it is an important part of the research and evaluation process and does not deserve to be neglected for the reasons just mentioned. This chapter provides you with an introduction to basic concepts and issues associated with project management. Because project management constitutes a discipline of practice in its own right, this chapter is simply intended to provide a basic overview to the student so those basic issues are understood. By the conclusion of this chapter, the student should have developed an understanding of what project management is about; how following sound principles of project management practice contribute to more effective, efficient, and hence more likely successful project outcomes; and how following good practices contributes to ethical research and evaluation work in service of evidence-based public management.

Basic Principles of Project Management

While the discipline of project management involves specialized training and expertise, we will start our overview by presenting a brief outline of four essential elements that constitute a basic approach to understanding project management and its effectiveness in practice. A first element is the management of resources used for completing the project. A second element is management of the project timeline and all the project tasks contained therein. A third element is an overview of how to understand, assess, and account for the scope of the project, which includes its goals, objectives, and basic requirements in areas such as management of the data that are gathered. And the fourth element is the consideration of the financial aspects of managing a project—that is, we will discuss the issue of project budgeting and understanding project costs.

Managing a Project Team

A first step in the development of any project management plan is to take account of all people, equipment, and other materials that are necessarily involved in the actual execution of the project. For instance, if we are thinking about a construction project, obviously the equipment would involve heavy machinery; the people would include not only those doing the actual construction labor but also those involved in other administrative tasks for the project, such as securing proper building permits and the like; and materials would involve construction supplies.

Of course, equipment and materials for conducting a social science research project or a program evaluation are very different. The people are quite analogous: you have the research investigators to account for, as well as other administrative support staff involved. If the work is being done within a university setting, it is common that a project will utilize student research assistants (typically graduate students). The equipment involved is typically only going to consist of computers and/or perhaps specialized analytic software (e.g., a statistical software package or a geographical information systems package)—and much of the time, that equipment is already available for use and is not going to require a special purchase for the project being undertaken. There are exceptions, however. For example, if the project involves a social psychological lab experiment, there are likely to be other types of equipment utilized that are associated with that laboratory. But overall, most materials used for a general social science research project or a program evaluation will not require a major expenditure of project resources if those responsible for conducting the research are professional researchers, consultants, or program evaluators.

This means for the most typical case of social science research and program evaluation, the key resource item to be managed is project personnel. There are different ways a project team might organize itself, but it is quite common for a single person to be identified as the lead project investigator. Other persons responsible for developing the research concepts, for defining the research approach, for key research tasks, and for writing the original project proposal itself are likely to hold a position of co-investigator. Additionally, a project might have other senior personnel who are not listed as investigators but serve in a limited capacity on the project. Likewise, student researchers, often graduate assistants, serve as key project team members (when the work is being conducted in a university setting).

In a formal sense, the project's leader is referred to as the **PRINCIPAL INVESTIGATOR**, which can be defined as the lead scientist who has the formal responsibility for project completion, for directing all project research tasks, and for reporting project results (i.e., findings) to the entity that funded the project. The funding entity might be a government agency, such as the National Science Foundation or the National Institutes of Health at the federal level; or a state government agency; or a project client who might be a private for-profit firm; or it might be a nonprofit organization. The logic of having a principal investigator is twofold. First, it allows a single point of responsibility between the funding entity and the project team, which is a useful relationship in terms of legal and financial accountability for the work promised to be performed.

There are several key considerations that contribute to good working relationships within a project team and overall management of the collective effort. Here is a list of principles of good team management to keep in mind:

- Active participation is important: individuals are more supportive of things they help create.

- Active participation not only includes helping design the overall project, but also having a meaningful role and voice in ongoing project plans and decisions.

- Team decision-making processes should be geared toward problem solutions rather than dwelling on problem identification.

- Communication channels should be open and consistent within the team.

- Task expectations should be clearly defined and task responsibilities clearly assigned.

- As the project work is being completed, the team should have a process for identifying unforeseen difficulties in the work and a means for discussion on how such challenges can be addressed.

Managing Time: Planning for Task Completion

As noted in the previous section, one part of defining the structure of the project team is to create well-defined project roles generally, and to assign task responsibilities to specific individuals. That is, as the project team develops the overall nature of the project, its goals and objectives—a research design plan, a key part of project management, will be to create a well-defined timeline for task completion. There are various ways an investigator or a whole team of investigators can proceed in setting out a specific set of action or task items for the project.

One possible way to proceed is to set out an action plan for the project. The idea of **ACTION PLANNING** for a project is to provide a detailed listing of the tasks that the team of research or evaluation investigators need to accomplish for specific parts of the project (see Figure 20.1). This kind of planning can also include creating defined process rules—meaning rules for meetings, how decisions will be made, who can contribute to what decisions, and revisions of action plan items and so forth.

To start this planning approach, the team should follow several basic guidelines:

- Make an explicit list of project goals and objectives. A goal is a general intention for the project (e.g., develop a better understanding of how training programs work in the field of emergency management), while an objective is a more specific and concrete action to be taken—an action step (e.g., develop specific measures of student comprehension before and after an NIMS training session).

- Develop a process for considering/examining the various ways in which the research or evaluation work can be designed—and then select the best approach.

- Develop a process for detailing how participants and resources needed for conducting the research or evaluation project will be utilized.

- Identify both strengths and weaknesses of the research design, and identify potential solutions corresponding to potential challenges the project work might encounter.

Action planning is one way to approach structuring project goals, objectives, and tasks. Another common way to describe this aspect of project management is to proceed with planning tasks and how they'll be done to develop a work plan. A **WORK PLAN** can be defined as a document that provides details on all project tasks that are needed to produce the research or evaluation project's major deliverable or deliverables. (A **PROJECT DELIVERABLE** is simply the tangible output produced by the project, such as the creation of a data set or a report analyzing those data or evaluation that produces a plan for improvement in organizational processes or similar products.) The work plan also provides very specific details about when the tasks should occur and how much time it will take to complete them. Further, creating key time points (often referred to as

> **Class Exercise:** Break into groups and have a group discussion of past experiences with collaborative or group work. Did the experiences you had correspond to these basic principles of team management? Evaluate those experiences using the above list of principles as a framework for recalling and assessing the effectiveness of those projects.

Figure 20.1 An Action Plan Form

PROJECT ACTION PLAN		
Core Project Goal:		
Project's Period of Performance:		
Key Action Item	Responsible Party	Target Completion Date
Threats to Task Completion:		
Response to Possible Threats:		
Key Milestones:		

progress milestones) to judge how well the project is proceeding and whether it will be completed is the other basic component of a work plan. Action plans or work plans are more or less the same way to approach planning for a project. Differences between the two are only subtle ones—an action plan is often used to help outline the overall process of developing a project overall, while a work plan generally doesn't include a discussion of decision processes but instead is a document geared toward laying out specific tasks, completion dates, and responsible parties.

A key tool in developing a work plan for a project is to use a Gantt chart (Figure 20.2). A **GANTT CHART** is a chart that visually depicts an overall project time line, with identification of key milestone task dates (their start and finish) and the overall

Class Exercise: Think about, and then outline how a work plan is related to a project's deliverables. For example, think about what the main deliverable might be for the Amity Homeland Security project. How would you develop a work plan that ultimately allowed that deliverable to be realized? What would it contain? Develop an outline and discuss why you included those elements.

Figure 20.2   A Sample Gantt Chart

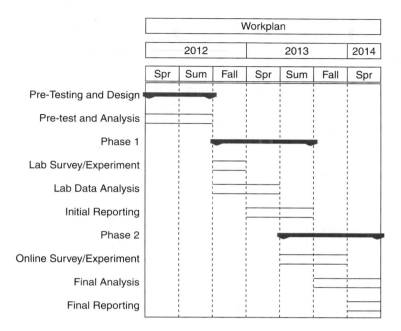

relationship between the project work tasks. Gantt charts are an extremely common tool. They are very useful for showing and clarifying how the project work is going to be accomplished according to a time line.

Putting Knowledge into Practice: How to Create a Gantt Chart

Creating a Gantt chart is an extremely helpful—and most would probably say necessary—element of project planning generally and a work plan specifically. There are specialized software packages that permit the development of a Gantt chart. However, because most PC users have access to the MS Excel program, we can say a few words about using Excel to create such a chart. While Excel does not have a Gantt application per se, it can be produced easily using the bar chart function. There are three simple steps to follow in doing so. First, create a variable in the spreadsheet with a task identifier (e.g., "Task 1"), add a second variable for the start date for the task, then a third variable for the number of days of work completed on the task, and then a final variable column for the number of days of remaining work time. Second, create a stacked bar chart using Excel's Chart Wizard and be sure to create it as a horizontal bar chart. Third, simply format the chart to look something like Figure 20.2.

There are specialized software packages that permit the development of a Gantt chart. However, because most PC users have access to the MS Excel program, we can say a few words about using Excel to create such a chart. While Excel does not have a Gantt application per se, it can be produced easily using the bar chart function. The key is to simply make a stacked horizontal bar chart with proper data specification and label specification.

To consider additional details in doing such project timeline planning, the reader should refer to the eTextbook for additional exercise questions that will help the reader see the logic of performing this task.

Project Scope and Data Management

The idea of a scope of work document is another essential element of any research or evaluation project. A **SCOPE OF WORK STATEMENT** can be defined as analogous to a contract; it lays out the specific details about what specific project tasks will be pursued, and it provides specific details on the end products of the project (i.e., the project deliverables). Scope work statements are written to support a formal project agreement between the funding agency and the team performing the work; it commits a researcher or a research team to certain tasks and a time line in support of producing the agreed-upon deliverable(s).

As a scope of work statement is written, along with the work plan, the project team should also develop a **RISK MANAGEMENT PLAN** or statement. Doing so is a standard feature of an overall project management approach to a new work effort. While the risks for a standard research or evaluation project are not the same as other types of projects (e.g., various risks/challenges associated with completing a major construction project), they do exist. They can include risks such as not completing all or parts of the project on time, not being able to collect or gather the intended measurements, or the potential for noncooperation or participation of research subjects that would be necessary for successful completion of the project. As a result, the team of investigators should create a plan for identifying, analyzing, prioritizing, and controlling any risks associated with the project. The value of a risk management plan is that it helps identify where a project might fail—and thus forces the project plan to develop contingencies if those risks are actually realized during the implementation of the project. In other words, the risk management plan should describe procedures for contingency planning, how the planning team will track risks, how the team will evaluate those risks, and how the team can respond to risks.

Along with a risk management plan, the project team also needs to establish an explicit plan, or at least protocols, for data management or control. A **DATA MANAGEMENT PLAN** is simply a statement of guidelines for exactly how the team of investigators will collect, store, document, and potentially share (i.e., disseminate) project data with other researchers or interested parties. We have covered data collection processes at length in prior chapters. However, we have not discussed the issue of data storage. There will be some research projects where the data gathered are sensitive (e.g., human subjects data) and require privacy. There are several considerations in storing such data files. A first is that the principal investigator and coinvestigators have a responsibility to ensure that those data are stored in a secure location (e.g., locked storage containers if there are hard copies of data materials, password protected, and security enabled server storage for electronic data files) and that no one other than the investigative team is granted access. Second, after initial data collection is completed, to ensure confidentiality of those data (if we are dealing with individual human subjects, for instance), identifying information tied to any specific case in the data file should be removed.

Another practice that should be followed for all research projects is to develop a written codebook, which allows researchers to record the details of data collection processes. A **DATA CODEBOOK** is a document that provides a detailed explanation or definition of measurement items in the study as well as details about how and when those data were gathered. Similarly, the data management plan should also establish a procedure by which project data can be shared with others. It is not uncommon for the project funder to request that the gathered data be made available for use by other interested researchers. It is also not uncommon for individual researchers to request a data set for replication purposes or use in a related project or research endeavor. The data management plan provides for guidance to allow for an orderly dissemination of those data.

Example 20.1—Case Discussion: Amity DHS

Colton has been given the task of assessing the relative effectiveness of training for the NIMS among relevant Amity government personnel; he will serve as project principal investigator along with a team of coinvestigators. The overall goal of the project is to measure training effectiveness; this will be accomplished by comparing the pretraining scores of individuals on a questionnaire of NIMS knowledge to the scores on the same instrument following employee completion of the NIMS self-study course. This is a quantitative measure of performance; one that Colton argues is a reasonable indication of effectiveness. Further, by looking at the change in scores by employee occupation (e.g., first response personnel versus public health personnel), Colton will be able to investigate whether general knowledge of emergency management issues is relevant to training effectiveness. With that in mind, Colton decides to develop a work plan and assign a series of tasks and develop a project time line. He expects that the overall project will take five months.

Questions about the Example: How would you proceed in developing a work plan? For this kind of project, what would the scope of work statement look like? What would be the core content of a work plan? Could you develop a Gantt Chart to map out a set of tasks and milestone dates?

Project Budgets and Costs

The last major element of project management is to engage in planning and develop guidelines over the development of a project budget and appropriate costs that fall under that budget. The project budget is developed in association with the scope of work. That is, once specific activities are determined necessary to produce the project deliverables, the investigators craft a budget required to support that work effort. For a typical research or evaluation project, planning the budget includes accounting for personnel costs (i.e., the researchers involved), supplies and equipment (such as computer equipment, printing of documents), travel costs (for on-site data gathering or presentations of research findings), and other contracted services costs (for instance, paying a survey firm to conduct a telephone survey or paying a transcription service to transcribe audio files of recorded interviews).

When the budget is developed—in association with the scope of work—a budget justification (sometimes called a budget narrative) is also written. The **BUDGET JUSTIFICATION** is a formal document that describes and explains the rationale for each line item in the overall project budget. Those line items are statements that describe each line item in the budget, each with its own descriptive section. The sections of a budget form and its justification will always include the following categories (line items):

- **Personnel**—These costs include salary for the principal and coinvestigators, other senior personnel, and/or (if the work is done at a university) graduate research assistants. Likewise, the costs for the personnel working on the project also include their fringe benefits (which includes employee health insurance, sometimes a contribution to a retirement plan, or similar items).
- **Equipment**—Items such as laptop computers purchased for use by investigators specifically for the project's data collection process.
- **Travel**—Appropriate travel costs to plan for and budget include any travel needed to complete project work (such as conducting in-person interviews, making site visits to review an organization or some event in person, or to visit a data archive location, etc.) or any travel that directly benefits the project (such as presenting research results at a professional conference). The budget justification will necessarily provide details on where and why for the travel activities, a breakdown of airfare, hotel, ground transportation, per diem rates (for meals and expenses), conference registration fees, and the like.
- **Other direct costs**—This line item includes materials and supplies that could include such typical research items as communication charges (e.g., telephone use charges, postage costs if a mail survey is used), subcontract costs (such as hiring a survey firm to conduct a telephone survey for the project), software (such as a statistical software package needed to perform the analysis outlined in the scope of work document), or any other similar costs directly related to the project's completion.

Those costs listed above are what is known as direct costs—which are items fundamental to the completion of the project and directly related to the specifics of producing the deliverables promised. However, planning a project budget will also include accounting for any administrative overhead charges. This is true of a public entity like a university as well as a private consulting firm. These administrative overhead charges are referred to as indirect costs, and they must be included in a project budget plan, the actual budget, and they must be explained in the budget justification. These indirect costs—the administrative overhead charge, which is usually referred to as a facilities and administrative (F&A) costs in a university setting, are appropriate project charges. They are general organizational expenses that are incurred as the result of the organization existing to conduct its work. The F&A indirect cost line item captures a whole host of costs that exist separate from the specific details of the research

> **Class Exercise:** Create a list of what budget items you would expect for the National Helping Hands case, and a list of budget items you would expect for the Amity Department of Homeland Security case. How would you explain and justify those project costs?

or evaluation project, such as rent; utilities; and operational staff salaries, such as the human resources staff, information technology staff, etc., which provide support to the organization in a general way but do not work on a specific task item as specified in the scope of work document.

Award Administration

In addition to the four major elements of project management just discussed above, we can also think about several basic considerations in applying for project funding and what to do after receiving such a project award.

Applying for Grants or Contracts

There are a wide variety of organizations that fund research and evaluation work, and there are a wide variety of reasons for doing so. The federal government through entities like the National Science Foundation (NSF) and the National Institutes for Health (NIH) fund a great deal of natural and social science research. Other federal agencies likewise routinely provide research and evaluation funding within their specific policy area. The same is true with state and local government: state and local agencies will commonly fund research or program evaluation projects in support of agency analytic and evaluative needs. The major difference between federal funders and state and local funding is that the former frequently funds basic science or science for knowledge generation, while on the other hand, state and local governments are more likely to fund applied research or evaluation projects. That is, state and local government will frequently contract out data gathering, analysis, and evaluation services to private consulting firms or university researchers. Similarly, nonprofit organizations will commonly contract with consultants or university researchers to conduct data collection or evaluation work on their behalf. (While private firms commit significant resources to activities like market research, those kinds of project fall outside the public management domain.) And finally, private foundations are another major source of funding for research and evaluation work. Most foundations have a specific mission area and focus, and many support basic policy research on topics of interest to those missions.

While there are other sites, Grants.gov is the federal government's main portal for a listing of, and the place to apply for, federal grants for research. Grants.gov is where all federal agencies post solicitations and grant announcements—which can be thought of as an invitation to submit an application to receive project funding.

There are perhaps at least three major considerations in deciding to develop a proposal to pursue funding for a project. The first is fairly straightforward: eligibility. Again, if we focus our attention on federal funding, we should make note of the fact that it is not unusual for federal grant solicitations to have restrictions on who can receive which award. Categories of eligible recipients commonly include state agencies (or state governments more broadly), universities, and nonprofit organizations. Second, another practical concern is whether there is sufficient time to develop an effective proposal. It is extremely commonplace for a researcher or evaluator to learn of a proposal solicitation only shortly before a submission deadline. Further, it is not uncommon (especially for nonfederal funders) by the time the proposal solicitation is publicly disseminated, the proposals are due in a very short time frame. Thus, if there is insufficient time to complete a sound proposal, the investigators may not want to waste their energy on a weak submission. Finally, perhaps most important of all is whether the investigators can develop a strong team to submit the proposal. Grants solicitations are usually fiercely competitive from any funding agency; this is especially true at the federal level. Grant proposals are reviewed not only on the content of the ideas presented, but on the expertise, quality, and track record of the investigators making the proposal. Thus, it is important to build a high quality team for any proposal submission if one expects a reasonable chance at success in winning funding for a project.

Award Reporting and Monitoring

A critical part of project management not yet discussed is the topic of monitoring and award reporting. These two activities are in actuality a subset of the work plan. The work plan should specify who is responsible for monitoring the implementation of project work and who is responsible for making reports on project progress to the funding entity. However, because they are a relatively unique category of tasks (i.e., distinct from the other research or evaluation-related tasks), we discuss them separately here.

As might seem intuitive, monitoring of the task schedule outlined as part of the project work plan is important because it helps ensure that project milestones are met. But meeting a schedule is only one part of monitoring. At the same time, it is important to recognize that monitoring also should be done to ensure that the substantive objectives associated with the project are also being met as outlined in the project objectives and overall management plan. There are two ways to approach project monitoring. For large and complex research or evaluation projects, a separate contractor might be brought in to provide ongoing monitoring and evaluation of the project itself. That is, a third party is hired to examine the team's work, check progress, and guarantee internal feedback to ensure the project stays on track. For large projects, it is common that such a third party evaluator be stipulated as a feature of the award proposal itself. Another way to approach monitoring is to simply have a designated person in charge of routinely checking progress and guaranteeing the work plan is being followed. This often falls to the principal investigator.

Closely related to tasks related to monitoring are tasks related to reporting. Virtually all project funders expect some level of progress reporting and some form of final project report (which is often considered a separate item from the substantive deliverables of the project). Award reporting is straightforward: depending on how long the life of the project is, the funder might expect a quarterly report, a semiannual report, or an annual report on progress. Given the project will have both scope of work and work plan documents, the person in charge of submitting the award report (typically the principal investigator) will provide a statement on progress toward goals and objectives, including whether major milestones have been met (or not).

Working with Clients

While not a formal part of project management planning, it is important for investigators to understand what potential problems or challenges they are likely to encounter when conducting research and evaluation work. Thinking about potential problems is important because if our data collection process is compromised or biased in some way, then of course we will not have valid and reliable results. Two common issues to take note of are communications with clients and having an awareness of the political context within which research and evaluation work is undertaken.

Understanding Communication Needs with Clients

A common challenge that any researcher or evaluator will face at one time or another is communication with a funder or client. This is especially true in the evaluation world, where much of the substantive work is applied—and by definition, is designed to assess with an eye toward understanding where changes or improvements can be made. Working with such a client and project goal is very different than receiving a research grant from the NSF to do original policy research for the sake of generating new knowledge in a subject area. As a result, clear channels of communication between the team of evaluators and the client are a key characteristic of project success. There are several basic features of such communications that a researcher or evaluator should be aware of. First, communication on research subjects (such as research design, sampling techniques, or the like) can be abstract and unfamiliar to a client. Whoever is the lead point of contact with the client (typically the principal investigator) should know that she or he might well have to play an educational function when communicating with the client to prevent incorrect assumptions or an inability to understand the risks involved with producing final project deliverables.

Class Exercise: Do you think there might be challenges in dealing with clients who do not have training in research methods? Imagine a client who expects you to do a purposive sample—even though that is not beneficial to the project—because they do not understand probability sampling. How would you go about explaining the concept and importance of random sampling?

As a result, a good practice is to establish a formal protocol for investigator—client communications. This can include regular meetings, routine e-mail contact, and the like. It also means a typically effective model of such communication is to have a single point of contact between the investigator team and the client organization. This will reduce any potential confusion of messages and information exchange. In essence, the expectations of the evaluators and the clients must be known and fostered throughout the evaluation. Communication is key throughout the entire process. This allows for meaningful dialogue and a time frame in which final evaluation product should be expected. The ability to nurture the relationship between both parties and compromise on issues should always be considered.

Understanding Potential Political Implications of Research and Evaluation

Research and program evaluation in the public sector almost always carries some degree of political consequence. This is not to say that the investigators might have done anything unethical or inappropriate in a given situation—but the statement is an acknowledgment that programs, policies, and organizations in the governmental sector (and much to the same degree in the nonprofit sector) tend to face special attention and scrutiny because of operating in a context of expected public trust. Further, regardless of the content of objective research findings, interested parties are likely to see such results through an ideological lens and might well challenge the results solely on that basis.

The ethic of research and evaluation is to follow sound methodological practices in order to produce valid, reliable, and clearly understandable results. That said, it is useful for a researcher to understand the intent of a client. In some cases, there will be no discernible intent or agenda other than producing the project results that are being funded. But in other cases, a client may have a vested in the results of the study. The researcher or evaluator has to be clear that his or her ethical obligation is to maintain the integrity of the research process. There can be no ambiguity on that point, and this should be communicated to a client who might fund a project with a desire to see a particular end result. It is important to understand the political and ideological viewpoint of any funder, as well as how other interested parties might be seeing the project work. The key is to communicate clearly project goals and objectives, to be transparent in all work activities, and to set clear expectations that the work will be handled in such a forthright manner. Setting expectations creates a safeguard for both parties.

Ethical Considerations in Conducting and Completing a Project

As had been noted at other points in this text, ethical concerns and the consequences of the failure to remain ethical have significant consequences for public sector research and evaluation. In the simplest sense, a researcher or evaluator has several core obligations. One is the ethical obligation to follow standard human subjects protections protocols in all instances. And while the typical research or evaluation project related to public policies or public management issues typically do not involve significant potential harms to individuals participating, there is in fact the possibility of adverse employment consequences for the study participants if the policy or program being studied is politically sensitive. Further, part of the ethical obligation toward protecting human subjects is to make sure they are given full and appropriate information about study design, intent, and purpose—regardless of level of risk. Moreover, securing explicit consent for participation is important in all cases of research, but is important to emphasize here because subjects relevant to the public sector domain, and issues of evidence-based management, do have a general risk of public scrutiny, which is a harm unique to this area and a bit different than many other types of social science research.

Following good practices with respect to human subjects is only one core ethical obligation. Another set of obligations for researchers and evaluators is a guiding principles document produced by the American Evaluation Association (AEA). The AEA first approved the "Guiding Principles for Evaluators" in 1994 and then updated that document a decade later in 2004. Those principles identified five basic and all-encompassing principles to provide program evaluators with guidance on what constitutes ethical work efforts. The principles include systematic inquiry, competence in an evaluation performance, integrity/honesty, respect for people, and responsibilities for general and public welfare. Each of those principles is defined by the AEA in the "Guiding Principles" document as follows:

- **Systematic Inquiry**—Evaluators conduct systematic, data-based inquiries.
- **Competence**—Evaluators provide competent performance to stakeholders.
- **Integrity/Honesty**—Evaluators display honesty and integrity in their own behavior and attempt to ensure the honesty and integrity of the entire evaluation process.
- **Respect for People**—Evaluators respect the security, dignity, and self-worth of respondents, program participants, clients, and other evaluation stakeholders.
- **Responsibilities for General and Public Welfare**—Evaluators articulate and take into account the diversity of general and public interests and values that may be related to the evaluation.

Example 20.2—Case Discussion: National Helping Hands

Colton has been given the task of assessing the relative effectiveness of training for the NIMS among relevant Amity government personnel; he will serve as project principal investigator along with a team of coinvestigators. The overall goal of the project is to measure training effectiveness; this will be accomplished by comparing the pretraining scores of individuals on a questionnaire of NIMS knowledge to the scores on the same instrument following employee completion of the NIMS self-study course. This is a quantitative measure of performance: one that Colton argues is a reasonable indication of effectiveness. Further, by looking at the change in scores by employee occupation (e.g., first response personnel versus public health personnel), Colton will be able to investigate whether general knowledge of emergency management issues is relevant to training effectiveness. With that in mind, Colton decides to develop a work plan and assign a series of tasks and develop a project time line. He expects that the overall project will take five months.

Questions about the Example: How would you proceed in developing a work plan? For this kind of project, what would the scope of work statement look like? What would be the core content of a work plan? Could you develop a Gantt Chart to map out a set of tasks and milestone dates?

Conclusion: How Project Management Relates to Evidence-Based Management Practices

Principles and concepts of project management are often not covered in detail—or sometimes not at all—in research methods textbooks. This is a mistake if one is interested in the idea of evidence-based management practices for the public sector. There are three reasons why those concepts and principles are important to evidence-based public management.

First, precisely because we are mainly talking about the public or nonprofit sector in this text, we make note of the fact that public agencies or nonprofit organizations (supported by philanthropic giving) have special expectations placed upon them. There is a public trust that comes with expenditures of such funds, and therefore, following careful project management practices both improves the quality of project deliverables, as well as helps guarantee successful project completion. Careful planning, appropriate expenditures, and efficient use of a project's budget contribute to overall confidence in the quality of the research product and make it more likely that the results of a study can and will be utilized by the client.

Second, proper research methods do not occur in a vacuum. Understanding how and why a public manager is going to use the results of a research or evaluation project is an important part of project management. This does not mean tailoring results to a client's preferred outcome. Not in the slightest. Instead, what it means is making sure that the research effort's deliverables are directly applicable to the management needs of the client organization. The client may or may not find the results of a study to be what they wish. But as long as the study matches to the project plan and promised deliverable, then the client will be able to utilize the evidence presented in their decision-making processes and organizational actions.

Last, evidence-based management is premised on the notion that quality data (i.e., valid and reliable measurement and analysis) can be used to inform management decisions and policy or program actions. The concepts and principles of sound project management contribute directly to data quality. Most any person with research experience will admit that if a project is poorly designed and managed, the quality of data gathered in the process is very likely to suffer. As a result, the more effective a researcher is in project management, the more likely he or she is to produce a quality research result. In turn, that means the client organization will have a more effective resource (the results of the study) to inform their decisions and practices.

Suggested Readings

A quick and cursory search on the topic of project management will lead the reader to various commercial project management software and tutorial sites. Perhaps a better place to start a more careful consideration of practices, guidelines, and ethics is to look at the Project Management Institute's website http://www.pmi.org. That institute is a nonprofit professional association of project management professionals and is a good starting point for learning more about this subject area.

Flashcards & MCQs

Vocabulary

ACTION PLANNING—A process of providing a detailed listing of the tasks that the team of research or evaluation investigators needs to accomplish for specific parts of the project.

BUDGET JUSTIFICATION—A formal document that describes and explains the rationale for each line item in the overall project budget.

DATA CODEBOOK—A document that provides a detailed explanation or definition of measurement items in the study as well as details about how and when those data were gathered.

DATA MANAGEMENT PLAN—A statement of guidelines for exactly how the team of investigators will collect, store, document, and potentially disseminate data with other researchers or interested parties.

GANTT CHART—A chart that visually depicts an overall project time line, with identification of key milestone task dates (their start and finish) and the overall relationship between the project work tasks.

PROJECT DELIVERABLE—The tangible output produced by the project, such as the creation of a data set, a report, or a plan for improvement in organizational processes or similar products.

PRINCIPAL INVESTIGATOR—The lead scientist who holds the formal responsibility for project completion, for directing all project research tasks, and for reporting project results to the entity that funded the project.

PROJECT MANAGEMENT—The process used to structure a set of research or evaluation tasks undertaken within a specific time frame and within a defined budget in order to ensure the efficient and effective completion of the project's stated objectives.

RISK MANAGEMENT PLAN—A planning document that identifies, analyzes, prioritizes, and controls the range of possible risks associated with completing the project.

Useful
Websites

SCOPE OF WORK STATEMENT—A document that lays out the specific details about what specific project tasks will be pursued and what are the project deliverables.

WORK PLAN—A document that provides details on all project tasks that are needed to produce the research or evaluation project's major deliverable or deliverables.

Review Questions

- Are there any differences between action planning and work plans?
- What is a Gantt chart, and how is it used as a project management tool?
- What are the several core elements of project management?
- Why do projects have a principal investigator?
- Why would a complex project contract with a third party evaluator, while a smaller less complex project might not have to use such a resource?

CHAPTER 21

Presenting Research

Learning Objectives

✓ Identify the multiple audiences to whom one might present public affairs research

✓ Compare and contrast different methods of presentation including written, spoken, and visual presentation techniques

✓ Understand how to integrate the results of various analytic techniques in presentations

Cases in Research

Case A—National Helping Hands

The manager of National Helping Hands (NHH) has been conducting a variety of research projects into the impact that their member organizations have had in disaster relief. In the end, the results of her research into disaster nonprofits will only improve the management of disasters if the word gets out. This will prove to be quite a challenge given the diverse nature of the disaster nonprofit audience. In the end, the researcher decides to create a pamphlet for distribution to NHH member organizations and to present the results at the upcoming national meeting. Now the work must begin on designing an effective pamphlet and research presentation.

Case B—Dewey School District

The investigation of teacher turnover in the Dewey Independent School District (Dewey ISD) had a clear audience—the district superintendent. The superintendent chartered and paid for the study to provide her with specific information. The primary goal of presenting the results is to design a report that the superintendent will find easy to read and compelling. However, the information may be of interest to other audiences. The researcher's secondary goal, then is to distribute the results more broadly to an audience of other school superintendents and academic researchers with interests in teacher turnover.

The Fundamentals of Presentation

Any results from public affairs research are of limited use if they are never communicated to other people. Academics spend a lot of time writing up the results of their research for other academics—but they are not the only one who report on research to other people. Practicing managers have to write up research as well. This can come in many forms. Practicing managers may write up internal memos for employees or summarize the results for their superiors (including, potentially, elected officials or the public generally). Managers may also write up results to share with other managers directly about what has worked in their offices. Presenting results of research has become one of the most effective tools for proving your skills as a manager and improving your career prospects. This chapter will review how to present the results of research. While there are many ways to present research, this chapter focuses on written presentations (like report or memo writing) and oral/visual presentations (like PowerPoint™ style slide presentations—hereafter just referred to as slide presentations).

To begin the process of preparing any report on you research, you need to know a few things about the context of the report.

Know Your Audience

You must first know your audience. Any report of your research is an act of communication. You are trying to tell something to someone (or many people). How you do this should depend on your audience. Consider the following example. Imagine that you wanted to put together a presentation about the importance of recycling for your organization (let's say, a local city management office). The presentation will differ radically if you are giving that presentation to a group of schoolchildren rather than your city manager. The presentation you would give at a city hall-style meeting would even differ from that which you would give to your coworkers.

For any particular audience, you need to establish a few parameters for a presentation (whether the presentation is written or oral). First, you must consider the educational background of the audience. You need to present your results in a manner that your audience will understand. Of course, you should avoid complicated language in a presentation for school children. Most presentations, though, need to be careful not to be more complex than the audience can comprehend—even among adults. College textbooks, for example, are typically written at between an 8th and 10th grade reading level. This is an appropriate target for just about any public report.

Second, you must consider the familiarity of an audience with specific terms that may be relevant to your audience. This may or may not be related to level of education. You could present a social media strategy to a class of high school students and not worry about the audience being unfamiliar with Twitter™ or other social media sites. The same sites could be largely unfamiliar to an audience of highly educated, but older, adults. You need to avoid any terms that

Class Exercise: What audiences do you think are common for presentations by public managers?

will be unfamiliar with your audience—unless the purpose of the report is to educate the audience on that subject.

Know Your Mode of Communication

Communication can take place in a variety of formats: a written report, a slide presentation, an Internet video, etc. Each of these formats is a different mode of communication. You need to know the mode you are using to develop the report as well as its strengths and limitations. A written report is just one example of a mode of communication. Writing a paper is quite different than designing an effective slide presentation. It would be poor practice (and likely get you either laughed at or people would just leave your presentation) if you simply pasted large segments of a paper onto slides. Even within papers, writing a short paper (say two–three pages or a single web page) requires different strategies than writing an entire book.

Class Exercise: Other than written reports and slide presentations, what other forms of communicating your research are available?

We will address the specific limitations of two key modes of reports later in this chapter: written reports (like memos or papers) and oral/visual presentations with slides.

Know Your Argument

Throughout this book, we have emphasized that research tools are designed to provide answers as part of managerial arguments. Information serves to inform arguments over what managers should or should not do. All of the reports of your research should support arguments related to managerial action. The argument should be central in your mind as you design any report. For every part of the report, you should tie choices back to the question, "How does this make my argument clear?"

One way to focus on your argument is to consider what the **TAKE-AWAYS** are for your talk. A take-away is a specific piece of information that you want your audience to retain. Of course, the audience won't remember everything. You likely can only leave them with 3–4 bits of information that they will remember for more than a day. If your argument is at the center of your presentation, the components of your argument should be your TAKE-AWAYS.

The Audiences of Public Affairs Research

As a public manager, you may find yourself reporting to a variety of audiences. This section will review some of the potential audiences with broad strokes. You will need to consider whether the specific audiences you report to possess the characteristics described in each of these sections. However, these general discussions will illustrate the thought process needed to assess your audience.

Internal Audiences—Internal Managers

The most obvious audience for reports on public affairs research is other public managers. To some extent, this is the easiest audience to whom you will report. In assessing their characteristics as an audience, you can use yourself as a model. What sort of presentation would you appreciate? What sort of questions would you ask about a report?

There is an important limitation to assuming that all other public managers are like you. If all public managers knew what you know now, the report would be unnecessary. The fact that you did the research project has made you atypical in important ways. You may have become familiar with or have adopted specific jargon. You should be intimately familiar with the methods you used in your research and the details in the field that you studied. You cannot assume that all public managers will have the same information specific to the report. If the managers are internal to your organization, they may be familiar with internal organizational jargon (e.g., names of specific rooms, shorthand names for specific commonly used forms, etc.) but not with jargon that is part of your research process (e.g., spuriousness, experiment, etc.). Managers from other organizations may not even be familiar with the internal organizational jargon and will need these terms defined.

If you are reporting within your own school about the results of your research into retirement decisions, you can rely on the other school principals and managers within the district office to be broadly familiar with jargon related to education management—maybe less so with jargon specific to human resource management. You may have to write the report in a way that many of your audience members unfamiliar with human resource law and theory or the jargon of research methods can still understand what you have found.

Internal Audiences—Line and Staff

You may also need to report to members of your organization other than management. Your research may provide insight into how best to carry out work within the organization. Getting this information to the people who can put the lessons into practice will require reporting to them in a manner that will be clearly understood. Again, you have to carefully consider the communication needs of this audience. Nonmanagement employees within the organization may be quite diverse, so one should be hesitant to make too many strong assumptions about what they may or may not know. In the light of such uncertainty, it is best to err on the side of reporting in a plain manner by explaining any jargon.

This comes with a risk. Explaining too much jargon or speaking too plainly (especially if such plain language comes across as condescending) can alienate your audience. You will have to balance these risks.

Nonmanagement employees within your organization are also likely familiar with much of the jargon of the organization. However, there may be some jargon terms that are specific to management and some jargon that is specific to other segments of the organization. When at all possible, you want to tailor your organization to the specific jargon of your target audience to better signal that you are a member of their community—as indicated by your use of a common language.

Just like jargon, different modes and formats of communication may be customary within an organization—or not. You need to use the customary forms of communication unless you have a very specific reason for surprising people with a new form of communication. For example, if the members of your organization are used to receiving printed memos, you would not want to rely on e-mail to send important messages. Similarly, if the organization customarily uses video presentations or visual slide presentations as training methods, you would not want to rely on paper memos. As with jargon, you want the mode of communication to be as familiar and comfortable as possible to the audience (if you want them to actually pay attention).

External Audiences—Academic Audiences

You may find yourself reporting to an academic audience. Some important innovations in our understanding of public management have emerged out of the experiences of practicing managers who reported on innovations they had conducted within their own organizations. Now commonplace strategies like introducing competition, increasing worker flexibility, and the like were popularized based on reports of experiences within actual organizations.

Writing for academics is peculiar—and who can say that with more conviction than a dyed in the wool academic? Academic audiences look for different aspects of reports on public management research than do practitioner audiences. In academic writing, there is an expectation of a detailed explanation of the research methods one used in a study. This is often left to a footnote or an appendix (if included at all) for practitioner audiences. For academic audiences, the methodology is a core part of the report and without convincing this audience of the legitimacy of your methodology, you will not convince them to even continue paying attention to your report.

Academic audiences also look for detailed connections between any given report and the long literature in public management. At times, the majority of a report is devoted to reviewing previous work and popular theories. Just as with the research methods, this is a section that is generally quite short in audiences other than academics. It is certainly appropriate with all audiences to acknowledge your intellectual debts to other work; academic audiences expect to see quite a bit more of this than anyone else.

Finally, you can make some assumptions about the education levels of academic audiences. To be on the safe side, you can write for a college graduate—but I would not assume much more than that for any but the most specialized academic audience. Presenting to an audience of academics who specialize in budgeting may allow you to make some assumptions about the audience's familiarity with budgeting jargon. Writing to an audience of academics who specialize in social work, similarly, opens up a world of potential jargon on which you can rely. With general academic audiences, it is rarely safe to assume any jargon, though. Here you must be quite careful to assess the diversity of your audience.

External Audiences—Political Officials

As a public manager, you may be asked to report to political officials that oversee your specific organization. A transportation office may be asked to report to the city council or a mayor on the status of a large project. You may even have to present to political officials who have no formal role in overseeing your organization. The director of NHH may be asked to provide a presentation to an official from the Federal Emergency Management Agency (FEMA) or a congressional committee. The Dewey ISD superintendent (or a manager acting as her delegate) may be asked to brief a local city council on the results of research. Such presentations can be wonderful opportunities to illustrate the professionalism of your organization—or an opportunity to reveal the opposite.

When preparing for political officials, it is essential to consider their background. Political officials may not be familiar with the jargon or technical background of your specific organization. The city council may not know much about the specifics of human resource planning or disaster relief. They are generally intelligent and interested people, though. They will become bored and frustrated if you talk down to them with overly simplistic presentations or material that fails to answer their questions.

Under these conditions, you should carefully ask about the goals of the presentation for the political officials. What is it that they want to get out of the presentation? Do they want a progress report on a project? Do they want the results of an evaluation project? What sorts of questions do they have that your presentation is supposed to answer? The last thing you want to do is waste the officials' time with a presentation that does not address the topic they wanted to hear about in the first place. The best way to avoid this is simply to ask them what they want to hear about and design a presentation for them as an intelligent, engaged, but nonexpert audience.

External Audiences—The Public

Finally, you may find yourself reporting on your research to the public in general. This may be as simple as trying to get the word out about a new program in your office to information about a problem the community is facing. Reporting to the public raises a number of difficulties for communication.

You must be quite conservative in your use of jargon and complex language or sentence structure. In an extreme case, you may want to communicate to members of the public who do not speak the predominant language. If you want to reach these communities, you may need to translate your message into another language. Even within the predominant language, you can assume very little about reading or vocabulary levels. Reports to the public need to be written in as simple a language with as simple a structure as possible.

You must also keep in mind how hard it is to capture and retain the attention of the public. Members of the public are not generally required to read reports from local agencies or organizations. If a member of the public begins reading or viewing a research report, she is under no obligation to finish the report. It is vital in these circumstances to create a report that is both simple to understand and sufficiently compelling to continue reading. A detailed written report running 50 pages with extensive footnotes will be read by few members of the public. On the other hand, a short video or graphic-intensive flier may be able to get information out to a general audience.

Putting Knowledge into Practice: Creating a Presentation for a Public Audience

Mel at National Helping Hands was asked to summarize the results of her research into disaster relief in a way that the manager could share with the public. Mel had to decide how to share the results of her research with a broad audience (possibly including journalists, members of local church groups, and other stakeholders in her organization) in a way that was both simple and accurate.

She abandoned the goal of summarizing the statistical analysis that she had completed. It would be hard to explain how to interpret the results to a broad audience. Instead, she decided to provide a series of representative stories of the disaster relief activities she had heard about from her members in the course of her research. This approach allowed her to make the stories personal, on a human scale, and compelling. The report could then include graphics and images to reinforce the point of the image without being difficult to interpret statistics and graphs. Mel knew she would have plenty of technical details and statistics in the full report.

Written Presentations for Public Affairs Research

There are a variety of modes of reporting your research, but this chapter will focus on two. The first mode on which the chapter will focus is written presentations. You are likely quite familiar with written reports on research. Every research paper you have written is a written report on research. You may even have to write such a paper for this course. It is worth considering, despite your possibly extensive experience with this mode of reporting, the specific strengths and limitations of written reports of research and strategies to help you communicate as effectively as possible within them.

The Advantages of Written Presentations

One of the defining characteristics of bureaucratic organizations is their reliance on written reports and records. It is worth considering why written reports and records have proven to be so useful. The same qualities that have made written records ubiquitous in contemporary offices are advantages to written reports.

Written records are conveniently consistent. Whenever you read them, they look the same. With the printed version of this book, the words you are reading will always be the same (assuming the book is not destroyed in some unfortunate accident or defaced in some way). Once the pages are printed, their contents are permanent. This is not the case with electronic documents where patches can later change the contents of the book. That consistency is an advantage for many purposes. The legal code, for example, is based on knowing that the language of the laws will not change except through formal processes. The code itself is printed, and people can read it knowing that other people looking at the same text will see the same thing. With a printed management report, you know that what you are reading won't change between when you first read it and later readings. If the NHH report lists all nonprofit organizations active in emergency planning, that list won't change once the report is printed.

The consistency of the printed report is important in that it allows **ASYNCHRONOUS** readings. An asynchronous reading is one where there is a separation in time between the creation of the report and the reader. That sounds more complicated than it is. You can write a report on Monday and give it to a supervisor to read on Wednesday—and he can actually read it. That is an asynchronous reading. This characteristic is an important source of flexibility. An oral presentation (assuming there is no one recording the presentation) is synchronous in that the audience has to be listening to the presentation as it is delivered. This is quite a limitation—only recently overcome with the inexpensive availability of recording technology.

> **Class Exercise:** What techniques have your found useful in revising your own term papers in the past?

Finally, and most important, written reports can be revised significantly before they are turned over to the audience. It should be the case in class that you revise any assignment many times before you turn it in for a grade. This is much more strongly the case for any report you write in your capacity as a public manager. With a written report, you can carefully consider every word and every image within your document. In an oral presentation, you may improvise and come up with words at the time of the presentation, but with a written report such improvisation is not required. This is the key reason that people pay greater attention to written reports than simple oral presentations. If you see a written report, you know that someone has carefully considered the content. The content is not improvised or hastily assembled.

The Disadvantages of Written Presentations

Of course, written reports have some serious disadvantages as well. You will need to develop written reports in a way that takes advantage of the strengths of the mode of presentation while compensating for its weaknesses.

The flipside of the consistent and asynchronous nature of written reports is that these reports cannot adapt to their audience. If a section is not clear, there is no opportunity to try again. The author is not present with the audience so he or she cannot watch to see if there are questions. Instead, people will just ignore the material they do not understand. You have to explain your point right the first time because you will not likely get a second opportunity.

Given this limitation, you must take care to ensure that your written reports are sufficiently engaging to keep people reading. Since you, as the author, are not present to see the audience read the report, there is little pressure for the audience to actually read it. You have to make them want to read the report. This is difficult in a world of distractions. Written reports are easy to put down and assume that you will get back to them later. If your audience puts the report down, though, you run the risk that they will never pick it up again. At the very least, you need to write the report such that the reader can pick it up anywhere and still understand your point. At best, you want to write a report that is so sufficiently engaging and easy to read that they will not put the report down in the first place.

Key Strategies for Written Presentations

Given their advantages and disadvantages, there are some key strategies to keep in mind for effective written reports.

Structure and Sectioning
With any but the shortest (two–three pages) written report, you will want to use structure and sectioning to help the reader understand your argument. Remember, you will not be with the reader to clarify your argument or to explain any part of the report. The report needs to speak for itself. One way to do this is for the structure of the report to parallel the outline of your argument. It should be clear with every section in the paper why that section follows the one that precedes it and what role the section plays in the argument as a whole. Readers should never be left wondering why you are dwelling on a specific subject.

The best practice for ensuring that your structure helps communicate your argument is to write from an outline. An outline can start with a small number of points that represent the components of your argument. You can then elaborate on each of these points with more detailed subpoints in your outline. Slowly you can continue elaborating until you have all of the points you want to cover within the report emerging naturally out of the original core argument.

Keeping your outline in mind, you can review the structure to make sure that there are no extraneous components of the report. Inessential components of your report are the areas where the readers are most likely to put down the report and never pick it up again. These are also the points where readers are most likely to lose track of your argument in the report as a whole.

You should let the structure of the report show through the sectioning of the report. It is best to have enough section headers (introducing and setting apart various sections, subsections, etc.) that you go no longer than a page or two without some section or subsection heading. This heading reminds your reader where she is in your argument and also reminds you to help the reader understand where she is within your argument.

Formatting Text

You can also use formatting of text to communicate your point. We live in an era of exceptionally inexpensive typesetting technology. Any word processor gives you a variety of options to use text formatting to emphasize the most important components of your argument. You can make words bold, italic, colored, or take on many other characteristics. In previous generations of writing technology (like typewriters), these formatting choices were quite difficult to accomplish, but style guides worked around these limitations. These older style guides include preferences for underlining the titles of books (as just one example) instead of italics because on a typewriter changing to italics required physically changing pieces of the typewriter. Electronic word processors have made all of this quite simple, though. Now you can use all of these strategies to emphasize key terms, phrases, or sentences within your report.

You should use formatting like this with caution, though. Readers who were raised in a publishing world that deemphasized such formatting (like bold font, etc.) may see such efforts as juvenile. Extensive use of formatting is seen by some as informal and inappropriate for formal communications (like memos or reports at work). You will have to consider your audience in this regard. Formatting is a powerful tool but one that can turn off some audiences if used too extensively.

Integration of Figures

Sometimes words are not enough. You need to include visual representations of processes of research results to communicate the results of your research. In these cases, a picture (as it is often said) can be worth a thousand words. Just as new word processor technology has made the use of text formatting easier than ever, the creation and inclusion of figures and images is now easier than ever. Figures can be a powerful tool for making your argument and should be considered carefully.

Class Exercise: Bring in a selection of graphics from newspapers and news websites. Discuss the strengths and weaknesses of various attempts to use graphics and figures to support the author's argument.

The key to including effective figures is having a specific goal in mind for every figure. You should carefully consider whether each figure is truly necessary. If you are convinced that a figure is the best way to communicate a point, you should invest the time to create and the space to accommodate a figure within a text. If you are not sure if the report is necessary, try to write the report without the figure. While figures are excellent tools, they are time consuming to create and can distract from your argument if not necessary to the report.

With written reports, it is particularly important to consider how people will view your report and the figures you include. One of the less obvious complications of the asynchronous nature of written documents is that people may read your report in ways that you had not anticipated. The use of websites to distribute reports complicated this environment further. If the NHH organization chose to release a report on the best practices for nonprofits in emergency planning via their website, they may have some people reading the report online, some on mobile devices (laptops, tablet devices, or even their phones), and some may print the report out for future reading. With the former set of devices, some documents may be completely unreadable in alternative formats (phones are particularly bad about rendering documents with figures). Even printing brings along with it complications. Still only a minority of managers make color copies of reports. If your figure uses different colors, the figure may be difficult to decipher with a black and white print out. Always keep the variety of ways that readers may observe your report (and particularly your figures) in mind when writing such a document.

Slide Presentations for Public Affairs Research

While written reports were the most common form of reporting for managers a decade ago (almost to the exclusion of other modes of communication), it is increasingly common for managers to instead provide presentations with a combination of an oral presentation and a series of slides projected onto a screen. Software packages like PowerPoint™ (from Microsoft) and Impress™ (as part of the Open Office™ suite of free software), along with easier technologies to project images from computers onto screens, have made the approaches affordable and popular. We refer to these as slide presentations.

The Integration of Oral and Visual Presentations

The distinguishing element of these types of presentations is the integration of oral (audio) and visual elements. If the presentation included a series of slides without any oral explanation, you would have an inefficient written report. If you had an oral report with no visual accompaniment, you may have trouble with people remembering what you had recently said and how the presentation comes together as an argument (with oral presentation, people cannot circle back to earlier parts of the presentation if they get lost—as they can do with written presentations). Bringing together both visual and oral components offsets the disadvantages of each individually. The quality of this sort of presentation depends most on how well you integrate the oral and the visual elements of the presentation.

The Advantages of Slide Presentations

The chief advantage of integrated oral/visual presentation is that they can be responsive to the audience. Unlike written reports, slide presentations are synchronous. The presenter is there at the same time as the audience. If the audience member has a question, she can ask the presenter. In a broader sense, the presenter can assess the audience and adapt the presentation (typically only the oral component) to the needs of the audience. If the audience seems confused or asks questions, the presenter can offer clarification. The responsiveness of the presentation to the audience is the chief advantage of these styles of reports. To the extent that a presenter does not react to the audience, the presentation could just as well have been a written report.

The flexibility and responsiveness of slide presentations make these reports more engaging to the audience. Audience members are more likely to pay attention to a report if they feel that the presenter is paying attention to them. This ability to retain the attention of the audience is an important reason why slide presentations have become so popular. The level of engagement makes audience members pay more attention and results in greater retention of information and acceptance of the report.

The Disadvantages of Slide Presentations

The engagement opportunities present in slide presentations bring their chief disadvantage. For the presentation to have the opportunity to connect the presenter with the audience, both must be present at the same place at the same time. This can present quite an obstacle for presentations. You cannot simply save a presentation for later consultation—as you can with written reports. This type of presentation requires some level of commitment and, possibly, costs in the form of transportation time and the commitment to devote a specific period of time.

The requirement for the audience and the presenter to be present at the same place and at the same time is slowly giving way to advances in technology. There are more options emerging every year for remote observation of presentations. Some technologies allow you to post slides and then accompany the slides with audio through conventional phone technology or through online programs like Skype™. These advances make it possible for audience members to be spread across space.

The linking of audience and presenter in time is a thornier issue. Even if you can watch a presentation from across the globe, you can only ask questions and engage the presenter if you are watching the presentation in real time. It is possible to ask questions of a presenter long after the presentation is over—but this is no different than with written reports and is hardly the level of engagement that distinguishes slide presentations from other modes of presenting information.

Key Strategies for Slide Presentations

Putting together an effective slide presentation requires careful strategies as did writer reports. It is important to keep in mind the distinctive elements of slide presentations. You want to create a good slide presentation—not a poor written report that happens to be in slide form.

Balancing Visual and Oral Elements
The art of creating an effective slide presentation is the careful balancing of visual and oral elements. If you wanted to rely entirely on visual elements, you could just create a document or a video. If you just wanted to rely entirely on oral communication, the slides themselves would be unnecessary. The best slide presentations are those that use the oral and visual elements in a complementary fashion. A balance of the visual and oral elements allows each to reinforce the other effectively.

The key to balancing visual and oral elements is to make sure that you (and your argument) are the central element of the presentation. You do not want (as the presenter) to become a part of the audience observing the visual elements. Similarly, you do not want the audience to deem your visual elements to be unnecessary. The best way to keep this balance is to start with the oral component of the presentation. Once you have a plan for what you will say, you can design visual elements to support the oral presentation. The visual elements can include summaries of your points as you are speaking or figures that illustrate relationships between key concepts.

> ### The Three Times to Tell Your Audience Anything
>
> Preview—"Tell them what you are going to tell them."
>
> Argue—"Tell them."
>
> Review—"Tell them what you told them."

It is important to keep in mind the difference between slide and written presentations. If you are having trouble understanding a point in this textbook, as an example, you can go back a page or so to review what you have read. This gives you a second opportunity to understand a key point. With a lecture or slide presentation, you cannot simply rewind a few minutes if you get lost. It falls to the presenter to make sure that no one in the audience is left behind. If a member of the audience does get lost, she is likely to simply ignore the rest of the presentation.

A simple technique helps to avoid losing members of the audience. Tell the audience what you want them to remember three times—a preview, the argument, and a review. Repetition reinforces your key point to your audience so that they will remember your central argument.

Repetition serves a purpose similar to detailed structure within a written document. Audience members are more likely to understand an argument if they see the relationships between the parts of your presentation. An occasional reminder of the whole argument will serve this purpose. It is much more common that people lose the audience because of a lack of review than that they bore the audience with excessive review—so don't be hesitant to include many opportunities for review and references to the whole of the argument.

It is also important to consider what audience members are most likely to remember. It is generally the case that people remember the beginning and the end of any presentation. It is much less likely that members of the audience will remember the details of the middle of your presentation. This has two important implications. First, you should concentrate your attention on making the beginning and the end of your presentation as impressive as possible. Those will be the parts of the presentation that will serve as the basis for people's impression of you. Second, you must include everything you want the audience to remember in the beginning and end of the presentation (preferably both). If you have narrow ranges of the presentation that audience members are likely to remember, you want to make them count. The three components of repetition make this easy. You should include the outline of your argument in the preview and review components—which just happen to be the parts of the presentation the audience members will remember.

Less Is More   The need to create memorable presentations can tempt one to go overboard with pictures and other visual elements. The ability to reinforce your points with images and words is quite powerful. With some moderation, visual aids can make points more easily understood and remembered. However, including too many visual elements simply creates a series of distractions. You want people to focus on your argument—possibly with the help of visual elements—not the visual elements themselves. Having too many cartoons or detailed images creates competition for the key points of your argument.

Text can also create problems for presentations if you use too much of it. Garr Reynolds, an expert on the creation of slide presentations, refers to slides with too much text as "slideuments." On one level, this is a clever combination of document and slide. Slideuments often result when one treats a slide as one would a written document. If you really want people to read large segments of unchanging text (like large quotes), you should create a written document—not a slide presentation. Asking the audience to read large segments of text puts them out of the mode of listening to the presenter and into a passive reading mode. This makes the genius of the term "slideument." Slides with too much text become monuments to be stared at rather than components of an interactive presentation experience.

There is no definite guideline for how much text or too many images are too much. A good starting point is to have no more than 24 words per slide. You may exceed this number in some circumstances and may want fewer in others. You will have to gauge your audience and the nature of your argument. It is easier to tell if a slide has too much text: If audience members spend more of their time watching the slides than the presenter, there are probably too many images or words. The presenter should be the center of the audience's attention to ensure that he or she can read the audience and change the presentation as needed. If the audience becomes passive consumers of the visual presentation, you lose the interactive component that makes slide presentations unique.

Conclusion: Final Reminders on Reporting

It is important to remember a few key points that apply to all types of presentations.

First, many people will know you primarily from the reports of your research and your work. Your presentations will be the source of their first impressions of you—as well as many impressions later. If people see your presentations are filled with errors (misspelled words, grammatical errors, strange formatting errors, etc.), their impression of you will be that you are lazy or careless. If your presentation is carefully prepared and well argued, the positive impression may be lasting.

Second, you have the opportunity to manage the impressions that your presentations create. You can avoid creating the impression of carelessness if you invest time in proofreading and practicing your presentation. You should read through your report (including any visual elements like slides) many, many times before anyone actually sees it whom you do not know well. You can, and should, rely on friends and trusted coworkers to review your reports. These are people whose impressions of you will not be soured by finding a typo. Anyone whose opinion may be influenced by errors, though, should only see material you have carefully revised.

Third, your time during a report to make changes is much shorter than your time before you release a report. If you release a written report, you have no chance at all to revise the text. If you are conducting a slide presentation, you can modify the presentation to meet audience needs, but you will have to do so quickly in response to signals from the audience. In both of these situations, you have much more time to scrutinize your report before you send it off. You should value you your prerelease time with your report and spend as much time as you can to make the report error free before release.

Suggested Readings

There are many excellent books on how to design effective presentations and reports. Advice for writing reports comes from different sources depending on the nature of the research it contains. For writing reports relying primarily on qualitative evidence, we recommend Wolcott's *Writing Up Qualitative Research*. For writing text that relies on tables of quantitative results, a good place to start is *The Chicago Guide to Writing about Numbers* or *The Chicago Guide to Writing about Multivariate Analysis*. An important complement to this material is the literature on the effective use of graphics. The works of Tufte—notably *The Visual Display of Quantitative Information*—is the standard starting point.

There is a similarly voluminous literature on effective design of slide presentations. The same Tufte who wrote classic texts on data visualization also wrote a powerful critique of poor practices common in slide presentations: *The Cognitive Style of PowerPoint*. More general advice is available in Duarte's *Slide:ology* and Reynolds's *Presentation Zen: Simple Ideas on Presentation and Delivery*. The emerging consensus by those whose livelihoods depend on slide presentations is that simple, clear presentations are best despite all of the bells and whistles that software makes available to us.

Flashcards
& MCQs

Vocabulary

ASYNCHRONOUS—Taking place at different points in time.
TAKE-AWAY—A specific piece of information that you want your audience to retain.

Useful
Websites

Review Questions

■ What are the limitations of a written report relative to a slide presentation?

■ What concerns would shape a presentation intended for the general public?

Discussion Questions

■ What strategies would you use to identify the needs of the audience if you have been asked to present to an agency in a different state about programs working at your home office?

■ What sorts of reports would be effective for NHH to get out the word about the work of their member organizations? What are the strengths and limitations of each type of report?

■ What limitations would be present in developing a webpage to report on your research?

CHAPTER 22

Conclusion: Bringing It All Together

Introduction

Throughout this book, we have introduced a wide variety of tools that you can use to conduct public affairs research and evaluation. With each tool, we introduced specific examples of how you might put these tools to work in the sort of research projects that public or nonprofit sector organizations might conduct to support key management objectives. In this final chapter, we will explore alternative visions of each of our core cases to illustrate how various tools can tie together. While the previous discussions of the cases focused on narrow slices of time, these narratives will emphasize the choices that one can make and how these choices impact the development of the research project over time.

In other words, this conclusion chapter provides you with a "big picture" look at the overall process of conducting research by highlighting the various types of decisions you will have to make as you execute a research project or a program evaluation. All of these issues have been covered earlier at various points in the text, but seeing how the ideas are all linked together—the key concepts and techniques you have learned over the course of this book—is a useful way to think about how you will translate this knowledge to your own project work.

As a means of summarizing the research process, Table 22.1 presents a simplified version of the progression of elements in conducting a research project. We would emphasize that this is only a summary table. As you now know, topics such as data analysis can be quite complex and demanding efforts in their own right. But one way to think about a research or program evaluation project is to consider what you will be doing at the basic six phases, or steps, of a process. You will start any project with conducting a preliminary review of relevant documents of prior research—including getting a handle on prior theoretic claims on a topic, and sometimes having either informal or formal conversations with subject matter experts (as discussed in chapters 3 and 4). Likewise, you will map out a project management plan (as discussed in chapter 20) to make sure you can execute the project effectively. At a second phase (or step, if you prefer), you will develop your central research question, other key questions that follow from it, and lay out hypotheses you will wish to test (as discussed in chapter 3). In conjunction with those activities are those that follow from your initial preliminary investigation work, such as writing an annotated bibliography or a literature review that you will perhaps use later in a formal report (as discussed in chapter 4). You will also create and implement a specific research design for the project, which carries with it key choices over what to measure and exactly how to measure it—issues covered in chapter 5. After doing all this project work, next you move to collecting the data you need to answer your questions; chapters 9–11 outlined a variety of data collection techniques and processes. After gathering your data, you of course need to analyze those data and interpret the results in order to answer your research questions (as was explained and illustrated in a number of different ways in chapters 12–20). The research process is completed when you present and disseminate findings to various audiences, as was covered in chapter 21.

Again, the phases presented in Table 22.1 serve only to illustrate in summary form what the research process is comprised of—it does not address the reality of overlapping features of these phases overlapping—nor does it capture the great complexity of questions and issues within each phase. But it does serve as a concise reminder of what you, as a research or evaluator, will have to do to complete a project successfully.

We return to our cases one last time to show how some key questions and decision across these phases play out in practice as research and evaluation projects are implemented (Table 22.1).

National Helping Hands

The executive director of National Helping Hands (NHH) wants to get a better sense of the contributions made by its member organizations to community disaster planning, relief, and recovery. Initially, he is looking for a dollar amount. Ideally, he would like to be able to establish that members of NHH contribute, say, $20 billion dollars a year in disaster-related services to communities affected by disasters in the United States—funded at no charge to the recipients of the assistance. This is a noble goal, but quickly it becomes clear that such a number will be difficult to find and to justify. It is not clear how much any single member of the organization contributes, in part because measuring their contribution is quite difficult. It is also difficult to define who is part of the nonprofit sector's effort but not formally a member of NHH. Any specific number would require answers to controversial questions like these. This leads to a working relationship with a university researcher, Melanie, who the executive director asked to conduct a research effort to get a better handle on possible answers to these kinds of key questions.

Table 22.1 Phases of the Research Process: An Illustration of Key Elements

Phase	Phase One: Preliminary Investigation and Project Planning	Phase Two: Framing Questions and Hypotheses	Phase Three: Structuring the Design of the Project	Phase Four: Data Collection	Phase Five: Data Analysis and Interpretation of Results	Phase Six: Dissemination of Results
Activities	Conduct background review of theory and prior findings on the topic; Review key documents or available data sets; Secure human subject protection approval	Establish core research question and subsidiary questions for the project; Establish key research hypotheses to test; Write a literature review and/or annotated bibliography	Establish a research design for the project; Make key measurement decisions; Assess implications of validity and reliability issues based on the research design selected	Create and implement measurement instruments; Implement data collection strategy (i.e., execute a survey, conduct field interviews, etc.)	Conduct data analysis, interpret results, review reliability and validity of gathered data	Produce formal reporting of project results to funding agency, client, or other researchers

(Continued)

Table 22.1 Phases of the Research Process: An Illustration of Key Elements (*Continued*)

Possible Key Questions to Ask and Decisions to Make					
What kind of prior research work needs to be reviewed and what to do if there are not established sources of data on the subject? Should you conduct either formal or informal interviews with subject matter experts? Will your study attempt to develop new theoretic arguments on the subject?	Based on the review of existing theory and research, what is the key question your project is intended to address? What is the basis for key hypotheses to test?	What design fits best with the research question and the realistically possible data that can be gathered? A true experiment, a quasi-experiment, or a non-experiment? What are the strengths and weaknesses of each design option relative to the data needs demanded by the core research question?	Given a project research question, what is the best data collection strategy? If the best strategy is not feasible, what are the next best alternatives?	What are the appropriate statistical tests to perform—if you are working with quantitative data? What is the best way to assess and interpret qualitative data that have been gathered?	What kind of audience will receive the report? What is the best way to structure the reporting document to meet the needs of the target audience? What are the best ways to try to disseminate the study's findings to a target audience?

While keeping the ultimate goal of finding a dollar amount to summarize the contribution of NHH members, Melanie approaches her research task by first seeking answers to two simpler, more realistic questions. First, she decides to focus on a single event—a recent flood disaster. Her hope is that the process of defining, in very detailed terms, the contribution of nonprofit organizations in a specific event will serve as a model for generating a contribution estimate for other cases. For this purpose, she develops a research question asking "What contribution did nonprofit organizations make in the recent flooding operation?" Second, she wants to start getting a rough assessment of individual members' contributions. She needs a separate, second research question. For this, she decides on the following question: "What contribution did member organizations make to disaster relief and recovery operations in 2010?" This will require getting responses from the dozens and dozens of members (and few, if any, of the members will even know the exact dollar value of their contributions to community relief and recovery efforts). She decides to pursue these research streams concurrently in that they are not intended to inform each other in any formal way, as shown in Figure 22.1.

For the first research question, "What contribution did nonprofit organizations make in the recent flooding operation," and first part of the overall project, Melanie chooses a

Figure 22.1 Illustration of Decisions of the Core Research Questions and What Research Design to Choose

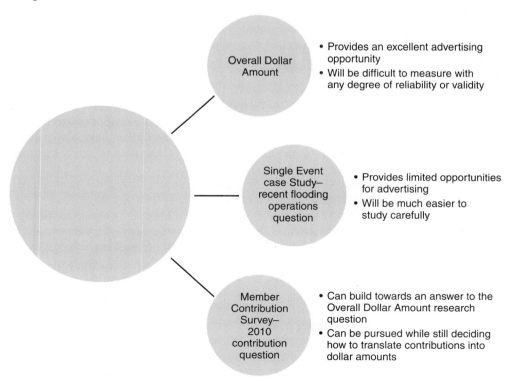

recent disaster in a remote, interior area of Alaska as a case study. This case is one where several NHH organizations were actively engaged, and so she has access to many key members of the recovery effort. The remoteness of the location may make the case atypical in key respects, but the access to key participants is seen as outweighing this disadvantage to the case. The remoteness also influences the sorts of research methods that one can use to assess who is involved and what they contributed to disaster recovery in the small rural communities affected by the flooding disaster. The project starts with a series of phone calls with key stakeholders in the area, but quickly it becomes clear that visiting the site of the disaster and talking to local people in person will be important because of the inability to reach intended interview subjects by telephone. This requires a shift from phone-based interviews to in-person interviews (along with all of the complications involved with travel).

> **Class Exercise:** Looking at Figure 22.1, we see how two phases of the research process are closely linked: Melanie has worked her way through her core research questions, and she has chosen two different research design approaches to answer them. Using what you have learned, discuss the nature of the two design choices and how they relate to the core research questions she has posed. Does this research design strategy make sense to you? Are there other ways you would have proceeded in setting up the project?

As Figure 22.2 shows, there are different strengths and weaknesses associated with the two types of interview techniques. There are trade-offs, but Melanie—as principal investigator on the project—organizes a research team to conduct a series of field interviews due to the nature of data collection needs in the post-disaster environment. The researchers travel to Alaska to visit interviewees in person and record their interviews using a small digital voice recorder.

After returning from the field, Melanie hires a firm to transcribe the audio recordings to text documents for eventual analysis. This turns out to be more complicated than expected. The initial series of text files are unusable due to transcription errors. As a result, Melanie has to send the recordings back to the transcription service with additional instructions for successful transcription (including clarification of some common jargon). Even then, Melanie sends the results of the second round of transcriptions to members of the research team for proofreading and correction. Only after these various steps are the interview transcripts ready for analysis.

Concurrent with the field interview process in Alaska, Melanie is also overseeing a national survey of member organizations. The design of the survey instrument proved to be quite a challenge. People in different parts of the country use different language to describe what they do and how they do it. They also have very different ways of internal accounting of their operational practices, so to try to measure those differences in a single survey instrument is a challenge. To help overcome this problem, she collects a focus group of the leaders of various member organizations. The focus group serves as a means to pilot test potential survey questions and work out these measurement problems. After the various questions have been vetted through the focus group, Melanie oversees a large Internet survey of member organizations. After working with another member of the project team, who is responsible for developing and implementing the

Figure 22.2   Illustration of Key Decisions over How to Gather Data

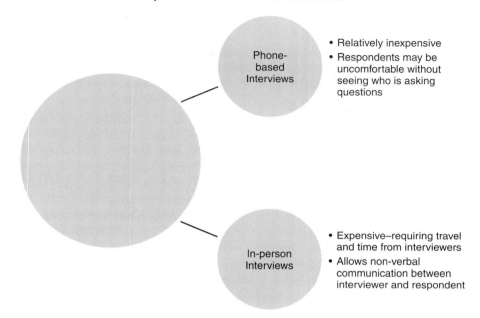

- Relatively inexpensive
- Respondents may be uncomfortable without seeing who is asking questions

Phone-based Interviews

In-person Interviews

- Expensive—requiring travel and time from interviewers
- Allows non-verbal communication between interviewer and respondent

online survey, Melanie's team, given the close connection between NHH and its member organizations, succeeded in getting most (85%) of the organizations to respond to the survey. The result is a database of responses cataloging efforts nationwide (Figure 22.3).

The two research streams are integrated under the same project—but actually answer quite different research questions. The case study provides a critical assessment of nonprofit contribution at the level of a specific event. The survey provides an assessment of perceived contributions at the organizational level. Each stream provides its own set of information. The survey may provide insight into the number of events that member organizations have worked on over the last year. This information can be combined with information on nonprofit contributions from the case study to generate projections of total contribution—based on the admittedly strong assumption that the case study generated information that is typical.

The next phases in the research process are to conduct an analysis of the gathered data and then to produce and disseminate a formal report on the study's findings. The entire motivation for the study was to illustrate the importance of nonprofits in disasters. As a result, the dissemination of research findings is exceptionally important to the mission and purpose of NHH. After Melanie and her research team have completed the data collection, analysis, and report writing, they turn those materials over to NHH. The executive director decides to focus on the organization's website as the mechanism to get the word out to NHH stakeholders and to others NHH interacts with such as federal and state emergency management agencies, key philanthropic donors to NHH, and the like. The executive director works with his team at NHH to refine the two documents,

Figure 22.3   Illustration of Strengths and Weaknesses of Data-Gathering Strategies

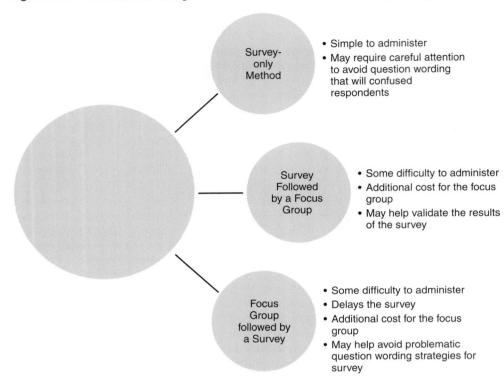

provided by Melanie and the research team, to better meet the specific dissemination style of NHH (i.e., to put into a format and narrative style that is typical of NHH published reports). First, the NHH website will have a number of pages devoted to the study with a graphic-rich review of the results of the research intended for a broad audience. Second, the research team puts together a written document providing the results in greater detail—possibly over 40–50 pages. This document, often called a white paper, serves as a means to reach more technical audiences, including experts in the field (Figure 22.4).

Summary of the Case Discussion

The case of the NHH research project just outlined highlights several key decision points in the research process. The discussion also pointed out several key challenges that a researcher typically will face. For example, we saw that Melanie had a broad mandate from the executive director at NHH—perhaps overly broad. Therefore, she re-framed that information challenge as two distinct research questions. This was a challenge because it posed the need for two different research design strategies (a case study and a cross-sectional survey, which we can define as a nonexperimental research design). Likewise,

Figure 22.4   Illustration of Decisions over Research Dissemination Strategies

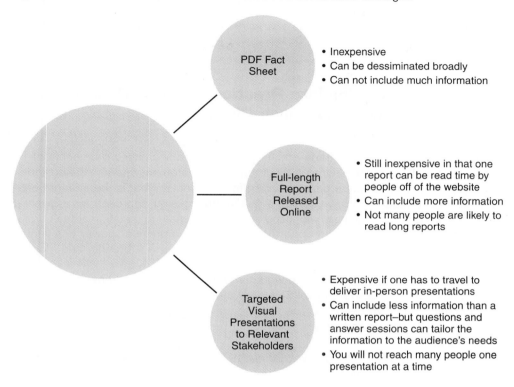

- PDF Fact Sheet
  - Inexpensive
  - Can be dessiminated broadly
  - Can not include much information

- Full-length Report Released Online
  - Still inexpensive in that one report can be read time by people off of the website
  - Can include more information
  - Not many people are likely to read long reports

- Targeted Visual Presentations to Relevant Stakeholders
  - Expensive if one has to travel to deliver in-person presentations
  - Can include less information than a written report—but questions and answer sessions can tailor the information to the audience's needs
  - You will not reach many people one presentation at a time

we saw that the data collection process was a bit messy (e.g., Melanie and her team had lots of problems with interview transcription, which undermines the quality and potentially even the reliability of the data gathered if such problems were not addressed and corrected).

These types of decisions and challenges were highlighted in the case discussion, but as the reader will note, not all phases or elements of the research process were discussed. The case description did not cover the initial phase or elements of the research process; that is, we did not cover how Melanie and her research team did a review of prior research on disasters and nonprofit organizations, nor did we see an illustration of how the research team put together a project plan, or how the team proceeded to apply for human subjects protection review and approval to conduct interviews and a survey. Likewise, once the team had their data gathered, they obviously would have had to make critical decisions about the most effective way to analyze those data given the needs of the research questions.

While the "Putting Knowledge Into Practice" box below gives the reader an opportunity to tackle some of those research issues and questions in greater detail, the purpose of the case discussion here—as with all the case discussions throughout the text—is to illustrate the kinds of decisions a researcher has to make in practice. What those decision points also demonstrate is that you, the reader, have been equipped with sufficient knowledge to understand the nature of these questions and sufficient knowledge to further develop the skills as you are responsible for your own research and evaluation projects.

Putting Knowledge into Practice: How to Think About Key Trade-offs in Research Choices

As you have come to learn over the course of reading this text, the research process involves a great many trade-offs. For instance, a researcher will be confronted with questions such as what is the strength of one quasi-experimental design versus another to structure data gathering for a project? What is the strength of using a case study approach versus a quantitative design approach for a given project? Should you use a very focused and narrow research question at the core of a project (i.e., giving you an opportunity to produce a precise answer to a very specific element of a policy or program), or should you use a broader and more general question?

There are several key issues to work through. As the material covered in this book has pointed out, starting with a clearly defined set of questions is essential to pursuing effective research. The importance of making those questions very clear will help you make key decisions about research design and variable measurement.

Consider the fairly straightforward question of defining a unit of analysis and the NHH example we've discussed above and elsewhere in this book. Melanie might have chosen an individual organization as her unit of analysis, or a category of disasters (e.g., all flood or hurricane disasters over a given time period), or an individual household (i.e., in order to study the cost and impact of disaster relief efforts in a given community). These are three very different units of analysis, and each carries with it certain characteristics that help drive choices over structuring a research design or defining the key variables to measure for those units.

Which is the best way to proceed? There is no correct answer to that question. It depends on the ultimate purpose of the project, what data are realistically obtainable, what are the possible ways one might measures the crucial aspects of a policy or program or individual and/or organizational behavior. What is key for a researcher or an evaluator is to have a clear understanding of the strengths and weaknesses of what choices are made, to understand the implications of those choices, and to clearly convey to the audience how and why those choices were made.

How does a researcher know which is the best option to choose? Unfortunately, there is not an easy answer or a rule of thumb that can be offered. The real answer to the question is this: it depends. While that might not seem a satisfying answer, it is the only one that can be offered.

To see what these kind of critical decisions look like in practice, and what the trade-offs are for any choice a researcher makes, the reader can look to the eTextbook for additional illustrative exercise questions regarding decisions and challenges one faces in the actual practice of research work.

Dewey Independent School District

The superintendent of the Dewey Independent School District (ISD) needs to find out about the retirement intentions of teachers within her district. The goal is to predict the number of teachers who intend to retire each year so that the district can develop a strategic human resource plan. This is a classic case of an organization needing an internal evaluative assessment to make critical management decisions that will support its operational effectiveness.

The superintendent has a relatively simple program evaluation problem. She is interested in the intentions of employees within her district—all people whom she can relatively easily reach with a survey. Furthermore, the intention to retire will be easy to identify. You can simply ask people what their intentions are. You have to ensure confidentiality to protect respondents from potential retaliation. You also can't be sure that people know what they will be thinking two years from now about retiring (some may change their minds in the meantime). However, this is a relatively simple program evaluation project.

With limited resources, the superintendent cannot staff the program evaluation internally. As a result, she contracts with an independent center for education policy research located at one of the state's major research universities to conduct the evaluation. Kelly from the education policy center will serve as the principal investigator (PI) on the contract with the Dewey ISD. Because the project is a relatively simple one, and the budget is small, Kelly will only require some limited effort from another research staff person, Andre, from the education policy center and some additional administrative support from the center's staff. She maps out a project plan of 12 weeks to complete the project. Because she will be collecting data via a survey, she immediately meets with school district personnel and a few teachers from schools in the district to help her craft a survey instrument. As soon as she completes that preliminary work, she submits an application for human subjects review to the Institutional Review Board at the university in which her research center is located.

At the same time, Andre has done a review of similar school districts in the state on the matter of how they have handled retirements and other human resource management decisions. He reviews several similar evaluation studies on strategic human capital management that are relevant to public sector organizations. In addition to helping Kelly while she wrote the survey instrument (mostly through editing assistance and helping with a pretest of the instrument's measurement items), Andre wrote a short summary of the substance of these human resource management issues, which will later be used in the final report.

As noted, the project budget is not particularly large, and the researchers from the university decide they do not want to attempt a census of all teachers in the schools of the Dewey ISD. Instead, Kelly and Andre decide the best course of action is to take a sample of the teachers and infer what the population levels values are (specifically, how many teachers in the entire district intend to retire over the next three years). They estimated a cost item in the project budget to cover a survey of about 100 teachers (out of about 1,000), and this was an acceptable course of action to the school district superintendent.

However, after the original project proposal was made to the client (the superintendent of the school district), Kelly and Andre begin to be concerned about the possible pitfalls of merely taking a simple random sample of 100 teachers. After more reflection (and after the award period had started for the project), they decide they need to be sure that their sample avoids the most obvious potential problems of nonrepresentativeness by using a stratified random sample with the teachers stratified by campus and age. As she thinks through this challenge, Kelly approaches the superintendent and asks for, and receives, permission to adjust the project plan slightly. Kelly reduces one project budget item (she reduces some of Andre's budgeted effort on the project slightly) and thus is able to reallocate the small amount of funds to cover another 100 surveys, which allows her to selectively oversample teachers over the age of 50. The short survey was a hard-copy mail survey, so the reallocation of funds was extremely small.

The key point was that Kelly felt it not only a good idea but a basic ethical obligation to inform the client that she decided that a slight alteration to the project's research design would produce a better analytic result.

Analyzing the data that Kelly and Andre had collected proved simple. The initial evaluation question was purely descriptive: how many teachers report that they intend to retire within three years (extrapolated from the sample)? However, Kelly opts to push the data a little farther to see what it is that is convincing people to retire. Are people retiring as planned at a specific age? Are those deferring retirement saying that they intended to but can't afford to anymore? Are there specific campuses likely to be hit particularly hard by a cluster of retirements? The simple survey instrument served to provide insight into all of these questions.

After receiving Kelly's report, the superintendent developed a presentation to the school board. The presentation included a summary of the evaluation's key findings as well as the superintendent's own interpretation of the significance of those results. She emphasized the survey results as a means to explain the nature of the upcoming retirement wave and serve as the foundation for a strategic human resource management plan

---

Class Exercise: Kelly's evaluation project really mostly required a descriptive assessment of the data gathered to answer the question of a projected level of teacher retirements in the school district. But given that Kelly pushed a little further with her analysis, discuss what kinds of items she likely included in her measurement instrument. Also discuss whether you think these additional questions were needed or were useful to the district's superintendent.

for the district. The school board was impressed with the care taken in developing such a proactive approach to human resource management.

Summary of the Case Discussion

The case of the Dewey ISD human resource strategy evaluation again provides several useful insights into how a research project functions in practice. This was a relatively simple and straightforward project, and it was able to be completed in a fairly short amount of time (three months) from the initial contract agreement to the final report produced by the project's PI. The case illustrates how sometimes an investigator will change her research or data collection strategy after the project has begun. Here, Kelly decided she needed to alter the design from a simple random probability sample to a stratified sample.

There is one other key item to take note of in this case. The dissemination portion of the evaluation study was left to the client. In this case, the evaluator delivered a report to the client. This was an evaluation effort specific to the organization (the school district), and as such, Kelly and her colleagues at the education policy center were not intending to conduct a study as generalizable research. Their work ended when they fulfilled the key-delivered specific in the project's contract: a report assessing future teacher retirements within the Dewey ISD. After the data and the report were delivered to the superintendent, Kelly, Andre, and the research center had no more connection to those data. It is entirely possible that Kelly could have wanted to use those data for more generalizable research, but that would have been a question for her to negotiate as the project contract was agreed to. In other words, she could have requested use of those data to produce an academic paper on the subject of strategic human resource management within a public school setting. But for the purposes of this case, she did not. She simply conducted an evaluation for the superintendent, who used the study findings to inform key future management decisions.

Putting Knowledge into Practice: What to Think About When Producing an Evaluation Report

One common type of expected deliverable for a research or evaluation project is the writing of an evaluation report. Such reports will vary by project and by the needs of the audience, but there is a fairly general structure to those kinds of reports.

The discussion in Chapter 8 provided a basic template for the structure of a case study report. Any evaluation report will be more or less follow that basic report structure. Likewise, chapter 21 provides a detailed discussion of issues related to reporting results and dissemination of findings. There are several key considerations to keep in mind when you are writing an evaluation report. First, as has been emphasized elsewhere, always be completely explicit about research design strategies, measurement strategies, and analytic choices made. The reader of a report should not have any uncertainty about how or why you produced what you did. Second, either in the narrative portion of the report or in accompanying appendices, always provide complete information about data collection processes and complete information about the evidence being used. For instance, it is most helpful for a reader to see complete distributional information on all the variables used in the analysis. Given space or narrative flow considerations, such detailed information might not always make sense in the main body of the report. But such information should be provided, so you might include that information in a report appendix. Third, it is extremely important to know the needs of your audience. A report should not "talk above" the heads of potential reader with advanced quantitative analysis that the typical reader will not have a familiarity. But at the same time, a report should not strive to "dumb down" the presentation to the point it has little analytic value. As in most things in life, writing evaluation reports should strive for a balance.

To get practice at writing up the results of an evaluation effort, the reader may go to the eTextbook and complete several exercise problems associated with this case. You will find a data set for the Dewey survey, which will then provide you with an opportunity to run an analysis and write up the results following the guidance provided in the exercise.

Grover's Corner Department of Transportation

The director of Grover's Corner Department of Transportation (DOT) wants to draw more people to light rail. His hope is that more attractive amenities will draw more people to use this form of public transportation. Given the stakes for the project, the director decided to invest a substantial sum of money into this research project. The large budget allowed for a diverse mixed methods research strategy engaging the core research question: "what amenities would draw you to use public transportation?" The director tasks an internal policy research analyst with leading a team to execute a research effort designed to answer this question directly. Several DOT staffers are trained to do this kind of research work, but they also do not have all the expertise needed to address all the research needs. As a consequence, some portions of the project are contracted out to consultants with very specific research skills and expertise.

The research project started with a brief but in-depth investigation phase to better understand how people are currently using the light rail service. This involved a series of field visits to light rail sites conducted by trained ethnographic observers. The goal was to observe how people used the light rail currently as well as early evidence of what improvement may be possible. Following the careful observational study to define a baseline, the head analyst responsible for supervising the project initiated two concurrent research designs: a series of focus groups and individual interviews with users recruited from current light rail users. The focus groups provide an opportunity to see users interact with each other and build on each other's comments while the individual interviews dig deep into specific individual preferences. The information gathered from these two interview protocols provide a basis for a much broader survey project of both actual and potential users of the light rail system. The director purchases a survey sample for his city from a marketing research firm to get a representative sample of the entire population—rather than only those who currently use light rail.

The survey revealed that there were specific amenities that people wanted to see at light rail stations to make the stations a realistic alternative to personal automobiles. The most prominent finding was the need for ample and inexpensive parking. The staff policy research analyst provided a comprehensive and detailed report of all the research findings. In turn, the Grover's Corner DOT director makes a presentation of the findings and their implications to several meetings of regional directors of transportation as well as to planning groups within his community. Given the value of the data generated (and the expense invested), the director also chooses to write papers based on the results for transportation planning professionals across the country as well as academicians interested in urban planning and transportation choice.

Amity Department of Homeland Security

The Amity Department of Homeland Security has succeeded in securing a large federal grant to pay for training of its office members. The details of Amity's grant proposal mainly centered on a plan to conduct a series of simulations involving not only members of the homeland security office but also the various other offices within the city government that often work with them during emergency or disaster incidents. A common condition of federal grants like this one is that an awardee (e.g., the city of Amity in this case) conduct an evaluation of the funded effort to ensure both fidelity to the details of the original proposal and to assess whether the project worked as intended. This condition was certainly welcomed by the Amity homeland security director, who wants to be able to evaluate whether the exercise actually improves the performance of her organizations— so that she can know whether to make similar investments in the future. As a result, she tasks Heather, the head of exercises and training for the department, to oversee the evaluation of the project.

Evaluating the success of the training program proves to be quite tricky for Heather and the staff she worked with on the evaluation. Of course, the Amity proposal did not want to wait until there was an actual event that required the skills included in the exercise. So Heather needs a strategy to evaluate performance outside the context of a specific event. The good news is that with the relatively small number of participants (10–15), it will be easy to collect data from each of them. Furthermore, since all of the participants work closely with her or for organizations with which she has had long-time relationships, she will have little trouble ensuring participation of the various parties from the simulation.

The grant proposal did not allocate a large share of the overall budget to the required evaluation effort. However, the small number of participants in the simulation exercise series has made the requirement for evaluation small scale. With only about a dozen participants, there are significant limitations on the use of statistical assessments for evaluation. Heather decides to include a pretest/posttest design on some key indicators of performance, including knowledge of the relevant plans and the different partners on which the organization relies. With a small number of participants, little more than a simple comparison of means test is appropriate. To complement the simple quantitative tests, Heather also conducts a series of interviews with participants about what they learned during the exercise. Given the ease of access to the participants, she chooses to repeat interviews and the quantitative assessment of plan knowledge months after the simulation exercise series was completed. She is interested to see whether any gains in knowledge are retained over time.

Heather is obligated to produce a final evaluation report to the homeland security director. This report will be used in final reporting to the United State Department of Homeland Security at the end of the project period as defined by the grant award. There is no external public constituency to which the evaluation results are reported. They go to a project officer who reviews the outcome of federal emergency and homeland security exercise grants. However, the Amity director does share the information formally to the directors of other organizations who sent participants to the simulation at follow-up meetings within the city. That discussion is fairly informal and is not presented to those city officials in the same way as it would be in a general public meeting. However, Heather also writes a report of the lessons learned from the simulation exercise (what type of knowledge was improved by the simulation, which mistakes were made in the planning and administration of the simulation itself). This is a "For Official Use Only" document and is not shared with the general public unless a specific request by a citizen is made to the office.

> **Class Exercise:** Discuss the logic of the research design for this evaluation. Is it sound? Could you think of a more effective way to assess the performance of the exercise participants?

Summary of the Case Discussion

The case of the Amity Department of Homeland Security is a very useful illustration of how research principles are put into practice as an evaluation study. The case highlights several challenges: a small project budget and the limitation of a small sample size, which prevents much statistical leverage over key relationships. The case also highlights the fact that not all research findings dissemination is intended for broad audiences. In fact, it is not uncommon for an internal evaluation study for a government agency to remain as just that—an internal resource that is not shared with the general public.

While the research design and analytic questions are not particularly challenging in the case (e.g. a simple pre- and posttest measurement approach, with a comparison of means between the two time periods—assessed as a simple paired samples t-test), the case is also interesting as a nice illustration of the utility of good empirical evaluation work to inform management decisions. That is, doing this kind of evaluation work is a common requirement of grant-funded projects for a reason: it obligates the organization to systematically check whether the logic of their planned program effort is truly working in practice. In turn, that evaluation research is critical information for the organization to learn how to improve performance—just as the department director and Heather were trying to do in this case.

Springfield Housing Department

Christina, senior program manager at the Springfield Housing Department, has long suspected that there were a number of people who were eligible for housing assistance within her community that were not applying. Her primary concern was identifying the barriers that existed within the application process that may be filtering out eligible people. She has already tasked some internal staff resources to conducting some research and evaluation work for the department.

The issue of challenges in housing during a severe economic downturn has also attracted the attention of public policy researchers. Dr. Sarah Jones, a professor from the flagship campus of the state's public university system, contacts Christina to let her know that she has just received a federal research grant to conduct a study of those particular issues. Indeed, Christina was not at all unique in her attention to difficulties in matching the eligible target population with housing assistance services.

Christina and Dr. Jones meet for a preliminary and informal discussion of what efforts have been undertaken by the Springfield Housing Department. After several other such discussions with other public officials and nonprofit organization representatives, and after doing a new review of prior housing research (Dr. Jones is a noted expert on the subject, but she still needs to read current research continuously government reports, and review other relevant public documents to stay current on what is happening with the policy domain), Dr. Jones makes several critical project choices. She decides on a mixed methods project to investigate whether there were barriers to application that she could address.

Dr. Jones's grant has two coinvestigators, and together they elect to have three streams of research: a field research study of local offices, a survey of recipients of funding, and a series of follow-up interviews. Dr. Jones and her colleagues make an early project management decision to run the field research effort concurrently with the other two components. The field research involves observation and document analysis from the actual housing office sites. The survey involves a sample of recent housing assistance recipients (n = 200) with some general questions about the application and assistance process. The survey was preceded by a small (n = 6) focus group just to ensure that the questions were easy to read by the intended respondents (i.e., a standard method of pretesting a measurement instrument).

The survey generated data in its own right, but Dr. Jones and her colleagues see the analytic value of following up with more in-depth interviews of a small number of respondents. Dr. Jones did not intend the in-depth interviews to replicate the representativeness of the larger sample. Instead, she wanted to focus on respondents who reported that they had experienced significant problems applying for assistance. Furthermore, she wanted to interview a set of respondents who reported diverse problems—some focusing on transportation, some on child care, etc.

The field notes and in-depth interviews generated rich textual data that the researchers analyze in NVIVO™. The survey resulted in a database of responses that the director analyzed in STATA™. She wrote a short report based on the results that she circulated to the managers of her local offices and other housing department managers in other parts of her region. (This kind of report can be described as a policy white paper.) The report served to raise awareness of some key barriers and steps that offices can take to make applications easier—like alternative office hours.

Further, we can also take note of the distinction between applied report writing for practitioners and more general academic writing. One audience for this research work is Christina and other Springfield officials. In this sense, they can be defined as the "receivers" for a nonacademic white paper that Dr. Jones produced. By receivers, we mean to indicate that a research report is directed to very specific individuals or organizations who will have the greatest interest and understanding of the implications of the findings reported. A second audience would be other researchers, often academic ones, who have a general interest in the topic area because they also do work on the same types of issues. Dr. Jones might well attempt to publish a paper on the subject in a research journal that is relevant to these kinds of substantive topic concerns.

Summary of the Case Discussion

Research being done around housing assistance eligibility, as highlighted by the Springfield case, reveals several interesting aspects of research work in general. First, this is generalizable research that speaks both to an academic audience interested in these policy and management questions in the housing domain and to practitioners like Christina, who can make use of the findings. This is important because public managers do not necessarily have to conduct such research analyses themselves in order to utilize findings when engaging in evidence-based decision making. That is, Christina can refer to current research from a field in order to help inform her decisions.

Second, this kind of research contributes to a network of policy experts. For example, not only will other academics read this, the dissemination points to the fact that you can produce an academic article for one audience and a more focused technical report for practitioners in another field. Making such a distinction in audience is important as they have different needs. The case discussion above, highlighting the issue of report "receivers," is extremely important because effective dissemination of research efforts in a public management sense requires an understanding of who will make use of the findings and how they are likely to want to use those findings for their policy and management decision-making needs.

Conclusion: How the Case Illustrations Relate to Evidence-Based Management Practices

As these vignettes have illustrated, public managers face diverse research demands in diverse circumstances. Sometimes a public agency or nonprofit organization will have internal research and evaluation staff to do this kind of work. At other times, with limited resources or expertise, that evidence gathering and assessment work will be contracted out to other individuals or organizations. For those researchers or evaluators, a research or evaluation problem might have a lot of time and many resources to conduct that work. Other times, they might have to conduct their research on a deadline without the resources to conduct expensive research protocols (like large surveys, long-term observational studies, etc.). In the end, public or nonprofit managers have to find the best research and evaluation methods available to tackle a specific problem given the constraints they face.

This book addresses the needs of practicing public managers by providing a toolset from which you can draw research tools. In each of the preceding vignettes, public managers could have chosen different tools under other circumstances. Research projects are not about using the best research strategy to tackle all of your research questions—they are about choosing the best available research tool that is appropriate. With this book, look into it like a toolbox and consider the various tools you have. In the end, you will have to choose one (or more) and get to work. While some choices in research are better than others, the worst projects are the ones you never conduct at all—and the worst decisions are those based on no evidence to speak of.

This book, while a toolbox, is only a beginning. Please take this book as an invitation to start developing your own toolbox. You may find that you rely on field observation a great deal and want to get a better version of that specific tool. You can take the rudimentary tool from this toolbox and replace it by reading more broadly on field research and observational studies. The recommended readings in each chapter provide a kick-start to such efforts. You may add entirely new tools (e.g., network analysis) or more advanced versions of the tools you see here (e.g., more advanced statistical tools for analyzing large surveys). Each of these new tools can go into the toolbox. In the end, you will have a personally tailored toolbox and a set of tools in which you can trust.

Index